THE
POOR
HALF BILLION
IN SOUTH ASIA

THE
POOR
HALF BILLION
IN SOUTH ASIA

What is Holding Back Lagging Regions?

edited by EJAZ GHANI

OXFORD
UNIVERSITY PRESS

THE WORLD BANK

OXFORD
UNIVERSITY PRESS

YMCA Library Building, Jai Singh Road, New Delhi 110 001

Oxford University Press is a department of the University of Oxford.
It furthers the University's objective of excellence in research, scholarship,
and education by publishing worldwide in

Oxford   New York
Auckland   Cape Town   Dar es Salaam   Hong Kong   Karachi
Kuala Lumpur   Madrid   Melbourne   Mexico City   Nairobi
New Delhi   Shanghai   Taipei   Toronto

With offices in
Argentina   Austria   Brazil   Chile   Czech Republic   France   Greece
Guatemala   Hungary   Italy   Japan   Poland   Portugal   Singapore
South Korea   Switzerland   Thailand   Turkey   Ukraine   Vietnam

Oxford is a registered trademark of Oxford University Press
in the UK and in certain other countries

Published in India
by Oxford University Press, New Delhi

© World Bank 2010

The moral rights of the author have been asserted
Database right Oxford University Press (maker)

First published 2010
Second impression 2011

The findings, interpretations, and conclusions expressed herein are those of the author(s)
and do not necessarily reflect the views of the Executive Director of the International Bank
for Reconstruction and Development/The World Bank or the governments they represent.
The World Bank does not guarantee the accuracy of the data included in this work.
The boundaries, colours, denominations, and other information shown on any map
in this work do not imply any judgment on the part of The World Bank concerning
the legal status of any territory or the endorsement of acceptance of such boundaries.

ISBN-13: 978-019-806884-6
ISBN-10: 019-806884-0

Typeset in Adobe Garamond Pro 10.5/12.7
by Eleven Arts, Keshav Puram, Delhi 110 035
Printed in India at Anvi Composers, New Delhi 110 063
Published by Oxford University Press
YMCA Library Building, Jai Singh Road, New Delhi 110 001

Contents

List of Tables and Figures   vii

Preface   xv

The Poor Half Billion in South Asia: An Overview   1
 Ejaz Ghani

I IMPROVING GROWTH IN LAGGING REGIONS

1. Development Disparities and Peculiarities   29
 Ejaz Ghani

2. Are Lagging Regions Catching Up with Leading Regions?   64
 Ejaz Ghani, Lakshmi Iyer, and Saurabh Mishra

3. New Economic Geography and Market Access   90
 Maarten Bosker and Harry Garretsen

4. Do Lagging Regions Benefit from Trade?   137
 Pravin Krishna, Devashish Mitra, and Asha Sundaram

5. Is Growth Constrained by Institutions?   178
 Ana M. Fernandes, Maddalena Honorati, and Taye Mengistae

6. Education Policies and Outcomes in Lagging Regions   209
 Dhushyanth Raju

II A NEW APPROACH TO REDUCING POVERTY

7. Is Decentralization Helping the Lagging Regions?   257
   Lakshmi Iyer, Ejaz Ghani, and Saurabh Mishra

8. How Important is Migration?   294
   Çağlar Özden and Mirvat Sewadeh

9. Stimulating Agricultural Growth   323
   Ejaz Ghani and Surabhi Mittal

List of Contributors   341

Tables and Figures

TABLES

1.1	Per Capita Income and Poverty Headcount Ratios in South Asia (2005–7)	33
2.1	Convergence of Per Capita GDP and Household Consumption across Countries	67
2.2	Convergence in Per Capita Incomes across Regions of South Asia and States of India	70
2.3	Poverty Convergence across Countries Headcount Ratios Based on Poverty Line of $1.25 a Day	73
2.4	Convergence in Measures of Poverty Severity and Depth	76
2.5	Poverty Convergence in South Asia	78
2.6	Convergence in Health Indicators	83
2.7	Convergence in Education Indicators across Countries	85
2.8	Convergence in Social Indicators within South Asia	86
3.1	South Asia Compared with the Rest of the World	93
3.2	Comparing South Asian Countries	95
3.3	Leading and Lagging Regions Compared	100
3.4	South Asia Trade Patterns	112
3.5	Impediments to Trade	115
3.6	Market Access and GDP per Capita	124

3.7	Coastal and Border Population	125
3.8	Focus on Landlocked Regions	126
4.1	Poverty, Regional Inequality, and Geographical Measures by Country	146
4.2	Summary Statistics for Protection and Poverty Measures	148
4.3	Trade Liberalization Dates	150
4.4	Trade and Poverty—Overall Sector Dependent Variable: Log (DD Poverty Measure)	156
4.5	Trade and Poverty—Rural Sector Dependent Variable: Log (DD Poverty Measure)	157
4.6	Trade and Poverty—Urban Sector Dependent Variable: Log (DD Poverty Measure)	158
4.7	Trade and Poverty—Overall Sector Dependent Variable: Log (GoI Measure)	159
4.8	Trade and Poverty—Overall Sector Dependent Variable: Log (ODR Measure)	160
4.9	Price Transmission Regressions Dependent Variable: Log (Unit Price for Sector)	162
4.10	Production of Export Goods in Lagging Versus Leading States Dependent Variable: Output in Industry-state/Total State Output	165
4.11	Trade Liberalization and Productivity Dependent Variable: Log (Net Value Added)	166
4.12	Trade, Poverty, and Lagging Regions in South Asia	168
4.13	(a) Inequality (b) Poverty	170
4.14	Infrastructure and Inequality Indicators for 2007	173
4.15	Adult Literacy in South Asia	174
5.1	Regressions of Property Rights and Contracting Institutions on Historical Determinants	187
5.2	Regressions of GDP per Capita on Property Rights and Contracting Institutions	190
5.3	Indicators of Access to Finance	193
5.4	Indicators of Security of Property Rights	195
5.5	Indicators of Regulatory Costs	198
5.6	Indicators of Labour Regulations in India	200
5.7	Firm Performance, Contracting, and Property Rights Institutions	203

5.8   Getting Around Weak Contracting Institutions   204

6.1   School Participation Rates, India   215
6.2   School Participation Rates, Pakistan   217
6.3   School Participation Rates, Bangladesh   219
6.4   School Completion Rates, India   222
6.5   School Completion Rates, Pakistan   224
6.6   School Completion Rates, Bangladesh   225

7.1   Extent of Fiscal Decentralization in South Asia and
       the World   260
7.2   Major Revenue Sources and Expenditure Categories
       for National and Subnational Governments in
       South Asia   264
7.3   Fiscal Transfer Arrangements in South Asia   272
7.4   Level of Administrative Decentralization in South
       Asia and the World   283
7.5   Measures of Political Decentralization in South Asia
       and the World   287

8.1   Results of Gravity Estimation of Migration Flows
       between States in India, 2000   311

9.1   Contribution of Agriculture in South Asia   326
9.2   Agricultural Sector Contribution in Leading and
       Lagging Regions of India   326
9.3   Estimated Increase in Income with Increase in
       Productivity in Lagging Regions, India   328
9.4   Ordinary Least Squares Results: Regressions for
       Access to Food (South Asia)   333
9.5   Ordinary Least Squares Results: Regressions for
       Access to Food (India)   334
9.6   Ordinary Least Squares Results: Regressions for
       Access to Food (India)   335
9.7   Road Density in India   336
9.8   Per cent Area under Irrigation in India (2005–6)   337

APPENDIX TABLES
A1.5   Poverty Dataset Time Period   58
A9.1   Variables Definitions and Data Sources   338

FIGURES

1	Poverty Rates and Real GDP per Capita in South Asia and East Asia	4
2	Number of Poor People in South Asia, East Asia, and Sub-Saharan Africa	5
3	Problems of South Asia are Concentrated in Lagging Regions	6
4	Conflict (1998–2004)	7
5	Conflict is Concentrated in Poor Regions of South Asia	8
6	Poverty is Concentrated in Lagging Regions in India but in Leading Areas in China and Brazil	12
7	Different Types of Fiscal Transfers to Lagging Regions in India (2005–6)	16
8	Social Service Expenditures across Indian States (2006–7)	20
9	High Concentration of Informal Jobs in South Asia	21
1.1a	Comparing Change in Poverty and Change in Income (1977–2007)	34
1.1b	Comparing Change in Poverty and Change in Consumption (1977–2007)	35
1.2a	Change in Inequality and Change in Consumption Growth (1997–2007)	37
1.2b	Change in Inequality and Change in Growth in Indian States (1994–2005)	38
1.3	Comparing Poverty Reduction and Growth in the Indian States in a Global Setting	39
1.4	Comparing Change in Adult Literacy Rate with Income Growth (1990–2006)	40
1.5	Comparing Change in Secondary Education and Growth (1990–2006)	42
1.6	Comparing Change in Infant Mortality and Growth (1990–2007)	43
1.7	Comparing Child Malnutrition Rates in Indian States in a Global Setting (2005)	44
1.8	Comparing Immunization Rates in South Asia	45
1.9	Comparing Female Labour Force as a Share of the Total Labour Force (2005)	47
1.10	Problems of South Asia are Concentrated in Lagging Regions	48

1.11   South Asia's Lagging Regions have Poverty Mass
        and Leading Regions have Economic Mass   50–1

2.1   Is There Convergence in Per Capita GDP across
        Countries?   66
2.2   Sigma Divergence of per Capita Incomes   69
2.3   Is There Convergence of Per Capita Incomes across
        States of India?   70
2.4   Is There Convergence in Headcount Ratios
        (absolute level)?   72
2.5   Is There Convergence in Headcount Ratios
        (proportional reductions)?   74
2.6   Convergence in Infant Mortality Rates across
        Countries (absolute change)   81
2.7   Convergence in Infant Mortality Rates across
        Countries (proportional change)   82

3.1   South Asia's Leading and Lagging States   98
3.2   Regional Income Disparities in South Asia   102
3.3   The Bell Curve   105
3.4   Market Access and GDP per Capita at the National
        Level   110
3.5   South Asian Migration Patterns (2000)   118
3.6   Regional Income per Capita and South Asian
        Market Access   121
3.7   National and International (South Asian) Market
        Access and GDP per Capita   122
3.8   Distribution of South Asia's Largest Cities across
        Its Regions (2000)   128
3.9   Urbanization and Population Density   129

4.1   Production of Export Goods in Leading and
        Lagging States   164

5.1   Rule of Law and Per Capita Incomes   179
5.2   Property Rights and Contracting Institutions in
        South Asia   188

6.1   Evolution of HDI Values, South Asian Countries
        (1975–2005)   210

6.2   Evolution of Enrolment Rates, South Asian Countries   211
6.3   Minimum Competency Rates in Language and
       Mathematic Assessments among Rural Primary
       School Students, Indian States (2006 and 2008)   230
6.4   Primary School Student Achievemet in Sri Lanka
       Provinces (2003 and 2007)   232

7.1   Subnational Revenue and Expenditure Shares, India   261
7.2   Provincial Revenue and Expenditure Shares over
       Time, Pakistan   262
7.3   Transfers from Central to State Governments in
       India (2006–7)   267
7.4   Transfers from Federal to Provincial Governments,
       Pakistan (2004–5)   269
7.5   Transfers from Federal to Provincial Governments,
       Sri Lanka (2004)   270
7.6   Lagging Regions and Fiscal Transfers in India
       (2005–6)   274
7.7   Lagging Regions and Types of Fiscal Transfers in
       India (2005–6)   276
7.8   Lagging Regions and Fiscal Transfers in Pakistan   278
7.9   Lagging Regions and Fiscal Transfers in Sri Lanka   281
7.10   Per Capita Development Spending across Districts
       of Bangladesh   281
7.11   Administrative Decentralization and Development
       Outcomes (cross-country)   284
7.12   Social Service Expenditures across Indian States
       (2006–7)   286
7.13   Number of Government Tiers and Human Capital
       Investments   288

8.1   Main Patterns of Migration 1990s, India   297
8.2   Main Migration Corridors   298
8.3   Distribution of Migrants by Origin and Destination
       in India   299
8.4   Migration Patterns by Education Levels   300
8.5   Inter-state Migration between Leading and Lagging
       Regions in India (1990s)   302
8.6   Net Migration Flows among Leading and Lagging
       States by Education Level   303

8.7   Distribution of Migrants by Origin and Destination
         in Pakistan   305
8.8   Main Patterns of Migration in Pakistan   306
8.9   Main Corridors for the Low-Skilled and High-Skilled   307
8.10   Distribution of Migrants by Origin and Destination
         in Sri Lanka   308
8.11   Main Patterns of Migration in Sri Lanka   309
8.12   Income Relative to the Rural Poverty Line of
         Rural Unskilled Non-migrants and Rural–Rural
         Unskilled Migrants   315
8.13   Income Relative to the Urban Poverty Line of
         Urban Unskilled Non-migrants and Urban–Urban
         Unskilled Migrants   317
8.14   Income Relative to the Urban Poverty Line of
         Urban Skilled Non-migrants and Urban–Urban
         Skilled Migrants   319

9.1   Diverging Yield in Rice and Wheat in Regions of India   327

APPENDIX FIGURES
A1.1   Real GDP per Capita of States in South Asia (2004)   53
A1.2   Economic Mass (2004–5)   55
A1.3   Poverty Rates by State in South Asia   56
A1.4   Number of Poor People by State in South Asia   57

Preface

South Asia presents an interesting paradox, it is the second fastest growing region in the world, and it is also home to the largest concentration of people living in debilitating poverty. While South Asia is at a much more advanced stage of development, it has many more poor people than Sub-Saharan Africa.

Even as growth has reduced poverty rates in South Asia, the poverty rates have not fallen fast enough to reduce the total number of people living in poverty. The number of people living on less than $1.25 a day increased from 549 million in 1981 to 595 million in 2005. Most of the poor live in India, and their numbers have increased from 420 in 1981 million to 455 million in 2005.

Social indicators, such as human development and gender parities, have also not kept up with the pace of income growth. More than 250 million children are undernourished and more than 30 million children do not go to schools. More than one-third of adult women are anaemic. The share of female employment in total employment is also extremely low.

How can South Asia be an emerging global economic powerhouse and yet have high poverty rates, poor human development indicators, and huge gender disparities? Can high-income growth co-exist with dismal social outcomes? The answer depends on where one looks. National averages hide vast regional disparities and are misleading. A subnational focus sharpens and also explains the paradox of South Asia. This is the focus of this volume.

The leading regions in South Asia have done extremely well. They are the envy of other middle-income countries. Millions of people in leading regions have come out of poverty. Poverty in the leading regions can be eliminated in a generation, provided high growth can be sustained. The story of lagging regions is very different. Growth and poverty reduction have turned out to be extremely challenging. The gap between lagging and leading regions has increased.

Poverty, human misery, and gender disparities in South Asia are largely concentrated in the lagging regions. The distinction between lagging and leading regions is so sharp that they seem to be anchored in two different centuries. What are the causes of these spatial disparities in income, poverty, and human development? What should and what can public policies do? This is what this volume is all about. The volume recognizes that there are limits to growth in lagging regions, and that economic geography, globalization, and institutions will only lead to further concentration of economic activity in leading regions. With a focus on the poor half billion of South Asia, the essays in this volume put into perspective the colossal task ahead to eradicate poverty and enable inclusive growth. They not only provide fresh perspectives on spatial disparities but also provide innovative short-term and long-term policy solutions to overcome the limits to growth and escape poverty traps.

We examine the well-being of the poor half billion in South Asia from four different perspectives. First, we analyse spatial disparities in income, poverty, human development, and gender disparities within countries and across countries in South Asia in a global setting. Second, we examine if poverty acts as a barrier to growth. Poverty traps can occur if certain regions are unable to make the required improvements for growth or because they are not able to generate enough productivity improvements. Third, we explore why certain regions are growing, while others are lagging behind. We focus at the subnational level on the role that economic geography, globalization, and institutions (business climate, education) have played in growth, and whether they will continue to favour growth in the already-prosperous regions. Fourth, we ask whether policymakers should wait for growth to lift all boats or take direct policy actions to reduce poverty. We discuss a range of solutions spanning fiscal policy, human mobility, education, and agriculture. There is no one right way, or a universal fix in development. Pluralism in development has great value. The challenge is to find out what works best, in what context, and in what setting.

Are regional development policies and area-based policies that promote equitable growth a solution? Regional development policies aimed at promoting equitable growth is not a solution for two simple reasons. First, empirical evidence shows that convergence of per capita income between lagging and leading regions is neither a necessary nor a sufficient condition for achieving poverty and social convergence. Poverty and social convergence can co-exist with (widening or reducing) income divergence. Second, regional policies that promote balanced growth could lower overall growth rate itself and, therefore, slow down the pace of poverty reduction. It lowers growth when it targets the creators of wealth and the concentration of economic activity. South Asia has numerous examples of such failed regional policies.

While economic growth is critical for poverty reduction, reviving growth in lagging regions will take time. There are limits to growth in lagging regions since economic geography, institutions, and globalization will continue to favour economic concentration in the leading regions. This has been the experience in Brazil, China, Europe, Japan, and USA. South Asia is no exception.

Policymakers should primarily *invest in people* when it comes to lagging regions, and *invest in places* when it comes to leading regions. Such interventions will reduce human misery, increase migration to growth poles, and reduce spatial disparities.

Policymakers should give a high priority to increasing pro-poor fiscal transfers to lagging regions. Poor regions have a low base of economic activity to tax, and typically these regions have lower revenues. This revenue constraint prevents them from expanding safety nets and investing in human capital and hampers the delivery of government services. Achieving equity through fiscal transfers can ensure a level playing field. This equity is particularly important if the government services are important inputs into future growth potential, such as in developing a healthy and educated workforce. Simply directing additional financial resources to lagging regions will not be sufficient. It needs to be complemented with an increase in capacity, accountability, and governance.

The escape from poverty and human misery need not be slow. Not so long ago, Bihar, the poorest state in India, was known for its law and order problems (extortion, carjacking, kidnapping) and low growth. However, with the restoration of law and order, improved governance, increased use of fiscal transfers, and greater market integration and human mobility, Bihar has now started to turn a corner. So can others.

South Asia is at a critical stage of historical transformation and time is of the essence. There is no room for complacency. Growing disparities could stifle growth itself, and if not handled well, could undermine the security of development.

23 June 2010   Ejaz Ghani

The Poor Half Billion in South Asia
An Overview

Ejaz Ghani[*]

Poverty is the worst form of violence.

—Mahatma Gandhi

South Asia is the second fastest growing region in the world after East Asia. India has attracted global attention as an emerging economic powerhouse. The other South Asian countries including Bangladesh, Bhutan, Nepal, Pakistan, and Sri Lanka have also done well. Growth has reduced poverty rates. But poverty rates have not fallen fast enough to reduce the total number of poor people.

It is worrying that the number of people living in poverty has actually increased in a region which is growing so rapidly. South Asia has the largest concentration of people living in debilitating poverty on earth. It has more poor people than Sub-Saharan Africa. Nearly 600 million people live on less than US$ 1.25 a day (Ravallion et al. 2009). More than

[*]I am grateful to the participants at the review meeting in December 2009 for comments, and in particular, to peer reviewers Pranab Bardhan, Kaushik Basu, and Homi Kharas. I would like to thank E. Cardoso, P. B. Mehta, B. Debroy, A. Kraay, M. Ravallion, N. Yoshida, E. May, M. Pigato, J. Newman, R. Murgai, C. Astrup, D. Dasgupta, S. Kathuria, S. Mozumdar, and S. Ramalingam for suggestions/comments. I am grateful to S. Mishra for excellent research support and Jennifer Casasola for her assistance with the tables and figures. Any errors are my responsibility. The views expressed here are those of the author and do not necessarily reflect those of the World Bank.

250 million children are undernourished. More than 30 million children do not go to schools. More than one-third of adult women are anaemic. The share of female employment in total employment is extremely low. Misery and conflict have increased.

How can South Asia be an emerging economic powerhouse and yet have high poverty rates, poor human development, and huge gender disparities? Can high economic growth co-exist with dismal social outcomes? The answer lies in where one looks. National averages hide vast regional disparities and are misleading.

South Asia is a land of sharp contrast and mind boggling disparities. It has more pronounced regional disparities than the rest of the world. It is a land of two Asias. A lot of attention has been given to 'Asia Shining'. There is another side of 'Asia Suffering'. The distinction between the two is so sharp that they seem to be anchored in two different centuries. The gap between the two has widened.

The rich regions have experienced rapid growth, thanks to the benefits of *economic geography* (Krugman 1999), *globalization* (Bhagwati 1978), and *institutions* (Acemoglu et al. 2001). Firms, workers, and households have benefited from three key drivers of growth—scale economies, knowledge spill-overs, and calibrated risk management. Growth has contributed to more growth. They seem to have hit a virtuous circle. Some leading regions in India are the envy of middle-income countries. Poverty in leading regions can be eliminated in a generation, provided high growth can be sustained (Devarajan 2006). But the poor regions are doing no better than many Sub-Saharan African countries.

The problems of South Asia—poverty, dismal social outcomes, conflict, and gender disparities—are concentrated in the poor regions. Their growth potential is limited. This is further compounded by the weak capacity of the state to deliver social services. They seem to be trapped by the dual failure of market and the state.

What should be done to address the giant task still ahead to eradicate the largest concentration of poverty on earth? What are the challenges that the region faces as it undertakes the historic transformation from low income to middle income?

Growth, poverty, human development, and gender disparities in this volume are examined from four different perspectives.

1. It examines if the problems of South Asia are concentrated in certain regions by analysing *spatial disparities* in income, poverty, human development, and gender disparities within countries and across counties in South Asia in a global setting.

2. It examines if poverty acts as a barrier to growth, that is, it generates *poverty traps*. This can occur if certain regions are unable to make the required improvements for growth or because they are not able to generate enough productivity improvements.

3. It explores the *reasons behind regional disparities*, that is, why certain regions are growing, while others are lagging behind. It focuses at the subnational level on the role that economic geography, institutions, and globalization have played in growth and poverty reduction, and whether they will continue to favour growth and poverty reduction in the already-prosperous regions.

4. It asks the big question in development economics whether *policymakers should wait for growth to lift all boats or take direct policy interventions to reduce poverty*. Is it growth that will reduce poverty, or will poverty reduction sparkle growth? It examines a range of solutions spanning fiscal policy, human mobility, social service delivery, and agricultural development.

GROWTH AND POVERTY

The fact that the total number of poor people has increased in a rapidly growing region raises the question whether growth contributes to poverty reduction? Has the pace of poverty reduction in South Asia kept up with global trends on poverty reduction? The answer is yes to both.

In early 1980s, South Asian countries adopted pro-growth policies. Policymakers improved economic management, focused on the private sector as the engine of growth, and opened up to global markets. These reforms, along with increased domestic savings and investments, paid off. It increased South Asia's real gross domestic product (GDP) growth rate to 5.3 per cent per year (1980–2000) from 3.7 per cent per year (1960–80). Growth accelerated further to 7 per cent per year during the period 2000–8. The global financial crisis moderated growth during 2009, but South Asia has bounced back faster than other regions. Although the growth momentum has been led by India, other countries have also shown growth dynamism.

Figure 1 compares poverty rate ($1.25 a day poverty rate) and real GDP per capita in South Asia with East Asia. Both regions have a large population of around 1.5 billion each. In East Asia, the poverty rate fell dramatically from 77 per cent in 1981 to 16 per cent in 2005. This was helped by rapid growth in China, the largest country in East Asia, where the pace of poverty reduction has been fast. In South Asia, poverty reduction was modest, falling from 59 per cent in 1981 to 40

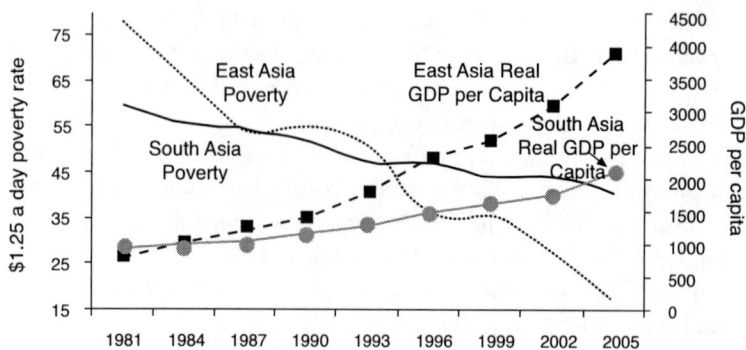

FIGURE 1   Poverty Rates and Real GDP per Capita
in South Asia and East Asia

Source: World Development Indicators (WDI), World Bank (2009).
Note: '$1.25 a day poverty rate' is the percentage of the population living on less
than $1.25 a day at 2005 international prices.

per cent in 2005. This was helped by India, which reduced its poverty
rate from 60 per cent in 1981 to 42 per cent in 2005. These estimates are
based on World Bank research which provides the most comprehensive
estimate of poverty in developing countries. Updated poverty estimates
are published every few years, based on the most recent global cost-of-
living data as well as on country surveys of what households consume
(Ravallion et al. 2009).

Cross-country comparisons suggest that the pace of poverty reduction
in South Asia, conditional on income growth, matches the global trend
(see Chapter 1). The point, however, is not whether South Asia has kept
up with the 'average' global pace, but whether it could do even better. The
region has not done as well as some of the better performers. South Asia's
average poverty rate remains more than double compared to East Asia.
It is much higher compared to other low- and middle-income countries
(Chapter 1).

Figure 2 compares the total number of people living on less than $1.25
a day in South Asia, East Asia, and Sub-Saharan Africa. In East Asia, the
number of poor people fell from 1.07 billion in 1981 to 316 million
in 2005. During the same period, it has increased in South Asia from
549 million to 595 million. It has increased in India from 420 million
people to 455 million. The total number of poor people in South Asia
is double that of Sub-Saharan Africa.

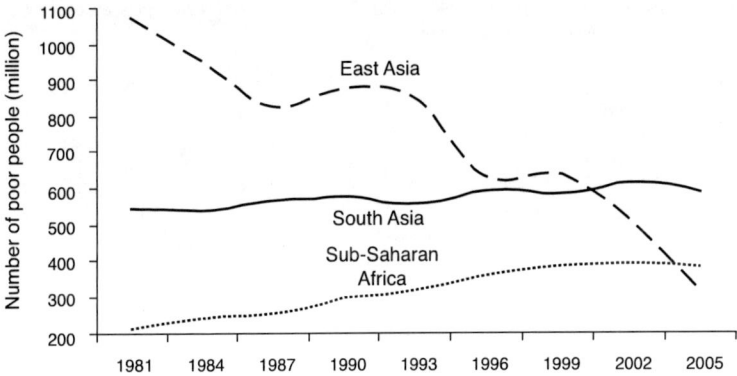

FIGURE 2   Number of Poor People in South Asia, East Asia,
and Sub-Saharan Africa

Source: *WDI*, World Bank (2009).
Notes: Poverty rate is the number of people living on less than US$ 1.25 a day
at 2005 international prices. South Asia regional aggregate includes Afghanistan,
Bangladesh, Bhutan, India, Maldives, Nepal, Pakistan, and Sri Lanka. East Asia
Pacific includes China.

Human development indicators have improved but they have not
kept up with the pace of income growth. Malnutrition rates, for example,
remain too high for South Asia's stage of development. Most of the
malnourished children will remain in poverty, since undernourishment
in early childhood leads to irreversible damage. Learning difficulties
increase the chance that children will drop out of school and never find
productive or regular employment as adults.

Despite a global female revolution in the last 50 years, gender
disparities are deeply embedded in South Asia. Afghanistan has some of
the worst gender disparities in the world. Attacks on schools in Afghanistan
are increasing at an alarming rate, and attacks are aimed at girls, in
particular, to keep them out of school. Female labour force participation
rates remain among the lowest in the world despite rapid growth.

Are problems of South Asia concentrated in certain regions? Figure 3
compares economic and social outcomes in lagging and leading regions.
Poverty rates in lagging regions are nearly double compared with leading
regions. The incidence of extreme poverty, that is, how far households are
from the poverty line as measured by poverty gap and poverty gap square,
is much higher in lagging regions. Poverty mass (number of poor people)
is much bigger. The availability of physical and human infrastructure like

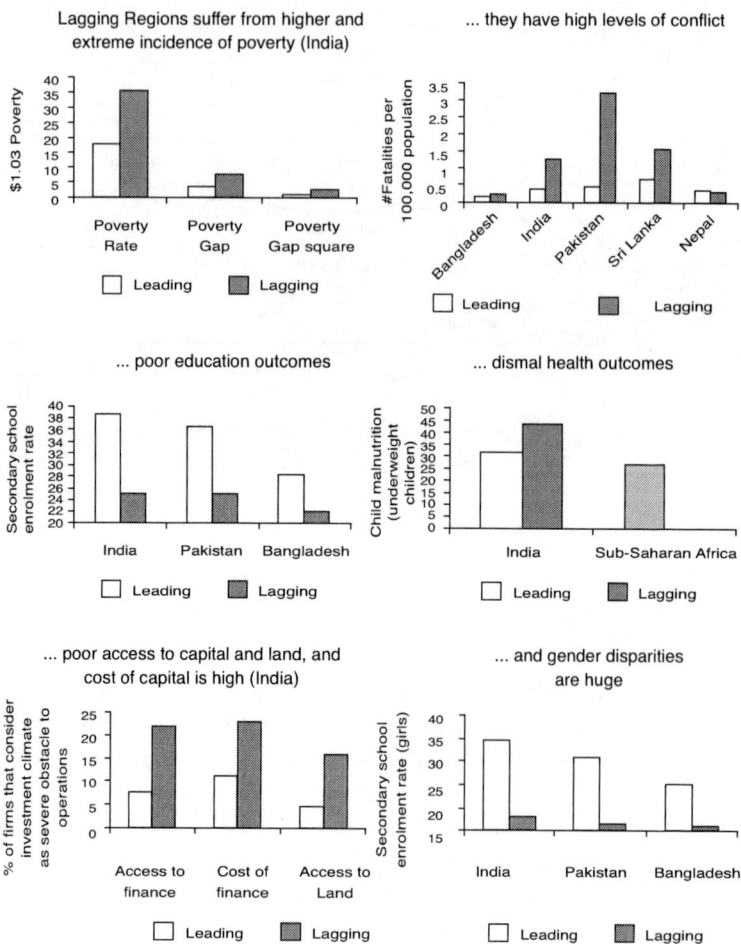

FIGURE 3   Problems of South Asia are Concentrated in Lagging Regions

Sources: World Bank staff estimates using National Sample Survey Organisation (NSSO) data for poverty estimates for India. Conflict data are from World Incidents Tracking System. Secondary school enrolment data from World Bank staff estimates using National Survey data. Child malnutrition data are from *WDI*, World Bank (2009).

Notes: Poverty figures are for Indian states in 2005. The national poverty line for India is international $1.03. Poverty gap is the mean distance below the poverty line as a proportion of the poverty line. Poverty gap square is the mean of the square distances below the poverty line as a proportion of the poverty line. Malnutrition prevalence is for underweight children below the age of five for Sub-Saharan Africa and the per cent of children under age three for Indian states. See Chapter 1 for data sources.

electricity, piped water, sanitation, roads, education, and healthcare are much worse in lagging regions. Firms face bigger restrictions in accessing credit and land assets in lagging regions. Law and order problems are a big concern.

Conflict rates are high in South Asia for its stage of development. The presence of conflict poses significant development challenges. Figure 4 plots conflict rates (number of people killed in conflict incidents normalized by population) and real per capita income for a large group of countries. The downward sloping line suggests that countries that have low per capita income have higher conflict rates. This is consistent with other findings that have reported higher conflict rates in low income countries (Collier et al. 2003).

Relationships between conflict, income, and poverty are more complex than is commonly assumed. Such relationships are not very tight, and there are many outliers, as shown in Figure 4. But what is even more striking in Figure 4 is that the outliers seem to be concentrated in South Asia (Ghani and Iyer 2010). Except for Bangladesh, all South Asian countries are above the line. Things have started to improve as civil wars in Nepal and Sri Lanka have ended. But ongoing conflicts have continued in Afghanistan and Pakistan.

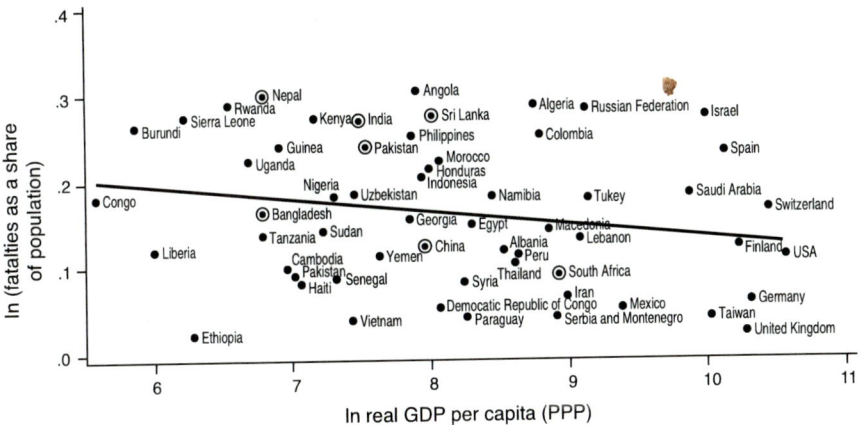

FIGURE 4 Conflict (1998–2004)

Source: Global Terrorism Database II, 1998–2004 (2008).
Notes: The figure takes the arithmetic mean for fatalities and income per capita for the period 1998–2004. Fatality is the number of total confirmed fatalities for the incident. The number includes all victims *and* attackers who died as a direct result of the incident.

Is conflict concentrated in poor regions? There are many types of conflict, including internal and external conflict or state-to-state conflict. The majority of conflicts in the developing world are now internal conflicts. While people-to-people conflict (ethnic conflict, Hindu/

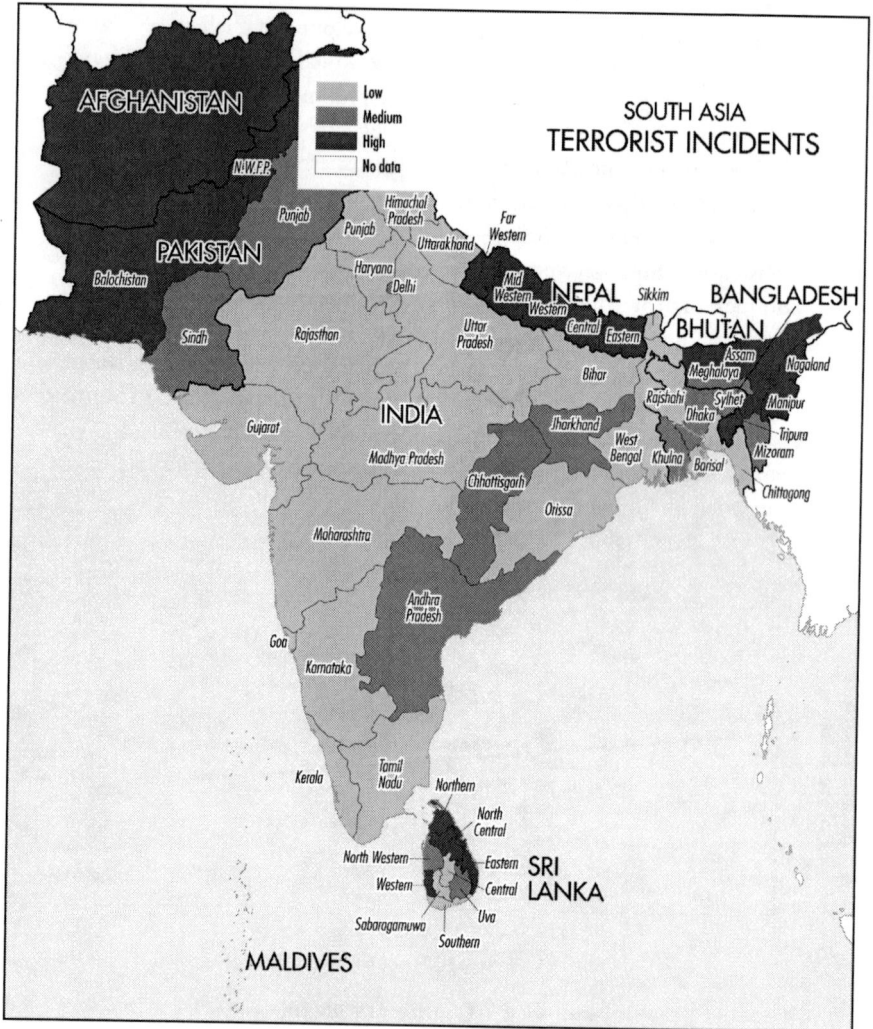

FIGURE 5   Conflict is Concentrated in Poor Regions of South Asia

Source: MIPT data was collected by the National Memorial Institute for the Prevention of Terrorism (MIPT), in collaboration with the National Counter Terrorism Center (NCTC).

Muslim riots) has declined over time, conflict against the state (or terrorism directed against the state) has increased. Conflicts against the state are perpetrated by a relatively organized group of non-state actors, and directed specifically against the apparatus of the state with the intent of destabilizing the state. They pose the greatest challenge to political stability and the ability of the state to implement development.

Figure 5 shows that in Afghanistan, Bangladesh, India, Nepal, Pakistan, and Sri Lanka, conflict is concentrated in the lagging regions. Lagging regions have experienced more than three times the number of conflict incidents per capita, compared with leading regions, and almost twice as many deaths per capita in such incidents. The lagging regions in Pakistan (Balochistan, Federally Administered Tribal Areas [FATA], and North-West Frontier Province [NWFP]), India (Naxalite insurgency in Bihar, Chhattisgarh, Jharkhand, and Orissa), Sri Lanka (North), and Nepal have attracted global attention.

Leading regions too have poverty and conflict, but rapid growth and stronger institutions have helped them to manage poverty and conflict better. The adverse consequences of poverty and conflict are more severe in regions that have weak institutions, poor geography, and are not integrated with markets. These are also the characteristics that limit growth in poor regions.

WHAT IS HOLDING BACK POOR REGIONS?

Are poor regions catching up or falling further behind rich regions? A divergence in poverty rates would suggest that lagging regions are trapped in poverty. A divergence in social outcomes would suggest there are social traps. If such traps exist, then policymakers may need to revisit prior beliefs about development theory and practice. If growth fails to pull people out of poverty, then policymakers may need to change their policy focus.

People can be trapped in poverty, when poverty itself becomes a constraint to growth. This occurs in regions that display characteristics of high conflict, low savings or investment rates, dismal education or health outcomes, poor access to credit or property rights, and incomplete insurance markets which increase the risks of crop failures, floods, and droughts (Banerjee and Duflo 2007). Poverty traps limit choices of economic agents, whether individuals, households, or firms, to fully express their economic potential. These traps can become a vicious cycle.

But not all economic and social outcomes have spatial characteristics. Education traps, for example, could be non-spatial. The poor in leading regions may never receive an education and hence never get out of poverty, as is the experience with the poor in developed economies. Health outcomes can be relatively independent of spatial income trends. Non-income factors (better access to ideas, knowledge, and information through television, mobile phones, and the Internet) may be as important to health outcomes as trends in spatial incomes.

Poverty traps may be local rather than regional. Leading regions have 'poor districts' and lagging regions have 'rich districts'. For example, some of the northern parts of Karnataka state, a leading region in India, are not different on many socio-economic parameters from poorer parts of lagging regions like Bihar and Uttar Pradesh and Sub-Saharan Africa. The same is true for areas around Dharmapuri in Tamil Nadu, a leading region in India.

Poverty traps at the local level are difficult to examine without a long time-series of micro panel data and strong assumptions. Given data limitations, we focus on the definition of an area that has administrative and data coherence and that can be used as a key instrument from a policy and development perspective. We focus at the state level data.

Poverty Traps

In Chapter 2, we examine whether poverty and social traps exist across three different types of space—within countries, across countries in South Asia, and globally. We consider convergence and divergence trends in income and poverty, health, and education outcomes.

Our empirical analysis uncovers four main findings.

1. Per capita incomes are not *converging* across leading and lagging regions of South Asia.
2. Despite this lack of convergence in per capita incomes, we see that areas with higher levels of poverty (lagging regions) achieve a greater reduction in the percentage of people living below the poverty line, as well as in measures of poverty depth and severity. They do not, however, achieve faster proportionate reductions in these poverty indicators.
3. Education indicators converge substantially but not in measures of health.
4. Finally, all these trends for the regions of South Asia are similar to the trends we observe across developing countries as a whole, with the exception that South Asia shows much *slower convergence* trends than the global sample. For instance, we see greater proportionate reductions in the squared poverty gap measure among initially poorer countries, but not among initially poorer regions within South Asia.

All in all, these results provide for cautious optimism on progress in the lagging regions. There is little evidence of persistent poverty traps at a regional level in South Asia, or even among developing countries as a whole. However, we do not see lagging regions catching up with leading regions in terms of per capita income or in health indicators or even in proportionate terms for poverty.

What explains huge disparities? Limited mobility (new economic geography), inability to benefit from trade (globalization), and high cost of doing business and high conflict rates in lagging regions (institutions) explain the limits to growth in lagging regions. We turn to them now.

New Economic Geography

The economic geography of lagging and leading regions is examined in Chapter 3. We find that economic mass is concentrated in the leading regions in all South Asian countries. This is not unique to South Asia—it has happened in Brazil and China.

As countries develop, economic activity gets concentrated in leading regions that are better located to take advantage of scale economies, risk management, and knowledge/technology spill-overs. This in turn concentrates economic mass in the leading regions. Bigger economic opportunities in leading regions, in turn, encourages people to migrate from lagging to leading regions, in search of jobs, which in turn increases the number of poor people in leading regions. Economic mass and poverty mass (number of poor people) thus converge in the same area. This can start a virtuous cycle of development which is good for growth and good for poverty reduction (*World Development Report* 2009).

Poverty mass in South Asia, unfortunately, is still concentrated in lagging regions. Figure 6 compares the spatial locations of poverty in Brazil, China, and India. In all three countries, *poverty rates* are much higher in lagging regions. This is where their similarity ends and differences begin. *Poverty mass* is concentrated in the coastal leading regions of Brazil and China. But in India and other South Asian countries, poverty mass is still concentrated in lagging regions. This asymmetry in the spatial location of economic mass and poverty mass is confirmed by lower migration and urbanization rates in South Asia compared with Brazil and China. India, which has a population size similar to that of China, has a migration rate of around 3 million people per year compared to around 7 million workers who migrate every year in China.

Because poverty mass is concentrated in lagging regions, regional development disparities are more pronounced in South Asia. It is not just

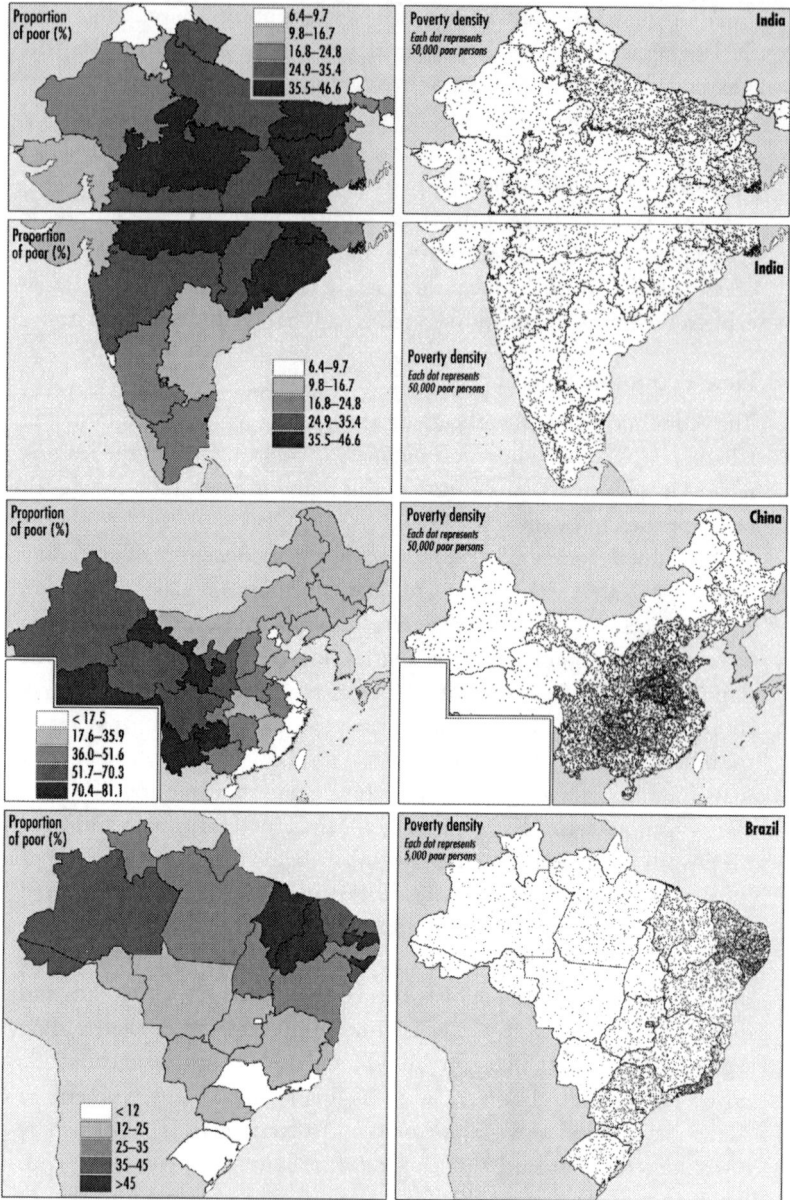

Proportion of poor (%)	
	6.4–9.7
	9.8–16.7
	16.8–24.8
	24.9–35.4
	35.5–46.6

Poverty density
Each dot represents 50,000 poor persons
India

Proportion of poor (%)

	6.4–9.7
	9.8–16.7
	16.8–24.8
	24.9–35.4
	35.5–46.6

Poverty density
Each dot represents 50,000 poor persons
India

Proportion of poor (%)

	< 17.5
	17.6–35.9
	36.0–51.6
	51.7–70.3
	70.4–81.1

Poverty density
Each dot represents 50,000 poor persons
China

Proportion of poor (%)

	< 12
	12–25
	25–35
	35–45
	>45

Poverty density
Each dot represents 5,000 poor persons
Brazil

FIGURE 6   Poverty is Concentrated in Lagging Regions in India
but in Leading Areas in China and Brazil

Source: World Development Report (2009).

labour mobility, but other factors such as globalization and institutions that also help explain why poverty remains concentrated in lagging regions.

Globalization

We examine whether globalization (through trade channels) is inclusive in South Asia in Chapter 4. Are the benefits of globalization shared equitably between lagging and leading regions?

Evidence shows that trade globalization has contributed to accelerated growth, but its benefits are spread unevenly across lagging and leading regions. Trade liberalization is associated with reduced poverty, but its effect is much greater in leading regions. The expected transmission of international prices to domestic prices with openness to trade is less perfect in lagging states than in leading ones. Growth and poverty reduction in lagging regions are impeded by the lack of exposure to international markets, as opposed to another commonly argued factor—the competition to domestic production from international trade.

The benefits of globalization are concentrated in leading regions because production benefits from economies of scale and market forces induce production to agglomerate in leading regions. The lagging regions do not have the same level of access to international trade, because weak infrastructure and institutions result in high transportation costs and a high cost of doing business.

Institutions

We examine the critical role institutions have played in the development of South Asia in Chapter 5. We distinguish between two key dimensions of institution: property rights institutions and contracting institutions. At the national level, we find that while India has poor performance on contracting institutions, it fares reasonably well on measures of property rights institutions. The reverse is true for Bangladesh.

Property rights institutions matter more for growth than contracting institutions. India's good performance on property rights institutions has not yet had the development impact that cross-country analysis would suggest. In contrast, Bangladesh stands out in the opposite direction, with a predicted income level based on its institutional quality that is much lower than its actual income level. It may be that India has a great deal of scope for future growth given its good institutional performance, while Bangladesh's current relatively high income levels (given its weak institutional quality) are more likely to be unsustainable.

Do institutions differ between leading and lagging regions? We document important institutional differences using micro data. We find that lagging regions exhibit a substantially poorer institutional environment. Firms are more difficult and costlier to set up in these regions, and once set up, they have greater difficulties in raising formal external finance. Property rights are also less secure in lagging regions.

Weak institutions limit the economic choices of households, firms, and workers in poor regions. For example, farmers, who constitute the majority of the labour force in lagging regions, find risk hard to bear. So they spread their risk by not specializing in any one occupation. They work part-time outside agriculture to reduce their exposure to farming risk, and keep a foot in agriculture to avoid being overly dependent on their non-agricultural jobs. Their access to credit is restricted, or the cost of credit is too high. Financial and credit markets inherently suffer from moral hazard and adverse selection problems. But these problems are worse in lagging regions because of weak property rights and contracting institutions. The poor have very little collateral to secure loans and, therefore, lenders hesitate to trust them with a lot of money. Land titles are also difficult to obtain in lagging regions. Given poor institutions (market distortions, poor access to credit, and weak property rights), entrepreneurs attach greater risk premiums to the expected returns on investment projects in lagging regions than they attach to the expected returns on projects in leading regions. Hence, as a response to lower risk-adjusted expected rates of returns, investments in lagging regions tend to be lower. Stronger institutions can reduce the cost of doing business and accelerate growth. At the heart of growth processes are governance institutions that determine access to opportunities (credit, land, education, and health) which can either accelerate or stifle growth.

Education

In Chapter 6, we compare the trends on education outcomes in lagging and leading regions. Evidence shows that education indicators in lagging areas in India and Pakistan are worse than in leading areas, with girls in Pakistan facing a particularly large disadvantage. With the exception of primary school participation and completion in India, the gaps between leading and lagging areas in these two countries appear not to have narrowed over the recent past.

In Bangladesh, participation and attainment outcomes between the leading division of Dhaka and the other divisions (all lagging) do not appear to be different. The provinces in Sri Lanka appear to have comparable outcomes at the primary and secondary level; evidence also shows lagging provinces are catching up to the leading Western province in student achievement. The differences that do exist are between the lagging North and Eastern provinces (which until recently were under conflict) and the leading Western province. In general, the battle of closing the education divide between lagging and leading areas has shifted from the primary level to the secondary level and higher education.

WHAT SHOULD BE DONE?

What should policymakers do to reduce spatial concentration of poverty? Are regional development policies and area-based policies a solution? Can growth be the total solution? Or should policymakers take direct policy interventions to reduce human misery?

Regional development policies aimed at promoting equitable growth is not a solution for two simple reasons. First, empirical evidence shows that convergence of per capita income between lagging and leading regions is neither a necessary nor a sufficient condition for achieving poverty and social convergence. Poverty and social convergence can co-exist with (widening or reducing) income divergence. Second, regional policies that promote balanced growth could lower overall growth rate itself and, therefore, slow down the pace of poverty reduction. It lowers growth when it targets the creators of wealth and the concentration of economic activity. A prime example of this is investment license *raj* in India, which promoted investments in the lagging regions but failed to increase growth rates. South Asia has numerous other examples of such failed regional policies.

Growth should not be the total solution, given limits to growth in lagging regions. Growth is important but reviving growth will take time. In the short run, policymakers should consider taking direct policy interventions to reduce poverty through pro-poor fiscal transfers. This should be accompanied by increased market of integration of regions that are not doing too well with regions that are doing well. Human mobility is a good example of market integration that promotes inclusive growth. A precondition for direct policy interventions to reduce poverty and promote inclusive growth is reducing conflict. Solutions will depend on local conditions and context, and they will vary within countries and across countries.

Pro-poor Fiscal Transfers

The existing transfers from the central government do not adequately correct for human and infrastructure deficiencies of lagging regions. Chapter 7 explores this theme. In most countries, fiscal transfers, through a system of inter-state transfers, ensure equity across subnational regions. This equity is important for economic and political reasons. Poorer regions have a lower base of economic activity to tax, and typically these regions have lower revenues. This revenue constraint prevents them from expanding safety nets, investing in human and physical capital, and hampers the delivery of government services. Achieving horizontal equity through fiscal transfers can ensure a level playing field. This equity can be particularly important if the government services are important inputs into future growth potential, such as in developing a healthy and educated workforce. Growing regional disparities can cause political tensions, and fiscal transfers can offset some of these disparities.

The performance of South Asian countries in achieving horizontal equity is mixed. The systems of inter-state fiscal transfers in South Asian countries transfer a greater amount of resources to poorer regions, suggesting that they are working to achieve greater equity. However, this outcome usually occurs when pro-poor redistribution has explicit rules. Simply directing financial resources to lagging regions may not be sufficient and may need to be complemented with increases in capacity, accountability, and participation at the local level.

When we look at the different components of fiscal transfers in India, it is clear that horizontal equity is being achieved only through the tax-sharing schemes of the Finance Commission (see Figure 7A).

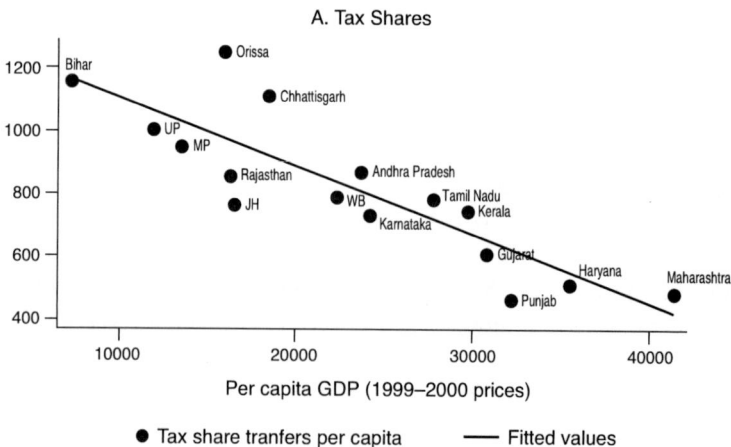

A. Tax Shares

B. State Plan Schemes

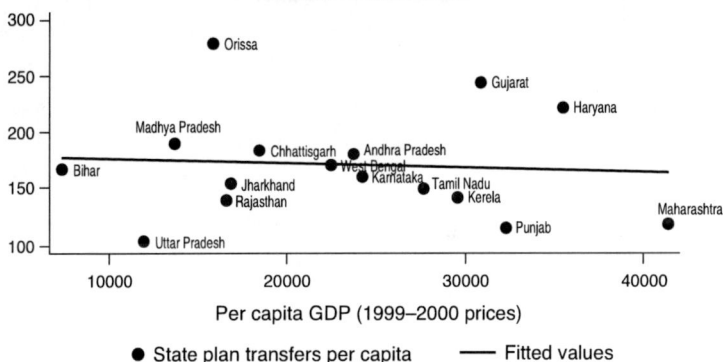

State plan transfers per capita — Fitted values

C. Discretionary Schemes

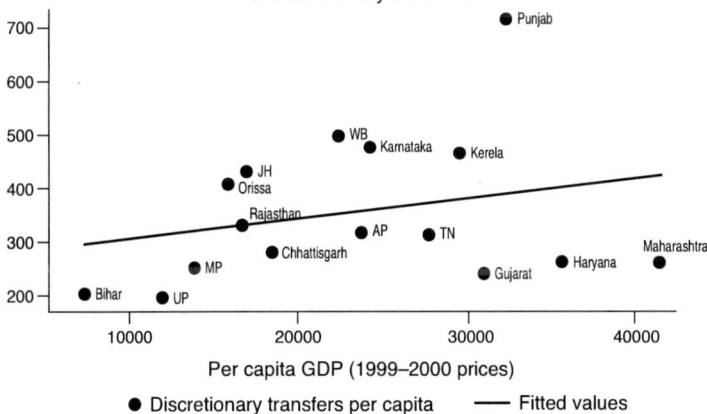

Discretionary transfers per capita — Fitted values

D. Food Subsidy (sales)

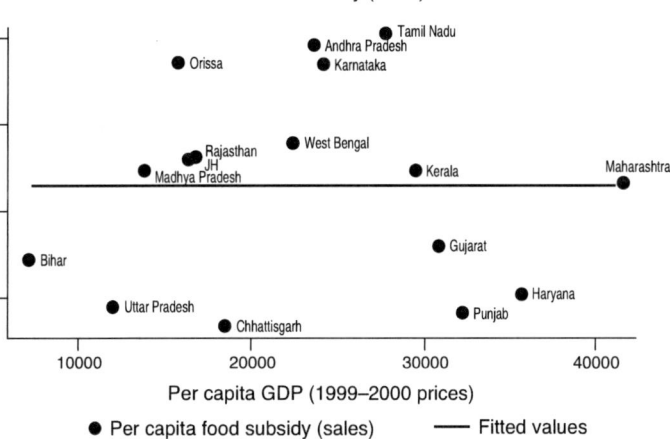

Per capita food subsidy (sales) — Fitted values

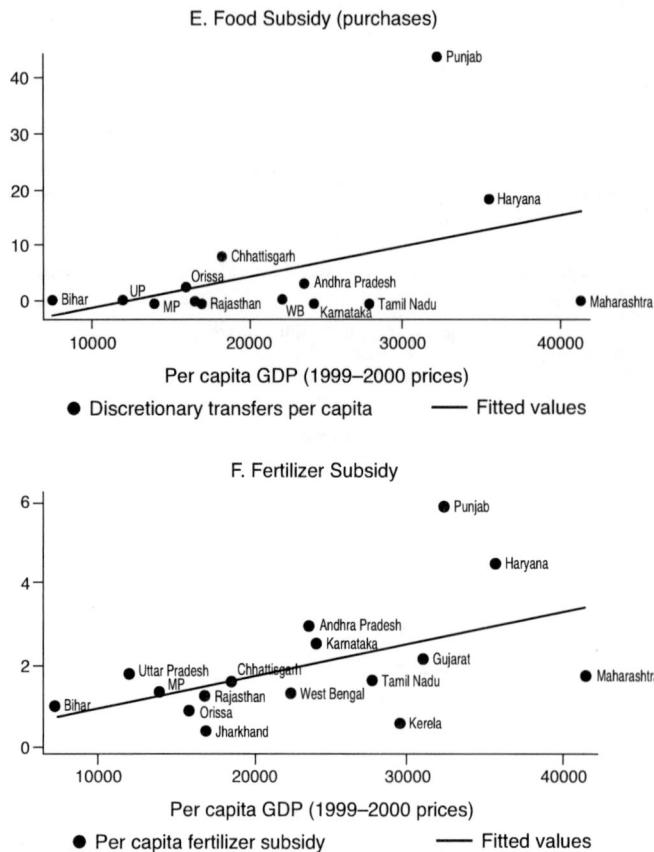

E. Food Subsidy (purchases)

F. Fertilizer Subsidy

FIGURE 7   Different Types of Fiscal Transfers to Lagging Regions
in India (2005–6)

Sources: Indian Public Finance Statistics, 2007–8, Ministry of Finance; and Food
Corporation of India for food subsidy allocation.
Notes: States in India can obtain resources from the central government in three
main ways. The first consists of tax shares and grants decided by a non-political
Finance Commission. Centrally-sponsored schemes give various ministries grants
to their counterparts in the states for specified projects either wholly funded by the
centre (central sector projects) or requiring the states to share a proportion of the
cost (centrally-sponsored schemes). These are wholly discretionary and often are
not coordinated with Planning Commission transfers. In addition to these explicit
transfers from the centre to the states, a number of 'hidden' or 'implicit' transfers
arise from the large subsidies given by the central government for food and fertilizers,
the existence of subsidized borrowing resources for the states from the central
government or government-owned financial institutions, and tax exportation. The
largest component of fiscal transfers in India comes from the tax-sharing schemes,
for which the Finance Commission has an explicit mandate to help poorer states.

Discretionary schemes show higher per capita expenditures in the richer states (see Figure 7C). Food subsidies per capita are roughly uniform across poor and rich states, that is, if we assume that all subsidies are used for the sale of food by the Food Corporation of India (see Figure 7D). Conversely, if we allocate food subsidies on the assumption that all the subsidies are spent in food procurement through above-market procurement prices, then the highest levels of subsidies are given to the leading states of Punjab, Haryana, and Maharashtra (see Figure 7E).

The true picture is probably a mix of production and consumption subsidies, but the conclusion is that these food subsidies are not significantly higher in poorer regions. If we look at the second-largest source of subsidies, fertilizers, we see that this subsidy benefits richer regions much more than poorer regions, because the richer regions tend to consume more fertilizer (see Figure 7F). If the subsidies are meant to improve welfare programmes and investment levels in lagging regions, they need to be targeted to those regions, rather than to a specific good or service that may be consumed more heavily in richer states.

The food subsidy mainly helps better-off farmers and consumers in leading regions where the public distribution system has more effective coverage. The lagging regions do not have effective access to subsidized food grains. The subsidies on petrol and diesel also mainly accrue to better-off regions, and they undermine the development of more effective electricity distribution network, which keep villages in darkness. The success of mobile telephones in rural areas shows that subsidies are not necessary to reach the lagging regions.

In Pakistan and Sri Lanka, we see poorer regions obtaining a higher level of per capita fiscal transfers. In Sri Lanka, the highest levels of per capita funding have been allocated to the North-East Province, the centre of a long-running Tamil separatist movement. In this sense, fiscal transfers appear to address a political problem as well. In Bangladesh, however, no explicit mandates direct resource transfers toward poorer regions. The World Bank's recent public expenditure report on Bangladesh raised the concern that poorer regions are being allocated lower levels of per capita development funding.

Because subsidies reduce fiscal space for other things, the poorer states spend considerably less on social services, including education and health care (see Figure 8). A key source of budget deficit is commodity-related subsidies (fuel, fertilizers, food) (Devarajan et al. 2006). One way of overcoming the resource problem would be to divert resources from

Social Services per Capita

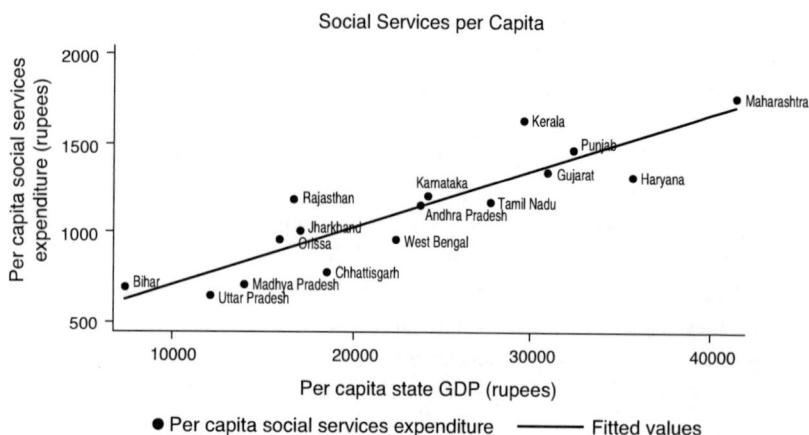

FIGURE 8   Social Service Expenditures across Indian States (2006–7)

Source: Indian Public Finance Statistics 2007–8, Ministry of Finance, Government of India (2008).

existing subsidy-oriented programmes towards better targeted safety net, education, health, and infrastructure.

Human Mobility

Removing barriers to human mobility is an integral part of economic development and poverty reduction. Labour mobility, like all other reallocation mechanisms, should allow labour to move to geographic areas and economic sectors, where the demand and the returns are much higher. Chapter 8 examines labour mobility. South Asia suffers from exceptionally low human mobility. In India, Pakistan, and Sri Lanka, inter-state migrants rarely constitute more than 6 per cent of that state's population. Despite large potential gains from migration, people in South Asia stay in their regions.

Globalization has exploded mobility of goods and capital flows, but human mobility remains unduly restricted. Unlike the explosive growth in global trade and global capital, the share of international migrants in the world's population has remained stagnant at around 3 per cent over the last 50 years, despite reduced cost of travel, increased demographic pressures (aging population in developed economies and a young population in South Asia), growing employment opportunities, and cheaper communications and travel costs.

Labour migration benefits poor areas through two key channels: remittance flows and a wage-pull effect, as excess lower skilled labour in one area migrates to another. Most migrants maintain strong links with their home communities and send remittances. These remittances transfer some of the benefits of growth from the leading to the lagging areas. Migration has contributed to reducing differences in non-agricultural wages across provinces. Migration integrates labour markets. By pulling up wages in lagging regions, migration benefits non-migrants in these regions.

Cross-country evidence shows that the size of informal labour markets is inversely related to income, so workers move from informal to formal labour markets as income increases (see Figure 9). India and most South Asian countries are huge outliers on this—they have much bigger informal labour markets, for their stage of their development. Labour market distortions have slowed the pace at which workers move from informal to formal markets, or from rural to urban areas. Barriers to mobility include labour market restrictions and state-specific social welfare programmes. If migrants are not eligible for certain welfare programmes outside their state, then they will have lower incentives to move. Similarly, deficiencies in rural land ownership laws and rules and distortions in urban housing markets create additional mobility costs.

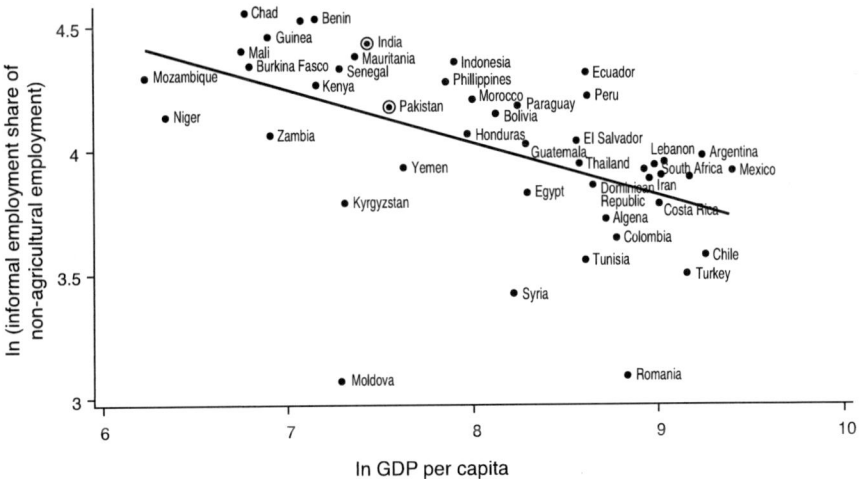

FIGURE 9   High Concentration of Informal Jobs in South Asia

Source: OECD (2009).
Notes: This figure uses the latest available data, 1995–9 or 2000–7. Informal employment being defined as the non-coverage by social protection, it is measured by the response to the question on coverage in labour force surveys.

Social and cultural barriers also affect mobility. Linguistic barriers can create significant costs for the unskilled and the uneducated.

Gains of labour mobility are not equally shared between educated and uneducated migrants. The gains are much higher for skilled workers. In India, the mobility rate increases with the education level. The mobility of university-educated people is much higher than the mobility of the unskilled workers. A range of empirical evidence supports the positive impacts of migration on poverty reduction, human development, and gender disparities. Migration tends to empower the traditionally disadvantaged groups, in particular women.

Stimulating Agriculture

Slow agricultural growth has constrained economic opportunities for the vast majority of poor people in lagging regions. Both market failure and state failure are more acute in agriculture than in manufacturing and services sectors. Farmers in lagging regions are less integrated into state-supported structures, such as crop and livestock extension systems, price support systems, provision of credit, cooperatives, and networks for processing and marketing.

Policymakers should consider recasting agriculture in the new environment of globalization, growing domestic demand, and supply chains. Both productivity gains and supply chain efficiency need to be improved. A precondition for this is to create a business environment conducive to private sector participation. The private sector should realize profits from its investment in supply chains and to be confident that returns from future commitments are justified by the risks which this investment entails. Technology can play a key role in connecting farmers directly to broader, deeper, and global markets. The food price crisis of 2007–8 has served as a 'wake up call' for policymakers and has created an opportunity to revisit existing agricultural policies. This is examined in the last chapter.

CONCLUSION

South Asia is the second fastest growing region in the world. Growth has reduced poverty rates. But poverty rates have not fallen fast enough to reduce the total number of poor people.

The problems of South Asia—poverty, social dismal outcomes, conflict, and gender disparities—are concentrated in the lagging regions. South Asia has more pronounced regional development disparities than the rest of the world. There are limits to growth in poor regions, since economic geography, institutions, and globalization will continue to favour economic concentration in the leading regions. History shows that this has been the development experience of Brazil, China, Europe, Japan, and USA. South Asia is not an exception.

So what should be done? There is no 'one right way' or a 'universal fix' in development (Rodrik and Rosenzweig 2010). Pluralism in development has great value. The challenge is to find out what works best, in what context, and in what settings.

While economic growth is critical for poverty reduction, reviving growth in poor regions will take time. Meanwhile, policymakers should consider direct policy interventions to reduce poverty. Such direct policy interventions can have double dividend—it will reduce human misery, which in turn, could *spark* growth.

A high priority should be given towards increasing pro-poor fiscal transfers. Poor regions have a low base of economic activity to tax, and typically these regions have lower revenues. This revenue constraint prevents them from expanding safety nets, investing in human and physical capital, and hampers the delivery of government services. Achieving equity through fiscal transfers can ensure a level playing field. This equity is particularly important if the government services are important inputs into future growth potential, such as in developing a healthy and educated workforce. Simply directing financial resources to lagging regions, however, may not be sufficient. It will need to be complemented with increase in capacity, accountability, and participation at the local level.

Pro-poor fiscal transfers and improved governance should be accompanied by increased market integration and human mobility. Removing barriers to human mobility is an integral part of economic development and poverty reduction. Labour mobility, like all other reallocation mechanisms, allows labour to move to geographic areas and economic sectors, where the demand and the returns are much higher. It promotes growth and reduces poverty. The experience of Nepal and several other countries has shown that migration can be the single most important driver of poverty reduction and human development. Migration also empowers the traditionally disadvantaged groups, in particular women.

The escape from human misery need not be slow. Not so long ago, Bihar, the poorest state in India and in whole of South Asia, was known for law and order problems, extortion, carjacking, kidnapping, and low growth. However, with the restoration of law and order, improved

governance, increased use of fiscal transfers, and greater market integration
and human mobility, Bihar has started to turn a corner. So can others.
South Asia is at a critical stage of historical transformation. Time is of
the essence. There is no room for complacency.

REFERENCE

Acemoglu, Daron, Simon Johnson, and James A. Robinson. 2001. 'The Colonial
    Origins of Comparative Development: An Empirical Investigation', *American
    Economic Review*, 91 (5): 1369–1401.
Acharya, Shankar and Rakesh Mohan. 2010. *India's Economy: Performances and
    Challenges, Essays in Honour of Montek Singh Ahluwalia*. New Delhi: Oxford
    University Press.
Ahluwalia, Montek, 2002. 'Privatization: From Policy Formulation to
    Implementation. The View from Inside', Annual Fellows Lecture, Center for
    Advanced Study of India, University of Pennsylvania, April 2002.
Ahmed, Sadiq and Ejaz Ghani (eds). 2007. *South Asia—Growth and Regional
    Integration*. New Delhi: Macmillan Press.
Ahmed, Sadiq, Saman Kalegamma, and Ejaz Ghani (eds). 2010. *Promoting
    Economic Cooperation in South Asia*. New Delhi: Sage Publications.
Banerjee, A. and E. Duflo. 2007. 'The Economic Lives of the Poor', *Journal of
    Economic Perspective*, 21 (1): 141–67.
———. 2006. 'The Economic Lives of the Poor', Working Paper No. 0629,
    MIT Department of Economics.
———. 2004. 'Growth Theory through the Lens of Development Economics',
    in Steve Durlauf and Anne Philippe Case (eds), *Handbook of Economic
    Growth*, Volume 1A.
Banerjee, Abhijit Vinayak, Roland Bénabou, and Dilip Mookherjee (eds). 2006.
    Understanding Poverty. New York: Oxford University Press.
Bhagwati, J. and T.N. Srinivasan. 2002. 'Trade and Poverty in the Poor Countries',
    American Economic Review Papers and Proceedings, 92(2): 180–3.
Collier, Paul, V.I. Elliott, Hårvard Hegre, Anke Hoeffler, Marta Reynold-Querol,
    and Nicholas Sambanis. 2003. *Breaking the Conflict Trap: Civil War and
    Development Policy*, Oxford: Oxford University Press.
Devarajan, Shanta. 2006. *Can South Asia Eliminate Poverty in a Generation?*
    Washington, D.C.: World Bank.
Devarajan, Shanta and Ejaz Ghani. 2006. 'Oil Price Shocks, Fiscal Adjustment
    and Poverty Reduction in South Asia', Mimeo, World Bank, Washington,
    D.C.
Ghani, Ejaz (ed.). 2010. *The Service Revolution in South Asia*. New Delhi: Oxford
    University Press.
———. 2010. 'Do Cities Matter?', World Bank South Asia Blog on Ending
    Poverty, World Bank.

Ghani, Ejaz and Lakshmi Iyer. 2010. 'Conflict and Development', VoxEU, 23 (March).

Ghani, Ejaz and Sadiq Ahmed (eds). 2009. *Accelerating Growth and Job Creation.* New Delhi: Oxford University Press.

Kelkar, Vijay. 2010. 'On Strategies for Disinvestment and Privatisation', 26th Sir Purshotamdas Thakurdas Memorial Lecture. Available at www.iibf.org.in/documents/ptmllecutre_jan2010.pdf.

Krugman, Paul. 1999. 'The Role of Geography in Development', *International Regional Science Review,* 22 (2): 142–61.

Panagaria, Arvind. 2009. *India: The Emerging Giant.* New Delhi: Oxford University Press.

Ravallion, Martin, Shaohua Chen, and Prem Sangraula. 2009. 'Dollar a Day Revisited', Policy Research Working Paper No. 4620, World Bank, Washington, D.C.

Rodrik, Dani. 2009. *One Economics, Many Recipes: Globalization, Institutions, and Economic Growth.* Princeton, NJ: Princeton University Press.

Rodrik, Dani and Mark R. Rosenzweig (eds). 2010. *Handbook of Development Economics,* Volume 5 (Handbooks in Economics). Amsterdam: North-Holland.

Subramanian, Arvind. 2009. *India's Turn: Understanding the Economic Transformation.* New Delhi: Oxford University Press.

I

Improving Growth in
Lagging Regions

1

Development Disparities and Peculiarities

Ejaz Ghani*

South Asia is home to 1.5 billion people. It has attracted global attention for its economic growth. India and other South Asian countries are seen as emerging powerhouses. While growth moderated in 2009 as a result of the global financial crisis, it has bounced back faster in South Asia than in other regions.

The region has also attracted global attention for high rates of poverty and conflict. It has the largest concentration of poor and conflict-affected people. More than 1 billion people live on less than US$ 2 a day. Even more strikingly, 600 million of the poor live on less than US$ 1.25 a day (Chen and Ravallion 2009). Development in South Asia has been markedly uneven (Bardhan 2009; Ghani and Ahmed 2009; Chaudhuri and Ravallion 2007; Devarajan 2006; Purfield 2006; Sen and Himanshu 2004; Dreze and Sen 2002).

This chapter examines success, opportunities, and challenges facing South Asia. How do Afghanistan, Bangladesh, Bhutan, India, Maldives, Nepal, Pakistan, and Sri Lanka compare with the rest of the world

*I am grateful to S. Mishra for research assistance, Jennifer Casasola for her assistance with the tables and figures, and to participants at the review meeting in December 2009 for comments/suggestions. In particular, I would like to thank K. Basu, P. Bardhan, H. Kharas, E. Cardoso, D. Dasgupta, E. May, L. Iyer, A. Kraay, J. Newman, M. Ravallion, R. Murgai, P. Joddar, and M. Pigato. Any remaining errors are my responsibility.

on growth, poverty, conflict, human development, and gender outcomes? Has poverty reduction matched income growth? Has human development kept up with income growth? Have gender disparities declined? Do national level comparisons hide vast disparities at subnational levels? Are South Asia's problems concentrated in the lagging regions? What explains the disparities—geography, institutions, or globalization? What can be done to promote inclusive development?

We compare poverty in South Asia from three different spatial perspectives: global, regional, and within country. Although the focus is on poverty, we also examine other development indicators including conflict, education, health, and gender outcomes, since they are important for escaping from poverty (Banerjee and Duflo 2004, 2006). Without freedom from illness, freedom from illiteracy, and freedom from inequality of opportunity, escaping from poverty will remain elusive for poor people.

This chapter presents three key empirical findings. First, South Asia is a poor region as its poverty rate is much higher than the average poverty rate in low and middle-income countries and is more than double compared with East Asia. Growth has been instrumental in reducing poverty. When we compare *change* in poverty, conditional on income growth, South Asia's performance matches the global trend. But they can do even better. India and other South Asian countries have not done as well as China. Indeed, poverty rates have not fallen fast enough to reduce the total number of poor people in South Asia. The total number of poor people has actually increased.

Second, human development outcomes have not kept up with income growth. South Asian countries compare dismally in a global setting on most human development and gender outcomes (Devarajan 2006). Primary education completion rates in South Asia are among the lowest in the world. Out of every 100 students that enter the primary education cycle, fewer than 10 graduate out of secondary education (World Bank 2009a). More than 30 million children, mostly poor, do not go to primary schools. On any given day, anywhere between 20 and 25 per cent of government teachers and health workers in India are absent from the schools and clinics they serve (Kremer et al. 2005; Chaudhary et al. 2005; Das and Hammer 2004).

South Asia's performance on health outcomes are puzzling (Deaton 2007; Das et al. 2006; Duflo 2005). Despite rapid income growth, child malnutrition rates, infant mortality rates, and immunization rates remain dismally low. More than one-third of adult women in India are anaemic

(Deaton and Dreze 2009). India has much higher child malnutrition rates than Sub-Saharan Africa. Most of the malnourished children will remain in poverty, as children who are undernourished in early childhood tend to suffer irreversible damage. Learning difficulties increase the chance that children will drop out of school and will be unable to find productive employment as adults. So poverty will persist.

Income growth should stimulate human development. People demand more and better education and health as incomes increase. South Asian countries have achieved first-generation goals on educational attainment. Improvements in adult literacy have outpaced income growth in South Asia compared with the global norm. But they have yet to fully address second-generation human development reforms. In particular, South Asian countries are lagging behind in secondary education compared to East Asia (World Bank 2009d). Secondary education is critical in breaking the intergenerational cycle of poverty, in an increasingly knowledge-intensive and globalized world. Secondary education is more important than primary education for poverty reduction in South Asia, given that service-led growth is more skill intensive compared with manufacturing-led growth (World Bank 2010).

The world has experienced a female revolution, but gender disparities remain huge in South Asia (Das and Desai 2003). Pakistan has one of the lowest ratios on the share of female employment in total employment. In India too, female participation in the labour force is extremely low. The school enrolment rate for girls is low and they account for just 34 per cent of total enrolment in Afghanistan and 41 per cent in Pakistan.

Third, the problems of South Asia are concentrated in the lagging regions. National-level comparisons hide huge disparities at subnational levels. A massive divide exists between lagging and leading regions. Lagging regions in India, Bangladesh, and Pakistan are not doing any better than some Sub-Saharan African countries.

This is worrying because poverty and conflict are both concentrated in lagging regions. Growth remains low and volatile because of conflict (institutions), limited mobility (economic geography), and weak effects of trade in transmitting price signals to lagging regions (globalization). If this goes unchecked, lagging regions could plunge into a low equilibrium trap of poverty, conflict, and human misery (Banerjee et al. 2006; Purfield 2006; World Bank 2006; Sen and Himanshu 2004). Growth will help, but there are limits to growth in lagging regions. Growth can never be equalized between lagging and leading regions (World Bank 2009d), nor will growth be sufficient to reduce poverty, conflict, gender disparities, and human misery (Banerjee and Duflo 2007).

The leading regions are also home to poor people. However, the way out of poverty for them is better understood. If double-digit growth rates can be attained, poverty can be eliminated (that is, they can reduce income poverty rates to single digits) in a generation (Devarajan 2006). The prospects for achieving double-digit growth rates is bright provided reforms can be accelerated and infrastructure improved. However, under the current growth conditions, lagging regions will not be able to achieve the United Nation's Millennium Development Goals by 2015.

The rest of the chapter is organized as follows. First, we compare the pace of poverty reduction conditional on income growth in South Asia with the rest of the world. Second, we examine how South Asia has performed on human development and gender outcomes. Third, we discuss where the poor live, and why poverty, conflict, and dismal social outcomes are concentrated in lagging regions.

GLOBAL COMPARISON OF POVERTY REDUCTION

Table 1.1 shows South Asia's position in a global setting. South Asia is a poor region, with per capita income in all South Asian countries below $2,000 in 2007 ($4,500 in purchasing power parity terms). By this standard, the World Bank classifies Bangladesh, Nepal, and Pakistan as low-income countries, and India and Sri Lanka as lower-middle-income countries. A high proportion of South Asia's population lives in poverty: half of Bangladesh's population consumes less than $1.25 per day (which corresponds closely to the poverty lines used in the poorest countries and expressed in terms of 2005 US dollars, adjusting for differences in purchasing power, across different currencies). The corresponding headcount ratios for India and Pakistan are 42 per cent and 23 per cent, respectively. Poverty rates in South Asia are a lot higher than the average levels for low—and lower-middle-income countries.

Growth is associated with poverty reduction. The $1.25 a day poverty rate for South Asia fell from 60 per cent in 1981 to 40 per cent in 2005. But the poverty rate has not fallen fast enough to reduce the total number of poor people. In India, the total number of poor people living on less than $1.25 a day has actually *increased* from 420 million people in 1981 to 455 million in 2005 (the poverty rate as a share of the total population came down from 60 per cent in 1981 to 42 per cent in 2005 (Chen and Ravallion 2009).

TABLE 1.1   Per Capita Income and Poverty
Headcount Ratios in South Asia (2005–7)

Country	Per capita GDP (current $)	Per capita GDP (PPP current $)	Poverty headcount ratio at $1.25 a day (PPP) (% of population)	Poverty headcount ratio at $2 a day (PPP) (% of population)
Bangladesh	431	1241	49.6	81.3
India	1046	2753	41.6	75.6
Nepal	367	1049	55.1	77.6
Pakistan	879	2496	22.6	60.3
Sri Lanka	1616	4243	14	39.7
South Asia	949	2532	40.3	73.9
East Asia & Pacific	2366	4954	16.8	38.6
China	4076	1715	15.9	36.3
Thailand	6009	2472	0.4	11.5
Vietnam	2363	711	21.5	48.4
Low income countries	618	1520	25.3	47.3
Lower middle-income countries	2008	4610		

Source: World Bank (2009c).
Notes: Per capita GDP data are for 2007. Poverty data are from 2005 for Bangladesh, India, and Pakistan; from 2004 for Nepal; 2002 for Sri Lanka; 2005 for China; 2004 for Thailand, and 2006 for Vietnam. Poverty is defined as the per cent of the population living in households with consumption or income per person below the US$ 1.25 and US$ 2 poverty line at 2005 international prices. To measure poverty in the world by the standards of what poverty means in low-income countries, the data that goes into the analysis actually uses the poverty lines that are actually used in poor countries. The new poverty lines $1.25 a day, which is the average poverty line of the 15 poorest countries in the world. The international poverty line is based on nationally representative primary household surveys conducted by national statistical offices or by private agencies under the supervision of government or international agencies and obtained from government statistical offices and World Bank Group country departments.

Do changes in poverty in South Asia, conditional on growth, match global trends? Figure 1.1a compares change in poverty rate ($1.25 a day) and change in real gross domestic product (GDP) per capita in Bangladesh, India, Nepal, Pakistan, and Sri Lanka with the rest of the world. Each dot in Figure 1.1a represents a country.[1] The vertical axis shows annual change in log poverty rate, and the horizontal axis shows annual change in real GDP per capita controlling for initial log poverty. We control for initial poverty rate as it affects subsequent changes in income growth. The figure clearly shows that changes in poverty rates are inversely associated with changes in income growth—that is, an increase in income is associated with poverty reduction, as expected. We cannot infer anything on causality from this figure.

The change in poverty in South Asia matches the global trend. They are all in the southeast quadrant of Figure 1.1a, except Nepal and Pakistan which are in the southwest quadrant. But they have not done as well as some better performers like China, Malaysia, Thailand, and Vietnam (all to the right of India in the southeast quadrant). There are differences even within South Asia. India has experienced a slightly slower pace of poverty reduction compared with Bangladesh and Sri Lanka.

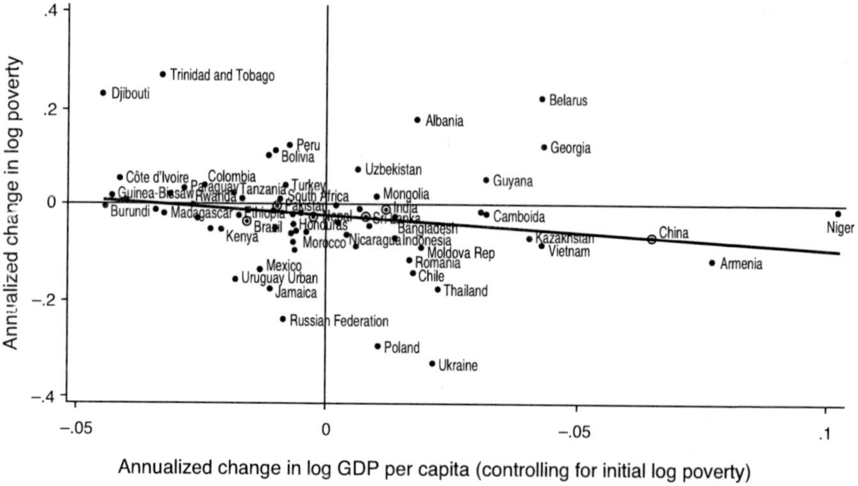

FIGURE 1.1a   Comparing Change in Poverty and Change
in Income (1977–2007)

[1]We are grateful to Martin Ravallion for providing us the World Bank Povcal dataset on poverty. Only the latest time periods in the dataset have been changed to get a sense of poverty reduction from historically to most recent trend. For details on time period used please refer to Appendix A1.5.

Poverty reduction has been a subject of long academic debate in India. It has been argued that the slow pace of poverty reduction in India stems in large part from the well-known divergence between consumption as measured in the National Sample Survey (NSS) and that measured by the National Accounts System (NAS) (see Himanshu 2009; Deaton 2008, 2007, 2005b, 2004; Ravallion 2008, 2003, 2000; Deaton and Kozel 2005; Deaton and Tarozzi 2005; Deaton and Dreze 2002). The poverty measures are based on mean consumption from the NSS. A large share of the gap between the two measures of private consumption in India can be attributed to differences in the definition of consumption used. Additionally, it also can be attributed to overestimation of household consumption in the NAS, which is calculated residually (at the commodity level), given the likely underestimation of intermediate (non-household) consumption in India's NAS. It may well be that poverty in India is high relative to NAS consumption (and GDP) but

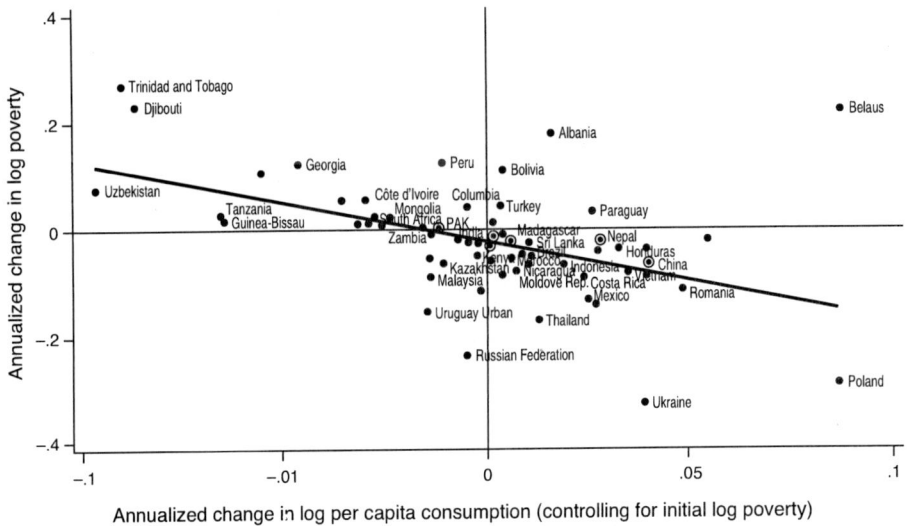

FIGURE 1.1b   Comparing Change in Poverty and Change in Consumption (1977–2007)

Sources: World Bank (2009b, 2009c).
Notes: The horizontal axis controls for log initial poverty levels. Poverty rate is defined as the per cent of the population living in households with consumption or income per person below the international US$ 1.25 poverty line. The sample includes 91 countries. Change is for the time period 1977–2007.

that poverty in India is not high conditional on mean consumption measured from the NSS.

Figure 1.1b compares annual change in poverty rate and annual change in household survey mean consumption per capita for the same sample of countries shown in Figure 1.1a. The pace of poverty reduction in South Asia matches or exceeds global trends. But they have not done as well as better performers like China. So, when we replace annual change in real GDP per capita with annual change in household survey mean consumption per capita, the finding still holds that the pace of poverty reduction in Bangladesh, India, Nepal, and Sri Lanka matches global trends, but does not match the pace of poverty reduction in the better-performing countries.

Whatever the relative merits of different methodologies used (household survey mean consumption or national accounts private consumption), the main difference concerns the *level* of poverty. There is much less disagreement on *changes* in poverty (Banerjee et al. 2006). That changes in poverty in South Asian countries have not done as well as the better performers is consistent with other findings in the literature that have concluded that the pace of poverty reduction in India is slow compared with that in China (Ravallion and Dutt 2009).

Why have South Asian countries not done as well as some of the better performers like China? Both China and India have roughly the same population, but the poverty *rate* in India is a lot higher than in China. Poverty rate depends on average income and how it is distributed across people, that is, inequality. We have seen in Figures 1.1a and 1.1b that India has experienced a slower economic growth relative to China. This slower growth in part explains the higher poverty rates in India. What about inequality?

Is the poverty rate higher in India because inequality has increased more in India than in China? Figure 1.2a shows the annual change in household survey mean consumption (horizontal axis) against the change in inequality (vertical axis). The cross-country plot shows that an increase in inequality is not necessarily associated with lower growth. All South Asian countries as well as China are in the northeast quadrant suggesting that they have experienced an increase in both inequality and growth. Brazil and Thailand are in the southeast quadrant indicating that they have experienced a reduction in inequality. The figure shows that inequality in China has increased more rapidly than in India. But China managed to reduce poverty faster than India, despite rising inequality, because it has grown much faster.

Figure 1.2b compares change in inequality and change in consumption growth for the 17 largest states in India. These are big states in terms of population size. Bihar is 2.5 times bigger compared with Canada in population size. The figure shows that most Indian states (leading states have per capita incomes above national average, see Appendix A1.1) have experienced an increase in inequality.

Figure 1.3 compares the change in poverty and per capita consumption growth for Indian states in a global setting. The lagging regions are concentrated in the southwest quadrant suggesting that they have experienced slower growth and slower poverty reduction, compared to leading regions which are concentrated in the southeast quadrant, indicating that they have experienced faster consumption growth and poverty reduction.

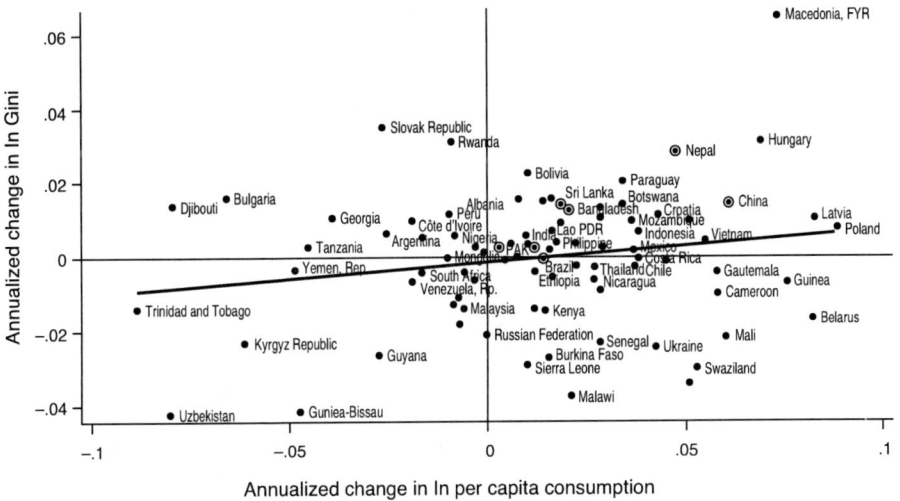

FIGURE 1.2a   Change in Inequality and Change in Consumption Growth (1997–2007)

Sources: World Bank (2009b, 2009c).
Notes: The sample includes 91 countries. Change is for the time period 1977–2007. Gini index is a measure of inequality between 0 (everyone has the same income) and 100 (richest person has all the income).

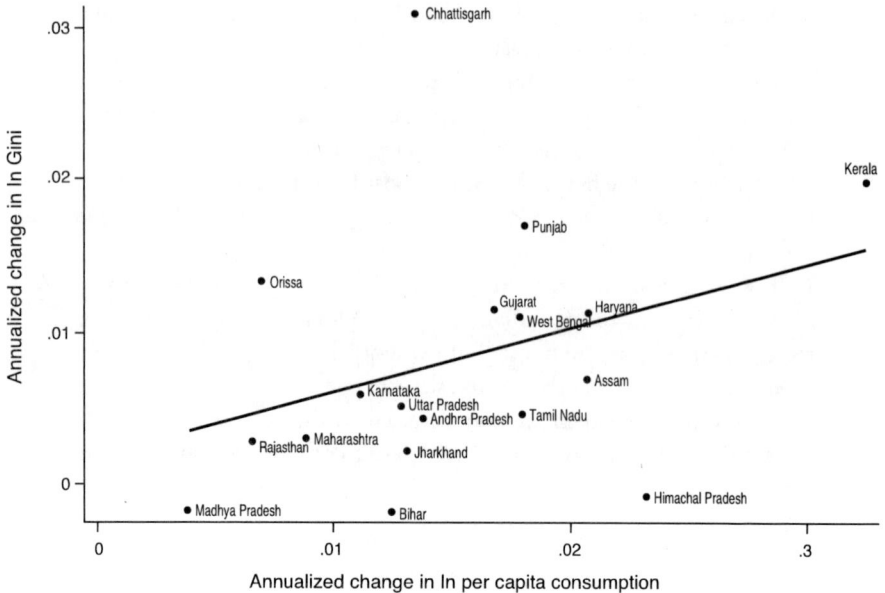

FIGURE 1.2b   Change in Inequality and Change in Growth in Indian
States (1994–2005)

Source: World Bank staff estimates using NSS 50th and 61st Rounds (National
Sample Survey of India 1993/4–2004/5).
Notes: The change in survey mean is estimated from rural prices. Time period used
for change is 1994–2005. Gini index is measure of inequality between 0 (everyone
has the same income) and 100 (richest person has all the income).

Most leading states in India have reduced poverty rates faster than
lagging states because they grew faster, which more than compensated
for the increase in inequality. Both Kerala and Haryana (leading states)
experienced an increase in inequality, but they have reduced poverty faster
because of higher consumption growth. Bihar and Madhya Pradesh,
where inequality decreased, have experienced a slower pace of poverty
reduction because of slower growth.

The relative merits of different methodologies and the statistical issues
related to the measurement of poverty in India and other South Asian
countries will not be resolved any time soon. This should not detract
policymakers from the bigger issue at stake, which is how to ensure that
growth is more inclusive. Human development and spatial locations of
growth are two critical factors that affect inclusiveness of growth. We
now turn to human development.

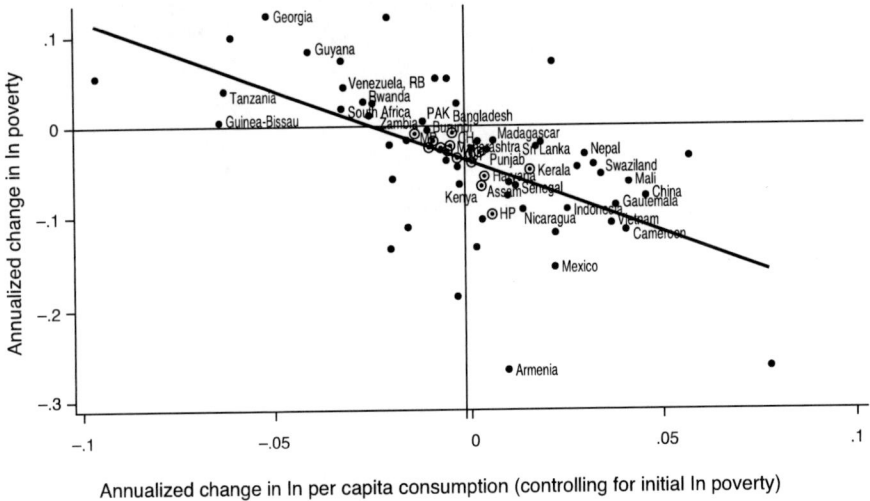

FIGURE 1.3   Comparing Poverty Reduction and Growth in the
Indian States in a Global Setting

Sources: World Bank (2009b, 2000c).

Notes: Y-axis controls for initial poverty levels. The data are representative of poverty rate for the per cent of the population living in households with consumption or income per person below the international $1.03 poverty line. The cross country sample has been brought down to $1.03 poverty line to match the poverty line representative for Indian states. The sample size, including Indian states, in the cross-country sample is 109. The cross-country change sample is for 1977–2007; change in poverty in Indian states is for 1994–2005.

GLOBAL COMPARISON OF HUMAN DEVELOPMENT AND GENDER OUTCOMES

South Asian countries have attracted global attention for centres of excellence in education and health facilities as well as for long-standing problems of illiteracy, poor health, meagre social protection, and social exclusion, including gender discrimination. Governments have failed to deliver services equitably and efficiently, given high teacher absenteeism, unqualified doctors, and low levels of accountability and voice to the poor people (Kremer et al. 2005; World Bank 2004b).

These problems of poor service delivery in education and health raise a big question. Has the pace of human development kept up with the pace of income growth? We address this by comparing annual changes

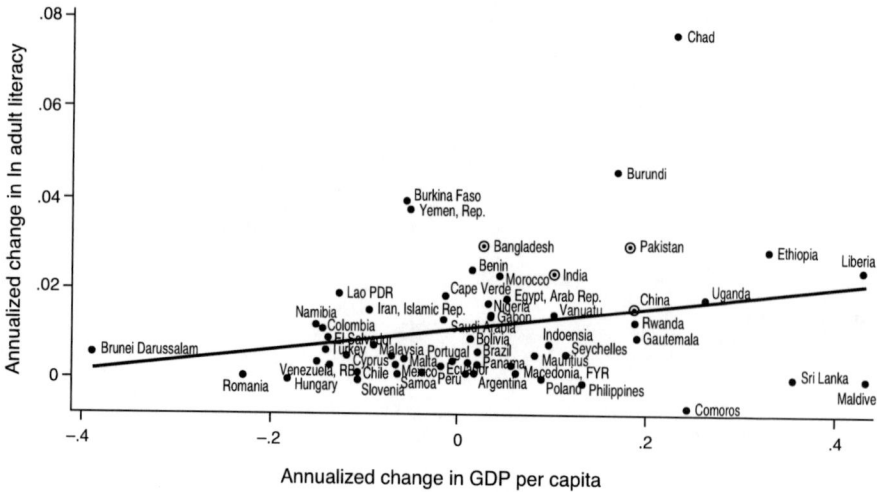

FIGURE 1.4   Comparing Change in Adult Literacy Rate with
Income Growth (1990–2006)

Source: World Bank (2009c).
Note: Adult literacy rate is defined as the percentage of people aged 15 and above who can, with understanding, read and write a short, simple statement on their everyday life.

in education, health, and gender outcomes conditional on growth in South Asia with the rest of the world.

Education

Figure 1.4 compares the annual change in adult literacy rate and annual change in real GDP per capita for 60 countries for the period 1990–2006. The upward sloping line shows that, as incomes increase, it stimulates demand for more education. Bangladesh, India, and Pakistan are above the trend line. They have experienced a faster pace of improvement in adult literacy than the global norm. This confirms that the pace of development in basic education matches income growth.

In countries where the public provision of education (and health) services is particularly low, private providers step in. In parts of India where public school absenteeism is the highest, the fraction of rural children attending private schools is also the highest (Chaudhury et al. 2005). Bihar, a lagging region in India, has more private schools per village compared with Tamil Nadu, a leading region (Muralidharan and Kremer 2007). Private schools are cropping up in rural Punjab province in

Pakistan, charging about US$ 2 per month in tuition. In urban Pakistan, all the growth in education enrolment is in the private sector. School management responsibilities in Nepal are devolving to communities.

Many private schools are less than ideal, however. While they have lower teacher absenteeism than the public schools in the same village, teachers are significantly less qualified in terms of having a formal teaching degree (Banerjee and Duflo 2006).

India and other South Asian countries have been successful in achieving first-generation education outcomes. Second-generation education issues are yet to be fully addressed. This inability to address these issues can be seen in their dismal performance in secondary education where South Asian countries lag behind the rest of the world. Secondary education plays a greater role in determining a country's economic growth and its people's standards of living—it provides huge beneficial impacts on health, raises the marriage age, reduces fertility rates, and improves child-rearing practices.

Figure 1.5 compares the change in secondary education and income growth for some 100 countries for the period 1990–2006. The experience of India, Nepal, and Pakistan match global trends, but they have not done as well as some of the better performers, like China and Thailand. India's gross enrolment ratio (GER) in secondary school is 40 per cent, compared with 70 per cent in East Asia and 82 per cent in Latin America.

The escape from poverty in South Asia has been more skill intensive. Growth has been led by the service sector, which is more skill intensive compared with manufacturing and agriculture. Wage regressions and poverty profiles show that workers with a secondary education find it easier to get jobs in the service sector. In India and other South Asian countries, 15 million young people will join the labour force every year for the next 10 years. These young men and women will need the knowledge, skills, attitudes, and experience to access better-paying jobs and escape from poverty.

Health

Health outcomes in South Asia are paradoxical (Deaton 2007; Patnaik 2007; Virmani 2007; Das et al. 2006; Duflo 2005; Chandrashekhar and Ghosh 2003; Haddad et al. 2003). Figure 1.6 compares change in infant mortality against income growth. Given concerns about data on health outcomes, we have restricted the sample to those countries for which we have household consumption and poverty data. The use of

Annualized change in ln secondary school enrolment

.1

.05

0

Malawi

Guinea Mali   Cape Verde

Burundi

Thailand

Djibouti

Oman

Ethiopia   Costa Rica
Bolivia   Tunisia
St. Lucia   Lao PDR
Colombia Turky
Mexico   Sudan

China

Venezuela
UAE   Pakistan
Madagascar   Italy   Nepal Indonesia   India
Uruguay Guyana
France   Chile
UK

Moldova

Kenya   Sweden   Ireland
Uzbekistan Japan USA Latvia   Poland Korea, Rep.
Ukraine   Cameroon   Belarus   Estonia
Switzerland Kazakhstan
Russia   Romania

−.05   0   .05   .1

Annualized change in ln GDP per capita

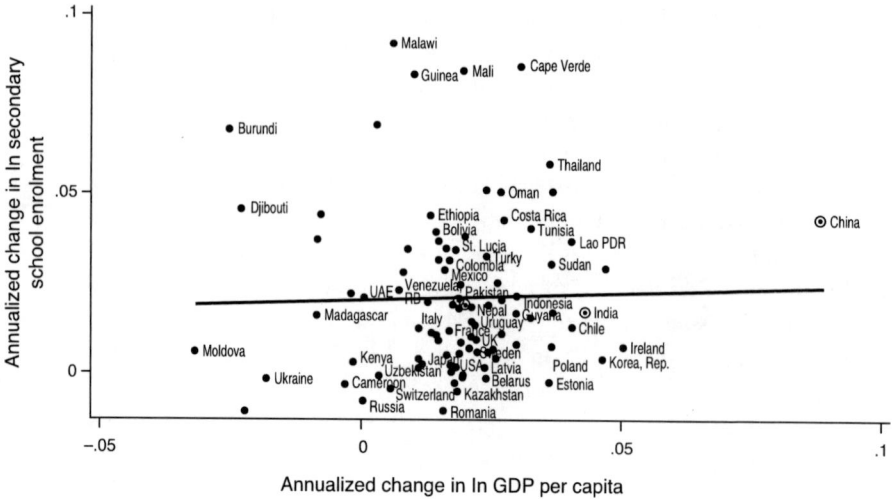

FIGURE 1.5   Comparing Change in Secondary Education and Growth
(1990–2006)

Source: World Bank (2009c).

Note: Secondary school enrolment change is for 1990–2006. Gross enrolment ratio is the ratio of total enrolment, regardless of age, to the population of the age-group that officially corresponds to the level of education shown. Secondary education completes the provision of basic education that began at the primary level and aims at laying the foundations for lifelong learning and human development, by offering more subject—or skill-oriented instruction using more specialized teachers.

consumption, rather than income, is motivated by the better quality of the consumption data in surveys (Deaton 2004).

Figure 1.6 shows that infant mortality falls with income growth, as expected. But South Asian countries have not done as well as the rest of the world in reducing infant mortality conditional on growth. A lot of variation exists within South Asia. India and Pakistan are way above the trend line, which suggests that reduction in infant mortality in these two countries has not kept up with income growth. These countries are performing worse than the global norm. Bangladesh and Nepal are below the line and seem to be doing much better in reducing infant mortality.

We compare the level of child malnutrition against real GDP per capita in 2005 in Figure 1.7. As incomes increase, child malnutrition falls. Once again, most South Asian countries are above the line—they have

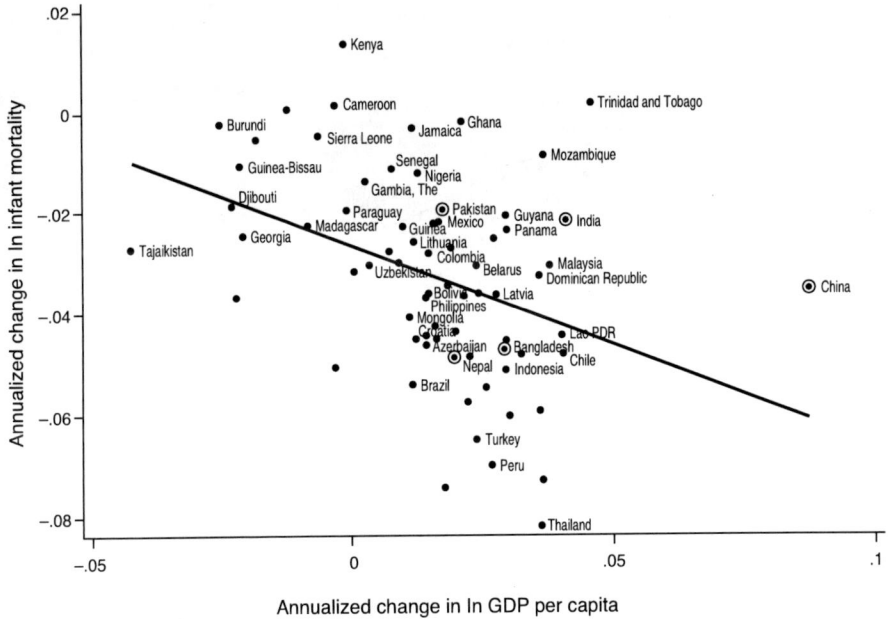

FIGURE 1.6   Comparing Change in Infant Mortality and Growth
(1990–2007)

Source: World Bank (2009c).
Note: Infant mortality is for the period 1990–2007. Infant mortality rate is the number of infants dying before reaching one year of age, per 1,000 live births in a given year.

much higher child malnutrition rates given their stage of development. Malnutrition rates in India and Pakistan are substantially higher. Similarly, Bangladesh and Nepal have much higher child malnutrition rates compared with Kenya. Despite unprecedented economic growth, South Asia has the highest rates of malnutrition and the largest numbers of undernourished children in the world. Undernourished children have higher rates of mortality, have lower cognitive and school performance, and are more likely to drop out of school.

Malnutrition rates at the subnational level within countries have a great deal of variation. Figure 1.7 compares child malnutrition rates for 17 large Indian states in a global setting. The figure shows that most India states are above the line. The lagging regions of India, such as Bihar,

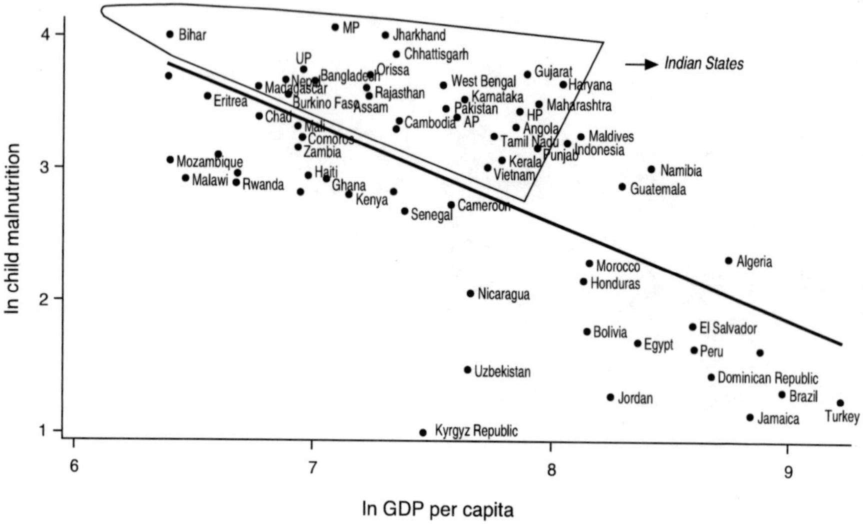

Bihar • MP • Jharkhand
• Chhattisgarh
UP
Bangladesh • Orissa → Indian States
Nepal • Rajasthan • West Bengal • Gujarat
Madagascar • Kamataka • Haryana
Eritrea • Burkino Faso • Assam • Pakistan • Maharashtra
Chad • Mali • Cambodia • AP • HP
Comoros • Angola
Zambia • Tamil Nadu • Maldives
Mozambique • Kerala • Indonesia
Malawi • Rwanda • Haiti • Vietnam • Punjab • Namibia
Ghana • Guatemala
Kenya
Senegal • Cameroon
Morocco • Algeria
Honduras
Nicaragua
Bolivia • El Salvador
Egypt • Peru
Uzbekistan • Dominican Republic
Jordan • Brazil
Jamaica • Turkey
Kyrgyz Republic

In child malnutrition (y-axis, 1 to 4)
In GDP per capita (x-axis, 6 to 9)

FIGURE 1.7   Comparing Child Malnutrition Rates in Indian States
in a Global Setting (2005)

Source: World Bank (2009c).

Notes: Malnutrition prevalence is for underweight children below the age of five for
the cross-country sample and the per cent of children under age three for Indian
states. Underweight is expressed in 2 standard deviation units from the median of
the 2006 WHO International Reference Population.

Uttar Pradesh, and Madhya Pradesh, have child malnutrition rates that
are much higher compared with India's leading regions. The malnutrition
rate in India (43 per cent) is also higher compared with Bangladesh (39
per cent) and Nepal (39 per cent).[2]

Figure 1.8 compares immunization rates in India with other countries.
The figure shows that India has one of the lowest immunization rates.
India's immunization rate is largely stagnant and is not keeping up with
economic growth but other countries have got very positive trends.
Nepal, Pakistan, and Bangladesh are improving and Sri Lanka is the
best performer. That health development has not kept up with income
growth suggests that non-income factors—technology, ideas, and access
to information—are as important as income growth.

[2]2006 for India, 2006 for Nepal, and 2005 for Bangladesh.

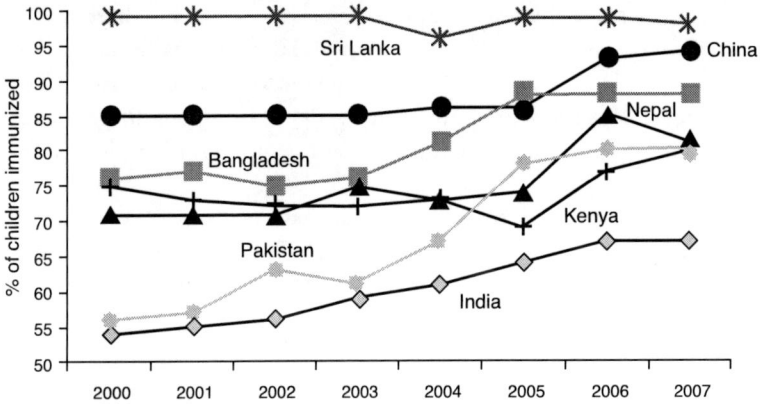

FIGURE 1.8   Comparing Immunization Rates in South Asia

Source: World Bank (2009c).
Notes: Child immunization measures the percentage of children ages 12–23 months who received vaccinations before 12 months or at any time before the survey. A child is considered adequately immunized against diphtheria, pertussis (or whooping cough), and tetanus (DPT) after receiving three doses of vaccine.

Social Protection

Social assistance programmes to protect the poor exist in all South Asian countries (World Bank 2006). These include Food for Work and Vulnerable Group Feeding in Bangladesh, Samurdhi in Sri Lanka, Zakat in Pakistan, and the Public Distribution System (PDS) and the National Rural Employment Guarantee Scheme (NREGS) in India.

The current mix of social protection programmes may not be well suited to addressing the risks facing the poor and vulnerable households in South Asia. Informal risk-sharing arrangements exist within poor communities (barter trade, remittances, religious and ethnic charities). But the poor are forced to inefficient risk management in times of shocks, that is, reducing consumption (quality and quantity); increasing labour supply (withdrawal of children from school; child labour). Evidence shows that at times of shocks, informal networks can also break down if all households are adversely impacted in the same manner and transfers are lumpy. The integration between regular social protection and disaster response programmes is limited. The response to the 2004 tsunami in Sri Lanka and the 2005 earthquake in Pakistan had to be developed almost from scratch.

Except for Bangladesh, South Asia largely has not used social protection schemes to provide incentives for human capital accumulation that can contribute to long-term reduction in vulnerability. Bangladesh (through its stipend programme for girls) is using conditional cash transfers (CCTs) to alleviate income poverty and to improve long-term earning potential.

South Asia needs social protection systems that have adequate coverage, flexibility to handle shocks, use IT innovations to improve delivery (for example, cash less systems, India RSBY), and better governance and accountability.

Gender Disparities

Over the last 50 years, the role women play in the economy and society in the industrial and developing world has been revolutionized. Around the world, the most striking forms of inequality, which include discrimination against women in access to basic services, employment, political voice, and resources within the household, have been largely reversed.

South Asian countries have made progress in reducing first-generation gender disparities, that is, girls' access to basic services such as primary education. They now are facing second-generation issues, such as women's access to employment and women's voice in political decision-making at the community, local, state, and federal levels. A good indicator of second-generation gender issues is the trend in female employment.

Figure 1.9 plots the share of the female labour force in the total labour force and real GDP per capita for 160 countries over the period 2000–5. It shows that gender disparities in employment are reduced with income growth. Bangladesh and Nepal are the star performers as they show higher ratios on female employment. India and Pakistan are the poor performers—worse than most Sub-Sahara African countries. Gender disparities are a bigger problem in the lagging regions of Pakistan and India.

CONCENTRATION OF POVERTY AND DISMAL SOCIAL OUTCOMES

The problems of South Asia are largely concentrated in the lagging regions. Figure 1.10 tells the story of lagging regions. These regions

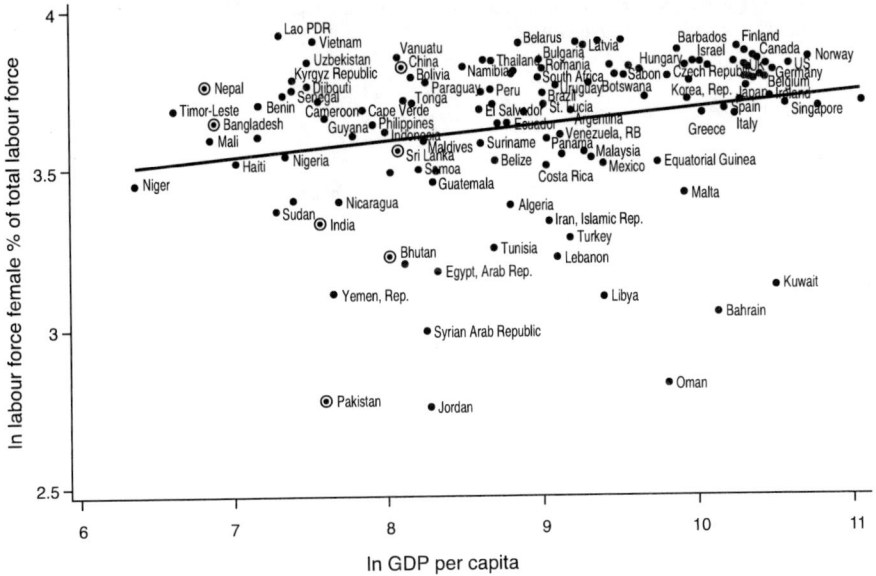

FIGURE 1.9 Comparing Female Labour Force as a Share of the Total Labour Force (2005)

Sources: World Bank (2009c); International Labour Organization (ILO 2008).
Notes: The female labour force as a percentage of the total shows the extent to which women are active in the labour force. Labour force includes people aged 15 and older who meet the ILO's definition of the economically active population. The plot takes averages for the period 2000–5.

have much higher poverty rates, a higher incidence of extreme poverty, higher conflict rates, dismal education and health outcomes, and huge gender disparities. Poverty rates in lagging regions are nearly double compared with leading regions. Other measures of poverty that take into account how far households are from the poverty line (poverty gap and poverty gap square) show that the incidence of extreme poverty is much higher in lagging regions. The availability of physical and human infrastructure like electricity, piped water, basic sanitation education, and health is much worse in lagging regions. The differences in healthcare and basic sanitation infrastructure can directly affect mortality. The statistics on infant mortality rates are startling. Child malnutrition rates are a lot higher in lagging regions. Poor families

Lagging Regions suffer from higher and extreme incidence of poverty (India)

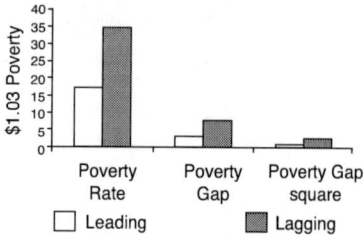

....they have high levels of conflict

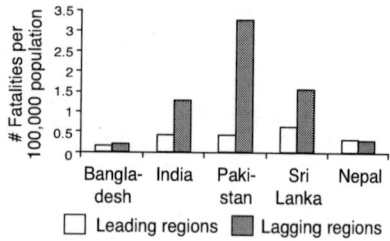

...poor education outcomes

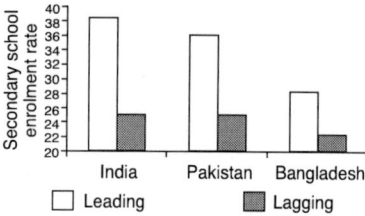

...dismal health outcomes

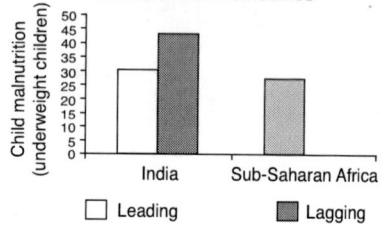

...poor access to capital and land, and cost of capital is high (India)

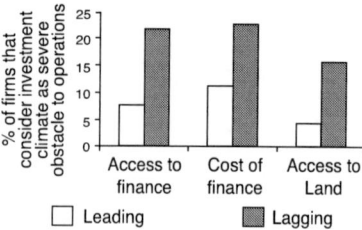

...and gender disparities are huge

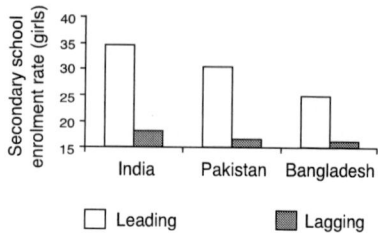

FIGURE 1.10 Problems of South Asia are Concentrated in Lagging Regions

Sources: World Bank staff estimates using National Sample Survey Organisation (NSSO) data for poverty estimates. Conflict data are from World Incidents Tracking System (2009). Secondary school enrolment data are from World Bank staff estimates using National Survey data. Child Malnutrition data are from *World Development Indicators* (*WDI*), World Bank (2009C).

Notes: Poverty figures are for Indian states in 2005. The national poverty line for India is international $1.03. Poverty gap is the mean distance below the poverty line as a proportion of the poverty line. Poverty gap squared is the mean of the squared distances below the poverty line as a proportion of the poverty line. Malnutrition prevalence is for underweight children below the age of five for Sub-Saharan Africa and the per cent of children under age three for Indian states. Underweight is expressed in 2 standard deviation units from the median of the 2006 WHO International Reference Population. For institutions, the variable is defined as the per cent of firms that consider investment climate constraint to be a major or severe obstacle to current operations by lagging and leading region.

tend to have more children, so the number of malnourished children in lagging regions is astounding. Gender disparities are huge as measured by the gap between lagging and leading regions in girls' secondary school enrolment rates.

Economic choices in lagging regions are constrained by their market environment. For example, there is no insurance market for crop failure. The farmers who find risk hard to bear tend to spread their risk by not specializing in any one occupation. They work part time outside agriculture to reduce their exposure to farming risk and keep a foot in agriculture to avoid being too dependent on their non-agricultural jobs (Banerjee and Duflo 2007). Credit tends to be expensive because contract enforcement in lagging regions is more difficult. The poor have little collateral to secure loans and, therefore, lenders hesitate to trust them with a lot of money. Lagging regions have weak market institutions (Acemoglu et al. 2001; Ahmed and Ghani 2007). So poor institutions slow the pace of economic expansion in lagging regions.

Figures 1.11a and 1.11b present a map of poverty mass and economic mass for South Asia. It shows that poverty mass (or number of poor people) is concentrated largely in the lagging regions. Because labour mobility is low in South Asia, poverty remains concentrated in lagging regions (see Chapter 3).

Figure 1.11b shows that economic activity is concentrated in leading regions. The economic mass in Pakistan is concentrated in the two leading regions bordering India (Sindh and Punjab). Most of the economic mass in India is found in the leading southern regions and around Mumbai and New Delhi. In Bangladesh and Sri Lanka, the bulk of economic activity takes place in the region surrounding the capital city (Dhaka and Western Province, respectively).

CONCLUSION

Despite rapid growth, South Asia faces significant challenges in poverty reduction, human development, and gender outcomes. These challenges are even bigger in lagging regions where growth is slower. Growth remains low in lagging regions because of conflict (institutions), limited mobility (economic geography), and weak effects of trade in transmitting price signals to lagging regions (globalization).

The current development strategy has worked well in leading regions which have experienced rapid growth and poverty reduction. It has not worked so well in lagging regions, where the problems of poverty,

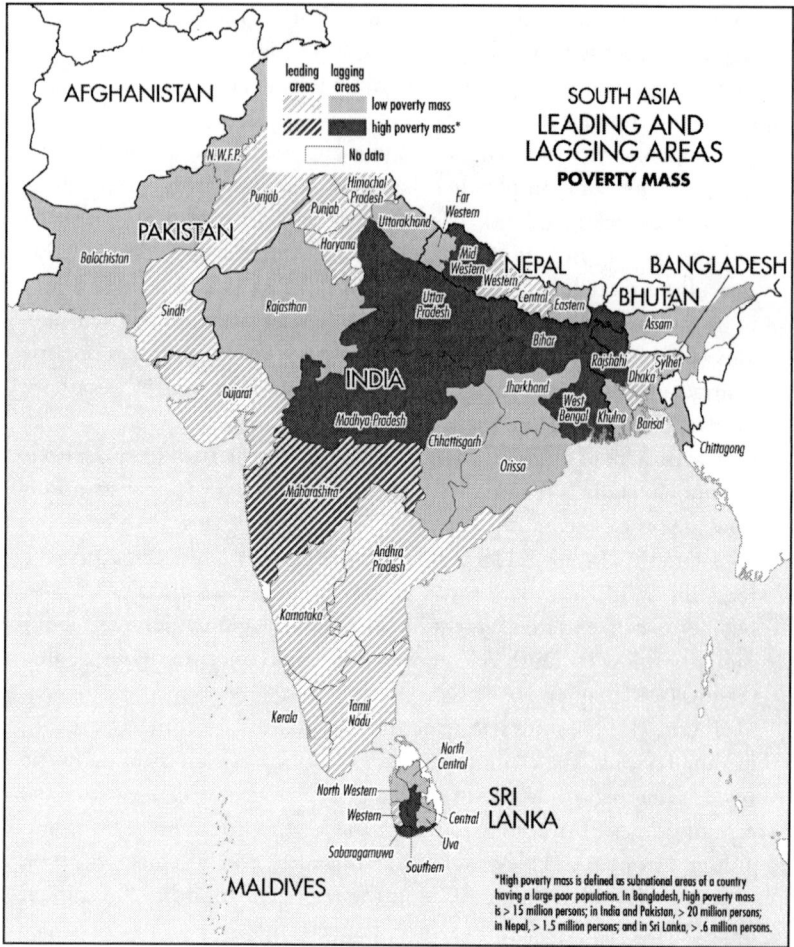

1.11a   Poverty Mass

FIGURE 1.11   South Asia's Lagging Regions have Poverty Mass and
Leading Regions have Economic Mass

Sources: For Poverty Mass: World Bank staff; Sri Lanka: Household Income and
Expenditure Survey (HIES 2002); Nepal: NLLS (2003–4); Bangladesh: HIES (2005);
Bhutan: International Monetary Fund Population figures for Nepal and Bangladesh
from comparative statement of per capita expenditure files. India: Directorate of
Economics and statistics of respective state government; Sri Lanka: Central Bank of
Sri Lanka; Bangladesh: *Statistical Yearbook of Bangladesh* (2002); Nepal (household

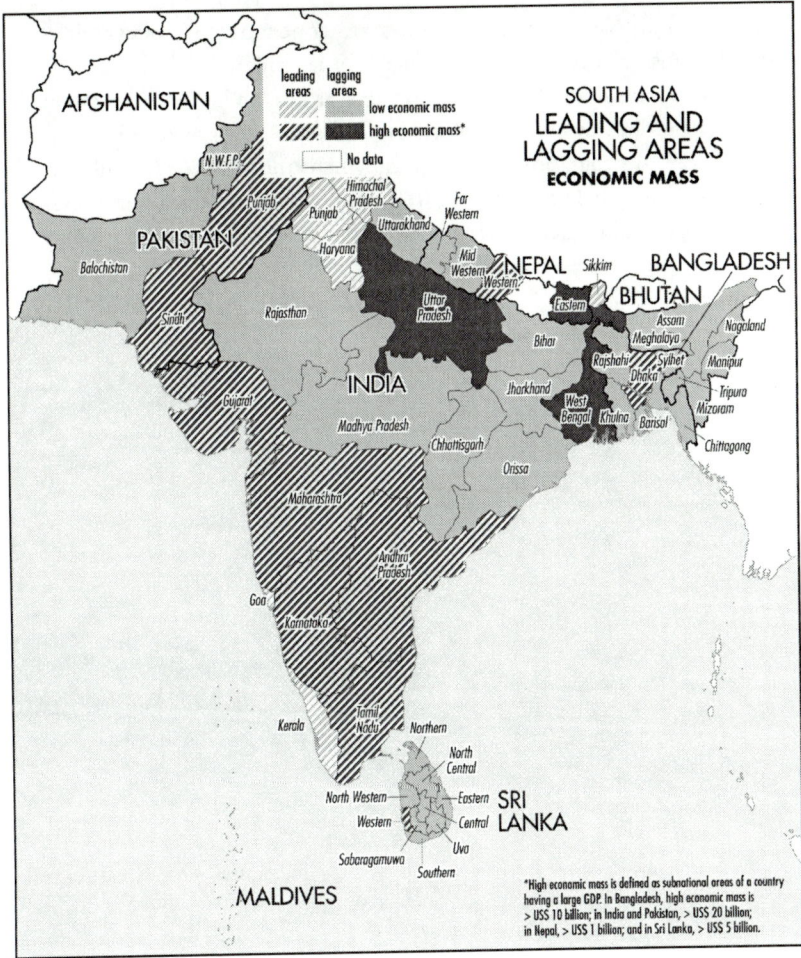

1.11b   Economic Mass

income per capita): Central Bureau of Statistics (CBS) and World Bank staff calculations using Nepal Living Standards Survey (NLSS I and II); Pakistan: World Bank staff; Afghanistan: World Bank (2009c).

Notes: Poverty Mass = National Poverty Rate x State Population. For India, data for poverty headcount rate are based on 2004/5; Sri Lanka: 2002; Pakistan: 2005/6; Bangladesh: 2005; Nepal: 2003/4; Bhutan: 2000; Maldives: 2004. Population data are in million. Population numbers for Nepal and Bangladesh are from 2006.

conflict, and dismal social outcomes are concentrated. Policymakers should consider a two-pronged strategy for lagging regions. First, foster growth, as is being done in leading regions, as growth is a key instrument to escape from poverty. But there are limits to their growth given the differences in geography, mobility, and institutions. Growth will take time. So policymakers in the short run should focus on direct policy interventions to reduce poverty, and human misery. The second strategy may have been overlooked in the lagging regions.

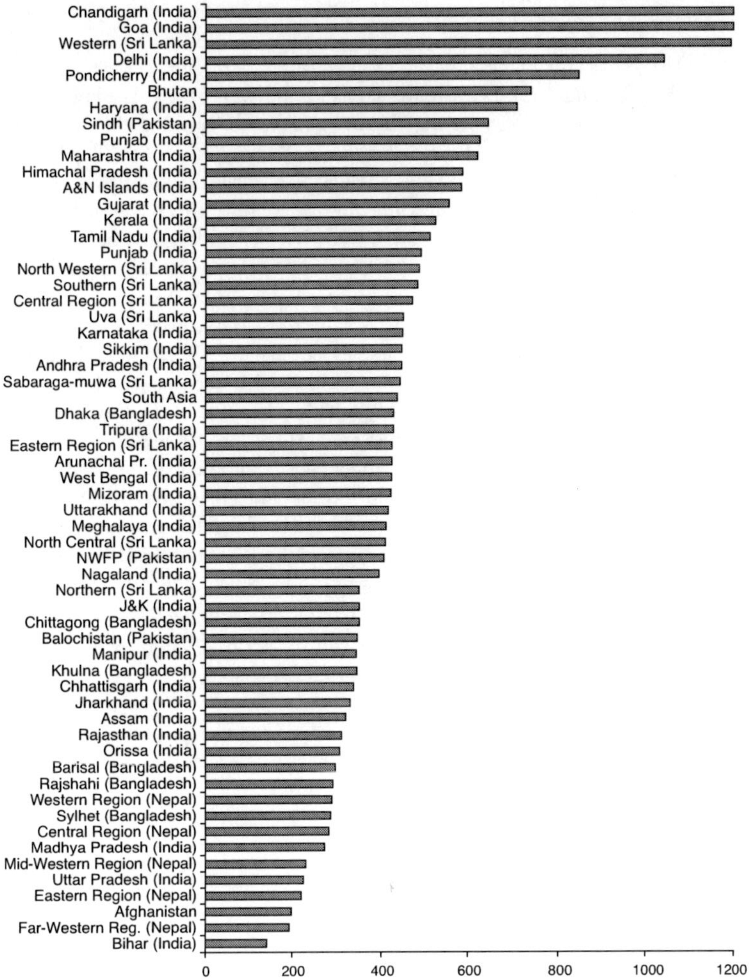
Chandigarh (India)
Goa (India)
Western (Sri Lanka)
Delhi (India)
Pondicherry (India)
Bhutan
Haryana (India)
Sindh (Pakistan)
Punjab (India)
Maharashtra (India)
Himachal Pradesh (India)
A&N Islands (India)
Gujarat (India)
Kerala (India)
Tamil Nadu (India)
Punjab (India)
North Western (Sri Lanka)
Southern (Sri Lanka)
Central Region (Sri Lanka)
Uva (Sri Lanka)
Karnataka (India)
Sikkim (India)
Andhra Pradesh (India)
Sabaraga-muwa (Sri Lanka)
South Asia
Dhaka (Bangladesh)
Tripura (India)
Eastern Region (Sri Lanka)
Arunachal Pr. (India)
West Bengal (India)
Mizoram (India)
Uttarakhand (India)
Meghalaya (India)
North Central (Sri Lanka)
NWFP (Pakistan)
Nagaland (India)
Northern (Sri Lanka)
J&K (India)
Chittagong (Bangladesh)
Balochistan (Pakistan)
Manipur (India)
Khulna (Bangladesh)
Chhattisgarh (India)
Jharkhand (India)
Assam (India)
Rajasthan (India)
Orissa (India)
Barisal (Bangladesh)
Rajshahi (Bangladesh)
Western Region (Nepal)
Sylhet (Bangladesh)
Central Region (Nepal)
Madhya Pradesh (India)
Mid-Western Region (Nepal)
Uttar Pradesh (India)
Eastern Region (Nepal)
Afghanistan
Far-Western Reg. (Nepal)
Bihar (India)
0
200
400
600
800
1000
1200

APPENDIX A1.1 Real GDP per Capita of States in South Asia (2004)
(constant US dollars)

Sources: India: Directorate of Economics and statistics of respective state governments; Sri Lanka: Central Bank of Sri Lanka; Bangladesh: *Statistical Yearbook of Bangladesh* 2002; Nepal (household income per capita): Central Bureau of Statistics (CBS) and World Bank staff calculations using Nepal Living Standards Survey (NLSS I and II); Pakistan: World Bank staff; Afghanistan: *World Development Indicators.*
Notes: A state is defined lagging if its per capita income is below the national average. For India, lagging states are Arunachal Pradesh, Assam, Bihar, Chhattisgarh,

(contd...)

Appendix A1.1 (contd...)

Jharkhand, Madhya Pradesh, Manipur, Meghalaya, Mizoram, Nagaland, Orissa, Rajasthan, Tripura, Uttar Pradesh, Uttarakhand, and West Bengal. Leading states in India are Andaman & Nicobar Islands, Andhra Pradesh, Chandigarh, Delhi, Goa, Gujarat, Haryana, Himachal Pradesh, Karnataka, Kerala, Maharashtra, Pondicherry, Punjab, Sikkim, and Tamil Nadu. For Bangladesh, Dhaka is leading and the rest Barisal, Chittagong, Khulna, Rajshahi, and Sylhet are lagging. In Nepal, Eastern Region, the Far-Western region and Mid-Western region are lagging whereas Central and Western regions are leading. For Pakistan, NWFP and Balochistan are lagging states whereas Sindh and Punjab are leading states. In Sri Lanka, the Western region is a leading state whereas Central Eastern, North-Central, North-Western, Nothern, Sabaraga-muwa, Southern, and Uva are lagging states In most developing and industrial countries, lagging regions are defined as those areas where growth and income seriously lag behind average national performance. This definition frequently has been applied to distinguish among high-income, middle-income, and low-income regions. Implicit in this argument is a definition of income and growth. But the economic variable used to define 'income' and 'growth' has implications for the definition of a 'lagging region'. There are important differences between 'GDP per capita' as a measure of income and growth and 'consumption expenditures' and 'disposable incomes', including transfers (government and private, including remittances from internal and external migration). Due to insufficient data at the regional level, GDP per capita for Bangladesh and Nepal are projections based on 2000 and 2003/04, respectively.

Maharashtra (India)
Punjab (Pakistan)
Uttar Pradesh (India)
West Bengal (India)
Andhra Pradesh (India)
Tamil Nadu (India)
Gujarat (India)
Karnataka (India)
Sindh (Pakistan)
Rajasthan (India)
Dhaka (Bangladesh)
Madhya Pradesh (India)
Kerala (India)
Punjab (India)
Haryana (India)
Bihar (India)
Orissa (India)
NWFP (Pakistan)
Rajshahi (Bangladesh)
Jharkhand (India)
Chittagong (Bangladesh)
Assam (India)
Chhattisgarh (India)
Western (Sri Lanka)
Khulna (Bangladesh)
J&K (India)
Himachal Pradesh (India)
Uttarakhand (India)
Balochistan (Pakistan)
Barisal (Bangladesh)
Sylhet (Bangladesh)
Eastern Region (Nepal)
Goa (India)
Western Region (Nepal)
Tripura (India)
Central Region (Sri Lanka)
Southern (Sri Lanka)
North Western (Sri Lanka)
Meghalaya (India)
Nagaland (India)
Manipur (India)
Sabaraga-muwa (Sri Lanka)
Mid-Western Region (Nepal)
Eastern Region (Sri Lanka)
Uva (Sri Lanka)
Arunachal Pr. (India)
Far-Western Reg. (Nepal)
North Central (Sri Lanka)
Mizoram (India)
Northern (Sri Lanka)
Sikkim (India)

0   5000   10000   15000   20000   25000   30000   35000   40000   45000   50000

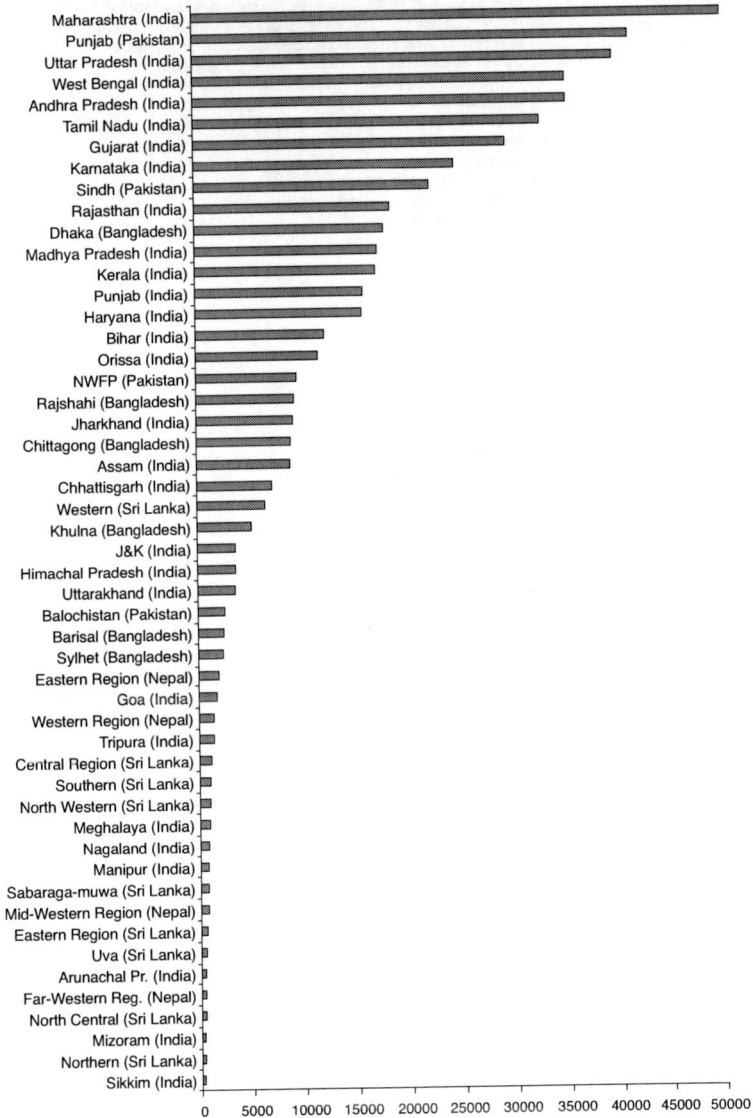

APPENDIX A1.2   Economic Mass (2004–5)
(GDP in constant US$, million)

Source: Same as Appendix A1.1.

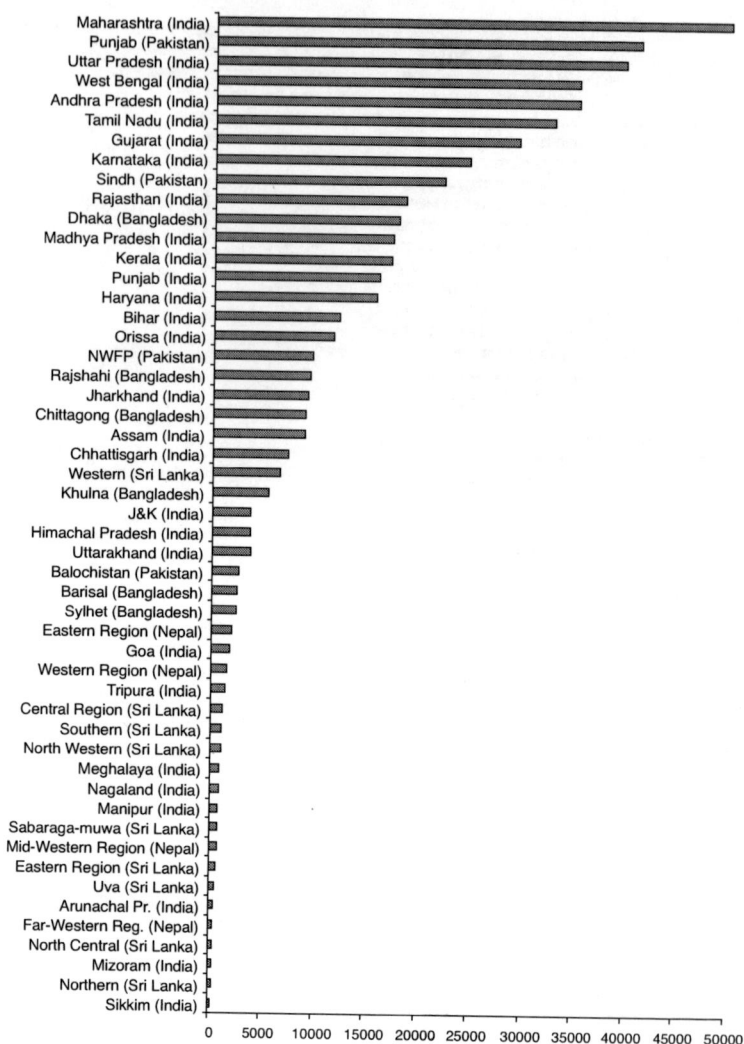

APPENDIX A1.3   Poverty Rates by State in South Asia
(per cent)

Sources: Pakistan: World Bank staff; Sri Lanka: Household Income and Expenditure Survey (HIES 2002); Nepal: NLLS (2003–4); Bangladesh: HIES (2005); Bhutan: International Monetary Fund; Maldives: Asian Development Bank.

Note: For India, data for poverty headcount rate based on 2004/5; Sri Lanka: data for poverty are based on 2002; Pakistan: 2005/6; Bangladesh: 2005; Nepal: 2003/4; Bhutan: 2000; and Maldives: 2004.

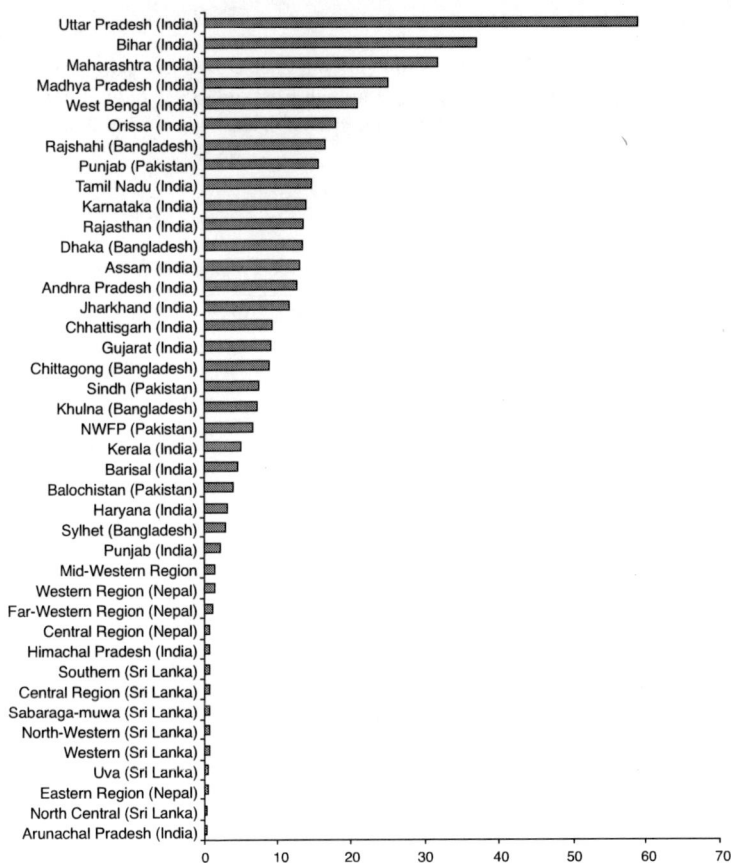

Chart showing number of poor people by state/region, with horizontal bars. X-axis from 0 to 70.

Uttar Pradesh (India)	
Bihar (India)	
Maharashtra (India)	
Madhya Pradesh (India)	
West Bengal (India)	
Orissa (India)	
Rajshahi (Bangladesh)	
Punjab (Pakistan)	
Tamil Nadu (India)	
Karnataka (India)	
Rajasthan (India)	
Dhaka (Bangladesh)	
Assam (India)	
Andhra Pradesh (India)	
Jharkhand (India)	
Chhattisgarh (India)	
Gujarat (India)	
Chittagong (Bangladesh)	
Sindh (Pakistan)	
Khulna (Bangladesh)	
NWFP (Pakistan)	
Kerala (India)	
Barisal (India)	
Balochistan (Pakistan)	
Haryana (India)	
Sylhet (Bangladesh)	
Punjab (India)	
Mid-Western Region	
Western Region (Nepal)	
Far-Western Region (Nepal)	
Central Region (Nepal)	
Himachal Pradesh (India)	
Southern (Sri Lanka)	
Central Region (Sri Lanka)	
Sabaraga-muwa (Sri Lanka)	
North-Western (Sri Lanka)	
Western (Sri Lanka)	
Uva (Sri Lanka)	
Eastern Region (Nepal)	
North Central (Sri Lanka)	
Arunachal Pradesh (India)	

APPENDIX A1.4   **Number of Poor People by State in South Asia**
(*million*)

Sources: World Bank staff estimates. Pakistan: World Bank staff; Sri Lanka: Household Income and Expenditure Survey (HIES 2002); Nepal: NLLS (2003–4); Bangladesh: HIES (2005); Bhutan: International Monetary Fund. Population figures for Nepal and Bangladesh from comparative statement of per capita expenditure files.

Notes: Poverty Mass = National Poverty Rate × State Population. For India, data for poverty headcount rate based on 2004/5; Sri Lanka: data for poverty are based on 2002; Pakistan: 2005/6; Bangladesh: 2005; Nepal: 2003/4; Bhutan: 2000; and Maldives: 2004. Population data used are in million. Population numbers for Nepal and Bangladesh are from 2006 because of insufficient data at the regional level for the corresponding year poverty numbers are available. Number of poor people in the lagging states of India was 209 million, whereas 92 million were residing in leading states. Similarly for Pakistan, 10 million poor people lived in lagging and 22 million

(contd...)

Appendix A1.4 (contd...)

in leading regions. For Sri Lanka, 3 million poor people lived in lagging and 0.5 million in leading regions. In Nepal, 2.9 million lived in lagging and 0.6 million in leading regions. For Bangladesh, 39 million lived in lagging and 13 million poor people in leading states.

APPENDIX A1.5   Poverty Dataset Time Period

Country	Initial survey year	Latest survey year	Time difference
Albania	1996.8	2005	8.2
Algeria	1988	1995	7
Argentina	1986	2005	19
Armenia	1998.5	2003	4.5
Azerbaijan	1995	2005	10
Bangladesh	1991.5	2005	13.5
Belarus	2000	2005	5
Bolivia	1990.5	2005	14.5
Bosnia and Herzegovina	2001	2004	3
Botswana	1985.5	1993.9	8.4
Brazil	1981	2005	24
Bulgaria	1989	2003	14
Burkina Faso	1994	2003	9
Burundi	1992	2006	14
Cambodia	1994	2004	10
Cameroon	1996	2001	5
Central African Republic	1993	2003	10
Chile	1987	2003	16
China	1981	2005	24
Colombia	1995	2003	8
Costa Rica	1981	2005	24
Cúte d'Ivoire	1985	2002	17
Croatia	1998	2005	7
Czech Republic	1988	1996	8
Djibouti	1996	2002	6
Dominican Republic	1986	2005	19
Ecuador	1987	2005	18
Egypt, Arab Rep.	1990.5	2004.5	14
El Salvador	1989	2003	14
Estonia	1995	2004	9
Ethiopia	1981.5	2005	23.5

(contd...)

Appendix A1.5 (contd...)

Country	Initial survey year	Latest survey year	Time difference
Gambia, The	1998	2003	5
Georgia	1996	2005	9
Ghana	1987.5	2005.5	18
Gautemala	1987	2006	19
Guinea	1991	2003	12
Guinea-Bissau	1991	2002	11
Guyana	1992.5	1998	5.5
Honduras	1990	2005	15
Hungary	1998	2004	6
India	1977.5	2004.5	27
Indonesia	1984	2005	21
Iran, Islamic Rep.	1986	2005	19
Jamaica	1988	2004	16
Jordan	1986.5	2006	19.5
Kazakhstan	1996	2003	7
Kenya	1992.4	2005.4	13
Kyrgyz Republic	1988	2004	16
Lao PDR	1992.2	2002.2	10
Latvia	1998	2004	6
Lesotho	1986.5	2002.5	16
Lithuania	1996	2004	8
Macedonia, FYR	1998	2003	5
Madagascar	1980	2005	25
Malawi	1997.5	2004.3	6.8
Malaysia	1984	2004	20
Mali	1994	2006	12
Mauritania	1987	2000	13
Mexico	1984	2006	22
Moldova, Rep.	1997	2004	7
Mongolia	1995	2005	10
Morocco	1984.5	2007	22.5
Mozambique	1996.5	2002.5	6
Nepal	1995.5	2003.5	8
Nicaragua	1993	2005	12
Niger	1992	2005	13
Nigeria	1985.5	2003.7	18.2
Pakistan	1987	2004.5	17.5
Panama	1979	2004	25
Paraguay	1990	2005	15

(contd...)

Appendix A1.5 (contd...)

Country	Initial survey year	Latest survey year	Time difference
Peru	1990	2005	15
Philippines	1985	2006	21
Poland	1996	2005	9
Romania	1998	2005	7
Russian Federation	1993	2005	12
Rwanda	1984.5	2000	15.5
Senegal	1991	2005	14
Sierra Leone	1989.5	2003	13.5
Slovak Republic	1988	1996	8
Slovenia	1998	2004	6
South Africa	1993	2000	7
Sri Lanka	1985	2002	17
Swaziland	1994.5	2000.5	6
Tajikistan	1999	2004	5
Tanzania	1991.9	2000.4	8.5
Thailand	1981	2004	23
Trinidad and Tobago	1988	1992	4
Tunisia	1985	2000	15
Turkey	1987	2005	18
Turkmenistan	1988	1993	5
Uganda	1989	2005	16
Ukraine	1996	2005	9
Uruguay Urban	1992	2005	13
Uzbekistan	1998	2003	5
Venezuela, RB	1981	2005	24
Vietnam	1992.7	2006	13.3
Yemen, Rep.	1992	2005	13
Zambia	1991	2004.25	13.25

Source: Martin Ravallion. PovcalNet, World Bank. Development Economics Research Group. Washington, D.C. (2009)

REFERENCES

Acemoglu, Daron, Simon Johnson, and James A. Robinson. 2001. 'The Colonial Origins of Comparative Development: An Empirical Investigation', *American Economic Review* 91 (5): 1369–401.

Ahmed, Sadiq and Ejaz Ghani. 2007. *South Asia: Growth and Regional Integration*. New Delhi: Macmillan Press.

Besley, Timothy and Robin Burgess. 2003. 'Halving Global Poverty', *Journal of Economic Perspectives*, 17 (3): 3–32.

Banerjee, A. and E. Duflo. 2007. 'The Economic Lives of the Poor', *Journal of Economic Perspectives*, 21 (1): 141–67.

————. 2006. 'The Economic Lives of the Poor', Working Paper No. 0629, MIT Department of Economics.

————. 2004. 'Growth Theory through the Lens of Development Economics', in Steve Durlauf and Anne Philippe Case (eds), *Handbook of Economic Growth*, Volume 1A.

Banerjee, Abhijit Vinayak, Roland Bénabou, and Dilip Mookherjee (eds). 2006. *Understanding Poverty*. New York: Oxford University Press.

Bardhan, Pranab. 2009. 'Notes on the Political Economy of India's Tortuous Transition', *Economic and Political Weekly*, XLIV (49): 31–5.

Chandrashekhar, C.P. and J. Gosh. 2003. 'Changing Utilization and Expenditure Patterns of Health Care in India'.

Chaudhuri, S. and M. Ravallion. 2007. 'Partially Awakened Giants: Uneven Growth in China and India', in L. Alan Winters and Shahid Yusuf (eds), *Dancing Giants: China, India, and the Global Economy*. Washington, D.C.: World Bank.

Chaudhury Nazmul, Jeffrey Hammer, Michael Kremer, Karthik Muralidharan, and F. Halsey Rogers. 2005. 'Teacher Absence in India: A Snapshot', *Journal of the European Economic Association*, 3 (2–3): 658–67.

Chen, S. and M. Ravallion. 2009. 'The Developing World is Poorer than We Thought, but No Less Successful in the Fight against Poverty', Policy Research Working Paper, WPS 4703, 2009/08/05, World Bank, Washington, D.C.

Das, J., J. Hammer, S. Devarajan, and L. Prichett. 2006. 'Will a Wealthier India be a Healthier India?', Presented at NBER/NCAER Conference on Growth in India, New Delhi.

Das, Jishnu, and Jeffrey Hammer. 2004. 'Strained Mercy: The Quality of Medical Care in Delhi', *Economic and Political Weekly*, 39 (9): 951–65.

Das, M., and S. Desai. 2003. 'Why are Educated Women Less Likely to be Employed in India? Testing Competing Hypotheses', Social Protection Discussion Paper Series No. 0313, World Bank, Washington, D.C.

Deaton, Angus. 2008. 'Price Trends in India and Their Implications for Measuring Poverty', *Economic and Political Weekly*, Special Article, 43 (6): 43–9.

————. 2007. 'Height, Health, and Development', Proceedings of the National Academy of Sciences of the United States of America, PNAS Col., 104 (33): 13232–7.

————. 2005a. 'Health and Wealth among the Poor: India and South Africa Compared', *American Economic Review Papers and Proceedings*, 95 (2): 229–33.

————. 2005b. 'Measuring Poverty in a Growing World (or Measuring Growth in a Poor World).' Review of *Economics and Statistics* 87: 353–78.

————. 2004. 'Measuring Poverty', in Abhijit Banerjee, Roland Benabou, and Dilip Mookherjee (eds), *Understanding Poverty*. New York: Oxford University Press.

Deaton, A., and J. Dreze. 2009. 'Food and Nutrition in India: Facts and Interpretations', *Economic and Political Weekly*, XLIV (7): 42–65.

———. 2002. 'Poverty and Inequality in India: A Re-Examination', *Economic and Political Weekly*, 7 September: 3729–48.

Deaton, A., and V. Kozel (eds) 2005. *The Great Indian Poverty Debate*. New Delhi: Macmillan.

Deaton, A. and A. Tarozzi. 2005. 'Prices and Poverty in India' (chapter 16), in Deaton and V. Kozel (eds), *The Great Indian Poverty Debate*. New Delhi: Macmillan.

Devarajan, Shanta. 2006. *Can South Asia End Poverty in a Generation?* Washington, D.C.: World Bank.

Dreze, J. and A. Sen. 2002. *India: Development and Participation*. New Delhi: Oxford University Press.

Duflo, A. 2005. 'Health Shocks and Economic Vulnerability in Rural India: Break the Vicious Circle', Centre for Micro Finance Research Working Paper, Center for Micro Finance, IFMR.

Ghani, Ejaz and Sadiq Ahmed. 2009. *Accelerating Growth and Job Creation in South Asia*. New Delhi: Oxford University Press.

Haddad, L., H. Alderman, S. Appleton, L. Song, and Y. Yohannes. 2003. 'Reducing Child Malnutrition: How Far Does Income Growth Take Us?', 17 (1): 107–31.

Henderson, J., V. Shalizi, and A.J. Venables. 2001. 'Geography and Development', *Journal of Economic Geography*, 1: 81–105.

Himanshu. 2009. 'Estimate of Consumption Expenditure from National from National Accounts and Household Surveys', Manuscript, Jawaharlal Nehru University, New Delhi.

International Labour Organization (ILO). 2008. Key Indicators of the Labor Market (KILM). Available at www.ilo.org/kilm, accesed in January 2010.

Kremer, M., K. Muralidharan, N. Chaudhury, J. Hammer, and F.H. Rogers. 2005. 'Teacher Absence in India: A Snapshot', *Journal of the European Economic Association*, 3 (2–3): 658–67.

Krugman, Paul. 1999. 'The Role of Geography in Development', *International Regional Science Review Science Review*, 22 (2): 142–61.

Munshi, K. and M. Rosenzweig. 2007. 'Why Is Mobility in India so Low? Social Insurance, Inequality and Growth', NBER Working Paper No. 14850.

Muralidharan, K. and M. Kremer. 2007. 'Public and Private Schools in Rural India', in P. Peterson and R. Chakrabarti (eds), *School Choice International*. Available at http://econ.ucsd.edu/~kamurali/public%20and%20private%20 schools%20in%20rural%20india.pdf, accessed in November 2009.

National Sample Survey of India. 1999–2000. 51st, 55th, and 61st Rounds. Available at http://mospi.gov.in/nsso_4aug2008/web/nsso.htm, accessed in November 2009.

Patnaik, U. 2007. *The Republic of Hunger and Other Essays*. Gurgaon: Three Essays Collective.

Purfield, C. 2006. 'Mind the Gap: Is Economic Growth in India Leaving Some States Behind?' IMF Working Paper 06/103, International Monetary Fund, Washington, D.C.

Ravallion, M. 2008. 'A Global Perspective on Poverty in India', *Economic and Political Weekly*, 43 (43): 31–7.

———. 2003. 'Measuring Aggregate Economic Welfare in Developing Countries: How Well do National Accounts and Surveys Agree?,' *Review of Economics and Statistics*, 85: 645–52.

———. 2000. 'Should Poverty Measures be Anchored to the National Accounts?', *Economic and Political Weekly*, 34: 3245–52.

Ravallion, M. and G. Dutt. 2009. 'Has India's Economic Growth Become More Pro-poor in the Wake of Economic Reforms?', Policy Research Working Paper No. WPS 5103.

Sen, A. and Himanshu. 2004. 'Poverty and Inequality in India 2: Widening Disparities during the 1990s', *Economic and Political Weekly*, 39: 4361–75.

UNICEF (United Nations Children's Fund). 2009. *State of the World's Children Report 2009*.

Virmani, A. 2007. 'The Sodoku of Growth, Poverty, and Malnutrition: Policy Implications for Lagging States', Working Paper No. 2/2007-PC, Planning Commission of India, New Delhi.

World Bank. 2010. *Service Revolution in South Asia*. Oxford University Press: New Delhi.

———. 2009a. Brief on Education in South Asia. Available at http://web.worldbank.org/WBSITE/EXTERNAL/COUNTRIES/SOUTHASIAEXT/0, contentMDK:21487829-pagePK:146736-piPK:146830-theSitePK:223547,00.html. Washington, D.C.: World Bank.

———. 2009b. *PovcalNet*. Washington, D.C.: World Bank.

———. 2009c. *World Development Indicators*. Washington, D.C.: World Bank.

———. 2009d. *World Development Report 2009: Reshaping Economic Geography*. Washington, D.C.: World Bank.

———. 2006. *Can South Asia End Poverty in a Generation?* Washington, D.C.: World Bank.

———. 2004a. *Making Services Work for the Poor*. Washington, D.C.: World Bank.

———. 2004b. *World Development Report*. Washington, D.C.: World Bank.

WHO (World Health Organization). 2006. International Reference Population.

World Incidents Tracking System. 2009. Available at http://wits.nctc.gov/, accessed in December 2009.

2

Are Lagging Regions Catching Up with Leading Regions?

Ejaz Ghani, Lakshmi Iyer, and Saurabh Mishra*

South Asia is home to nearly half a billion poor people. This high level of poverty persists despite the high economic growth in the region over the past decade. Are the economically lagging regions catching up with the leading regions of South Asia or are they falling further behind? The chapter examines the trends regarding convergence and divergence across the regions of South Asia. We consider the trends in several different human development outcomes: income and poverty, health, and education outcomes. Throughout the chapter, we compare these trends with the corresponding trends in a global sample of developing countries to assess whether South Asia conforms to global patterns.

A particular concern in this regard is whether poverty acts as a barrier to future growth, generating a 'poverty trap'. This can occur because poor areas are unable to make the required investments for growth, or because they are not able to generate enough productivity improvements. Several theoretical models have explored how credit constraints or other frictions can prevent required investments in physical or human capital in poor countries, thereby trapping them in poverty (see, among others, Banerjee

*We are grateful to Pranab Bardhan, Kaushik Basu, Charles Kenney, Homi Kharas, Aart Kraay, Martin Ravallion, and Nobuo Yoshida for valuable guidance. Any errors are our responsibility.

and Newman 1993; Galor and Zeira 1993; Piketty 1997). Poverty traps also can occur because of insufficient demand, which can discourage a productive investment, thereby leading to low incomes and a persistent low level of demand (Murphy et al. 1989). These poverty trap models suggest that we may not necessarily see convergence in incomes over time, and that some poor economies may be stuck in a poverty trap for an extended length of time.

Our analysis uncovers four main facts regarding convergence in South Asia. First, per capita incomes are not converging across the regions of South Asia. Second, despite this lack of convergence in per capita incomes, we see that areas with higher levels of poverty achieve a greater reduction in the percentage of people living below the poverty line, as well as in measures of poverty depth and severity. They do not, however, achieve faster proportionate reductions in these poverty indicators. Third, we find substantial convergence in education indicators, but not in measures of health. Fourth, we find that all these trends for the regions of South Asia and the states of India are similar to the trends observed across developing countries as a whole, with the exception that South Asia shows slower convergence trends than the global sample. For example, we see greater proportionate reductions in the squared poverty gap measure among initially poorer countries in the global sample, but not among initially poorer regions within South Asia.

Overall, these results provide for cautious optimism on progress in the lagging regions. There is little evidence of persistent poverty traps in South Asia at a regional level, or even among developing countries as a whole. We do not, however, see lagging regions catching up with leading regions in terms of per capita income, health indicators, or proportionate terms for poverty. Our analysis also does not rule out the presence of localized poverty traps at a level lower than the regional one. We conclude that a large role remains for policies to increase growth in the lagging regions, and to target poverty and human development more directly.

CONVERGENCE IN PER CAPITA INCOME AND CONSUMPTION

Given that South Asia has experienced high growth in the last decade, it is important to ask whether the lagging regions have improved their position in relation to leading regions during that time. This is the question of growth convergence. We will briefly review the sizeable literature in the cross-country context before we present results for South Asia.

Cross-country Results

What are the trends in the distribution of per capita incomes across countries? A well-established fact is that income per capita exhibited a greater variance across countries in 2000, as compared with 1960, although the spread is smaller when these figures are weighted by population, because the two most populous countries (India and China) have experienced particularly fast growth in the past two to three decades. The large differences in income per capita across countries are not a recent phenomenon and, in fact, some historical data indicates that these differences became particularly pronounced after the industrial revolution in the nineteenth century (Acemoglu 2009: chapter 1). The world income distribution also appears to exhibit 'twin peaks', as first pointed out by Quah (1993, 1997).

This persistence in cross-country income differences suggests that there has been little convergence—and indeed, that is what we find in the data. There is no evidence that countries at a lower level of gross domestic product (GDP) per capita achieve higher growth, as would be required for convergence to occur; in fact, low-income countries appear

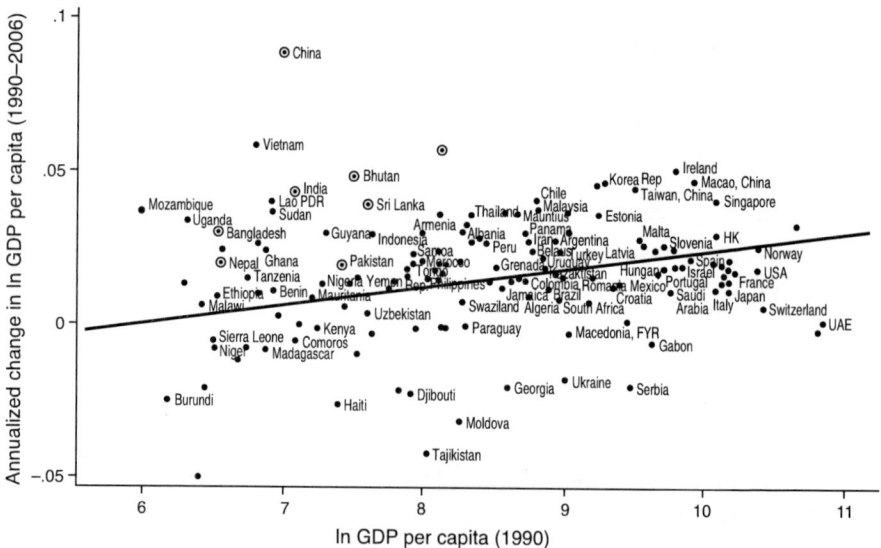

FIGURE 2.1   Is There Convergence in Per Capita GDP across Countries?

Source: World Bank (2009b).
Notes: PPP = purchasing power parity.
Time period is 1990–2006. GDP per capita is in 2005 PPP international US dollars.

to have slightly lower growth rates on average (see Figure 2.1), a fact also documented by Lopez and Serven (2009).

This lack of convergence is confirmed when we run a regression of per capita GDP growth between 1990 and 2006 on initial levels of per capita GDP. We find a positive coefficient on initial per capita GDP levels (see Table 2.1, column I), consistent with earlier cross-country studies on the topic. Despite this lack of unconditional convergence, the cross-country literature finds some evidence of income convergence if we compare data across countries that are similar in some respects. This is the 'conditional convergence' identified by Barro and Sala-i-Martin (1992), who estimate convergence of about 2 per cent a year after they control for variables such as male and female education levels (which might affect the rate of innovation and technology adoption), life expectancy (as a proxy for human capital), the ratio of public expenditures to GDP, the ratio of investment to GDP, the ratio of government consumption to GDP, and institutional quality measures such as political instability or the black

TABLE 2.1 Convergence of Per Capita GDP and Household Consumption across Countries

	Growth rate of GDP per capita 1990–2006		Growth rate of mean household consumption per capita	
	(I)	(II)	(III)	(IV)
ln initial GDP per capita (1990)	0.002*	−0.001	−0.01***	−0.02***
	(0.001)	(0.003)	(0.004)	(0.005)
Initial investment (% of GDP)		0.0007***		−0.0001
		(0.0002)		(0.0003)
Initial years of schooling (log)		0.009		0.02***
		(0.007)		(0.008)
Observations	166	97	74	50
R-squared	0.01	0.23	0.10	0.30

Sources: Initial investment (per cent of GDP) and GDP per capita are from World Bank (2009b). Consumption numbers are from country-specific survey years in the period 1977–2007 available at PovcalNet, World Bank (2009a). Years of schooling are from Barro and Lee (2001).

Notes: Robust standard errors are reported in parenthesis.

***represents significance at 1 per cent; **represents significance at 5 per cent; and *represents significance at 10 per cent.

market premium. A similar analysis using panel data regressions finds even higher rates of conditional convergence (Caselli et al. 1996).

We show one such regression in Table 2.1 (column II), when we control for initial levels of investment and education. We see that the positive coefficient on initial per capita income changes to a negative one; the coefficient on initial education is positive, suggesting that better education can lead to higher growth outcomes, but the relationship is not very strong. Growth responds strongly to changes in investment. In this restricted specification, however, we do not find much evidence of conditional convergence.

When we turn to per capita consumption (measured through household surveys), rather than incomes as a better measure of well-being, we find different results. In particular, we see a trend toward convergence, in contrast to the results for per capita income (Table 2.1, columns III and IV). Consumption growth is not significantly associated with investment growth, but countries with higher levels of education do achieve higher levels of consumption growth.

The differences between the results for income and consumption suggest that poverty can be reduced in poorer countries even if they do not achieve the highest levels of income growth. The issue of poverty convergence is explored in a later section of the chapter.

When we use the concept of sigma-convergence—that is, when looking at the variance of log per capita GDP across countries, we again see a consistent trend toward divergence, both across the world and across the countries of South Asia (see Figure 2.2). The first concept of beta-convergence (that is, poorer countries having faster growth) typically leads to the second sigma-convergence, but this is not guaranteed.

Convergence of Per Capita Incomes within South Asia

What can we expect to observe in terms of income convergence within countries or regions? The cross-country literature on conditional convergence suggests that we should see a strong degree of income convergence across regions of the same country, because these regions are relatively homogeneous with respect to many characteristics. Specific government initiatives could bring about such convergence to ensure equality. Indeed, the growth literature has documented significant unconditional income convergence among relatively homogeneous units, such as the different states of the United States, the countries of Europe, and the prefectures of Japan (see Barro and Sala-i-Martin 1999: chapter 11).

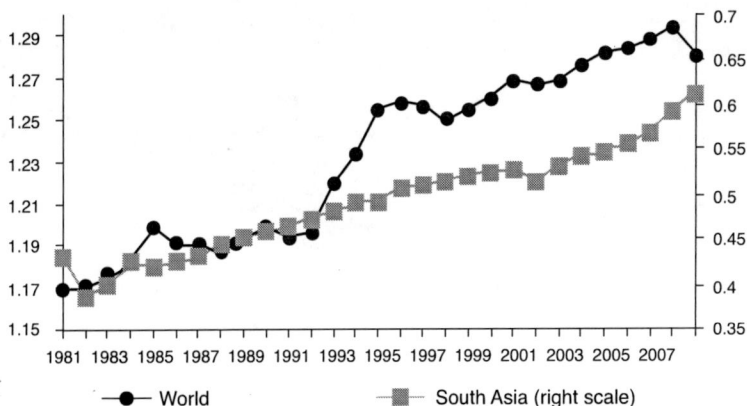

FIGURE 2.2   Sigma Divergence of Per Capita Incomes

Source: World Bank (2009b).
Note: The graph represents the standard deviation of log per capita income across the global sample and South Asian countries.

In this chapter, we present a similar analysis for the regions of South Asia. Similar to the cross-country findings, we find no evidence for convergence of per capita incomes across the regions of South Asia. In fact, we see a significant divergence of per capita GDP across the states of India (see Figure 2.3). This lack of unconditional convergence is documented for regions of South Asia and India in the regressions in Table 2.2. We are unable to run conditional convergence regressions as in the cross-country sample because of a lack of data on investment rates at the subnational level.

CONVERGENCE IN POVERTY

We turn now to the important question of whether poorer countries have been able to reduce poverty more swiftly than less poor countries. Despite the lack of unconditional convergence in per capita GDP growth rates documented in the earlier sections, the convergence trends in poverty could be different. We have noted that consumption appears to be converging in the cross-country sample, although GDP per capita does not show any convergence.

A major concern regarding poverty or other measures of income distribution is that the initial distribution of assets (labour, capital, entrepreneurial talent, technical skills, and so on) can have a direct effect

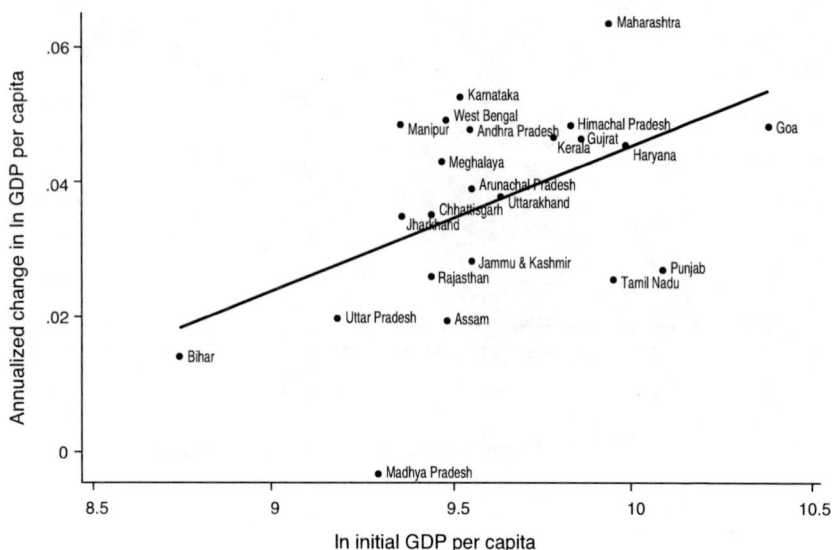

FIGURE 2.3   Is There Convergence of Per Capita Incomes across States of India?

Source: System of National Accounts (NAS), Ministry of Statistics, Government of India (2008).
Note: Time period for growth rates is 1994–2005.

TABLE 2.2   Convergence in Per Capita Incomes across Regions of South Asia and States of India

	South Asia (2000–2005)	South Asia (1994–2005)	India (1996–2005)	India (2000–2005)
	(I)	(II)	(III)	(IV)
ln initial GDP per capita (1990)	–0.001	–0.006	0.02***	0.01
	(0.006)	(0.009)	(0.007)	(0.01)
Observations	35	36	23	25
R²	0.002	0.02	0.23	0.05

Source: India: System of National Account, Ministry of Statistics, Government of India (2008); Sri Lanka: Central Bank of Sri Lanka; Pakistan: World Bank staff.
Notes: South Asia region includes states in India, Pakistan, and Sri Lanka. Robust standard errors are reported in parenthesis.
***represents significance at 1 per cent; **represents significance at 5 per cent; and *represents significance at 10 per cent.

on the patterns of growth that arise. The initial distribution of assets, coupled with the pattern of specialization and growth, can have differing implications for poverty reduction, and for the extent to which economic growth is pro-poor. Theoretical papers predict a range of potential relationships between the initial distribution of assets in the population and subsequent growth and occupational choice outcomes (see the brief review in Banerjee and Duflo 2003). Several papers have empirically examined the link between initial income inequality and subsequent GDP growth rates, with widely different results. Initial papers such as Deininger and Squire (1998) found a negative link between inequality and growth, while others such as Forbes (2000) found a positive link, and Banerjee and Duflo (2003) find a non-linear relationship.

A more recent literature has examined the links between poverty and growth. Again, the results are mixed. Kraay (2006) finds that economic growth is mostly pro-poor, while Ravallion (2009) finds no convergence in poverty rates around the world. The latter finding can be reconciled with the former if poorer areas fail to have any growth, a finding documented in Lopez and Serven (2009). In this section, we examine whether measures of poverty are converging, both across countries and within the South Asian region. Our analysis parallels that of Ravallion (2009), but includes measures of poverty depth and severity in addition to the headcount ratio.

Cross-country Trends on Headcount Ratio

We investigate convergence trends in poverty rates both at the cross-country and regional levels. In all our analysis, poverty is measured by the headcount ratio—that is, the proportion of population with per capita consumption below a specified poverty line. The most widely used international poverty line are $1.25 a day and $2 a day (Chen and Ravallion 2008). We will show the results using the poverty line of $1.25 a day; all the results remain similar when we use the $2 a day poverty line (results available on request).

We find that countries with an initially higher level of poverty experience greater absolute reductions in the poverty headcount ratio (see Figure 2.4). The y-axis of Figure 2.4 represents the average annual reduction in the headcount ratio in percentage points, where the headcount ratio is the proportion of the population consuming less than $1.25 a day.

These trends are shown to be statistically significant in Table 2.3, column I. When we regress the absolute change in the headcount ratio

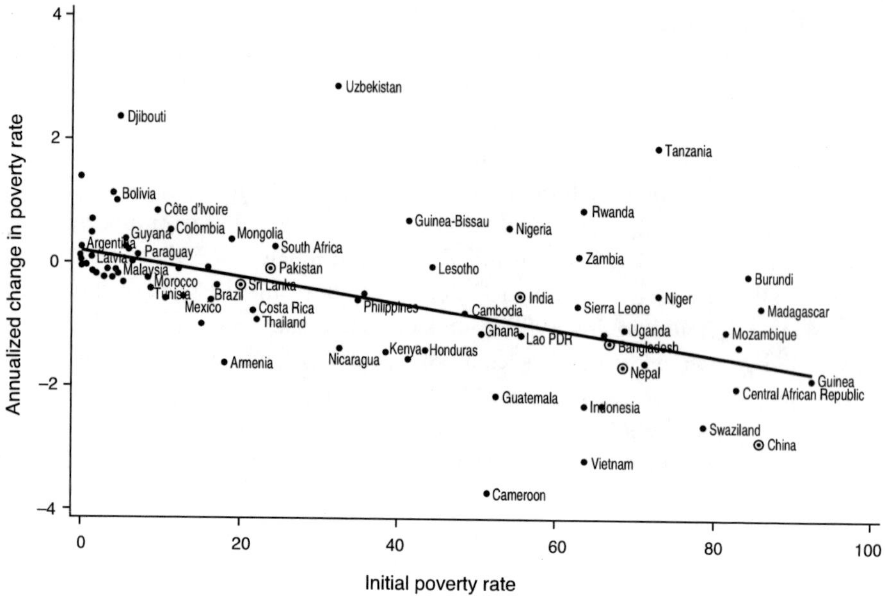

FIGURE 2.4   Is There Convergence in Headcount Ratios (absolute level)?

Source: World Bank (2009a).

Notes: Poverty rate is for $1.25 a day. Time period for change in poverty is for 1977–2007. Number of observations is 91.

on the initial poverty level, we see a negative and statistically significant coefficient, even after controlling for growth rates of per capita GDP. This negative relationship between poverty reduction and initial poverty holds even after controlling for per capita consumption rather than per capita GDP (column II), suggesting that more of the growth in per capita consumption is happening among the poor.

Using the reduction in headcount ratio tells us the absolute reduction in poverty—that is, if we multiply this reduction by the population of the country, it will tell us the number of people who have been raised out of poverty. This is obviously an important way to measure economic progress. When comparing across countries, however, we might face two issues with measuring only absolute changes in poverty. First, countries with low levels of poverty cannot display high values of poverty reduction. For instance, a country with a headcount ratio of 10 per cent can show a maximum reduction of 10 percentage points, whereas a country starting from a headcount ratio of 25 per cent might

TABLE 2.3 Poverty Convergence across Countries Headcount Ratios Based on Poverty Line of $1.25 a Day

	Annualized change in headcount ratio (absolute)			Annualized change in headcount ratio (proportional)	
			Initial poverty >10%		
	(I)	(II)	(III)	(IV)	(V)
Initial poverty (level)	−0.02*** (0.005)	−0.01** (0.004)	−0.032*** (0.010)		
Initial poverty (log)				−0.006 (0.01)	0.01 (0.01)
Growth rate of GDP per capita	−0.25** (0.12)		−0.30** (0.15)	−0.01*** (0.004)	−0.01*** (0.002)
Growth rate of per capita household consumption		−0.36*** (0.07)			
Observations	82	82	56	82	82
R-squared	0.97	0.71	0.34	0.13	0.48

Sources: World Bank (2009a, 2009b).
Notes: Robust standard errors are reported in parenthesis. ***represents significance at 1 per cent; **represents significance at 5 per cent; and *represents significance at 10 per cent. Poverty rate is defined as the per cent of population living in households with consumption or income per person below the international $1.25 poverty line. Annualized poverty change is for time period 1977–2007.

show a decline of 15 percentage points. The existence of a 'floor value' of zero, therefore, may not capture all the progress in a country starting from low levels of poverty.

We partially control for the existence of such a floor value by restricting our sample to countries that had a headcount ratio greater than 10 per cent in the initial period. Our results regarding convergence are robust to this restriction (see Table 2.3, column III). These results provide a basis for cautious optimism regarding progress in poor countries; in particular, they suggest that poor countries may not be trapped in poverty forever.

The second caveat to using absolute poverty change is the fact that reducing poverty from a high level might be easier than reducing poverty further from an already low level. The latter might reflect more entrenched factors leading to poverty, including low levels of education or health problems or even persistent beliefs about the value of effort (for example, 12 to 13 per cent of the US population has been under the national poverty line for more than a decade). In this sense, a reduction of poverty from 10 per cent to 5 per cent might involve a significantly greater policy effort than a reduction from 30 per cent to 25 per cent. Using a percentage change in poverty (or equivalently, a change in log poverty) gives a greater magnitude to poverty reductions starting from a low base. It avoids the 'floor value' problem. Ultimately, the choice of either absolute or log change depends on a normative viewpoint about which types of change we consider to be more relevant or more indicative of social welfare or policy effectiveness. A similar argument applies to other measures of well-being, which have a natural floor value, such as infant mortality.

When we consider percentage changes in poverty, we do not see any significant degree of convergence in poverty across countries (see Figure 2.5). In other words, although poorer countries do reduce absolute numbers of people living in poverty, they do not reduce them

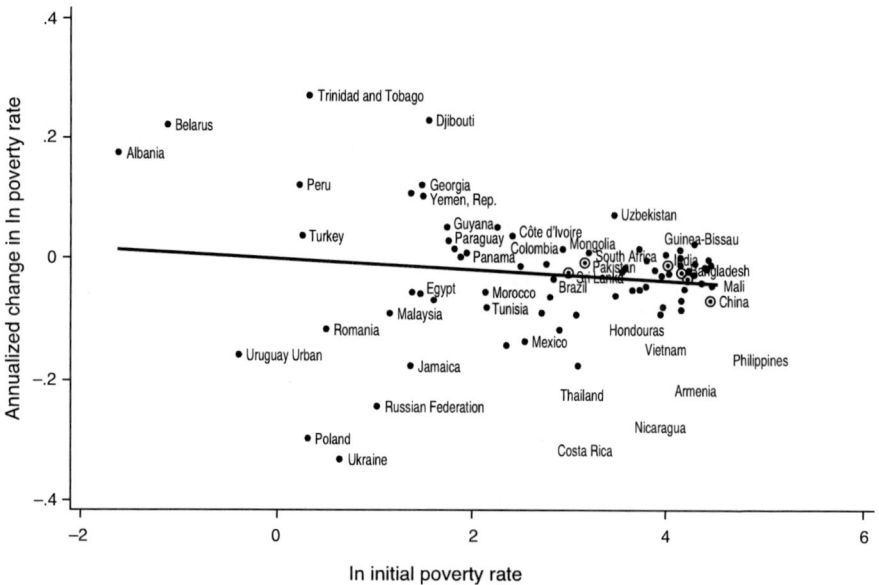

FIGURE 2.5   Is There Convergence in Headcount Ratios
(proportional reductions)?

Source: World Bank (2009a).
Notes: Poverty rate is for $1.25 a day poverty rate. Time period for change in poverty is for 1977–2007. Number of observations is 80.

proportionally faster than richer countries. In this sense, much work remains to accelerate poverty reduction in poor countries.

The lack of convergence in proportional terms is documented in Table 2.3, columns IV and V. The dependent variable is the annual rate of change in poverty (measured as the change in log poverty between two periods, divided by the number of years in between), and the main independent variable of interest is initial log poverty. We find no evidence of poverty convergence in this log specification, similar to the lack of convergence documented in Ravallion (2009).

Cross-country Trends in Depth and Severity of Poverty

In addition to the headcount ratio, we examine other measures of poverty, which take into account how far households are from the poverty line. This is particularly important in measuring extreme poverty, which may not be reflected fully in a simple comparison of headcount ratios. The two measures we consider are the Poverty Gap (PG) index and the Squared Poverty Gap (SPG) index. The PG is computed by measuring the gap between a household's per capita consumption and the poverty line, as a fraction of the poverty line figure. This figure is taken to be zero for households that are above the poverty line. The gap is then averaged over all households to obtain the PG index for a given country or region. The SPG is computed similarly, but the PG is replaced by its square for each household. The SPG measure therefore gives a greater weight to households that are far below the poverty line, and is thus interpreted as a measure of the severity of poverty. If some of the poorest households increase their consumption and come closer to the poverty line the SPG index will show a large reduction even if these households do not cross the poverty line (and therefore the headcount ratio shows no change).

Regressions using the PG or SPG measures show strong evidence of convergence across countries, with poorer countries showing the largest reductions in these indexes. This holds for absolute reductions as well as proportional ones. This result is encouraging. Even if poorer countries are not able to achieve huge reductions in the headcount ratio, they do appear to show the largest reductions in the depth and severity of poverty (see Table 2.4). Although the poorest show the largest increases in consumption, they are so far from the poverty line that this progress does not show up in equivalent changes to the headcount ratio.

Convergence in Poverty Indicators across South Asian Regions

We now examine similar trends at the subnational level within South Asia. Currently, we have subnational data on headcount ratios for most

TABLE 2.4 Convergence in Measures of Poverty Severity and Depth

	Annualized change in poverty gap				Annualized change in poverty gap squared			
	Absolute (I)	Absolute (II)	Proportional (III)	Proportional (IV)	Absolute (V)	Absolute (VI)	Proportional (VII)	Proportional (VIII)
Initial poverty gap (level)	-0.046*** (0.006)							
Initial poverty gap (log)		-0.029*** (0.005)	-0.024** (0.013)	-0.005 (0.01)				
Initial poverty gap squared (level)					-0.05*** (0.006)	-0.045*** (0.005)		
Initial poverty gap squared (log)							-0.045*** (0.015)	-0.025** (0.011)
Growth rate of GDP per capita	-0.104* (0.061)		-0.01*** (0.007)		-0.05 (0.037)		-0.022*** (0.009)	
Growth rate of per capita household consumption		-0.167*** (0.042)		-0.023*** (0.004)		-0.090*** (0.027)		-0.027*** (0.006)
Observations	82	82	82	82	79	79	79	79
R-squared	0.48	0.69	0.21	0.44	0.60	0.72	0.37	0.51

Sources: World Bank (2009a, 2009b).

Notes: Robust standard errors are reported in parenthesis. The regression results are restricted to the same sample as available in the proportionate change sample.

*** represents significance at 1 per cent; ** represents significance at 5 per cent; and * represents significance at 10 per cent.

Poverty rate is defined as the per cent of population living in households with consumption or income per person below the international $1.25 poverty line. Time period used is from 1977–2007. Poverty gap is defined as the mean distance below the poverty line as a proportion of the poverty line. Squared poverty gap is defined as mean of the squared distances below the poverty line as a proportion of the poverty line.

South Asia regions, as well as detailed data on various poverty measures for states of India.

The trends across South Asian regions are similar to our earlier results for the global sample. We see that regions with higher levels of poverty experienced greater absolute reductions in the headcount ratio (see Table 2.5, columns I and II). As in the global sample, however, they did not experience greater proportional reductions in the headcount ratio (Table 2.5, columns III and IV), suggesting that more needs to be done in these lagging regions to align them with the leading ones. When we look at measures of poverty depth and severity, we again see that the initially worse-off regions showed greater improvements on these measures than the initially better-off regions (see Table 2.5, columns V and VII). Unlike the global sample, the lagging regions do not show proportionally better performance in reducing the PG or the SPG measures (Table 2.5, columns VI and VIII). This is a worrisome sign that poverty reduction in the lagging regions of South Asia needs to be accelerated, especially with regard to extreme poverty.

What Explains Poverty Convergence?

Why might we observe convergence in absolute poverty rates even when we do not observe convergence in per capita incomes?[1] The poverty measures are based on income or consumption levels derived from household surveys. So one possibility is that these consumption numbers might be converging even if per capita GDP is diverging.[2] We call this explanation the 'GDP-consumption disconnect'. Detailed analysis of Indian household surveys reveals that household consumption grew much slower than overall GDP throughout the 1990s (World Bank 2009c). So this explanation is unlikely to explain the patterns of absolute convergence within South Asia.

Two possible explanations for these patterns are as follows: (i) inequality has fallen a lot in countries that are initially poor, or (ii) the sensitivity of the headcount to the mean is vastly larger in countries that are initially poor. The inequality channel has little a priori support: most studies find that inequality has risen in fast-growing countries

[1] We are grateful to Aart Kraay for motivating this analysis.

[2] This might happen for several reasons. For instance, if investments or exports are a large part of GDP, then divergence in those components might drive overall GDP divergence even if consumption is converging. The difficulties in reconciling GDP data from national accounts with data from household surveys are discussed in Deaton (2005) and Deaton and Kozel (2005).

TABLE 2.5 Poverty Convergence in South Asia

	Annualized change in headcount ratio (absolute)		Annualized change in headcount ratio (proportional)		Annualized change in poverty gap		Annualized change in poverty gap squared	
	South Asia (I)	India (II)	South Asia (III)	India, (IV)	India, absolute (V)	India, proportional (VI)	India, absolute (VII)	India, proportional (VIII)
Initial poverty (level)	-0.03*** (0.01)	-0.02* (0.01)						
Initial poverty (log)			-0.01 (0.01)	-0.002 (0.01)				
Initial poverty gap (level)					-0.03*** (0.01)			
Initial poverty gap (log)						0.001 (0.01)		
Initial poverty gap squared (level)							-0.04*** (0.01)	
Initial poverty gap squared (log)								-0.003 (0.01)

(contd...)

Table 2.5 (contd...)

	Annualized change in headcount ratio (absolute)		Annualized change in headcount ratio (proportional)		Annualized change in poverty gap		Annualized change in poverty gap squared	
	South Asia (I)	India (II)	South Asia (III)	India, (IV)	India, absolute (V)	India, proportional (VI)	India, absolute (VII)	India, proportional (VIII)
Growth rate of GDP per capita	-0.04	-0.06	-0.26	0.31	0.45	-0.10	0.03	0.02
	(0.07)	(0.07)	(0.30)	(0.31)	(1.19)	(0.33)	(0.72)	(0.39)
Observations	29	18	29	18	18	18	18	18
R-squared	0.21	0.14	0.05	0.02	0.31	0.003	0.46	0.002

Sources: India: World Bank staff calculations using the National Sample Survey Organisation (NSSO) 55th and 61st Rounds; Sri Lanka: Household Income and Expenditure Survey (HIES) (1996 and 2002); Pakistan: World Bank staff.

Notes: Robust standard errors are reported in parenthesis.

*** represents significance at 1 per cent; ** represents significance at 5 per cent; and * represents significance at 10 per cent. Regressions exclude the following outliers: Orissa for India and the Northern Province for Sri Lanka. Regressions exclude Nepal and Bangladesh because of a lack of data. South Asia includes states in India (1994–2005), Pakistan (1999–2005), and Sri Lanka (1996–2002).

like China and India. The most likely explanation, therefore, is that poverty reduction is much more sensitive to growth in initially poorer countries. Part of this sensitivity is due to the construction of poverty measures: as long as the poorest people increase their consumption levels, we will see sharp reductions in the poverty depth and severity (an increase in consumption among the non-poor does not affect these measures). If a lot of people live just below the poverty line, a small growth in consumption can move a lot of people above the line, resulting in a large decrease in the headcount ratio. And, in an initially poor country, a lot of people live both just below the poverty line and far below it, compared with those living in an initially not-so-poor country. Consumption growth in the no-so-poor country will affect a smaller proportion of the overall population and thus make a smaller change to the poverty measures.

In this sense, our results should be taken to reflect a partially optimistic picture: because we do find proportionate reductions in the depth and severity of poverty in the initially poor countries, we can say that some progress is being made, and that these countries need not be trapped forever in poverty. The picture in South Asia, however, is less rosy: we do not see proportionate reductions in either the headcount ratio or in the depth and severity measures.

CONVERGENCE IN HEALTH AND EDUCATION OUTCOMES

In this section, we examine whether other measures of well-being show signs of convergence. In part, this will provide a clearer picture of trends in welfare around the world, and allow us to see whether the poverty convergence results also are reflected in other types of outcomes.

Cross-country Trends in Health and Education

We consider outcome variables related to health status (infant mortality and life expectancy) and education attainment (secondary school enrolment, years of schooling, and adult literacy).[3] We find a substantial degree of convergence on the education indicators, but not on the health indicators.

Countries that initially had higher levels of infant mortality show greater decreases in infant mortality over time (see Figure 2.6), but we do not see

---

[3]These data are obtained from the *World Development Indicators* (World Bank 2009b) and the Barro and Lee (2001) data set.

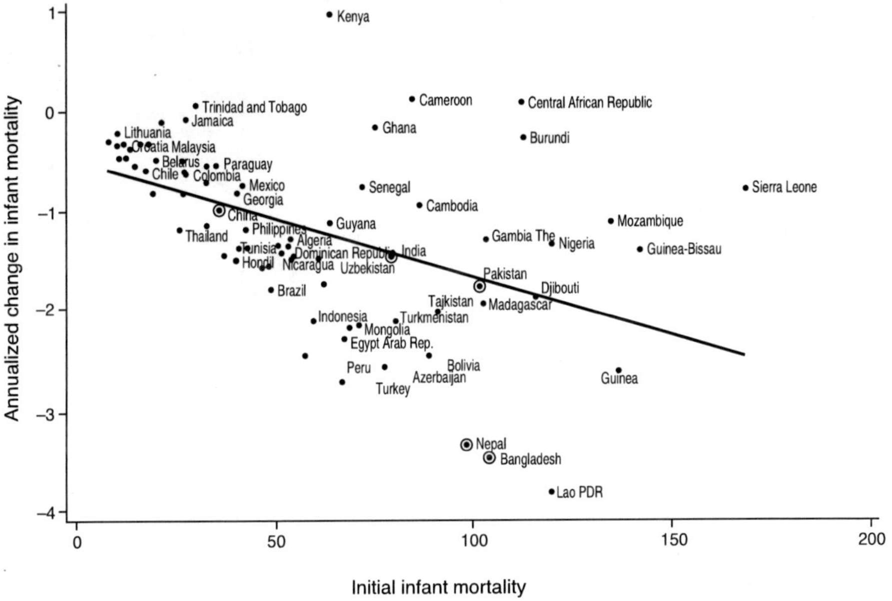

FIGURE 2.6   Convergence in Infant Mortality Rates across Countries (absolute change)

Source: World Bank (2009b).
Notes: Infant mortality rate is the number of infants dying before reaching one year of age, per 1,000 live births in a given year (1990–2006). The number of observations is 161.

greater proportional reductions in infant mortality in the countries that initially had higher rates (see Figure 2.7).[4] This mirrors the results for the poverty headcount ratio. Thus, although some progress is being made in the initially worse-off countries, it is not as rapid as we might like it to be.

The results for this partial convergence of infant mortality rates continue to hold even after we control for per capita GDP growth (see Table 2.6). Although we see the absolute convergence on these measures (see Table 2.6, column I), we see divergence rather than convergence when we consider proportional changes (see Table 2.6, column V). In other words, the reductions in infant mortality in the worst-off countries were rather small as a proportion of their initial levels.

[4]Infant mortality is measured as the number of deaths before one year of age, for every 1,000 live births.

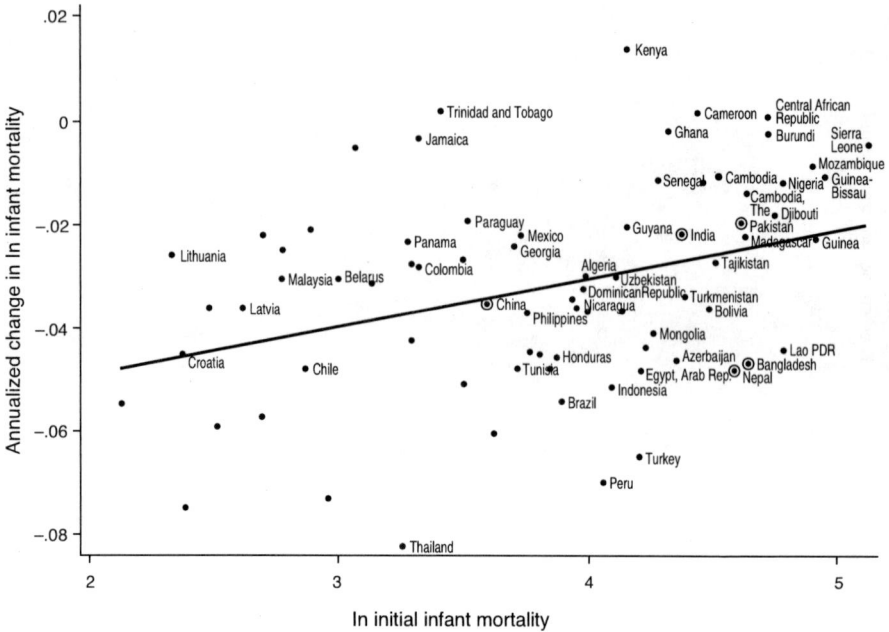

FIGURE 2.7   Convergence in Infant Mortality Rates across Countries
(proportional change)

Source: World Bank (2009b).
Note: The number of observations is 161.

We also show results for a different health measure, which takes into account mortality differences over all age-groups: life expectancy. On this measure, we do not see significant absolute increases in life expectancy among the initially worse-off countries (see Table 2.6, column II). In proportional terms we do see a trend toward convergence that is statistically significant at the 10 per cent level of significance (see Table 2.6, column VI).

The results on child malnutrition are similar to the trends in infant mortality: we see greater absolute reductions in countries that started with high levels of malnutrition, but no greater proportional reductions (see Table 2.6, columns III and VII). These data are available for a much smaller set of countries, however, than the samples for infant mortality or life expectancy measures.

Turning to education outcomes, we find a substantial degree of convergence across countries in secondary school enrolment rates, average

TABLE 2.6 Convergence in Health Indicators

	Absolute changes in health indicators			Proportional changes in health indicators		
	Infant mortality	Life expectancy	Child malnutrition rate	Infant mortality	Life expectancy	Child malnutrition rate
	(I)	(II)	(III)	(V)	(VI)	(VII)
Initial value of health indicator (level)	-0.01*** (0.003)	-0.004 (0.003)	-0.01*** (0.004)			
Initial value of health indicator (log)				0.006*** (0.002)	-0.008* (0.004)	0.001 (0.008)
Growth rate of GDP per capita	-0.12** (0.05)	0.02* (0.01)	-0.07* (0.04)	-0.31*** (0.12)	0.04* (0.02)	-0.52 (0.21)
Observations	73	91	48	73	91	48
R-squared	0.29	0.03	0.29	0.22	0.05	0.09

Source: World Bank (2009b).

Notes: Robust standard errors are reported in parenthesis. The regressions reported are restricted to the same sample of countries as the poverty convergence data. *** represents significance at 1 per cent; ** represents significance at 5 per cent; and * represents significance at 10 per cent. The regressions are restricted to sample where data on consumption and poverty are available. Infant mortality rate is the number of infants dying before reaching one year of age, per 1,000 live births in a given year (1990–2006). Life expectancy at birth indicates the number of years a newborn infant would live if prevailing patterns of mortality at the time of its birth were to stay the same throughout his or her life (1990–2007). Prevalence of child malnutrition is the percentage of children under age five whose weight for age is more than two standard deviations below the median for the international reference population ages 0–59 months (1990–8: initial and 2000–7) with average time period difference as nine years.

years of schooling, and adult literacy rates. Countries that started with lower levels of these indicators were able to generate larger increases in them over the past decade (see Table 2.7, columns I, II, and III). Of course, all of these measures have an upper bound, and hence this could be the mechanical effect of countries at the upper end not having the room to expand further on these indicators. These results also hold for proportional changes, which is more encouraging (see Table 2.7, columns IV, V, and VI). This trend suggests that the poor countries have been able to improve education outcomes to a much greater degree than health outcomes.

Such convergence of health and education outcomes across countries has been noted in other studies, including Kenny (2009) who attributes this phenomenon to the spread of technology and ideas. On the other hand, Deaton (2006) provides a useful word of caution in the interpretation of aggregate statistics, such as life expectancy (which can decline due to mortality changes at different points of the life cycle), and highlights the large gaps and poor quality of the data on health indicators in developing countries.

Social Indicators Convergence within South Asia

The convergence trends for social indicators across South Asian regions and Indian states are similar to the cross-country trends. Data from India show that states that had higher levels of infant mortality in 2000 managed greater absolute reductions in infant mortality over the next five years, but they did not achieve greater proportional reductions (see Table 2.8, columns I and V). We do not see statistically significant reductions in the child malnutrition rates across Indian states, although we do see worse-off states achieving somewhat higher reductions (see Table 2.8, columns II and VI). In terms of education, we see convergence in absolute and proportional changes in the education participation rate among children ages 11 to 15 years, but no statistically significant changes in the secondary school completion rate. As in the case of poverty depth and severity, convergence across the regions of South Asia does not appear to be as rapid as across the countries of the world.

Overall, our results suggest that it is possible for lagging regions to catch up with leading regions in terms of health and education outcomes, and with poverty rates, even if economic growth in the lagging regions does not exceed that in the leading regions. Our results also suggest that such convergence is not fast enough, in the sense that proportional levels are increasing similarly fast in leading regions. We see very few instances of 'reversal'—that is, lagging regions going ahead of leading regions in

TABLE 2.7 Convergence in Education Indicators across Countries

	Absolute changes in education indicators			Proportional changes in education indicators		
	Secondary school enrolment	Years of schooling	Adult literacy rate	Secondary school enrolment	Years of schooling	Adult literacy rate
	(I)	(II)	(III)	(IV)	(V)	(VI)
Initial value of education indicator (level)	-0.01*** (0.002)	-0.01*** (0.002)	-0.01*** (0.003)			
Initial value of education indicator (log)				-0.02*** (0.002)	-0.02*** (0.002)	-0.02*** (0.004)
Growth rate of GDP per capita	0.18*** (0.03)	0.02*** (0.008)	-0.38 (0.32)	0.22*** (0.06)	0.15*** (0.06)	-0.002 (0.005)
Observations	98	69	61	98	69	61
R-squared	0.23	0.34	0.58	0.66	0.73	0.84

Source: World Bank (2009b).

Notes: Robust standard errors are reported in parenthesis. *** represents significance at 1 per cent; ** represents significance at 5 per cent; and * represents significance at 10 per cent. Gross enrolment ratio is the ratio of total enrolment, regardless of age, to the population of the age-group that officially corresponds to the level of education shown (1990–2006). Expected years of schooling is the number of years a child of school entrance age is expect to spend at school, or university, including years spent on repetition (1990–2006). Adult literacy rate is the percentage of people age 15 and above who can, with understanding, read and write a short, simple statement on their everyday life (1990–2007). We take individual years because cross-country data on adult literacy are sparse.

TABLE 2.8 Convergence in Social Indicators within South Asia

	Absolute changes in social indicators				Proportional changes in social indicators			
	Infant mortality India	Child malnutrition rate India	Education participation rate, 11–15 years South Asia	Secondary school completion rate South Asia	Infant mortality India	Child malnutrition rate India	Education participation rate, 11–15 years South Asia	Secondary school completion rate South Asia
	(I)	(II)	(III)	(III)	(V)	(VI)	(VII)	(VIII)
Initial value of social indicator (level)	-0.01*** (0.003)	-0.01 (0.01)	-2.14* (1.10)	-0.03 (1.26)				
Initial value of social indicator (log)					-0.004 (0.004)	-0.01 (0.01)	-0.02** (0.01)	-0.009 (0.01)
Growth rate of GDP per capita	-0.10** (0.04)	-0.13 (0.04)	-0.15* (0.07)	-0.54 (0.12)	-0.17* (0.09)	-0.29 (0.11)	-0.19* (0.10)	-0.009 (0.003)
Observations	16	19	25	27	16	19	25	27
R-squared	0.44	0.29	0.40	0.07	0.12	0.22	0.49	0.03

Source: Planning Commission of India for Infant mortality and child malnutrition. NSS for education participation and secondary school completion rate (2008).

Note: Robust standard errors are reported in parenthesis. *** represents significance at 1 per cent; ** represents significance at 5 per cent; and * represents significance at 10 per cent. Infant mortality is per 1,000 live births (1994–2005). Child malnutrition is the per cent of children under age three years classified as underweight (1998–2005). Education participation rate is for 11 to 15-year-old children participating in education: India (1999–2005); Pakistan (1998–2005). Secondary school completion rate is for 20 to 24-year-olds completing the secondary stage: India (1999–2005); Pakistan (1998–2005).

any real sense. Therefore, more work is needed to bring lagging regions on par with leading regions.

POLICY OPTIONS AND CONCLUSIONS

Our results may provide some evidence for economic and social progress in lagging regions. On the positive side, we do see significantly greater absolute reductions in poverty and infant mortality, and significant increases in education indicators in initially poor countries and regions. This finding gives us hope that these countries are not trapped by their poverty. On the negative side, we see no evidence of convergence in per capita incomes and, in fact, observe divergence in many cases. We do not see greater proportionate reductions in poverty or infant mortality in initially poor places. Therefore, these regions are not catching up with richer regions fast enough, and more needs to be done to accelerate economic and social development in the lagging regions.

What can South Asian regions do to promote growth and social development in the lagging regions? This is the focus of the rest of the volume. The divergence in per capita GDP suggests that a key priority has to be generating greater growth in the lagging regions. This will require investments, such as greater physical infrastructure to improve connectivity; market integration of lagging regions with leading regions; and improvements in institutional quality to spur greater investment and productivity. A key institutional feature that needs to be strengthened is conflict management.

In addition to policies for greater growth, South Asia needs to directly address the social indicators in the lagging regions. This means greater funding for education and health services in lagging regions, as well as capacity building to enable better use of such funds. All of these factors are dealt with in greater detail in the remaining chapters of this volume.

The future growth prospects of South Asian countries are bright. The trend on poverty convergence and social convergence is positioning the region for faster growth, which is likely to be more pro-poor growth, and social development, which will be more pro-poor. This trend could become a virtuous circle, but there is no room for complacency.

REFERENCES

Acemoglu, Daron. 2009. *Introduction to Modern Economic Growth*. Princeton, NJ: Princeton University Press.

Banerjee, Abhijit and Esther Duflo. 2003. 'Inequality and Growth: What Can the Data Say?', *Journal of Economic Growth*, 1: 449–86.

Banerjee, Abhijit and Andrew Newman. 1993. 'Occupational Choice and the Process of Development', *Journal of Political Economy*, 101: 274–98.

Barro, Robert and J.W. Lee. 2001. 'International Data on Educational Attainment: Updates and Implications', *Oxford Economic Papers*, 53 (3): 541–63.

Barro, Robert and Xavier Sala-i-Martin. 1992. 'Convergence', *Journal of Political Economy*, 100: 223–51.

————. 1999. *Economic Growth*. Cambridge, MA: MIT Press.

Caselli, Francesco, Gerard Esquivel, and Fersnando Lefort. 1996. 'Reopening the Convergence Debate: A New Look at Cross-Country Growth Empirics', *Journal of Economic Growth*, 40: 363–89.

Chen, Shaohua and Martin Ravallion. 2008. 'The Developing World is Poorer than We Thought, but No Less Successful in the Fight against Poverty', Policy Research Working Paper 4703, World Bank.

Deaton, Angus. 2005. 'Measuring Poverty in a Growing World (or Measuring Growth in a Poor World)', *Review of Economics and Statistics*, 87 (1): 1–19.

————. 2006. 'Global Patterns of Income and Health: Facts, Interpretations, and Policies', WIDER Annual Lecture 10, Helsinki, Finland.

Deaton, Angus and Valerie Kozel. 2005. 'Data and Dogma: The Great India Poverty Debate', *World Bank Research Observer*, 20 (2): 177–99.

Deininger, Klaus and Lyn Squire. 1998. 'New Ways of Looking at Old Issues: Inequality and Growth', *Journal of Development Economics*, 57 (2): 259–87.

Forbes, Kristin. 2000. 'A Reassessment of the Relationship between Inequality and Growth', *American Economic Review*, 90 (4): 869–87.

Galor, Oded and Joseph Zeira. 1993. 'Income Distribution and Macroeconomics', *Review of Economic Studies*, 60: 35–52.

Household Income and Expenditure Survey (HIES). 2006/7. Department of Census and Statistics (DCS), Government of Sri Lanka.

Kenny, Charles. 2009. 'The Success of Development: Innovation, Ideas and the Global Standard of Living', book manuscript in preparation.

Kraay, Aart. 2006. 'When is Growth Pro-Poor? Evidence from a Panel of Countries', *Journal of Development Economics*, 80: 198–227.

Lopez, Humberto and Luis Serven. 2009. 'Too Poor to Grow', Policy Research Working Paper 5012, World Bank.

Murphy, Kevin M., Andrei Shleifer, and Robert W. Vishny. 1989. 'Industrialization and the Big Push', *Quarterly Journal of Economics*, 106: 503–30.

NSSO (National Sample Survey Organisation). 1983, 1994, and 2005. 55th and 61st Rounds. Government of India.

Piketty, Thomas. 1997. 'The Dynamics of Wealth Distribution and the Interest Rate with Credit Rationing', *Review of Economic Studies*, 64: 173–90.

Quah, Danny. 1993. 'Empirical Cross-section Dynamics in Economic Growth',
European Economic Review, 37: 426–34.

———. 1997. 'Empirics for Growth and Distribution: Stratification, Polarization
and Convergence Clubs', *Journal of Economic Growth*, 2: 27–60.

Ravallion, Martin. 2009. 'Why Don't We See Poverty Convergence?' Mimeo,
World Bank, Washington, D.C.

World Bank. 2009a. PovcalNet. PovcalNet Online Poverty Analysis Tool.
Available at http://web.worldbank.org/WBSITE/EXTERNAL/EXTDEC/
EXTRESEARCH/EXTPROGRAMS/EXTPOVRES/EXTPOVCALNET
/0,,contentMDK:21867101~pagePK:64168427~piPK:64168435~theSite
PK:5280443,00.html: World Bank.

———. 2009b. *World Development Indicators*. Washington, D.C.: World
Bank.

———. 2009c. 'Perspectives on Poverty in India: Stylized Facts from Survey
Data', draft report, World Bank, Washington, D.C.

3

New Economic Geography and Market Access

Maarten Bosker and Harry Garretsen

South Asia[1] has experienced sustained high growth rates over the past decades (World Bank 2007a, 2007b). This has helped significantly in reducing poverty throughout the South Asian region. These growth rates, however, mask significant differences not only between countries, but also between the growth experiences of different regions within the same country. Within each country, growth is typically concentrated in relatively few parts of the country. A clear distinction can be made between leading and lagging regions within each South Asian country. Such within-country disparities are viewed by many as a potential threat to future growth as tensions between the poorer and wealthier regions or states are likely to increase if current trends in regional inequality persist or even increase in the future. As outlined in the *World Development Report* (WDR, World Bank 2009b), a gap between leading and lagging regions can provide a major challenge for policymakers.

Recent insights from the so-called new economic geography (NEG) literature (World Bank 2009b: chapter 1; Fujita and Thisse 2002; Fujita et al. 1999; Puga 1999) suggest that increases in regional disparities may be a natural (though not inevitable) feature of the development process, and may even be warranted from an overall welfare perspective. This literature also shows that, once established, regional disparities

[1]South Asia comprises the following countries: Afghanistan, Bangladesh, Bhutan, India, The Maldives, Nepal, Pakistan, and Sri Lanka.

can be rather persistent and insensitive to policy-induced changes. At the same time, and depending on the interplay between NEG's three main ingredients (agglomeration economies, transport costs, and factor mobility), divergence is not the only outcome of the development process. It may very well be that at some point during the development process, the spreading of economic activity and hence convergence becomes dominant. Whatever the exact economic outcome, the NEG approach stresses that the overall economic development process will not necessarily be similar across regions. From the perspective of South Asia's lagging regions, the potential for successful government policy aimed at improving their fortunes crucially depends on what drives the observed regional inequality. Can its causes be targeted by policies to begin with?

The present chapter starts with a glance at the evolution of South Asia's economic geography at three different spatial scales. The first scale concerns South Asia's position in the global economy, comparing the evolution of the region as a whole to other developing world regions. At the second scale, we compare the economic development of each of the six (main) South Asian countries that together constitute the major part of the South Asian economy. And finally, and most important, at a third spatial scale of aggregation, we discuss the evolution of the subnational regional economies in detail, inter alia, by comparing the development of each country's lagging regions with that of its leading ones.

We briefly introduce the main building blocks of the NEG literature, introducing and summarizing its key elements. Their interplay of agglomeration economies, transport costs, and factor mobility comes to the fore in the key concept of market access.

After that, we link the basic facts of the region's economic geography to the NEG framework in order to establish the importance of NEG in shaping the regional distribution, and growth dynamics, of economic activity in South Asia. Our discussion is centred around the major role for market access in determining the spatial distribution of economic activity at three different spatial scales. In particular, it focuses on South Asia's economic geography as a whole, and each South Asian country's internal economic geography, as well as touching upon the urban–rural divide within each subnational region to get an idea about intraregional disparities.

Having established the potential relevance of NEG within the South Asian context, we suggest several policy guidelines that may not only further stimulate economic progress in general but also improve the future prospects for South Asia's lagging regions in particular. To preview our main findings:

1. South Asia has a lot to gain from increased economic integration, especially between the countries of the region itself. This would allow countries and subnational border regions, in particular, to exploit their potential market access and improve their economic situation.
2. This is especially so for currently lagging regions. Given their own small regional economies, many lagging regions are more dependent on good market access to other (larger) regions. Moreover, many of these regions are landlocked and/or in border areas; they in particular have a lot to gain from improved infrastructure and from improved integration of South Asian countries.
3. Urbanization levels in South Asia are the lowest in the world. Further urbanization will have positive effects not only on economic growth, but also on the urban–rural divide in terms of poverty.
4. Existing agglomeration patterns in South Asia will most likely persist, or even increase in the future.

STYLIZED FACTS ABOUT SOUTH ASIA'S ECONOMIC GEOGRAPHY

Before we discuss the basic ingredients of NEG and the empirical relevance of NEG for South Asia, this section presents some stylized facts about the region. In doing so, we focus on several (mainly) economic performance indicators and illustrate whether, and if so how, these stylized facts differ across three different levels of spatial aggregation. The three aggregation levels or spatial scales we distinguish are at an ever-increasing level of geographical detail: the South Asia region as a whole compared with other developing regions of the world economy, the individual countries within South Asia compared with each other, and, finally, the regional and urban development in each of the South Asia's countries, focusing explicitly on developments in the lagging regions.

South Asia Compared with the Rest of the World

Starting with the first spatial scale, Table 3.1 gives some stylized facts on South Asia's position in the world economy. As can be seen from the upper half of Table 3.1, South Asia is by global standards a poor region. Compared with the other (developing) world regions, South Asia's GDP per capita is low. About half a billion people (or half the world's poor) live in poverty on the South Asian subcontinent (see Chapter 1). Only Sub-Saharan Africa had a lower GDP per capita in 2005. This is the case despite the fact that the South Asian economy as a whole is quite large and has been the second fastest growing region (see the lower half of

Table 3.1) over the past decades. The relatively low GDP per capita levels are due to the fact that South Asia is a very populous region—indeed it is the second largest region in population terms.

A related and even more striking observation is that South Asia's level of population density is about 2.5 times higher than the second densest region, East Asia. It is quite interesting that South Asia's high population

TABLE 3.1   South Asia Compared with the Rest of the World

	GDP 2000 1$ billion	GDP per capita 2000 1$	GDP density 2000 1$/ km² (x 1000)	Popu-lation 2006 million	Popu-lation density # people /km2	Urbani-zation %	Poverty rate % < 1$ /day	Poverty rate % < 2$ /day
				Levels				
World region/ Year	2005	2005	2005	2006	2006	2006	2004	2004
East Asia & Pacific	10151	5384	639	1899	120	42.4	9.1	36.6
Europe & Central Asia	3899	8265	168	461	20	63.8	0.9	9.8
Latin America & Caribbean	4121	7482	204	556	28	77.7	8.6	22.2
Middle East & North Africa	1668	5450	186	311	35	57.5	1.5	19.7
South Asia	4102	2791	858	1499	314	28.8	30.8	77.1
Sub-Saharan Africa	1318	1774	56	782	33	35.8	41.1	72
				Growth				
Growth (unit):	GDP (%)	GDP per capita (%)		Popu-lation (%)		Urbani-zation (PPT)	Poverty rate % <1$ a day (PPT)	Poverty rate % < 2$ a day (PPT)
World region/ Period	1989– 2005	1989– 2005		1975– 2006		1975– 2006	1990– 2004	1990– 2004
East Asia & Pacific	260.3	200.2		51.2		23.1	–20.8	–33.2
Europe & Central Asia	4.2	2.3		19.6		7.9	0.5	5.5

(contd...)

Table 3.1 (contd...)

Growth (unit):	GDP (%)	GDP per capita (%)	Population (%)	Urbanization (PPT)	Poverty rate % <1$ a day (PPT)	Poverty rate % < 2$ a day (PPT)
World region/ Period	1989– 2005	1989– 2005	1975– 2006	1975– 2006	1990– 2004	1990– 2004
Latin America & Caribbean	56.1	21.8	75.1	16.4	–1.6	–4.1
Middle East & North Africa	91.7	36.6	113	13.3	–0.9	–2
South Asia	143.2	80.4	86.4	8.6	–12.2	–8.5
Sub-Saharan Africa	54	3.6	135.2	14.6	–5.6	–5.1

Source: World Bank (2009a).

Notes: GDP = gross domestic product; I$ denotes PPP-corrected international dollars; PPT = percentage point change. The year of observation may differ slightly; whenever no data was available for the indicated year, the closest year available has been used. Growth of GDP density and population density is the same as GDP and population growth, respectively (given that a region's area does not change).

density, or similarly high GDP density, which is generally considered as virtuous for economic development (World Bank 2009b), does not come along with a higher level of economic prosperity. We show that an explanation for this may be that South Asia's high population density does not coincide with a high degree of urbanization.

Compared with the other world regions in Table 3.1, South Asia has the lowest degree of urbanization (closely matched only by Sub-Saharan Africa, which has very low population density). South Asia's growth rate of urbanization has not matched its economic growth: South Asia was the second fastest growing region in GDP per capita terms, but its urbanization rate grew at a mere 8.6 percentage points during the last two decades (making it the least rapidly urbanizing developing world region). This combination of a high overall population density with a very low degree of urbanization (growth) is something that sets South Asia apart from the other developing regions in Table 3.1.

Comparing South Asia Countries

To see whether the above painted picture also emerges for each individual South Asian country respectively, Table 3.2 provides information on the

TABLE 3.2   Comparing South Asian Countries

	GDP 2000 1$ billion	GDP per capita 2000 1$	GDP density 2000 1$/ km2 (x 1000)	Popu- lation 2000 million	Popu- lation density # people /km2	Urbani- zation %	Poverty rate % < 1$ /day	Poverty rate % < 2$ /day
				Levels				
Country/ Year	2005	2005	2005	2006	2006	2006	2004	2004
South Asia	4102	2791	858	1499	314	28.8	30.8	77.1
Bangladesh	259	1827	1990	142	1090	25.1	41.3	84
Bhutan	–	–	–	1	14	11.1	–	–
India	3362	3072	1131	1095	368	28.7	34.3	80.4
Nepal	37	1379	262	27	190	15.8	24.1	68.5
Pakistan	328	2109	426	156	202	34.9	17	73.6
Sri Lanka	80	4088	1241	20	304	15.1	5.6	41.6
				Growth				
Growth (unit):	GDP (%)	GDP per capita (%)		Popu- lation (%)		Urbani- zation (PPT)	Poverty rate % <1$ a day (PPT)	Poverty rate % < 2$ a day (PPT)
Country/ Period	1989– 2005	1989– 2005		1975– 2006		1975– 2006	1990– 2004	1990– 2004
South Asia	143.2	80.4		86.4		8.6	–12.2	–8.5
Bangladesh	120.6	58.2		93.8		15.2	5.4	–2.4
Bhutan	–	–		45.2		6.5	–	–
India	153	92.4		78.4		7.4	–7.5	–5
Nepal	97.4	35.8		100.3		11	–	–
Pakistan	94.5	31.5		119.3		8.6	–	–
Sri Lanka	113	82.6		45.4		–4.4	1.7	1

Source: World Bank (2009a).

Notes: GDP = gross domestic product; I$ denotes PPP-corrected international dollars. The years of observation may differ slightly. Whenever no data was available for the indicated year, the closest year available has been used. Growth of GDP density and population density is the same as GDP and population growth respectively (given that a region's area does not change). The change in poverty rate is calculated over the period 1992–2000, 1993–2004, and 1990–2003 for Bangladesh, India, and Sri Lanka, respectively.

same set of indicators as Table 3.1, but for each of the individual South Asian countries, for which we have sufficient data, separately (Bangladesh, Bhutan, India, Nepal, Pakistan, and Sri Lanka).

Looking first at the GDP variables, two stylized facts about South Asia immediately come to the fore. First, there are very large differences between individual countries in terms of economic development. India and Sri Lanka notably have a significantly higher GDP per capita than Bangladesh, Pakistan, and Nepal. A similar pattern holds for economic growth over the last two decades, the region's overall above average economic growth performance can be mainly ascribed to India (and Sri Lanka) with Bangladesh, Pakistan, and Nepal lagging behind in terms of GDP per capita growth.

Second, India dominates the South Asian economy. This dominant position is above all due to its size. Out of the overall population of approximately 1.5 billion people for the region as a whole, more than 1 billion people live in India alone. This size difference is also apparent when one looks at overall GDP, India's economy accounts for over 80 per cent of the total South Asian economy. The dominance of India in the region or, put in NEG terms, the fact that it can be viewed as the core of the South Asian economy will be a main theme in our analysis.

In terms of the spatial concentration of people, Bangladesh stands out with a population density of almost 1,100 people per sq. km, almost three times as much as the second-densest country, India. The mountain kingdom of Bhutan's density of 14 people per sq. km stands in sharp contrast to this. Compared to this, the differences in terms of the urbanization level are much smaller among the South Asian countries. All countries have a low level of urbanization, which matches the finding for the South Asian region as a whole. Urbanization has increased most rapidly in Bangladesh, whereas the degree of urbanization in Sri Lanka even declined despite experiencing strong economic growth.

Subnational Level—Leading and Lagging Regions in South Asia

Finally, we turn to the third and most disaggregated spatial scale of our analysis. Tables 3.1 and 3.2 do not provide information on the differences *within* South Asian countries. In line with findings in the WDR 2009 for other developing countries, it turns out that the regional differences within each country are very pronounced for South Asia as well. To illustrate these regional differences, Figure 3.1 shows the spatial distribution of economic mass (GDP) and poverty mass (number of poor), respectively, across the *leading and lagging* regions of South Asia (see Chapter 1 for the exact definition of leading and lagging).

Some interesting geographical patterns show up in the location of leading and lagging regions in each South Asian country. Pakistan is characterized by an east/west divide with the western regions of Balochistan and the North-West Free Province lagging behind Punjab and Sindh, which both border India. In India, leading and lagging regions show a clear north/south divide instead (although the regions northwest of New Delhi and around Kolkata are an exception to this trend). In Sri Lanka only the region around its capital Colombo is characterized as being leading, and the same holds for Nepal and its capital Kathmandu (note that Nepal borders exclusively to India's lagging regions). In Bangladesh the capital city region Dhaka is characterized as leading together with Chittagong, which is home to its major international port (the regions bordering India are all lagging).

Besides showing the geographical distribution of leading and lagging regions, Figure 3.1b also shows that economic activity (total GDP) is not only distributed unevenly between the South Asian countries (see Table 3.2), but also between regions within the same country. The economic mass in Pakistan is concentrated in the two leading regions bordering India (Sindh and Punjab). Most of the economic mass in India is to be found in the leading Southern regions, around Kolkata, Mumbai, and (to the north-west of) New Delhi. In Bangladesh and Sri Lanka the bulk of economic activity takes place in the region surrounding the capital city (Dhaka and Western Province respectively). Similarly, Figure 3.1a, shows that in terms of poverty mass (the total number of people living on less than $1 a day) there exist substantial differences between regions in the same country: an indication that, besides economic disparities, social disparities within countries also are prevalent. In Pakistan, for example, poverty mass is concentrated in the leading regions where economic activity is concentrated, Sindh and Punjab. In India, however, we find the opposite: poverty mass is mainly concentrated in the lagging regions in and around the Ganges plains.

Complementing Figure 3.1, Table 3.3 shows that there exist substantial differences between each country's leading and lagging regions in several other indicators as well. In each country, the *lagging* regions have a *lower* GDP per capita, a *lower* population density, and they are *less* urbanized. However, they also tend to be home to a smaller part of each country's total population (with the notable exception of Bangladesh and Sri Lanka).

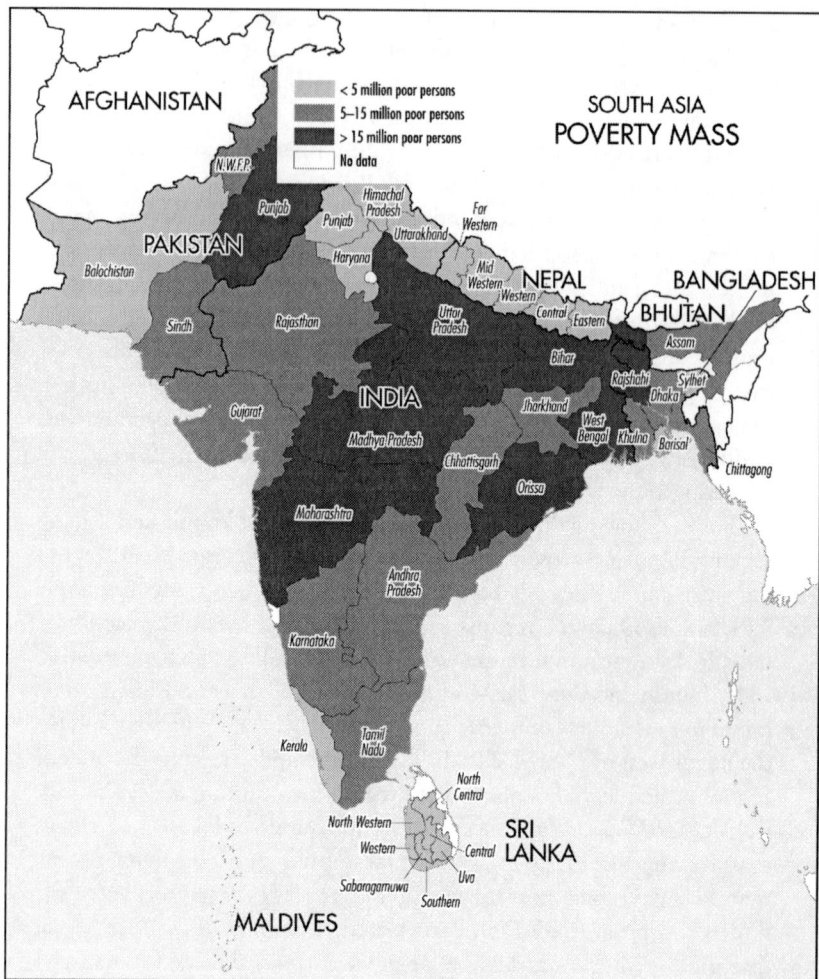

3.1a   Number of People

FIGURE 3.1   South Asia's Leading and Lagging States

Source: The classification of states into leading and lagging draws upon Honorati
and Mengistae (2007). They use a two-way classification, which follows Purfield
(2006) but uses more recent data.

Notes: Along the first dimension, states are compared by the level of development
attained by the early 1990s, measured by per capita income in 1994. Along the
second dimension, the comparison is in terms of recent growth performance,

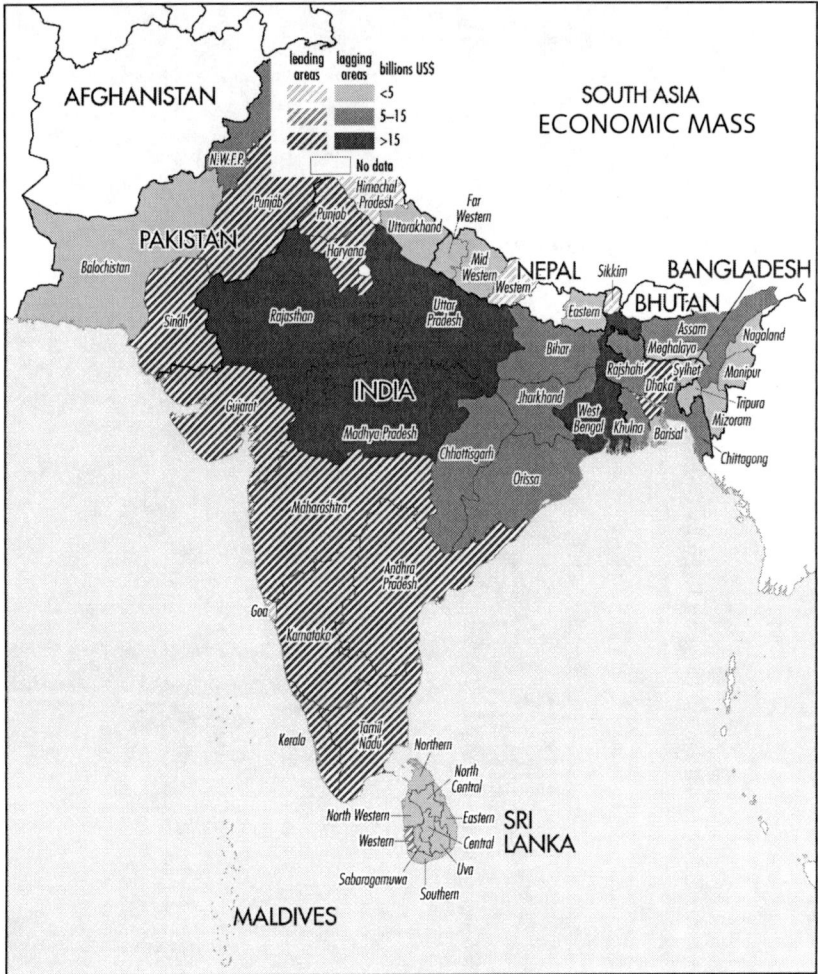

3.1b   GDP

measured by average annual growth rate in real GDP in the first decade since 1994. On the first dimension, states are grouped into a 'high-income' category and a 'low-income' group with the average state level per capita GDP of 1994 as the dividing line. Each of these two groups is then further classified into high-growth states and low-growth states with the average annual state level GDP growth rate for 1994–2003 as the cut-off point. The combined result is a four-quadrant grouping of states. Lagging regions are all 'quadrant-III states', having both low-income and low-growth states.

TABLE 3.3 Leading and Lagging Regions Compared

Variable	Year/Period	Bangladesh		India		Nepal		Pakistan		Sri Lanka	
		Lagging	Leading	Lagging	Leading	Lagging	Leading	Lagging	Leading	Lagging	Leading
% population	2001	69.1	30.9	48.4	51.6	45.6	54.4	20.8	79.2	71.4	28.6
% GDP	2005	62.3	37.7	32.3	67.7	38.9	61.1	17.1	82.9	51.7	48.3
Avg. GDP per capita (2000 I$)	2005	1366.4	1870.8	1793.9	3728	943.8	1261	1913.7	2347.7	2147.1	5203.0
Avg. population density (per km²)	2005	759.6	1372.4	285.4	319.7	123.7	224.3	174.1	332.7	246.5	1455.3
Avg. urbanization rate	2001	16	31.5	21.7	40.9	–	–	20.4	40.1	5.6	30.5
% urban population	2001	53.2	46.8	33.7	66.3	–	–	10.8	89.2	33.7	66.3
Avg. growth per year urbanization (PPT)	various	0.23	0.62	0.15	0.33			0.29	0.27	−0.27	0.79

(contd...)

Table 3.3 (contd...)

Variable	Year/Period	Bangladesh		India		Nepal		Pakistan		Sri Lanka	
		Lagg-ing	Lead-ing	Lagg-ing	Lead-ing	Lagg-ing	Lead-ing	Lagg-ing	Lead-ing	Lagg-ing	Lead-ing
Avg. annual GDP per capita growth (%)	various	4.36	8.07	2.75	5.11			3.53	2.87	3.27	4.34
Avg. annual population growth (%)	various	0	1.12	2.51	1.62	1.94	1.97	2.47	2.34	0.38	2.04

Source: Authors calculation using World Bank country sources data.

Notes: The period used to calculate growth rates differs between countries and variables, but generally span one or two decades. Indicators are only comparable between leading and lagging regions of the same country. The increase in urbanization for Bangladesh, India, Pakistan, and Sri Lanka is calculated over the period 1981–2001, 1991–2001, 1981–98, and 1981–2001, respectively. GDP growth for Bangladesh, India, Pakistan, and Sri Lanka is calculated over the period 1989–2003, 1995–2005, and 1996–2005, respectively. Population growth for Bangladesh, India, Nepal, Pakistan, and Sri Lanka is calculated over the period 1990–2003, 1995–2005, 1991–2004, 1995–2005, and 1996–2005, respectively. GDP (per capita) is measured in PPP-corrected 2000 1$.

When it comes to the changes over time in GDP per capita, population, and degree of urbanization (see bottom of Table 3.3), we see that Pakistan stands out. In Pakistan the gap between leading and lagging regions has decreased: the lagging regions are (be it very slowly) 'catching' up with the leading regions in terms of level of urbanization and income per capita. In Bangladesh and Sri Lanka, on the contrary, the leading regions have increased their lead over the past decades in terms of all three indicators: the leading region(s) has sustained (much) higher income per capita growth, its population has increased more rapidly, and more people have moved to the cities than in the lagging regions. In India we observe a largely similar pattern as in Bangladesh: regional disparities in urbanization level and income per capita are widening in India. The only exception is population growth: the lagging Indian regions are experiencing faster population growth.

Figure 3.2 further illustrates the regional income divergence in South Asia over the last decades: although average regional GDP per capita has increased over the period 1980–2005, the standard deviation of regional GDP per capita, and the difference in GDP per capita between the poorest and the wealthiest region have also increased, clearly showing that the differences between regions have grown much wider over the same period. So far, overall economic growth in South Asia has come along with increasing regional disparities. This observation will turn out to be important when we apply insights from the NEG approach to the case of South Asia and we will return to Figure 3.2 in our conclusions.

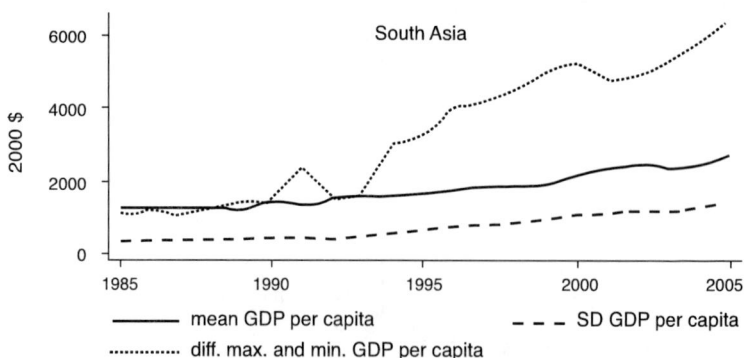

FIGURE 3.2   Regional Income Disparities in South Asia

Source: World Bank (2009a).
Note: GDP per capita is measured in 2000 1$ to correct for the differences in purchasing power between South Asian countries.

The stylized facts in this section provide a basic understanding of South Asia's economic geography at three different levels of spatial aggregation. The next question is how these facts can be explained, or, in the context of the present chapter, whether the NEG approach can be of use to get a grip on these facts and to explain the observed spatial differences that have clearly come to the fore from the stylized facts. We proceed in two steps. In the next section, we briefly introduce the main ideas behind and the main insights from the NEG literature. After this discussion of NEG's main insights, we analyse the data through an NEG lens to establish the potential relevance of NEG for the case of South Asia.

NEW ECONOMIC GEOGRAPHY—THE KEY CONCEPTS IN A NUTSHELL

The Main Ingredients

This section gives a brief overview of NEG theory.[2] The most important achievement of NEG is that it has put relative location back at the heart of mainstream economic analysis, stressing that a country or region is not an isolated island but is also affected by its relationship with other (nearby) countries or regions. Any NEG model has three basic elements: *increasing returns to scale, transport costs*, and *factor (labour) mobility*. The first two elements are not just part of NEG but are at home in any modern theory of location (Fujita and Thisse 2002). Increasing returns to scale, be it at the firm or industry level, ensure that firms want to concentrate their production across space and the existence of trade or transport costs ensures that firms are not indifferent as to where to locate in space.

Without trade or transport costs, that is, without costs of moving goods or people across space, but with increasing returns to scale still present, firms might also prefer one location (country, region, city) over

[2]For an extensive discussion of the NEG and its core models, see the (text)books by Fujita et al. (1999), Brakman et al. (2008), Fujita and Thisse (2002), Baldwin et al. (2003), or Combes et al. (2008). See also Krugman (1991), Venables (1996), Krugman and Venables (1995), Puga (1999) for the core models. Good reviews of and surveys on NEG are Neary (2001) or Ottaviano and Thisse (2004). For a survey on the empirics of NEG see Head and Mayer (2004), Combes et al. (2005), or Overman et al. (2003). Also, the central theme of the Word Development Report 2009 is to use the concepts of NEG to explain the (spatial) economic developments in different parts of the world. Empirical NEG papers that are specifically aimed at developing countries are, for instance, Lall et al. (2004), Deichmann et al. (2008), Amiti and Cameron (2007), Hering and Poncet (forthcoming), Amiti and Javorcik (2008), and Bosker and Garretsen (2008a).

others, but only if natural endowments differ across locations (that is, one region is more attractive than others a priori). The presence of trade costs makes NEG a theory that truly connects locations. In contrast to earlier important work in economic geography NEG explicitly does *not* consider locations as 'freely floating islands in space' (Fujita and Mori 2005).[3]

To then come up with a mechanism that allows for the degree of agglomeration, or more accurately the spatial distribution of economic activity, to be an outcome of the model, we need the third NEG element *factor mobility* in addition to increasing returns to scale and transport costs. Typically, in NEG the crucial mobile factor here is labour. If in a simple two-region NEG version of the world economy, the mobile (manufacturing) firms prefer region *North* over *South* in order to take advantage of the agglomeration economies in the *North*, these firms can only produce all in the *North* if either mobile workers also migrate *en masse* from the *South* to the *North* or if the pool of Northern manufacturing workers is increased by labour being released from other sectors (agriculture) in the *North* economy. The really novel element of NEG as introduced by Krugman (1991) is that it adds factor (labour) mobility to a model with increasing returns and transport costs (Brakman et al. 2008; Ottaviano and Thisse 2004). With factor mobility entering the story, the NEG models start to display cumulative causation: *firms want to locate where there is a large market demand for their goods, and a region's demand for goods depends on the location decision of workers, who in turn locate in a region where there is a large demand for labour, which in turn depends on the location decision of firms, and so on.* Or in NEG terms, both mobile firms and workers *ceteris paribus* prefer regions with a good market access, that is, they prefer to be located in or nearby large markets.

To what extent firms and workers prefer to be located in the agglomeration depends not only on the benefits agglomerations offer; agglomerations do, of course, also have downsides. For firms these can consist of having to pay higher wages, being faced with higher office rents, more traffic congestion, fiercer competition from other firms, and so on, compared to being located in the periphery. For workers, being located in an agglomeration also tends to come with several negative side effects, including among others higher crime rates, traffic jams, and higher costs of non-tradable goods such as housing or haircuts, than in the periphery.

---

[3]With transport costs but without increasing returns, the economy will be one of autarky or 'backyard capitalism' whereas increasing returns but costless trade across space implies that firms do concentrate their production in one location (cities) but they are indifferent in which exact location to choose.

Generally these congestion costs increase in the extent of agglomeration and as a result favour the spreading of economic activity across regions. The bottom line of the NEG approach is hence that the equilibrium spatial distribution, that is, the degree of agglomeration, depends on the mix of agglomeration and spreading forces. How this 'tug of war' between centrifugal and centripetal forces plays out in a particular case, like the South Asian region, depends on the specific economic circumstances at hand, like for example the degree of labour mobility, the level of transport or trade costs, or the quality of the infrastructure.

The interaction of agglomeration and spreading forces thus determines the observed spatial distribution of economic activity and, as a consequence, also the degree of dispersion in terms of living standards and more generally the quality of life. What the spatial outcome of this interaction can be in an NEG setting is most easily illustrated by using a figure from one of the main NEG models (Puga 1999). Figure 3.3 depicts how the evolution of a country's internal economic geography, that is, the distribution of economic activity across its two regions, could respond to an increase or decrease in transport to trade costs[4] in this *(highly stylized*

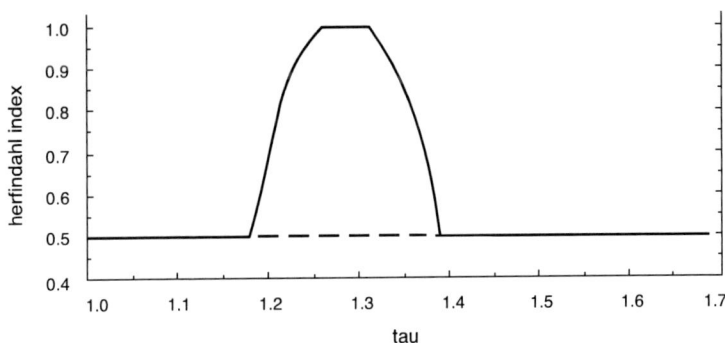

FIGURE 3.3   The Bell Curve

Source: Bosker et al. (2007). This is a replication of Figure 6 in Puga (1999).
Notes: The x-axis shows, *tau*, which stands for trade costs. Tau ranges from 1 (free trade) and increases from there with increasing trade costs. The y-axis shows the share of economic activity in one of the model's two regions (that is, economic activity is perfectly spread out when it is 0.5 and is concentrated in one region when it is 1).

[4]This figure actually emerges only in Puga (1999) in case of an inter-regionally immobile labour force. In case of inter-regionally mobile labour, his model would not yield a return to spreading (an equal distribution of economic activity across the two regions) for low trade costs. However, in other NEG models, the introduction of any

two-region) NEG model. It concisely illustrates the main insights from the theoretical NEG literature.

At *high* levels of trade or transport costs, it does not pay for firms to serve the national market from one of the two regions only. When trade costs fall, firms and people can at some point start to reap the benefits of agglomeration (thick labour and goods markets, knowledge spill-overs) by clustering in one of the two regions, while at the same time being able to serve the other region at lower costs.

Eventually, with trade costs falling even further, the benefits of agglomeration are overshadowed by its disadvantages, and firms and people move back to the periphery in search of lower wage costs, house prices, and less congestion.

To arrive at a better understanding of the mechanisms underlying Figure 3.3 and also to arrive at a categorization that will turn out to be useful for the discussion on the actual economic geography of South Asia in the second half of this paper, we will organize the remainder of our NEG discussion around the notions of market access, trade costs, and labour mobility.

Market Access, Trade Costs, and Labour Mobility

The main agglomeration benefit according to NEG theory can be defined broadly as having a good access to markets: markets for goods, factors of production, and ideas (Mayer 2008). Market access is arguably the central concept of the NEG. A particular region's or country's market access measures the extent of the market that can be easily reached from that region or country (a basic measure would be a region's own market size [GDP] plus the sum of its neighbouring regions' GDP, where the contribution of a particular neighbour to this sum is weighted by the costs involved in reaching that particular neighbour). In terms of Figure 3.3, the region with better market access will attract the bulk of economic activity once agglomeration becomes economically sustainable for low-enough levels of transport costs. This in turn will only reinforce that region's advantage (improving its market access even further), making it even more difficult for the lagging region to catch up in terms of economic activity.

Trade or transports costs are, besides the mass of economic activity itself, the most important component of market access. If trade were costless, each region would have exactly the same market access, and no

---

congestion force that does not diminish with lower trade costs (for example, housing in Helpman 1998), but increases with agglomeration, would result in a return to symmetry at lower levels of trade costs.

region would have an agglomeration advantage in terms of its location. Trade is far from costless, however, distance (affecting both transport costs and the time in transit) remains one of the major determinants of the extent of trade within and between countries (Disdier and Head 2008; Hummels 2007). But other costs, both tangible (tariffs, non-tariff barriers, legal/institutional differences, border controls) and non-tangible (language, cultural, or religious differences), affect the ease of doing business across borders. The role of trade costs in determining the distribution of economic activity clearly shows from Figure 3.3. With high trade costs, trade is almost absent and each region is basically a market of its own. As trade costs become smaller, people and firms find it easier (cheaper) to cluster together, taking advantage of the benefits that agglomeration offers, while still serving the other market. If trade costs decrease even further, location starts to matter less and less as each location can be reached at much lower cost. Depending on the degree of congestion in the agglomeration, this again makes peripheral regions attractive places and economic activity spreads across space.

The final ingredient from NEG that helps us understand the relevance of market access is the degree of labour mobility. In general, the more mobile the labour force (both between sectors and between regions), the more pronounced the agglomeration or dispersion patterns that will emerge. Labour mobility enforces any tendencies of firms to cluster. If labour can move freely between regions, agglomerations, once established, offer the earlier described benefits to its inhabitants and will attract even more people and firms from peripheral regions in search of jobs and workers, respectively. If instead labour tends *not* to move between regions, this will pose an additional spreading force. In this case, when more and more firms cluster in the agglomerated region, they will find it increasingly difficult to find employees (resulting in increasingly higher wages). In case of labour mobility, people in the peripheral regions would ease this tension on the labour market as they would respond to the higher wages in the agglomeration and move there.[5] These tensions will not be eased if labour does not, or is not allowed to, move between regions, and as a result firms will at some point start to move back to the peripheral regions that are attractive by offering a large pool of workers at relatively low cost. Despite the fact that in case of perfect labour mobility between

---

[5]In the Puga (1999) model, perfect labour mobility has the result that, as trade costs fall, economic activity does not move back to the periphery any more; instead agglomeration is the only stable equilibrium outcome for low levels of trade costs.

regions differences in economic activity between regions are much more likely to be present, differences in welfare levels between regions are much more likely to persist than when labour does *not* freely move between regions. In the case of perfect labour mobility, no one has an incentive to move between regions in equilibrium (if so, he or she would immediately improve his or her lot by moving to the other region). As a result, living standards are necessarily the same across regions in equilibrium. When labour is restricted in its movements, welfare differences are much more likely to persist as people do (or can) not move to places that provide them a higher standard of living.

The Empirical Relevance of NEG

With these basic NEG notions in mind, how do we proceed? In the next section our main vehicle to assess the relevance of NEG for South Asia will be various measures of market access and its underlying determinants such as trade, transport costs, and (labour) migration. As explained earlier, when it comes to agglomeration forces, NEG looks for the effects that interregional interdependencies, measured by the central concept of *market access*, have on individual regions. Besides that, we will also consider the role of *intra*regional agglomeration externalities stressed to be important by urban economic theory (Combes et al. 2005; Rosenthal and Strange 2004), and verify whether or not these *intraregional* agglomeration channels (measured by population density or the degree of urbanization) are more or less important for South Asia's regional economic development than the *inter*regional agglomeration effects stressed by NEG. We will see that both effects contribute significantly to shaping South Asia's geographical economic landscape.

Also we want to emphasize at this point that our discussion so far has mainly focused on the regional distribution of *economic* activity. However, the regional distribution of economic activity does not necessarily coincide with the regional distribution of living standards (as measured by social instead of economic indicators, for example, life expectancy, education attainment, and access to public services). Most relevant here is that the agglomeration of economic activity does not necessarily bring about large differences in quality of life between regions *in the long run*. Indeed, as extensively discussed in the WDR 2009, the overall trend in almost all developed countries is that during the growth process, we first observe divergence in both economic and social indicators between subnational regions, eventually followed by a convergence in living standard across regions. Although very important, a thorough discussion of the (different) development of living standards lies beyond the scope of this paper. The focus in this chapter will be on the (development of) regional *economic* disparities in South Asia; Chapter 1 offers a detailed overview of developments of other indicators of social well-being.

SOUTH ASIA FROM AN NEG PERSPECTIVE: THE ROLE OF MARKET ACCESS

Having explained the main insights from the NEG literature, this section turns to establishing the possible relevance of its central concepts in shaping South Asia's actual economic geography. In doing so, we will show that economic geography does not work only at the international level by affecting South Asia's overall chances of experiencing a growth spurt of the type witnessed in its Eastern Asian neighbours (or to put it differently, that it does not miss out on the next 'spread of industry' (Collier and Venables 2007). We will also, and maybe more important, show that economic geography works at the national and regional levels, possibly contributing to the large disparities between South Asian countries as well as between the leading and lagging regions within each individual country.

Our discussion of the empirical relevance of NEG for South Asia will centre around the notion of market access and, just like our previous empirical results, the discussion will be organized around three levels of aggregation: the global, national, and regional levels. We deal with the international aspects of South Asia's economic geography first by grouping the global and national dimensions together. Next, we turn to the regional economic geographies, the main focus of this report.

South Asia and the Rest of the World

We start by assessing the importance of market access, NEG's key concept, for the countries of South Asia. In Figures 3.4a and 3.4b, a country's market access in 1995 is plotted against its GDP per capita for all countries in the world. Figure 3.4a shows a country's market access *including* its own domestic market, whereas Figure 3.4b focuses purely on (foreign) market access to *other* countries' markets. Based on a methodology first used by Redding and Venables (2004), market access is constructed using bilateral trade data.

Both figures clearly show a positive relationship between a country's degree of market access and its economic prosperity. The difference between Figures 3.4a and 3.4b is also of interest, especially in case of

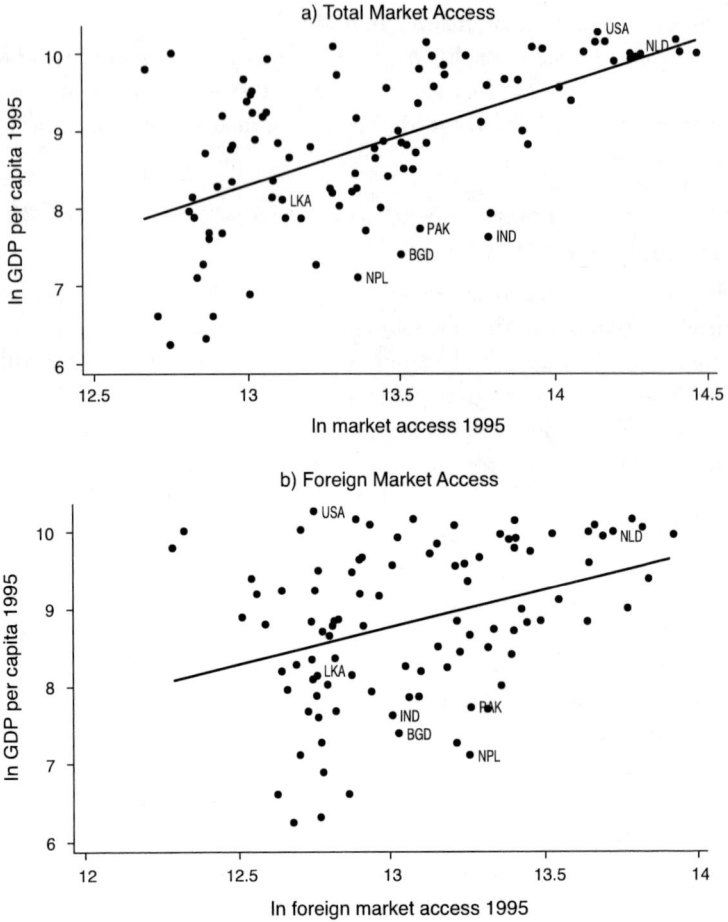

FIGURE 3.4   Market Access and GDP per Capita at the National Level

Source: Authors' calculations.

Notes: Market access is constructed in the same manner as in Redding and Venables (2004: sections 4.1 and 4.2), where we use the estimated coefficients of the following bilateral trade equation to construct Market Access (using data from CEPII for 1995 and employing PPML estimation following Silva and Tenreyro 2006): $X_{ij} = \alpha + \beta_1 \ln GDP_{ij} + \beta_2 \ln GDP_{ij} + \delta \ln D_{ij} + \gamma B_{ij} + \varepsilon_{ij}$, where X_{ij} denotes trade between importer i and exporter j, D_{ij} the distance (in km) between i and j, B_{ij} is a dummy variable that takes the value 1 if i and j share a common border, and ε_{ij} a well-behaved error term. Given that we also have information on each country's 'internal trade' (= total production—total exports), we also explicitly estimate the effect of internal distance (measured as $D_{ii} = 0.66(area_i/\pi)^{1/2}$). Results are available upon request. PAK, IND, NPL, BGD, and LKA denote Pakistan, India, Nepal, Bangladesh, and Sri Lanka, respectively. The straight line corresponds to the estimated coefficient on a simple regression of ln market access on ln GDP per capita.

India and Nepal. Nepal's ranking in terms of its foreign market access compared with total (foreign plus own country) market access indicates that the bulk of its market access is foreign (that is, India) whereas the opposite holds for India, consistent with the idea that the relevant market access for India comes first and foremost from the (very large) size of its own economy (54 per cent of its total market access is due to its own economy, compared with 38 per cent, 30 per cent, 26 per cent, and 10 per cent for Bangladesh, Sri Lanka, Pakistan, and Nepal, respectively).

The main message from Figure 3.4 is that for the five South Asian countries included in the analysis (Bangladesh, India, Nepal, Pakistan, and Sri Lanka), their GDP per capita is *lower* than expected on the basis of their market access. Or in graphical terms, all five countries lie below the straight line in Figures 3.4a and 3.4b that corresponds to the simple linear prediction (based on a simple regression of ln market access on ln GDP per capita) of a country's GDP per capita based on its market access. All South Asian countries are positioned well below this straight line. As a comparison, both the United States and the Netherlands are also indicated in the figure: the GDP per capita of these two countries corresponds nicely to their respective total market access (Figure 3.4a).

This finding immediately raises the question why South Asian countries have these sub-par scores when it comes to benefiting from their market access. Our measure of market access is based solely on the importance of each country's *geographic* access (on the bilateral distance between countries and on whether countries share a common border) to other countries as revealed by its trade performance. Roughly speaking, countries trade more when they share a common border and when they are closer to each other. Less trade, in turn, means a lower market access. The fact that such a *purely* geographically-based measure of market access severely over-predicts per capita income levels in South Asia is in our view due to the omission of other (non-geographic) determinants of a country's market access. Many other (implicit) barriers limit trade and thus market access. These barriers can for instance be related to a country's infrastructure, tariff, and non-tariff barriers, and a country's institutions. Can we find evidence that such barriers indeed diminish the positive effect of South Asia's relatively good *potential* market access? And if so, are these barriers predominantly present at the intra-South Asia, within country (regional), or the South Asia–rest of the world level? We try to get a glimpse of the answer in the remainder of this section.

International Trade

To understand why South Asian countries have a lower GDP per capita than one would expect based on their potential market access, we first turn our attention to the international trade patterns of the region and of each of the individual countries. Table 3.4 shows that, for the South Asian region as a whole, trade (as a per cent of GDP) is very low compared with other world regions. The importance of international trade has increased somewhat over the period 1990–2005, but the growth rates were far from impressive and lagged behind those of its East Asian neighbours and of Europe and Central Asia.

The South Asian countries also differ from *each other* in terms of openness to trade. Sri Lanka is a much more active trader, which partly reflects its particular position in South Asia being one of the main international transport hubs in the region (that is, its port facilities in Colombo). Also, landlocked Bhutan, Afghanistan, and Nepal are more

TABLE 3.4   South Asia Trade Patterns

Variable	Trade (% GDP)	Trade growth (PPT)	% exports within world region	% imports within world region
Year	2005	1990–2005	2005	2005
World Regions				
EAP	86.2	38.9	9.6	18.4
ECA	77.1	31.7	21.1	22.9
LAC	47.8	16.3	20.8	25.2
MENA	72.7	14.8	2.2	6.6
SSA	68.8	16.7	6.8	6.8
South Asia	43.5	23.3	4.7	3.1
South Asian Countries				
Afghanistan	68.1	–	20	37.8
Bangladesh	39.6	20	1.6	15.3
Bhutan	82	24.4	95	81.9
India	44.7	29	4.5	0.9
Nepal	48.7	17.1	54.3	27.7
Pakistan	35.2	–3.7	4.6	2.8
Sri Lanka	79.6	12.4	9.5	22.4

Sources: Data for the first two columns are from World Bank (2009a). The data on exports/imports within own region and to other South Asian countries are taken from World Bank (2007a: ch. 10).

Note: For EAP, the percentage of exports/imports within own region refers to low income EAP countries only (this makes for a better comparison with South Asia).

open to trade, partly reflecting their dependence on their coastal (South Asian) neighbours—it is also these three countries that trade relatively more with other South Asian countries (more on this later). The biggest economies of South Asia, however, are the ones trading the least: Pakistan, Bangladesh, and India are all very inward looking compared with international standards, partly reflecting the effect of years of import substitution policies.

Also, these three countries are the main drivers behind the extraordinarily low share of imports and exports with other South Asian countries. The share of exports to other South Asian countries is *below 5 per cent,* and the same share of imports is even lower (except for Bangladesh) for these countries, despite the potentially huge market that their neighbours constitute. The fact that trade between South Asian countries is much lower than the intraregional trade observed in other developing world regions is well documented (see World Bank 2007a: ch. 10 by Winters). It shows that most countries are much more oriented toward the rest of the world, not taking full advantage of the economic potential within the South Asian region that is clearly present when looking at the size of these economies (see Table 3.2). This trade pattern does not hold for the three landlocked countries (Afghanistan, Bhutan, and Nepal), but these three economies are dwarfed by those of their coastal neighbours (Table 3.2).

The earlier discussion shows that it seems to be the case that South Asia's major economies are focused towards world markets *but not* towards each other's (nearby) markets. *In terms of market access this means that South Asian countries 'underutilize' South Asian market access.* Given the (potential) market size in (border) regions, more economic integration that facilitates trade flows between countries could significantly increase South Asia's ability to fully utilize their potential good market access, boosting trade and contributing to GDP per capita growth. This is certainly the case for Pakistan (with a big share of Pakistan's population living in proximity to India) and also for Bangladesh. Barriers to trade between South Asian countries are manifold (see World Bank 2007b). Apart from being motivated from an economic point of view (each South Asian country has high tariffs in place to protect its own market) these barriers are also politically motivated and entrenched in a long history of disputes and conflicts, and substantial language and cultural differences. These barriers result in a trade-unfriendly geography that casts a shadow over the large potential for flourishing trade and interaction between the South Asian countries. This is also reflected in poor infrastructure connectivity between countries (see World Bank 2007a: ch. 8) and a focus on investment in domestic or within-country connectivity. India's Golden Quadrilateral, the almost completed 'superhighway' linking five of its major cities but lacking any direct connection to India's neighbouring countries is a good example (as are its planned North–South and East–West corridors).

Table 3.5 lists some of these trade impediments. They focus mainly on the quality of infrastructure within each country. Domestic infrastructure is arguably even more important for international trade in South Asia compared with other world regions, as a very large part of the South Asian population (in Bangladesh, India, and Pakistan in particular) lives in cities or regions that are *not* coastal, putting an extra cost burden on exporting or importing goods to foreign markets by making it more heavily dependent on national infrastructure quality.

Compared with other world regions, the extent of South Asia's road network fares reasonably well in terms of its road density but this is reflecting in part its high population density, which calls for more roads. When calculating road density as kilometres of road per inhabitant instead, South Asia falls behind Europe and Central Asia, and Latin America and is on par with East Asia. Also its road network has been expanding rapidly, compared with other world regions. In terms of its road network quality (essential for the quick handling of [international] trade by heavy trucks that haul containers over long distances), South Asia is an average region, but large differences exist between countries: In Bangladesh, only 25 per cent of roads are paved, in India and Pakistan this is about 50 per cent, and in Sri Lanka, which has the best quality of road network, 86 per cent of its roads are paved.

However, except for Sri Lanka and Bangladesh this percentage has fallen, showing that the increase in the total road network has (so far) not been matched by an equal increase in its quality. Besides road transport, a significant, although declining, share of freight and passenger transportation in the region is via rail. South Asia's railway network is virtually completely inherited from British colonial times, and although extensive in terms of network length, it is urgently in need of modernization. Furthermore, gauges used differ between countries and also sometimes even within countries, causing unnecessary delays (see World Bank 2007b).

South Asia's trade impediments towards intra-South Asia and international trade really stand out. Not only are South Asia's tariffs the highest in the world at an average 28 per cent in 2005, down from a staggering average 70 per cent in the 1980s (see World Bank 2007a: ch. 1),

TABLE 3.5 Impediments to Trade

Variable	Ports and terminals	Road density (km/100km^2)	Growth road network (%)	Roads (% paved)	Increase in % road paved	#documents to export	#documents to import
Year	2007	2000–6	1990–9	1999	1990–9	2007	2007
			World Regions				
EAP	–	14.3	5.6	20	2.8	7 (China)	6 (China)
ECA	–	8.2	–12.3	74.3	–2.3	4 (Germany)	5 (Germany)
LAC	–	4.4	9.4	22	0.5	8 (Brazil)	7 (Brazil)
MENA	–	1.9	–16.3	66.4	–3.1	6 (Egypt)	7 (Egypt)
SSA	–	1.6	31.6	12.1	–3.9	10 (Nigeria)	9 (Nigeria)
South Asia	–	37.6	20.7	30.8	–6.7	9 (avg.)	9 (avg.)
			South Asian Countries				
Year	2007	2000–6	1990–2003	1999	1991–9	2007	2007
Afghanistan	–	5.3	65.6	13.3	0	12	11
Bangladesh	2	183.8	27.2	9.5	2.3	7	9
Bhutan	–	17.1	244.6	60.7	–18.4	8	11
India	8	113.8	69.2	46.7	–0.6	8	9
Nepal	–	12.2	132.5	30.8	–7.4	9	10
Pakistan	2	33.5	50.4	55	2	9	8
Sri Lanka	2	150.5	4.6	85.8	53.8	8	6

Sources: World Bank (2007, 2009a, 2009b).

but also the administrative burden involved in importing and exporting is among the highest in the world. An average of nine documents are required for importing and exporting (see Table 3.2) and more than 20 signatures are on average required before one is able to import goods (see World Bank 2007b: ch. 1). In addition, South Asia's port infrastructure lags behind that of, for example, East Asia in terms of efficiency, capacity, and quality of infrastructural links with their hinterland, although capacity is rapidly increasing (see World Bank 2007a: chs 8 and 9). Most intra-South Asia trade, especially important for landlocked countries, uses the few overland transport corridors that are available—for example, only one access road connects India–Bangladesh and India–Pakistan. Delays on these routes are often extremely long because of long and uncoordinated customs and narrow and congested access roads.

To sum up, the impediments to trade, discussed earlier, inhibit South Asia from taking full advantage of its *potentially good market access*. In NEG terms, these high trade and transport costs hold back trade and weaken the link between potential market access and GDP per capita. Removing administrative and tariff barriers to trade, and improving domestic and international infrastructure will allow the countries of South Asia to reap even greater benefits of foreign markets. Especially intra-South Asian connectivity has scope for major improvements. South Asian economies potentially have a lot to offer each other in terms of market size, calling for an increased effort in facilitating exchange across international borders through increased regional integration, and major cross-border infrastructure improvements. Only removing these trade impediments will allow South Asian countries to take full advantage of their, in principle excellent, access to foreign markets, and other nearby South Asian markets in particular.

Migration

So far we have mainly focused on improving South Asian market access through increased trade facilitation. Apart from the possible relevance of trade and trade barriers to understand the somewhat weak relationship for South Asian countries between their market access and GDP per capita shown in Figure 3.4, factor mobility or, here, migration can also be relevant. If people are restricted in their ability to move toward those countries or regions where they can profit most from the benefits of good access to markets, this can also be a reason for the lower than expected degree to which South Asia's market access is reflected in its per capita income levels. In addition, from our previous discussion on NEG basics we know that labour (factor) mobility enables market access to change over time across space when workers are free to locate in whatever region that is expected to award them the highest income. As we explained earlier, factor mobility (both within and between countries) is thus an important mechanism in NEG through which agglomeration patterns can develop. Moreover, in the absence of sufficient mobility of labour, income disparities between regions can be expected to be much larger (and continue to widen) than when labour freely flows between regions or countries (Puga 1999, 2002).

In absolute terms the number of migrants in South Asia numbered 11.2 million in 2000, about 5 per cent of the world's total migrants. This is a large number of people, but migration in South Asia in *relative* terms is fairly low. International migrants constitute an average 0.8 per cent of the population in South Asia compared with an average 3 per cent for the world as a whole. This conveys a similar message as the trade statistics in the previous subsection, confirming South Asia's poor integration in the world economy compared with other (similar) developing world regions. Figure 3.5 gives additional information on migration patterns in South Asia,[6] depicting the major outward migration flows out of five different South Asian countries. A striking pattern emerges from these numbers.

First of all, and in contrast with international trade, *intra* South Asian migration constitutes the bulk of the international migration flows. Also, India is the top destination country for South Asian migrants from *all other* South Asian countries: Bangladesh, Nepal, Pakistan, and Sri Lanka. India constitutes the exception to this intra-South Asia migration rule: Indian emigrants mostly go to non-South Asia countries, in particular the United States, the United Kingdom (generally high skilled), and the Gulf States (generally low skilled). This pattern suggests that India, being South Asia's economic powerhouse (see Table 3.2) serves as the main locus of attraction for other South Asian countries, whereas the Indians themselves look for their fortune outside the South Asia region.

From an NEG perspective, restrictions limit people in being able to follow better economic prospects and tend to sustain or even increase existing disparities in income level. Not allowing people to follow the money—or the good market access—is another reason why South Asia's per capita income level is lower than expected on the basis of its *purely*

---

[6]Note that these numbers are generally considered to be a lower bound as illegal and/ or unreported migration flows are believed to be substantial.

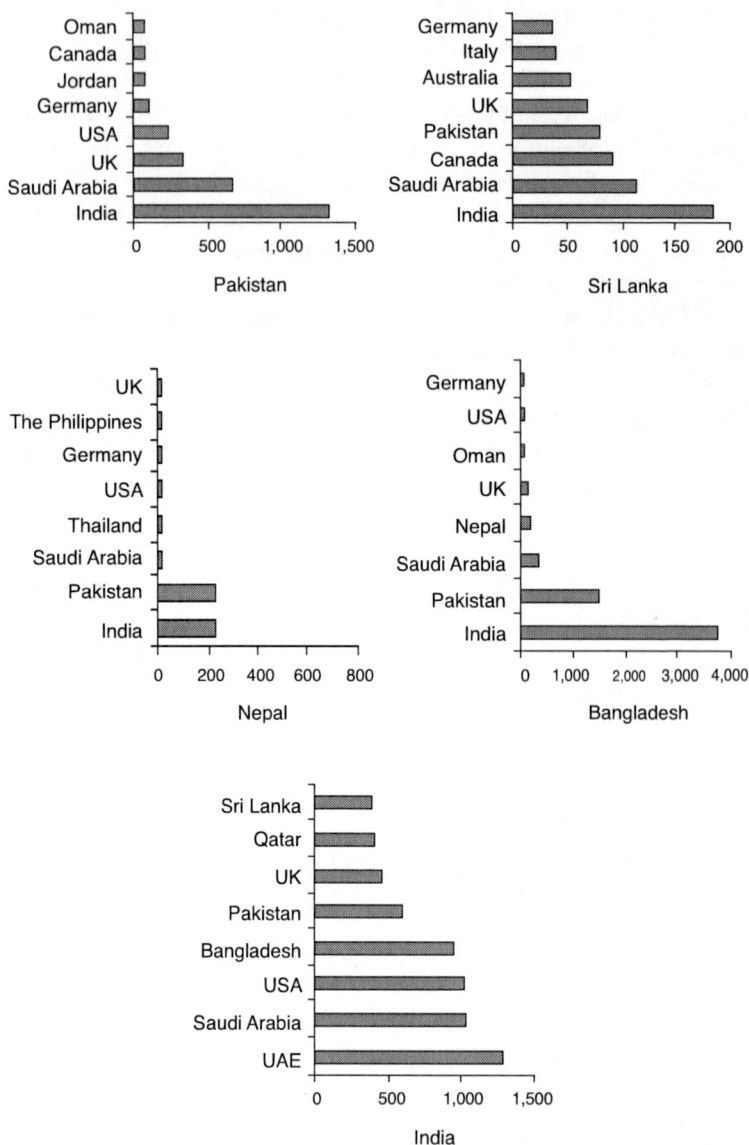

FIGURE 3.5   South Asian Migration Patterns (2000)
(in thousand)

Source: World Bank, presentation by Çaglar Özden, 22 April 2008. Available at
http://www.worldbank.org/sarintegration.

geographical market access. Alleviating restrictions to international labour mobility has in general proved to be a much slower (political) process than that of promoting more trade because of the social issues that it tends to raise (fear and/or discrimination against immigrants, and so on). This means that the prospect[7] of solving South Asia's underutilization of its geographical market access through increased international labour migration is much bleaker than through increased trade participation in world and intra-South Asia markets. Finally, given the current patterns of migration within South Asia and India's recent economic growth performance, alleviating these restrictions most likely would strengthen the patterns observed in Figure 3.5 even further—so that India would see an increased inflow of migrants from other South Asian countries whereas these other countries would experience a further outflow of people towards India in search of better economic opportunities. In NEG terms, fewer restrictions on migration would further reinforce the core–periphery pattern that already characterizes South Asia (India being the core and the other South Asian countries being the peripheral countries).

South Asia's Leading and Lagging Regions

Having established the role of economic geography for the South Asian region at the international level, we turn to assessing its relevance at the subnational or regional scale. In Table 3.3 and Figures 3.1 and 3.2, we documented stark differences between leading and lagging regions in each of the South Asian countries for which we have data available at the regional level. What can the insights from NEG tell us about the observed developments in income, market access, urbanization, and population levels at the subnational level? More specifically, what is the role of market access in creating the observed regional distribution of people and economic activity? Is it as relevant at the international level, or is its effect at this finer geographical scale overshadowed by the—more traditional—urban economic forces such as population density or urbanization measures? This subsection looks at these issues, focusing first on the role of market access (the *inter*regional distribution of economic activity), and then zooming in on the possible role for density and urbanization (the *intra*regional distribution of economic activity).

[7]Note that alleviating cultural, religious, and/or language difference are not so easily resolved by active government policy. In the case of South Asia, with its long history of violent conflict between countries, it may take some time before labour migration will increase further even when official institutional barriers are alleviated.

Market Access at the Regional Level

We start by calculating each region's market access. As we do not have information on interregional trade flows, we have to construct market access in a different, less sophisticated, way than we did when considering South Asia's countries' market access. More specifically, we construct each region's market access as the distance weighted sum of South Asia's GDP, that is:

$$MA_r = \sum_s GDP_s / D_{rs}, \qquad (3.1)$$

with D_{rs} the distance (in km) between the capital city[8] of region r and s. Each region's market access consists of not only its own regional economy, but also of the other South Asian regions' economies weighted by the transport costs involved (proxied simply by distance) to reach those other regions' markets.[9] Figure 3.6 plots this measure of market access against income per capita[10] for each of the South Asian regions in our sample.

It shows a weak positive relationship between GDP per capita and total South Asian market access, but this relationship is not significant, which suggests that market access to other South Asian regions is not a significant determinant of the observed income differences between South Asia's (leading and lagging) regions. This finding is very different compared with, for example, the finding of Breinlich (2006) for European regions, Hering and Poncet (forthcoming) for Chinese regions, or Amiti and Cameron (2007). Breinlich (2006), for example, shows that in Europe, with its common market crossing international borders, there exists a strong positive and significant relationship between market access and regional income levels. Our different finding for South Asia suggests that markets in South Asia are not very well integrated.

However, such a conclusion is rather premature. The measure of market access depicted in Figure 3.7 includes both other national as well as other international (that is, other South Asian) regions. In the

---

[8]Results do not change qualitatively when using distance between each region's largest city instead.

[9]Note that the size of a region's own economy is also included in this market access measure, it is weighted by its so-called internal distance that proxies for the average costs involved in shipping goods within one's own region (measured as $D_{ii} = 0.66$ $(area/\pi)^{1/2}$).

[10]Measured in 2000 international dollars to correct for purchasing power differences between countries.

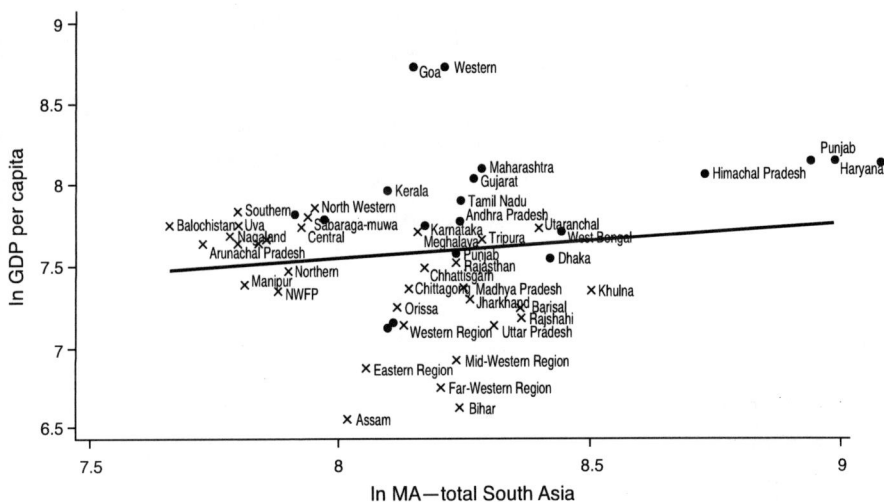

FIGURE 3.6   Regional Income per Capita and South Asian
Market Access

Source: World Bank (2009a).
Notes: Market access constructed as in (3.1). Regions marked by a ● are lagging regions, and those marked by a × are leading regions. Raw correlation between ln GDP per capita and ln MA is positive but not significant: 0.13 p-value [0.36]. The figure depicts the situation in 2004.

previous section, we documented that especially the lack of South Asian (economic) integration is likely to blame for the South Asian countries' underutilization of their market access at the international level. Given this lack of integration between South Asian countries, including both national as well as other South Asian regions in our measure of market access, could bias the results toward non-significance of regional market access. This is why we relate each region's income per capita to two different measures of market access, that is, national market access and South Asian market access in Figure 3.7:

$$MA_{r,c}^{country} = \sum_{s \in e} GDP_s / D_{rs}, \text{ and}$$

$$MA_{r,c}^{South\ Asia} = \sum_{s \notin e} GDP_s / D_{rs} \text{ respectively.}$$

(3.2)

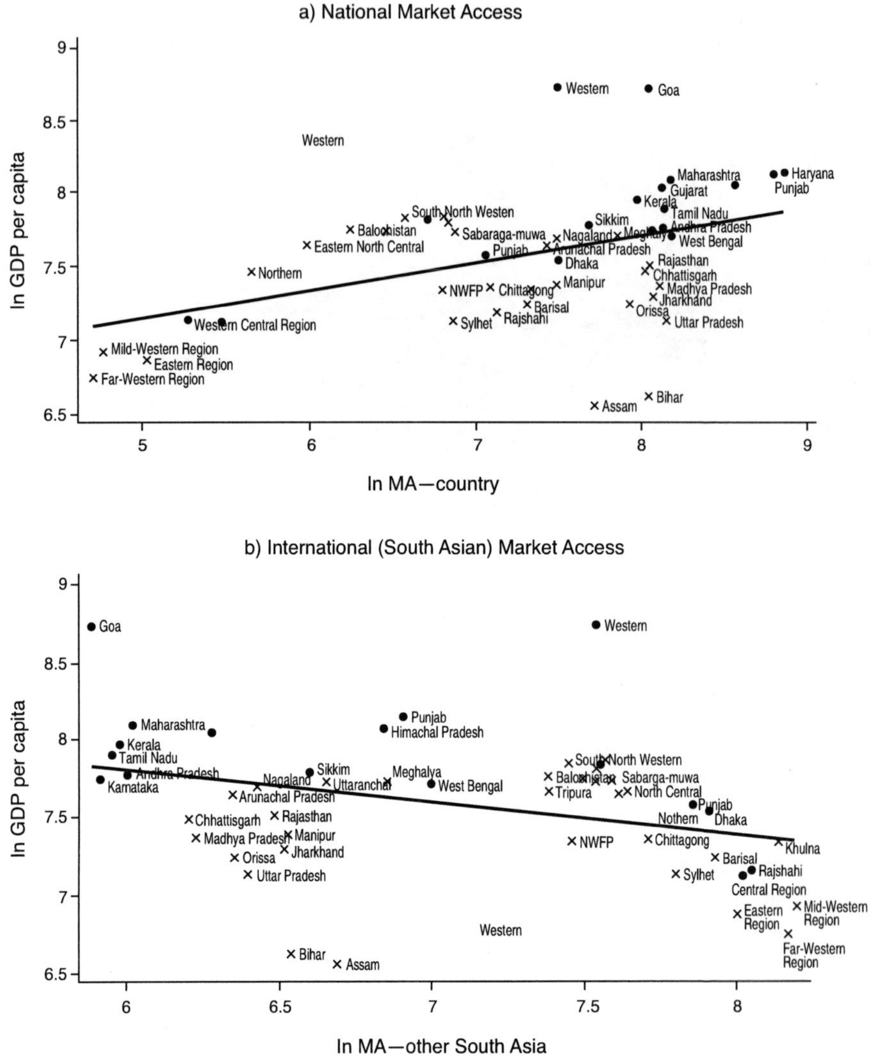

FIGURE 3.7   National and International (South Asian)
Market Access and GDP per Capita

Sources: Authors calculations and World Bank (2009a).

Notes: Market access constructed as in (3.2). Regions marked by a $\times$ are lagging regions, and those marked by a $\bullet$ are leading regions. Raw correlation between ln GDP per capita and ln national MA is positive and significant: 0.43 p-value [0.002], that between ln GDP per capita and ln international MA is negative and significant –0.38 p-value [0.003]. Both figures depict the situation in 2004.

The first measure constitutes a region's access to *national markets only* and the second measure to that of *other (foreign) South Asian regions*. The results confirm the lack of South Asian integration that came to the fore in the previous section. A region's income per capita strongly correlates with its *national* market access. This indicates that within each of the South Asian countries, we observe the main economic geography force of agglomeration at work: regions with better access to *national* markets outperform those that are not well connected to national markets. Note also that it is mostly the lagging regions that do not have good access to their national markets. This, combined with the fact that it is also these lagging regions that depend mostly on access to other markets (93 per cent of their total market access is derived from access to other markets, compared with 83 per cent for leading regions), suggests that economic geography plays an important role in the widening national disparities in terms of economic activity between leading and lagging regions.

When it comes to a region's access to foreign, that is to other South Asian, markets, we find no evidence of a positive relationship between GDP per capita and market access. Indeed, it seems even to be the case that those regions with relative better access to other South Asian markets tend to have a lower level of GDP per capita. This effect disappears after controlling for other factors apart from market access, such as urbanization or population density, that can leave their mark on GDP per capita.

This is in our view again a clear indication that it is the lack of integration between South Asian countries that is holding back regions from taking full advantage of their market access. For example, in terms of a potential market size, Pakistan's Punjab has in principle a lot to offer to India's Punjab, Himachal Pradesh, or Haryana. The same holds for India's West Bengal region to Bangladesh's (lagging) border regions, were it not for the large trade impediments that are present between them (see the previous section).

An objection to our use of regional market access is that it depicts only the relationship between a region's market access to national or other South Asian markets and omits the importance of access to foreign markets outside the South Asia region (the major trading partners of each of the countries we consider, see the previous section).

To see whether this makes a difference, Table 3.6 shows the results of a simple regression in which we relate a region's per capita income level not only to its national or South Asian market access, but also include a

TABLE 3.6   Market Access and GDP per Capita

	dependent variable: ln GDP per capita 2004					
	[1]	[2]	[3]	[4]	[5]	[6]
ln MA 2000 (own country)	0.30** [0.04]	– –	0.34** [0.03]	0.31** [0.05]	0.45*** [0.01]	0.72*** [0.00]
ln MA 2000 (*other* SA)	– –	0.09 [0.68]	–0.15 [0.51]	0.01 [0.99]	0.26 [0.18]	0.1 [0.68]
Landlocked	– –	– –	– –	–0.30*** [0.00]	–0.18*** [0.01]	–0.26*** [0.01]
Border	– –	– –	– –	0.05 [0.80]	0.07 [0.54]	0.06 [0.63]
Urbanization 2001	– –	– –	– –	– –	0.03*** [0.00]	– –
ln pop. density 2000	– –	– –	– –	– –	–0.22*** [0.00]	–0.29*** [0.00]
Urban primacy 2000	– –	– –	– –	– –	– –	0.02*** [0.00]
Country dummies?	yes	yes	yes	yes	yes	yes
No. obs.	46	46	46	46	45	37
R2	0.18	0.1	0.19	0.3	0.73	0.66

Notes: p-value, based on robust standard errors, is provided in brackets. ** and *** denote significance at the 5 per cent and 1 per cent, respectively. Country dummies are included in each regression to control for unobserved country-specific factors (for example, institutions) that can be expected to have a similar effect on all regions in the same country. Note that all variables are observed in an earlier year than GDP per capita so that reverse causality problems are arguably somewhat alleviated.

landlocked dummy as a proxy for a region's access to foreign markets.[11] Besides the landlocked dummy we also included a border dummy to check whether or not border regions take advantage of their excellent location to benefit from (land-borne) international trade.

The results in Table 3.6 confirm the message conveyed by Figures 3.6 and 3.7: only *national* market access has a positive influence on per capita regional income levels. This is also so when we include our landlocked dummy as a proxy for access to foreign non–South Asian markets. This, and the non-significance of being a border region, clearly confirms that

[11]Given that most of South Asian trade to the rest of the world is seaborne, we argue that this dummy variable is a good proxy for this.

border regions that are well-positioned to intra-South Asia international trade are not reaping the benefits of international trade, which they could reap if the continent was better integrated (67 per cent of South Asian border regions are classified as lagging, compared with 52 per cent of non-border regions). In contrast to being well positioned to pursue foreign trade with other South Asian nations, we do find a strong positive effect of being a region with direct access to the sea. Landlocked regions are lagging behind their coastal neighbours in terms of their income per capita (only 42 per cent of landlocked regions are classified as lagging, compared with 71 per cent of non-landlocked regions). Different from good access to other South Asian countries, being well positioned to trade with the rest of the world (and generally with countries outside the South Asia region) is beneficial for a region's economic prospects. Given our findings in Table 3.6, we focus in some more detail on South Asia's landlocked and border regions comparing some of the characteristics of these regions to their non-border or non-landlocked counterparts respectively.

Table 3.7 shows that in all South Asian countries except for India, a large part of the population lives within close range to an international border. For all these countries (see Table 3.8), this effectively means that most of their population lives close to the *Indian* border. In India, on the contrary, only a small part of the population lives close to the other South Asian countries. As will be become clear in the next subsection as well (see Figure 3.9) such a pattern is also discernible when one considers the distribution of the larger *cities* in South Asia.

Turning to Table 3.8 on landlocked regions and the evidence on the percentage of people living near the coast in Table 3.7, we see that South Asia's population (except for Sri Lanka) largely resides in the *landlocked, non-coastal areas*—setting it apart from any other region in the world (see World Bank 2009b). In Pakistan and Bangladesh this is

TABLE 3.7   Coastal and Border Population

Country	International Border		Coastline	
	< 25 km	< 75 km	< 25 km	< 75 km
Bangladesh	28.2	78.8	25.3	48.1
Bhutan	54.8	99.9	–	–
India	5.6	16.1	10.3	19.7
Nepal	44.1	95.2	–	–
Pakistan	13.8	42.2	7.1	8.3
Sri Lanka	–	–	47.3	88

Source: WDR 2009.

TABLE 3.8 Focus on Landlocked Regions

Variable	% population	% GDP	Avg. GDP per capita (2000 I$)	Population density	Avg. urbanization	% poor population	Poverty rate
	2001	2005	2005	2005	2001	2000–1	2000–1
Bangladesh	58.6	63.3	1464.1	958.9	19.5	60.5	48.6
(non-landlocked)	41.4	36.7	1436.8	764.5	17.6	39.5	48
India	52.3	39.3	2400.4	244.1	28.4	58	12
(non-landlocked)	47.7	60.7	2753.7	318	37.2	42	16
Pakistan	72	66.6	1842.6	370.8	24.1	70	36.9
(non-landlocked)	28	33.4	2418.8	136	36.4	30	37.1
Sri Lanka	34.6	24	2126.5	257.2	5.9	47.9	29.3
(non-landlocked)	65.4	76	2774.8	479.7	10.3	52.1	17.7

Source: Ahmed et al. (2010).
Note: Bhutan and Nepal are left out of this table as all their regions are landlocked.

also reflected in its economy: the bulk of economic output is generated in the landlocked—India bordering—regions of these two countries. In India and Sri Lanka, on the contrary, economic output *is* concentrated in its coastal, more urbanized regions, resulting in large differences in per capita income levels between its coastal and inland regions.

Combining our results, the overall picture that emerges is one where a region's access to *national* markets is an important determinant of its economic prosperity. Also, regions with good access to world markets (the non-landlocked regions) are doing better than their landlocked counterparts. But, until now, regions with in principle good market access to other South Asian markets—that is, border regions—have not been able to exploit this. Given the concentration of people and production in the Pakistani, Bangladeshi, Nepalese, and Bhutanese regions bordering India, it will most likely be those regions that have relatively the most to gain in terms of market access from increased South Asian integration, that is, access to the large Indian market. India does not need, it seems, to be so 'South-Asia minded'. It can rely largely on its own large economy and its relations with the rest of the world. This is not to say that India would not benefit from such increased South Asian economic integration, but to a lesser extent than the smaller South Asian economies given that India can rely much more on its own domestic economy and its rapidly increasing trade with the rest of the world.

Intraregional Division—Urbanization and Economies of Density

In the previous subsection, we have focused on the importance of the spatial distribution of economic activity, as measured by market access, across the South Asian regions. However, from an urban economics perspective, it is not so much the *inter*regional distribution of people and economic activity that matters but much more their *intra*regional distribution. In this section we focus more on this aspect of a region's economic geography, verifying to what extent the *intra*regional distribution of economic activity matters for a region's economic prosperity as well as assessing whether the conclusions reached about the relevance of the *inter*regional distribution of economic activity change once we allow the *intra*regional distribution to play a role as well.

Figure 3.8 below shows that also *within* the subnational South Asian regions, we find considerable differences in terms of the spatial distribution of people.

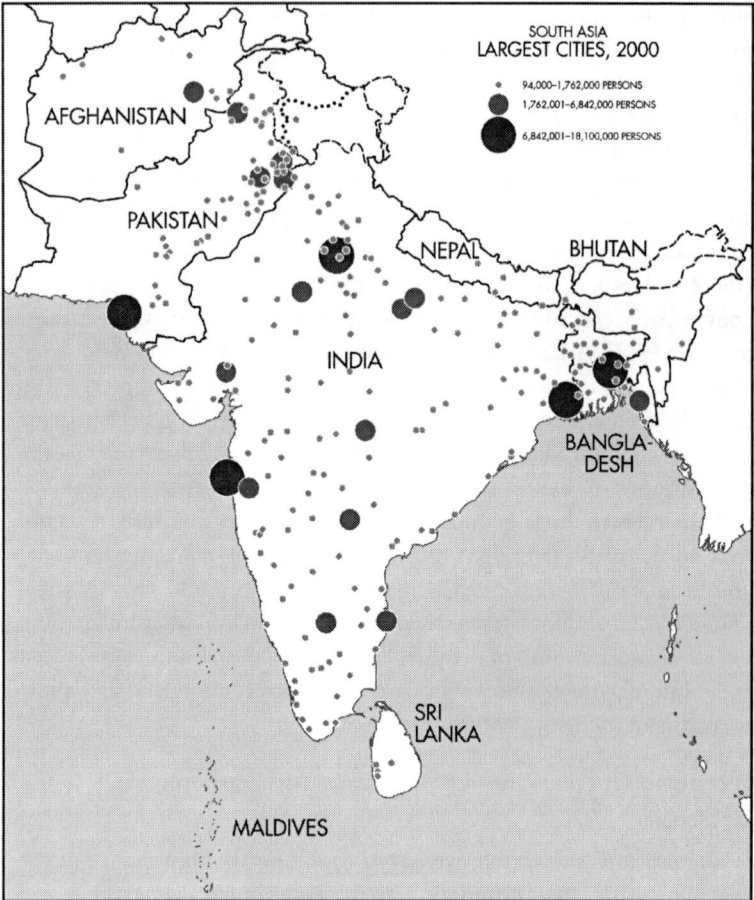

FIGURE 3.8   Distribution of South Asia's Largest Cities
across Its Regions (2000)

Source: World cities data available at http://www.econ.brown.edu/faculty/henderson/
worldcities.html.

Notice for example that several states are characterized by one mega-
city (West Bengal, Maharashtra, and Tamil Nadu, India; Dhaka and
Chittagong, Bangladesh; and Sindh, Pakistan); others are characterized
by several large and many medium-size cities (Rajasthan, Uttar Pradesh,
and Gujarat, India; Punjab, Pakistan); and yet others are characterized
simply by many medium-size cities (Madhya Pradesh, Bihar, and Kerala,

India). Does this spatial distribution of people within regions matter for a country's economic performance?

Given that we lack GDP or similar data at a lower spatial scale than the regional level, we assess the importance of the *intraregional* spatial distribution by regarding three different (but related) indicators. The first indicator is simply a region's population density, the second is a region's level of urbanization, and the third is the share of a region's urban population living in the largest city, so-called urban primacy. The first indicator tells us something about the effect of density per se; the second and third indicators are better linked to Figure 3.8 and tell us something about the within-region concentration of population (that is, how population is divided between a region's rural and urban areas, on the one hand, and how urban population is divided across a region's cities, on the other hand).

The fact that these three indicators do not necessarily coincide can be seen from inspecting Figure 3.9, which shows that there appears to be no relationship between population density and urbanization at the

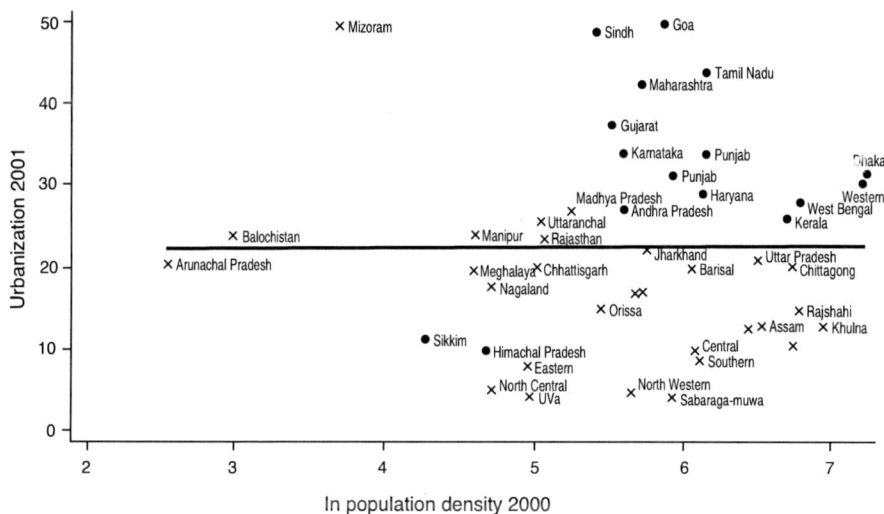

FIGURE 3.9   Urbanization and Population Density

Sources: World Bank (2009a). World cities database (compiled by J.V. Henderson 2001) is used to calculate urban primacy.
Note: Regions marked by a × are lagging regions, and those marked by a • are leading regions.

regional level in South Asia. The fact that population density in South Asia is high irrespective of the region being predominantly urban or rural is something that sets it apart from the rest of the world (see World Bank 2009b). Generally, a higher population density is associated with higher urbanization rates (see also the brief discussion on this issue around Table 3.1). The relation between urbanization and urban primacy, on the other hand, is very close (a correlation coefficient of 0.92)[12] in case of South Asia. This high correlation is interesting in itself as it indicates that in South Asia urbanization at the regional level is generally driven by one city in the region acting as the locus of attraction for rural and possibly also other cities' residents.

Next, to establish the importance of each of these three different indicators of *intra*regional density for regional economic development, we added them to our previous regression of ln GDP per capita on our two measures of market access. The last two columns in Table 3.6 show the results. Note that because regions' urbanization level is so strongly correlated with regions' urban primacy level (see above), it is impossible to distinguish clearly between the two concepts (causing problems with multi-colinearity). Urbanization and urban primacy go hand in hand in South Asia.

First of all the regression results indicate that all our conclusions in the previous subsection about the relevance of market access are not affected by also allowing the *intra*regional distribution to play a role. It is still the case that only national market access has a strong positive impact on income per capita levels, whereas market access to other South Asian regions does not have any significant impact. In addition to the role of market access, urbanization, or urban primacy for that matter (again given the almost one-to-one correspondence between urbanization and urban primacy), has a positive impact on income per capita. This latter finding shows that the intraregional distribution of economic activity also matters: there are clear benefits of the concentration of population in (a few) urban centres. Density in and of itself, as measured by population density, does not have a positive effect on income per capita, and even seems to be detrimental to a region's economic chances. In the case of South Asia the high overall density, in combination with comparatively low degrees of urbanization, reflects that many people live in rural areas and that the regions (and the country concerned) would be better off if for a given overall density level, relatively more people would live in cities.

[12]Corresponding scatter plot available upon request.

CONCLUSIONS AND POLICY RECOMMENDATIONS

Main Conclusions from an NEG Perspective

Combining all our empirical evidence at the international, interregional, and intraregional levels, we draw *three main conclusions* about the relevance of NEG in explaining South Asia's economic geography:

1. At the international level, every South Asian country underutilizes its potential market access. Market access matters for GDP per capita but it could matter a lot more if economic integration were to be improved. This holds in particular within the South Asian region. Trade and labour migration between South Asian countries is extremely low compared with other regions in the world. Economic interaction among the South Asian countries is hampered by a host of economic and non-economic impediments. Or, in the terminology of WDR 2009, *division* is a real issue in South Asia, holding back cross-national trade and migration. The gains from more economic interaction and especially more intra-South Asia trade are large in terms of increased market access and a higher GDP per capita. We expect that this would more clearly be the case for the 'smaller' South Asian countries than for India, which, given its status as South Asia's core economy, can rely to a large extent on its own large domestic market.

2. Also at the interregional level, market access, the key NEG variable, matters, but it is above all *national* market access that is important. Within each South Asian country the regions with good access to national markets (that is, a low *distance* in WDR 2009 terms) typically have a higher GDP per capita. The economic ties between South Asian countries are, on the other hand, relatively underdeveloped (confirming the evidence at the international level): good access to other South Asian markets (as most lagging border regions have) has no significant impact on regional income levels. Border regions in, for instance, Pakistan and Bangladesh might have a lot to gain from improved integration of their countries with India. The same holds for landlocked Nepal and Bhutan. Also within India the southern regions with good access to the sea (and thus generally to international, and not South Asian, markets) fare much better than its landlocked (border) regions.

3. Finally, at the interregional level, regions that are more urbanized (and usually have the bulk of urban population concentrated in one large city) are showing stronger economic performance than their more rural counterparts. In contrast to this positive urban concentration,

pure density effects seem to play little role at the regional level: a region's overall population density is not positively associated with its economic performance (perhaps because population density is generally really high in all parts of South Asia). Given that South Asia's degree of urbanization is low compared with other developing regions in the world, this leaves scope for aiming to encourage future urban–rural migration.

What the Future May Look Like

How can these findings be used to understand the present and future economic geography of South Asia from an NEG perspective? NEG considers first and foremost the spatial distribution of *economic activity and income* across space so we focus first on the question whether NEG can help us to understand the evolution of South Asia's regional differences in economic terms. In terms of the spatial distribution of economic activity NEG predicts, recall the bell curve (Figure 3.3), that certainly in its initial stages economic development goes along with large and probably increasing regional disparities. For South Asia, and determined in part by the observed differences in market access, this certainly seems to be the case at the regional level: leading regions are faring markedly better in economic terms than lagging regions. There are, in NEG terminology, distinct core–periphery patterns, both at the South Asian and at the national level (for the South Asian region as a whole, a core–periphery pattern is clearly visible with India, representing 80 per cent of the South Asia economy, being the core). More South Asian economic integration would, via its trade or factor mobility enhancing impact respectively, strengthen these current agglomeration patterns even further. This is not only true for the *inter*regional agglomeration differences, but also for the *intra*regional differences. Within each South Asian country, improvements in the infrastructure and more interregional labour mobility will most likely contribute to alleviating regional income differences but will tend to sustain or even strengthen core–periphery patterns between and within regions, so that we expect urbanization rates to continue to increase.

On the other hand, NEG theory also tells us that, as a result of the higher wages in agglomerations (that also tend to rise with the degree agglomeration), there could be a point (for instance, because labour mobility remains low) where firms start moving back to the peripheral regions to take advantage of the lower peripheral wages levels. If this happens, it will put a brake on agglomeration tendencies and, for low enough transport costs, could even lead to (renewed) spreading (see the bell curve in Figure 3.3). This bell curve–like scenario implies that further economic integration via increased trade will at some point put a brake on the process of agglomeration as the increased income differences between India, South Asia's economic core, and the other South Asian countries will start to act as a powerful spreading force (that is, firms previously located in India, will find the lower wages in other South Asian countries attractive and relocate there). But we expect this to be really only a long-term scenario. In line with the WDR 2009 and depending on the future policy measures, we expect that further economic development in South Asia will come along with an increased regional divergence of economic activity, at least in the years to come.

Stimulating Agglomerations while Empowering the Periphery

Based on the evidence in this chapter, this section finally provides several policy recommendations that are likely to help in bringing about a faster convergence in living standards between leading and lagging regions in South Asia. In our view the most important policy measures would be those that stimulate regional integration (both within and between countries), increase infrastructure investments (in quantity, but as important, in quality) in order for lagging regions and leading regions to become better connected, and reduce (growth hampering) congestion problems. Also, policy should be aimed at improving education, providing basic amenities, and addressing (un)official restrictions on labour mobility. It is extremely important to give the right incentives and opportunities to both firms and people to take advantage of the economic opportunities that are present not only in their own region but also in other (economically prospering) regions.

Our policy recommendations can be classified into two different categories:

1. International level: More economic integration seems to be a, or even *the,* key policy objective. Given the history of the region, with its cultural, religious, and other differences, we do not think that it will be easy to improve the connectivity between South Asian countries in terms of labour mobility. It seems more effective to try to stimulate intra-South Asia trade, and hence market access, by a reduction of trade costs and barriers. This can be done via the actual reduction of trade barriers by streamlining regulation between South Asian countries and reducing tariffs, but also by improving the interconnectivity through the development of better cross-

national infrastructure (transport corridors). Also within countries, connectivity should be improved by investing in the quantity and quality of infrastructure projects that will boost the region's market access. Moreover, formal and informal barriers to labour mobility should be removed.

2. Regional level: The main message is that policymakers should primarily invest in *places* when it comes to *leading* (urbanized) regions and in *people* when it comes to *lagging* regions. In leading regions, initiatives like export zones might help to give people increased incentives to develop economic activities that are able to compete on world markets and enhance local positive agglomeration economies. Also trying to reduce congestion problems in leading regions is a priority. On the contrary, in lagging regions they should above all invest in people: further investments and improvements in education and health in lagging regions are called for in order to give people a chance to take advantage (by moving there) of the economic developments in leading regions. After all, measures to increase labour mobility only make sense if this enables migration of a well-trained, well-qualified, and effective labour force from lagging to leading regions.

REFERENCES

Ahmed, Sadiq, Saman Kelegama, and Ejaz Ghani (eds). 2010. *Promoting Economic Cooperation in South Asia*. New Delhi: Sage Publications.

Amiti, M. and B.S. Javorcik. 2008. 'Trade Costs and Location of Foreign Firms in China', *Journal of Development Economics*, 85: 129–49.

Amiti, M. and L. Cameron. 2007. 'Economic Geography and Wages', *Review of Economics and Statistics*, 89 (1): 15–29.

Baldwin, R., R. Forslid, Ph. Martin, G.I.P. Ottaviano, and F. Robert-Nicoud. 2003. *Economic Geography and Public Policy*. Princeton, NJ: Princeton University Press.

Bosker, E.M. and H. Garretsen. 2008a. 'Trade Costs, Market Access and Economic Geography: Why the Empirical Specification of Trade Costs Matters', forthcoming in *Papers in Regional Science*.

———. 2008b. 'Economic Geography and Economic Development in Sub-Saharan Africa', Working Paper, University of Groningen.

Bosker, E.M., S. Brakman, H. Garretsen, and M. Schramm. 2007. 'Adding Geography to the New Economic Geography', forthcoming in *Journal of Economic Geography*.

Brakman, S., H. Garretsen, and Ch. van Marrewijk. 2009. *The New Introduction to Geographical Economics*. Cambridge: Cambridge University Press.

Breinlich, H. 2006. 'The Spatial Income Structure in the European Union—What Role for Economic Geography?', *Journal of Economic Geography*, 6: 593–617.

Collier, P. and A.J. Venables. 2007. 'Trade Preferences and Manufacturing Export Response: Lessons from Theory and Policy', *World Development*, 30: 1326–45.

Combes, P-P., G. Duranton, and H. Overman. 2005. 'Agglomeration and the Adjustment of the Spatial Economy', *Papers in Regional Science*, 84 (3): 311–49.

Combes, P-P., T. Mayer, and J-F. Thisse. 2008. *Economic Geography: The Integration of Regions and Nations*. Princeton, NJ: Princeton University Press.

Deichmann, U., S.V. Lall, S.J. Redding, and A.J. Venables. 2008. 'Industrial Location in Developing Countries', *World Bank Research Observer*, 23 (2): 219–46.

Disdier, A-C. and K. Head. 2008. 'The Puzzling Persistence of the Distance Effect on Bilateral Trade', *Review of Economics and Statistics*, 90 (1): 37–48.

Fujita, M. P.R. Krugman, and A.J. Venables. 1999. *The Spatial Economy: Cities, Regions, and International Trade*. MIT Press.

Fujita, M. and T. Mori. 2005. 'Frontiers of the New Economic Geography', *Papers in Regional Science*, 84: 377–407.

Fujita, M. and J-F. Thisse. 2002. *Economics of Agglomeration*. Cambridge: Cambridge University Press.

Head, Keith and Thierry Mayer. 2004. 'The Empirics Of Agglomeration and Trade', in J.V. Henderson and J.F. Thisse (eds), *Handbook of Regional and Urban Economics*, Vol. 4, chapter 59, pp. 2609–69. North-Holland, Amsterdam: Elsevier.

Helpman, E. 1998. 'The Size of Regions', in D. Pines, E. Sadka, and I. Zilcha (eds), *Topics in Public Economics*. Cambridge: Cambridge University Press.

Henderson, J.V., Z. Shalizi, and A.J. Venables. 2001. 'Geography and Development', *Journal of Economic Geography*, 1: 81–105.

Hering, L. and S. Poncet. Forthcoming. 'Market Access Impact on Individual Wages: Evidence from China', *Review of Economics and Statistics*.

Honorati, Maddalena and Taye Mengistae. 2007. 'Corruption, Business Environment, and Small Business Fixed Investment in India', Policy Research Working Paper No. 4356, World Bank, Washington, D.C.

Hummels, D. 2007. 'Transportation Costs and International Trade in the Second Era of Globalization', *Journal of Economic Perspectives*, 21: 131–54.

Krugman, P.R. 1991. 'Increasing Returns and Economic Geography', *Journal of Political Economy*, 99: 483–99.

Krugman, P.R. and A.J. Venables. 1995. 'Globalization and the Inequality of Nations', *The Quarterly Journal of Economics*, 110: 857–80.

Lall, S.V., Z. Shalizi, and U. Deichmann. 2004. 'Agglomeration Economies and Productivity in Indian Industry', *Journal of Development Economics*, 73: 643–73.

Mayer, T. 2008. 'Market Potential and Development', CEPR Working Paper, DP6798.

Neary, J.P. 2001. 'Of Hype and Hyperbolas: Introducing the New Economic Geography', *Journal of Economic Literature*, 39: 536–61.

Ottaviano, G.I.P. and J-F. Thisse. 2004. 'Agglomeration and Economic Geography', in J.V. Henderson and J-F. Thisse (eds), *Handbook of Regional and Urban Economics*, Vol. 4, pp. 2563–608. North-Holland, Amsterdam: Elsevier.

Overman, H.G., S.J. Redding, and A.J. Venables. 2003. 'The Economic Geography of Trade, Production and Income: A Survey of Empirics', in K. Choi and J. Harrigan (eds), *Handbook of International Trade*, pp. 353–87. Oxford: Basil Blackwell.

Puga, D. 2002. 'European Regional Policies in Light of Recent Location Theories', *Journal of Economic Geography*, 2: 373–406.

———. 1999. 'The Rise and Fall of Regional Inequalities', *European Economic Review*, 43: 303–34.

Purfield, C. 2006. 'Is Economic Growth in India Leaving Some States Behind?', IMF Working Papers, WP/06/103, Washington, D.C.

Redding, S. and A.J. Venables. 2004. 'Economic Geography and International Inequality', *Journal of International Economics*, 62 (1): 53–82.

Rosenthal, S.S., and W.C. Strange. 2004. 'Evidence on the Nature and Sources of Agglomeration Economies', in V. Henderson and F. Thisse (eds), *Handbook of Regional and Urban Economics*, Vol. 4, pp. 2119–71. North-Holland, Amsterdam: Elsevier.

Santos, Silva and Silvana Tenreyro. 2006. 'The Log of Gravity', *The Review of Economics and Statistics*, 88: 641–58.

Venables, A.J. 1996. 'Equilibrium Locations of Vertically Linked Industries', *International Economic Review*, 37: 341–59.

World Bank. 2009a. *World Development Indicators*. Washington, D.C.: World Bank.

———. 2009b. *World Development Report: Reshaping Economic Geography*. Washington, D.C.: World Bank.

———. 2007a. *South Asia: Growth and Regional Integration*. Washington, D.C.: World Bank.

———. 2007b. *Can South Asia Achieve Double Digit Growth?* Washington, D.C.: World Bank.

4

Do Lagging Regions Benefit from Trade?

Pravin Krishna, Devashish Mitra, and Asha Sundaram

After decades of post-imperial stagnation, South Asia has experienced impressive growth in recent years. From 1990 to 2005, the region's gross domestic product (GDP) grew at about 6 per cent annually—nearly twice the rate of the world economy. This acceleration in output growth took place in the context of a parallel increase in international trade—itself driven by a combination of declining trade barriers and transportation costs as well as technological changes. Between 1990 and 2005, South Asia's largest economy, India (accounting for nearly 75 per cent of regional GDP), more than doubled its trade-to-GDP ratio (from about 15 per cent to 35 per cent). Other countries in the region, including Bangladesh and Sri Lanka, also experienced impressive increases in their international trade. Greater international trade in the region, however, has raised some basic questions regarding the gains from trade: Who benefits from trade? Will greater international trade result in an increase in income inequality and poverty? Should we expect the benefits from trade to be uniformly distributed across lagging and leading regions within a country?

Basic international trade theory predicts that trade will increase the returns to the abundant factors in an economy: For the unskilled, labour abundant countries of South Asia, this is good news—the implication is that trade will raise the incomes of low-skilled workers, thus generating a reduction in poverty. It has, however, been argued that the benefits of trade may not spread uniformly across different regions within a country for a number of practical reasons. First, different regions may have different levels of access to international trade—lagging regions may not benefit from trade because transportation and other trade costs may be too high for these regions to interact with international markets. As the World Development Report (WDR, World Bank: 2009a) notes:

... for trade in goods and services, distance from markets implies time and monetary costs. The placement and quality of transport infrastructure and the availability of transport can dramatically affect the economic distance between any two areas ... two villages may have the same straight-line distance to a city, but one could be near a national highway, the other on an unpaved rural road.

Thus, the type and quality of roads and other transport infrastructure may affect the ability of lagging regions to benefit from trade.

Second, an important source of the gains from trade is the improvement in the allocation of productive resources in the economy. To achieve this improvement in production efficiency, however, it is important that factors of production, such as labour, are mobile and that labour markets are flexible to enable mobility. However, markets, in practice, are often characterized by a variety of rigidities. Importantly, the extent of labour market inflexibility also varies across countries. As Ramaswamy (2003) notes:

In India, firms employing more than 100 workers need to take prior permission from the government before retrenching a worker. In Sri Lanka, all firms employing more than 15 workers need consent of the Commissioner of Labor before dismissing a worker with more than one year of service. In Pakistan, permission from the labor courts is required for all firms with more than ten workers to close or to retrench more than 50 per cent of the workers. In Bangladesh, a worker can be retrenched after giving one month's notice to the concerned worker.

Furthermore, regions within a country may also vary in their labour market flexibility. Aghion et al. (2006) note in their study on the differential effects of trade liberalization across Indian states that, in India, 'labor market institutions started from a common nationwide framework, the Industrial Disputes Act, approved in 1947, which regulated industrial relations in the registered or organized manufacturing sector'. However, under the Indian constitution 'states were entitled to amend the Act, and amendments were in fact extensively introduced. As a result, labor market institutions gradually evolved, and there was a large extent of heterogeneity across Indian states at the time of the industrial policy reforms of the 1980s and 1990s.'

Third, recent insights from the literature on the 'new economic geography' suggest that increases in regional disparities may be a natural feature of the economic development process (Fujita et al. 1999). Specifically, if production is subject to economies of scale (so unit costs fall with larger scale in production), market forces may induce production to agglomerate in a few areas. In this case, the economic development process can be a lumpy one—with some regions growing faster than others do. Trade itself may affect agglomeration patterns and the location of economic activity. Trade liberalization may lead to an increase in the geographic concentration of economic activity—thus, possibly increasing (or decreasing) the extent of regional differences within a country. As WDR 2009 notes, in China, the coastal provinces—three areas known as the Bohai Basin, the Pearl River Delta, and the Yangtze River Delta—accounted for more than half of the country's GDP in 2005, but constitute less than a fifth of China's geographic area. This is a pattern of concentration of economic activity that has accelerated with the expansion of Chinese trade in recent decades.

The preceding discussion highlights contexts in which the effect of trade on poverty alleviation in developing countries may not be uniform—with the specific possibility that lagging regions may not see benefits from trade. It is these issues concerning the differential effects of trade openness on leading and lagging regions within countries in South Asia that this chapter is interested in studying. Using data from South Asia (primarily from India), we study empirically the extent to which trade liberalization affects differently lagging and leading regions within a country. In addition, we attempt to study the factors that inhibit market integration and prevent trade from positively affecting development in lagging regions. Our focus is on poverty—but we do also examine other variables of interest such as industry productivity.

To preview our findings: We find evidence that although trade liberalization is associated with reduced poverty, the effect is smaller in lagging states. A percentage point reduction in the tariff rate decreases poverty by 0.22 per cent in the leading states, while the effect is insignificant in the lagging states. Within leading states, the effects of trade liberalization are also larger in the urban rather than rural areas. A percentage point decrease in the tariff rate decreases poverty by 0.19 per cent in the rural sector and by 0.26 per cent in the urban sector in the leading states.

Lagging states are farther away from ports (on average about 25 per cent farther from the nearest port than an average leading state). For example, the north-eastern states in India that fall in the 'lagging category' are somewhat geographically isolated. This isolation from the rest of India is accentuated by the intermediate presence of Bangladesh, which makes distance by road to the nearest port quite large (more than 1000 km in some instances). Also, the quality of roads and highway connections in this sector lag behind most states. In contrast, Maharashtra is a leading state, and itself has the country's largest port, the city of Mumbai. In Pakistan, the North West Frontier Province (NWFP) faces a similar problem of remoteness, while the leading region of Sindh has the country's largest port, Karachi. How much does remoteness matter? We find that price transmission (from international prices to domestic prices) is less perfect in lagging states than in leading ones, especially in the rural sector. Our estimates for India suggest that, in the urban sector, a 1 per cent reduction in international prices implies a 0.61 per cent reduction in the unit price in the leading states but a 0.53 per cent reduction in the unit price in the lagging states. In contrast, in the rural sector, a 1 per cent reduction in international prices implies a 0.60 per cent reduction in the unit price in leading states but a 0.34 per cent reduction in the unit price in the lagging states. This, taken along with the findings concerning the links between trade liberalization and poverty reduction described earlier, suggests that it is the lack of exposure to international markets (and not the opposite cause—that is, competition from international trade) that is lowering the rate of poverty reduction in lagging regions relative to leading ones.

Finally, we see that trade liberalization has increased the productivity of Indian industry, while also finding that the increase in productivity due to trade liberalization is (weakly) smaller in lagging states. Specifically, a 1 percentage point reduction in the tariff rate increases productivity by 0.41 per cent across all leading states but only by 0.38 per cent in the lagging states. These results for India suggest that lagging regions and the extent of regional inequality limit the benefits of trade reform in a number of ways.

We study the links between trade and poverty alleviation further using data from other countries in South Asia—Bangladesh, Pakistan, Nepal, and Sri Lanka. We find that the effects of trade liberalization on poverty differ by the proportion on national population living in lagging regions. Countries with a smaller proportion of population in lagging regions benefit more from trade liberalization. Specifically, our results indicate that a percentage point increase in the proportion of population in lagging regions further depresses the annual growth in per capita GDP after trade liberalization further by 0.01 percentage points. We also find statistically weaker yet suggestive evidence that a percentage point increase in the proportion of population in lagging regions decreases the annual rate of decline in poverty following trade liberalization by an additional 0.01 percentage point. Even though small, since these effects are on the annual rate of growth or decline, these benefits can accumulate to something quite substantial over time.

The rest of this chapter proceeds as follows. In the next section, we briefly survey the existing empirical literature on the effects of trade liberalization. This literature has largely focused on the effects of trade on growth, inequality, and poverty reduction at the national level, paying relatively little attention to subnational variation in outcomes. Nevertheless, as we will point out, a few contributions in this literature have indeed discussed how a variety of economic, political, and institutional factors that vary at the subnational level may lead to differences in regional outcomes. In the sections that follow we discuss our data, our estimation strategy, and our empirical results. In the final sections we discuss the policy implications of the literature and our empirical analysis for South Asia. Finally, we present our conclusions.

TRADE, GROWTH, INEQUALITY, AND POVERTY

Early empirical demonstrations of the linkages between trade and growth include the well-known studies of Bhagwati (1978) and Krueger (1978). Analysing in detail a sample of developing countries including India and Turkey, these studies concluded that trade openness was indeed an important driver of economic growth. These conclusions are also consistent with the recent economic experience—as countries such as China and India have grown extremely fast after their economies became open to trade and foreign direct investment in recent decades. While these countries were also engaged in numerous domestic policy reforms at the same time, it would be hard to argue that international integration did not play an important role in supporting the growth outcomes there.

Other methodological approaches have also been used in the literature to explore the link between trade and growth. Hasan et al. (2007) list Wacziarg and Welch (2004), Edwards (1998), Sachs and Warner (1995), and Dollar (1992), each of whom, using cross-country growth regressions, found positive effects of trade on growth. However, Rodriguez and Rodrik (2001) have argued that results linking trade and growth are not particularly robust to the choice of openness measures. These inconclusive findings have inspired a vigorous debate regarding the limitations of both case-study and cross-country regression approaches in analysing the relationship between trade and growth. While the trade–growth nexus has not been decisively demonstrated in quantitative exercises, a combination of intuition and experience leads the majority of economists to believe that trade is good for growth (and at a minimum that trade does not harm growth).

An extensive literature has examined the impact of trade liberalization on inequality in developing countries (see Goldberg and Pavcnik [2004] and Winters et al. [2004] for comprehensive surveys). Since developing countries are mainly unskilled labour abundant, trade liberalization should result in specialization in unskilled labour-intensive sectors, pushing the unskilled wage up relative to the skilled wage. However, as Goldberg and Pavcnik (2004) point out, a casual examination of the data suggests that, if anything, there were large increases in inequality between skilled and unskilled workers in the years following trade reform in Latin America (with inequality increasing by 60 per cent between 1987 and 1993 for Mexico and by 20 per cent between 1990 and 1998 for Colombia). Rising skill premia suggest that factors other than (or which dominate) international trade (which, theoretically, should be shrinking skill premia in developing countries) may be at work in determining labour market outcomes. Several explanations have been offered in the literature.

First, returns to particular occupations that require a higher level of education may have increased—as has been observed in Mexico. At the same time, it appears that the fraction of skilled workers has risen across all sectors. Taken together, these facts point to skill biased technological change rather than international trade as the dominant driver of rising skill premia. On the other hand, the literature has also suggested that it may be trade liberalization that causes skill-biased technological change. For instance, in Colombia, demand for skilled workers was largest in those sectors that experienced the largest tariff cuts, suggesting that competition induces firms to pursue research and development (R&D) and invest in technologies and innovation. Finally, it has been argued that international trade has indeed contributed to rising inequality in developing countries because of the nature of production sharing in the global economy. Feenstra and Hanson (1996) have argued that industrial countries typically outsource production of less-skill-intensive intermediate goods to developing countries. However, these intermediate goods are relatively more skill intensive in developing countries. Outsourcing hence increases the relative demand for skilled labour in both industrial and developing countries, thereby increasing the skill premium. Overall, it appears that skill-biased technological change and international trade may both be relevant in understanding increased wage inequality in industrial and developing countries. Feenstra and Hanson (1996), study US trade data to conclude that both factors are quantitatively significant as well (with international trade explaining roughly 15 per cent of the increased wage inequality and skilled biased technological change explaining another 40 per cent).

The literature has also examined the question of the relationship between trade and poverty. On the one hand, it has been argued that if trade is good for growth, it should also lower poverty. For instance, trade liberalization increases productivity through cheaper intermediate inputs and import competition—and productivity improvements are clearly important for poverty alleviation in the long run. On the other hand, if productivity grows faster than output in the short run, there may be adverse consequences for employment. Equally, import competition may kill weaker domestic firms, pushing their employees into less-well-paying alternatives or unemployment—thereby raising poverty. In one of the relatively few studies to have examined the effects of trade on poverty using disaggregate household level data, Hasan et al. (2007) provide evidence for the poverty-reducing impact of trade reforms in India. Their study also shows that trade reform is associated with larger reductions in poverty in states with flexible labour laws, especially in the urban sector. Finally, their study finds weak evidence that, in addition to the effect of trade liberalization, deregulation reduces poverty in states with flexible labour markets.

Finally, the literature stresses the role played by domestic policy in ensuring that the poor benefit from trade reforms. Rodrik et al. (2002) find that the quality of domestic institutions interacts with trade liberalization. They use an instrumental variables approach to control for the endogeneity of trade and institutions to find that good institutions are important for growth. Hasan et al. (2003) contend that institutions that 'support economic freedom'—like freedom to trade with foreigners, property rights, and rule of law—are key to poverty reduction. Harrison (2006) stresses the need for investment in human capital, credit provision, and infrastructure for globalization to aid poverty reduction.

In closing this brief literature review, we should note that the most, if not all, of the papers in the literature are fraught with methodological issues—notably measurement error of various forms in data and difficult questions concerning identification and inference in the statistical analysis. Improved data and econometric methodologies are nevertheless constantly being brought to bear, and future research will most likely provide more decisive answers to these questions than has been possible to date until now.

DATA

Poverty

For India, the poverty and trade protection data used in this paper are from Hasan et al. (2007).[1] To measure poverty, we employ urban, rural, and overall poverty rates (headcount indices) by state based on National Sample Survey (NSS) household expenditure surveys, and urban and rural poverty lines for the years 1987–88, 1993–94, and 1999–2000. Different estimates of poverty are available for India because of differences in data and methods used.[2] To ensure that our results are robust to varied approaches to estimating poverty, we employ three different estimates for poverty rates.

The first set of estimates is from Deaton and Dreze (2002). The Deaton and Dreze (DD) poverty estimates improve upon official estimates by using better commodity weights for the consumer-price index (CPI), adjusting for the change in the NSS survey questionnaire in 1999–2000, and accounting for the differentials between urban and rural poverty lines implicit in the official poverty lines. Our second set of estimates is the official Government of India (GOI) poverty estimates adjusted for the change in the NSS expenditure survey questionnaire as proposed by Deaton (2003). The DD and GOI estimates are obtained from thick rounds of the NSS survey. The third set of poverty estimates used in this paper, developed by Ozler-Datt-Ravallion (ODR), was downloaded from LSE's EOPP Indian States Database website. These estimates are based on both thick and thin rounds of the NSS expenditure survey, although they do not correct for the new NSS survey questionnaire in 1999–2000.

For the other South Asian countries in our cross-country regressions, we use poverty data from the World Bank's PovcalNet database. This database incorporates the findings of the 2005 International Comparison Program (ICP). The poverty estimates combine the 2005 purchasing power parity (PPP) exchange rates for household consumption from the 2005 ICP with data from 675 household surveys across 116 developing countries spanning the period 1981–2005. The World Bank's official poverty estimates (as reported in the World Development

---

[1]Hasan et al. (2007) provide a more comprehensive discussion of the poverty and trade protection estimates used in this paper.
[2]See Hasan et al. (2007) for more details.

Indicators) use unit record household data whenever possible while PovcalNet uses grouped distributions. Our poverty variable is the percentage of population living in households with consumption or income per person below the poverty line. The poverty line is $38.00 per month at 2005 PPP. This is the World Bank $1.25 per day poverty line ($38=$1.25*365/12).

We use two other measures of well-being. The first is the per capita GDP in 2005 PPP US dollars obtained from the World Development Indicators 2009. The second is the Human Development Index (HDI) from the United Nations Development Program (UNDP) as an alternative measure of human well-being. The HDI is a composite index measuring the average achievements in a country in three dimensions of human development: a long and healthy life, access to knowledge, and a decent standard of living. The dimensions are measured by life expectancy at birth; adult literacy and combined gross enrolment in primary-, secondary-, and tertiary-level education; and GDP per capital in PPP US dollars.[3] HDI measures are available for the years 1975 through 2005 with gaps of five years in between.[4] Hence, we assume that the HDI is constant over five-year intervals in this period.

Measures of Regional Inequality

In our cross-country regressions for South Asia, we use the proportion of population in lagging regions within each country as a measure of regional inequality. We classify regions, states, and provinces within each country as leading and lagging based on data provided to us by the South Asia Poverty Reduction and Economic Management (PREM) team of the World Bank. Table 4.1 lists these regions, states, and provinces and their classifications. Next, we use region-, state-, province-, and national-level populations for each country to construct the proportion of national population in lagging regions. For Bangladesh, India, and Sri Lanka, we use population data provided by the World Bank. For Nepal, we use population data from the Statistical Yearbook 2005 (see Table 4.1), Central Bureau of Statistics, Government of Nepal. For Pakistan, we obtain population data from the Statistics Division,

[3]For details on the construction of the HDI see Technical Notes 1 in *Human Development Report 2007/2008*, UNDP.
[4]HDI are not comparable across time due to differences in methods used in calculation. Hence, we use Table 2 in the *Human Development Report 2007/2008* that provides trends in HDI from 1975 to 2005 with five-year gaps using the same methodology used for the construction of the 2005 HDI.

Ministry of Economic Affairs and Statistics, Population Census Organization, Government of Pakistan (see http://www.statpak.gov.pk/depts/pco/statistics/statistics.html). Data on populations are available only for census years. Hence, we use the populations in the beginning of the decade to calculate the proportion of population in lagging regions for the whole decade.[5] In the absence of such data, we use the population data for the next available year in the decade, and so on.

We use two other controls in our cross-country regressions of poverty on trade liberalization and its interaction with proportion of population

TABLE 4.1   Poverty, Regional Inequality, and Geographical Measures by Country

Variable	Country	Obser-vations	Mean	Standard deviation	Maxi-mum	Mini-mum
Proportion of population in lagging regions	Afghanistan	0				
	Bangladesh	27	0.72	0.02	0.69	0.73
	Bhutan	0				
	India Rural	17	0.61	0.01	0.6	0.62
	India Urban	17	0.42	0	0.42	0.42
	Maldives	0				
	Nepal	27	0.46	0	0.46	0.46
	Pakistan	40	0.17	0.01	0.17	0.18
	Sri Lanka	17	0.73	0.01	0.71	0.74
Coastline/(Coastline + Land boundary)	Afghanistan	48	0	0	0	0
	Bangladesh	48	0.12	0	0.12	0.12
	Bhutan	48	0	0	0	0
	India Rural	48	0.33	0	0.33	0.33
	India Urban	48	0.33	0	0.33	0.33
	Maldives	48	1	0	1	1
	Nepal	48	0	0	0	0
	Pakistan	48	0.13	0	0.13	0.13
	Sri Lanka	48	1	0	1	1
National average distance to capital city	Afghanistan	48	418	0	418	418

(contd...)

[5]We do not expect the proportion of population in lagging regions to vary greatly over a decade.

Table 4.1 (contd...)

Variable	Country	Obser-vations	Mean	Standard deviation	Maxi-mum	Mini-mum
	Bangladesh	48	165	0	165	165
	Bhutan	48	99	0	99	99
	India Rural	48	992	0	992	992
	India Urban	48	992	0	992	992
	Maldives	48	276	0	276	276
	Nepal	48	236	0	236	236
	Pakistan	48	661	0	661	661
	Sri Lanka	48	157	0	157	157
Percentage individuals in households below poverty line	Afghanistan	0				
	Bangladesh	7	50.25	4.21	43.03	56.11
	Bhutan	1	26.23	.	26.23	26.23
	India Rural	5	55.74	9.13	43.83	69.02
	India Urban	5	45.49	7.20	36.16	54.79
	Maldives	0				
	Nepal	2	61.78	9.42	55.12	68.44
	Pakistan	7	41.53	18.53	22.59	66.46
	Sri Lanka	4	16.31	2.62	13.95	19.96
Per capita GDP in PPP US$	Afghanistan	0				
	Bangladesh	28	797.10	164.41	614.12	1172.65
	Bhutan	28	2239.86	990.00	922.54	4567.53
	India Rural	28	1445.62	479.43	868.89	2598.59
	India Urban	28	1445.62	479.43	868.89	2598.59
	Maldives	13	3628.52	770.41	2520.01	5035.92
	Nepal	28	777.37	134.76	564.22	975.51
	Pakistan	28	1753.43	307.54	1190.90	2383.32
	Sri Lanka	28	2465.94	701.87	1553.16	4020.22
HDI	Afghanistan	0				
	Bangladesh	33	0.43	0.07	0.35	0.55
	Bhutan	3	0.58	0	0.58	0.58
	India Rural	33	0.51	0.06	0.42	0.62
	India Urban	33	0.51	0.06	0.42	0.62
	Maldives	3	0.74	0	0.74	0.74
	Nepal	33	0.41	0.08	0.30	0.53
	Pakistan	33	0.45	0.06	0.37	0.55
	Sri Lanka	33	0.69	0.04	0.62	0.74

Note: GDP = gross domestic product; HDI = Human Development Indicators; PPP = purchasing power parity.

in lagging regions. The first is the coastline in kilometres divided by the coastline plus the land boundary in kilometres. The second control is the national average distance to the national capital in kilometres. Data on coastlines, land boundaries, and average national distance to the capital are drawn from the World Development Indicators (World Bank 2009b). Table 4.2 provides summary statistics on the poverty, HDI, regional inequality, and geographic measures by country.

Trade Barriers for Poverty Regressions

Following Hasan et al. (2007), we look at both tariffs and non-tariff barriers (NTBs), and alternatively at a principal components aggregation of the two policy instruments as measures of trade protection. Protection measures by state by broad sector (urban, rural, and overall) are arrived at by weighting two-digit industry-level tariff rates and NTB coverage rates (constructed from Pandey 1999) for manufacturing, mining, and agricultural industries by state and sector employment shares. The NTB

TABLE 4.2   **Summary Statistics for Protection and Poverty Measures**

Variables	Average*		
	1987	1993	1999
Poverty measures			
Deaton-Dreze overall poverty rate	32.63	27.48	20.87
Deaton-Dreze urban poverty rate	21.15	16.93	11.62
Deaton-Dreze rural poverty rate	36.25	30.97	24.19
GOI overall poverty rate	36.58	33.63	26.52
GOI urban poverty rate	36.30	30.27	23.35
GOI rural poverty rate	36.07	33.82	26.91
ODR overall headcount index	40.28	36.66	31.28
ODR urban headcount index	36.46	28.12	22.53
ODR rural headcount index	41.34	39.12	33.70
Trade protection measures (Lagged by one year)			
Overall tariff	94.69	70.63	24.38
Urban tariff	131.49	93.84	36.72
Rural tariff	90.22	67.86	22.86
Overall non-tariff barriers	100	80.80	70.48
Urban non-tariff barriers	100	74.25	53.33
Rural non-tariff barriers	100	81.54	72.47

Notes: GOI = Government of India;
          ODR = Ozler-Datt-Ravallion.
       *The average is taken over the 15 major states.

measure is the proportion of the value of imports covered by NTBs. The weight for each industry in a state and sector is its employment share from the 1993–4 round of the NSS household data. We exclude non-tradables from our calculation of employment weights.[6] Thus, our state-level protection measures are inverse measures of the trade exposure of the labour force. Such measures make sense in the light of the fact that there is substantial inter-state and inter-industry labour immobility in India. Tariffs and NTBs are strongly correlated, and this prevents our estimates from being precisely estimated. We use principal components analysis, which combines correlated variables into a smaller set containing most of the variation in the data. Because the first principal component contains about 90 per cent of the variation for all industry groups in our case, we use it as a third measure of trade protection.

Table 4.2 presents summary statistics for the poverty and protection measures used in our trade and poverty regressions. Time plots of the three poverty and protection estimates (the tariff, NTB coverage rates, and the first principal component of the two) for the rural, urban, and overall sectors are available at http://faculty.maxwell.syr.edu/dmitra/hmu_appendix.pdf.

For our cross-country regressions, we use a dummy variable that is one after liberalization and zero before liberalization to study the impact of trade liberalization on trends in poverty. Years of trade liberalization for each of the South Asian countries are obtained from Sachs and colleagues (1995) and from Wacziarg and Welch (2003). Sachs and colleagues classify a country as closed to trade if it satisfies at least one of the following conditions: (i) NTBs covering more than 40 per cent or more of trade; (ii) average tariff rate of 40 per cent or more; (iii) a black market exchange rate that is depreciated by 20 per cent or more relative to the official exchange rate, on average, during the 1970s or the 1980s; (iv) a socialist economic system; or (v) a state monopoly on major exports. A country is classified as open if none of the above apply to it. They determine the trade liberalization date as the date after which a country remains open continually until the end of the sample period, which is 1994. Wacziarg and Welch (2003) update the Sachs et al. study and include trade liberalization dates for countries that liberalized after 1994 and before 2001, which is the end of their sample period. They disagree with Sachs et al. on trade liberalization dates for several countries,

[6]The size of the non-tradable part of economy is endogenous to protection given to tradable sectors and to factor endowments (controlled for by our state-specific fixed effects).

TABLE 4.3   Trade Liberalization Dates

Country	Trade liberalization year
Afghanistan	
Bangladesh	1996
Bhutan	
India	1994
Maldives	
Nepal	1991
Pakistan	2001
Sri Lanka	1977–83, 1991

Sources: Wacziarg and Welch 2003; Sachs et al. 1995.

one of which is India. Sachs et al. note 1994 as the year in which India can be classified as open, however, Wacziarg and Welch (2003) find that even though 1994 was the year that saw major tariff reductions in India, the country still had high NTBs, which were not below 40 per cent by the end of 2001. For the purpose of this study, we use 1994 as the year in which India liberalized trade. Table 4.3 provides liberalization dates for each of the South Asian countries in our sample.

Data for Price Transmission Regressions for India

Price data for price transmission regressions, also obtained from Hasan et al. (2007), are unit values for primary commodities computed using information on expenditures and quantities from the NSS consumer expenditure surveys for 1987–8, 1993–4, and 1999–2000. World prices for the same years are derived from the index of export prices in the World Trade Organization's International Trade Statistics handbook. Distance is measured as the weighted sum of the distances between a state capital and all ports, with the weights being the share of each port in overall cargo traffic.[7] Exchange rate data are from the International Monetary Fund (IMF) *International Financial Statistics* (IFS) database. Our tariff and NTB measures are at the commodity level.

Export Data for India

Export data are from the National Bureau for Economic Research–United Nations (NBER–UN) World Import and Export database (http://www.nber.org/data/) provided by Feenstra et al. (2005). The data are at the four-digit level of Standard International Trade Classification (SITC)

[7]For sources of distance data, see Hasan et al. (2007).

Rev 2. The data were matched with production data for manufacturing industries at the two-digit level from the Annual Survey of Industries, CSO, New Delhi.[8] Export and production data are for the years 1980 through 1997. To examine whether lagging states primarily produce goods in export-oriented industries, we use, as a regressor, the value of exports of each two-digit industry as a proportion of overall exports as a measure of export orientation. Net value added in each industry in a state as a proportion of overall net value added of all industries in that state has been used to measure specialization in each industry within a state.

Data for Productivity Regressions for India

For our productivity regressions, we use data on net value added, capital stock, and number of workers for each of 18 two-digit manufacturing industries in 16 Indian states from the Annual Survey of Industries. Tariff and NTB rates, constructed from Pandey (1999), are at the two-digit industry level and are from Hasan et al. (2007). We again classify Indian states as leading and lagging states based on data provided to us by the South Asia PREM team of the World Bank. The states of Assam, Bihar, Madhya Pradesh, Orissa, Rajasthan, Uttar Pradesh, and West Bengal are classified as lagging states.

ESTIMATION STRATEGY AND RESULTS

Trade and Poverty

For the period during which India experienced trade liberalization, we want to know whether the differences in the level of development between lagging and leading regions were becoming smaller or getting magnified over time. In other words, we are interested in finding out where development is taking place faster. As a starting point, we ask if poverty trends differ across leading and lagging Indian states, and if they

[8]The ASI data are at the 2-digit level of NIC, India. To match the NBER–UN world trade data with Indian production data, the world trade data were first converted to US NAICS 1997 using the concordance provided by Feenstra and Lipsey at http://www.nber.org/data/. During this process, some export data which Feenstra and Lipsey could not attribute to the 4-digit SITC level and hence attributed to a 3-digit SITC code were lost. We then aggregated the data to the 3-digit NAICS level. A concordance was then written between 3-digit US NAICS 1997 and 2-digit Indian NIC 1987. Data have been aggregated at the 2-digit level to reduce measurement error caused by the concordance. The world trade data are in nominal US dollars and the Indian ASI data in nominal Indian rupees.

are different, where are these trends higher. The specification we adopt for this purpose is as follows:

$$y_{it}^j = \gamma^j t + \eta^j t * \text{Lag}_i + \delta_i^j + \varepsilon_{it}^j \qquad (4.1)$$

where y_{it}^j is the logarithm of poverty in state i and sector j (where j = overall, urban, or rural) at time t, t is the time trend, Lag_i is a dummy variable that equals one if the state is a lagging state and is constant over the three years, δ_i^j are state fixed effects and ε_{it}^j is the error term. We expect a positive coefficient on the interaction between the time trend and the lag dummy if poverty has been rising faster or falling more slowly in lagging states.

Our main question in this chapter focuses on the impact of trade on poverty and the difference in this effect between the leading and the lagging states. We also want to control for trends or time effects common across all states to control for the decline in poverty that would take place in any case through poverty-alleviation programmes and other policies. It is actually quite possible that government programmes to reduce poverty are more concentrated in the lagging states. Not controlling for the differential in trend, which is driven by such policies, in fact makes finding a smaller poverty-reducing effect of trade in lagging more difficult. We work here with the following basic specification:

$$y_{it}^j = \alpha + \beta_1^j \text{protection}_{it-1}^j + \beta_2^j \text{Lag}_i * \text{protection}_{it-1}^j + \delta_i^j + \mu_t^j + \varepsilon_{it}^j \quad (4.2)$$

where protection $^j_{it-1}$ is the trade protection measure (the tariff, NTB coverage rate or Principal Component (i) lagged by one year and μ_t represents time fixed effects. Note that the level of protection here is at the state level and is arrived at from industry-level protection for various sectors and weighting them with their employment shares with the overall, urban, or rural sector. In deriving this measure, we restrict ourselves to tradable sectors. The state fixed effects control for time invariant unobservable state-specific factors like factor endowments or local government policy that might affect poverty and might be correlated with protection. While β_1^j identifies the impact of trade liberalization on poverty (in sector j = overall, urban, or rural) in leading states, β_2^j captures the differential effect on lagging states.

Price Transmission

After investigating whether trade affects poverty differently in leading and lagging regions, in the event we find a difference, we would like to find the causes for it. An important possible cause could be differences in the transmission of international prices and trade protection. We check for differences in the transmission of trade protection to domestic prices between lagging and leading states by running the following regression:

$$p_{cit}^{j} = \alpha + \beta_1 \text{protection}_{ct} + \beta_2 \text{protection}^{ct}*\text{Lag}_i + \beta_3 \text{world price}_{ct}$$
$$+ \beta_4 \text{world price}_{ct}*\text{Lag}_i + \beta_5 \text{exchange rate}_t + \beta_6 \text{inverse}$$
$$\text{distance}_i*\text{protection}_{ct} + \beta_7 \text{inverse distance}_i*\text{world price}_{ct} + \delta_i + \varepsilon_{cit}$$

(4.3)

where p_{cit}^{j} is the unit price of commodity c in sector j (rural or urban) in state i at time t. Protection$_{ct}$ is now a vector of protection measures including either tariff rates or NTB coverage rates or both at the industry level. Lag$_i$ is the lagging state dummy that equals one if a state is classified as a lagging state, δ_i are state fixed effects, and ε_{cit} is the error term. The coefficient β_2 will be negative if price transmission in lagging states is more imperfect than in leading states.

Exports

If protection and world prices are transmitted to the leading and lagging states to different degrees, and that causes the differential effects of trade on poverty in leading relative to lagging states, then this could happen through differences in the product mixes of the two types of states. The easiest thing that comes to mind here is to look for the importance of export goods in the overall product mix. We explore whether lagging or leading states produce export-oriented goods as a larger proportion of their output by running the following regression:

$$q_{kit} = \alpha + \beta_1 \text{exp}_{kt} + \beta_2 \text{exp}_{kt}*\text{Lag}_i + \mu_t + \varepsilon_{kit} \qquad (4.4)$$

where q_{kit} is output (measured by net value added) in industry k in state i at time t as a proportion of total output in state i at time t and exp$_{kt}$ is the value of exports from India in industry k at time t as a proportion of overall national exports at time t. If leading states specialize in net export goods and lagging states in other goods we would expect to see a negative β_2.

Productivity

While trade can affect poverty and incomes by making countries more specialized in certain goods and by increasing competition, trade can also force firms to be more efficient and can make them invest more in R&D. Thus productivity is expected to increase through trade, unless the loss in market size for domestic import-competing firms offsets this effect. However, due to the differential transmission across states, the effect of trade liberalization on productivity might differ across leading and lagging states. Also, factor markets can be more rigid in the lagging states, coming in the way of resource reallocation in response to trade liberalization. To estimate the trend in productivity and to see whether the trends are the same or different across leading and lagging states, we estimate the following regression:

$$\log q_{kit} = \alpha + \beta_1 \log K_{kit} + \beta_2 \log L_{kit} + \beta_3 t + \beta_4 t^* \text{Lag}_i + \delta_i + \zeta_k + \varepsilon_{kit} \quad (4.5)$$

where q_{kit}, K_{kit}, and L_{kit} refer to net value added, capital stock, and employment in industry k in state i at time t, and ζ_k are industry fixed effects. We expect a negative β_4 if productivity has been rising more slowly in lagging states. If the trends are actually different, this difference may be caused by the fact, trade affects the two types of states differently. To find this out we focus on the impact of trade policy on industry productivity in India by estimating:

$$\log q_{kit} = \alpha + \beta_1 \log K_{kit} + \beta_2 \log L_{kit} + \beta_3 \text{Lag}_i + \beta_4 \text{protection}_{kt}$$
$$+ \beta_5 \text{protection}_{kt}^* \text{Lag}_i + \zeta_k + \mu_t + \varepsilon_{kit} \quad (4.6)$$

where protection$_{kt}$ refers to either the tariff rate or the NTB coverage rate; μ_t are time fixed effects.

Trade and Poverty in South Asia

After running the above regressions for India, we need to generalize our findings to the extent possible with the limited data available for the other South Asian countries. To estimate the effects of trade liberalization on poverty and well-being in South Asia as a whole, we run cross-country regressions of the form:

$$h_{ct} = \alpha + \beta_1 t + \beta_2^* t^* T_{ct} + \varepsilon_{ct} \quad (4.7)$$

where h_{ct} refers to human development poverty in country c at time t and is measured by per capita GDP or percentage of population in households in poverty or the human development index (HDI); 't' is a trend, T_{ct} is the trade liberalization dummy that equals zero pre-liberalization and that equals one post-liberalization. To further study whether these trade liberalization effects on poverty trends depend on the proportion of national population in lagging regions, we estimate the equation:

$$b_{ct} = \alpha + \beta_1 t + \beta_2 {}^* t {}^* T_{ct} + \beta_3 {}^* t {}^* T_{ct} {}^* P \text{ Lagging}_{ct} +$$
$$\beta_4 {}^* t {}^* T_{ct} {}^* CB_{ct} + \beta_5 {}^* t {}^* T_{ct} {}^* \text{distance}_{ct} + \varepsilon_{ct} \qquad (4.8)$$

where P Lagging$_{ct}$; CB$_{ct}$ and distance$_{ct}$ are the proportion of the national population in lagging regions, the ratio of coastline to the total boundary and the national average distance to the capital city, respectively, for country c at time t.

Trade and Poverty for India

We start with the study of poverty trends in India and how they differ across leading and lagging states. This discussion is followed by an investigation of the effects of changes in protection on poverty, after controlling for common trends or time effects across states. As explained earlier, we allow the effect of protection on poverty to be different for leading and lagging states, mainly because price and protection transmission might be more imperfect in the lagging states. In addition, there are further imperfections in such states, some of which take the form of factor-market rigidities and can be partly responsible for the differential effects. We present these results in Tables 4.4, 4.5, and 4.6, where we use specifications (4.1) and (4.2), for overall and for rural and urban sectors, respectively. Column 1 of each table presents results for specification (4.1), where the DD poverty measure is regressed on a time trend, on the time trend interacted with the lagging state dummy, and on state fixed effects. In other words, we allow for the trend to differ between leading and lagging states and poverty to vary across states because of time-invariant, state-specific factors. Columns 2, 3, and 4 present results for specification (4.2), where the DD poverty measure is regressed on lagged protection, on lagged protection interacted with the lagging state dummy, and on state and time fixed effects. In other words, even controlling, through time effects, for the fact that poverty over time would change all over the country, for example, due to poverty alleviation programmes, we try to see whether protection and the reductions in them over time additionally affect how poverty changes in the various states. We also see how this variation in protection across states explains the variation in poverty across states. The variation in protection across states comes from the variation in the industrial composition of employment across these different states. However, because protection interacts with labour market institutions, distance from ports, and the quality of roads and road transportation, the effect of protection on poverty will be different for lagging and leading states. In columns 2, 3, and 4 of each table, the trade protection measures are lagged tariff rates, NTB rates, and the first principal component, respectively.

Results from column 1 of Tables 4.4, 4.5, and 4.6 indicate that poverty has been falling in all three sectors (urban, rural, and overall). Poverty seems to be falling faster in the urban than in the rural sector. This is not surprising because most of the trade liberalization took place in manufacturing and transmission of world prices, and trade policy is expected to be stronger in urban compared with rural areas. In addition, it is the urban sector that experiences industrialization and modernization. Though poverty is falling in all states, the positive and significant coefficient on the interaction between the time trend and the lagging state dummy suggests that it has been falling much more slowly in the lagging states.

Next we look at the differential effect of trade reforms as a possible cause for the differential trend. Here we control for time effects or trends

TABLE 4.4   Trade and Poverty—Overall Sector Dependent Variable: Log (DD Poverty Measure)

	(1) Time trend	(2) Protection = Tariff	(3) Protection = NTB	(4) Protection = Principal Component 1
Lagged protection		0.002	0.03**	0.19*
		(0.002)	(0.01)	(0.10)
Lagged protection*				
Lag		−0.01***	−0.01	-0.08*
		(0.002)	(0.004)	(0.05)
Time trend	−0.06***			
	(0.01)			
Time trend*Lag	0.02**			
	(0.01)			
Constant	5.76***	2.81***	0.37	3.46***
	(0.32)	(0.28)	(0.89)	(0.27)
State Fixed effects	Yes	Yes	Yes	Yes
Year Fixed effects	No	Yes	Yes	Yes
Observations	60	45	45	45
R-squared	0.93	0.96	0.96	0.96

Notes: Robust standard errors in parentheses. ***$p < 0.01$, **$p < 0.05$, *$p < 0.1$ Data are for years 1987, 1993, and 1999 for each of 15 Indian states. Lag is equal to one if state is a lagging state, zero otherwise. Tariffs and NTBs are expressed in percentage points. A 50 per cent tariff implies that the tariff variable equals 50.

that are common across all states, and see whether, after controlling for these common effects, we find an effect of protection on poverty that is different for lagging and leading regions. From columns 2, 3, and 4, some evidence suggests that trade protection is positively related to poverty in the leading states. From Table 4.4, column 2, disregarding the insignificance of the pure tariff term, a 1 percentage point decrease in the employment-weighted average tariff rate for a state decreases poverty there by 0.22 per cent overall in the leading states. From column 3, a 1 percentage point decrease in the NTB coverage rate decreases poverty by 3 per cent overall in the leading states, which seems rather large. Stronger results are obtained using the principal component combined measure of tariffs and NTBs. The coefficient of lagged protection is both positive and significant.

Next we look at whether the differential effect on leading versus lagging regions is more pronounced in urban or rural areas. From column 2 in Tables 4.6 and 4.7, a 1 percentage point decrease in the tariff rate reduces poverty more in the urban than in the rural sector of leading states. It

TABLE 4.5   Trade and Poverty—Rural Sector Dependent Variable: Log (DD Poverty Measure)

	(1) Time trend	(2) Protection = Tariff	(3) Protection = NTB	(4) Protection = Principal Component 1
Lagged protection		0.002	0.02*	0.13
		(0.002)	(0.01)	(0.11)
Lagged protection* Lag		−0.01**	-0.01	−0.08*
		(0.002)	(0.005)	(0.05)
Time trend	−0.05***			
	(0.01)			
Time trend*Lag	0.02*			
	(0.01)			
Constant	5.62***	4.01***	1.72	3.64***
	(0.34)	(0.37)	(1.25)	(0.30)
State Fixed effects	Yes	Yes	Yes	Yes
Year Fixed effects	No	Yes	Yes	Yes
Observations	60	45	45	45
R-squared	0.93	0.96	0.95	0.96

Notes: Robust standard errors in parentheses. ***$p < 0.01$, **$p < 0.05$, *$p < 0.1$. Data are for years 1987, 1993, and 1999 for each of 15 Indian states. Lag is equal to one if state is a lagging state, zero otherwise. Tariffs and NTBs are expressed in percentage points. A 50 per cent tariff implies that the tariff variable equals 50.

TABLE 4.6   Trade and Poverty—Urban Sector Dependent Variable: Log (DD Poverty Measure)

	(1) Time trend	(2) Protection = Tariff	(3) Protection = NTB	(4) Protection = Principal Component 1
Lagged protection		0.003	0.01	0.16
		(0.005)	(0.01)	(0.17)
Lagged protection*				
Lag		−0.004***	−0.01***	−0.10***
		(0.001)	(0.002)	(0.03)
Time trend	−0.07***			
	(0.01)			
Time trend*Lag	0.03***			
	(0.01)			
Constant	6.03***	2.45***	2.04*	3.47***
	(0.29)	(0.65)	(0.99)	(0.28)
State Fixed effects	Yes	Yes	Yes	Yes
Year Fixed effects	No	Yes	Yes	Yes
Observations	60	45	45	45
R-squared	0.91	0.96	0.95	0.95

Notes: Robust standard errors in parentheses. ***$p < 0.01$, **$p < 0.05$, *$p < 0.1$. Data are for years 1987, 1993, and 1999 for each of 15 Indian states. Lag is equal to one if state is a lagging state, zero otherwise. Tariffs and NTBs are expressed in percentage points. A 50 per cent tariff implies that the tariff variable equals 50.

decreases poverty by 0.19 per cent in the rural sector and by 0.26 per cent in the urban sector in the leading states. While the lagged protection measure always has the correct sign, it is significant in the case of NTB for the rural case and for the combined measure for the overall case.

However, not surprisingly and possibly due to differences in the transmission of world prices and protection, the impact of trade liberalization on reducing poverty is smaller in the lagging states (and sometimes goes in the opposite direction) as seen by the negative coefficient on the interaction between protection and the lagging state dummy. The negative coefficient on the interaction term is always significant when the tariff or the first principal component is used for measuring protection. From Table 4.4, column 2, a 1 percentage point decrease in the tariff *increases* poverty by roughly 0.8 per cent in lagging states in the overall sector. From Table 4.5, column 2, we see that in the rural sector a 1 percentage point decrease in the tariff also *increases* poverty by approximately 0.8 per cent, which is much higher than the increase of

0.15 per cent in the urban sector (Table 4.6, column 2). Since the pure tariff term is insignificant (that is, its effect is not precisely measured), it is difficult to say in all the above cases whether trade liberalization actually increased poverty in the lagging states or just whether the reduction in poverty in such states was smaller than in others. When NTB rates are used as a protection measure, the interaction term is no longer significant in the overall and rural sectors, but it is still negative. Thus, from our results, we conclude that while poverty has been decreasing across all states, it has been falling more slowly in lagging states. Besides, trade liberalization may have reduced poverty overall, but it actually could have increased poverty in the lagging states of the country. At the very least, the poverty-reducing effects of trade liberalization were not as large in the case of the lagging states. Our results also suggest that urban areas have benefited more from trade liberalization than rural ones.

To ascertain whether our results are robust to alternative measures of poverty, we use the GOI and ODR measures of poverty to estimate

TABLE 4.7   Trade and Poverty—Overall Sector Dependent Variable: Log (GoI Measure)

	(1) Time trend	(2) Protection = Tariff	(3) Protection = NTB	(4) Protection = Principal Component 1
Lagged protection		0.004*	0.03**	0.24***
		(0.002)	(0.01)	(0.08)
Lagged protection* Lag		–0.01***	–0.01**	–0.09**
		(0.002)	(0.003)	(0.04)
Time trend	–0.04***			
	(0.005)			
Time trend*Lag	0.02***			
	(0.01)			
Constant	4.87***	2.87***	0.86	3.47***
	(0.21)	(0.30)	(0.85)	(0.21)
State Fixed effects	Yes	Yes	Yes	Yes
Year Fixed effects	No	Yes	Yes	Yes
Observations	60	45	45	45
R-squared	0.94	0.96	0.95	0.96

Notes: Robust standard errors in parentheses. ***p < 0.01, ** p < 0.05, *p < 0.1. Data are for years 1987, 1993, and 1999 for each of 15 Indian states. Lag is equal to one if state is a lagging state, zero otherwise. Tariffs and NTBs are expressed in percentage points. A 50 per cent tariff implies that the tariff variable equals 50.

TABLE 4.8   Trade and Poverty—Overall Sector Dependent Variable:
Log (ODR Measure)

	(1) Time trend	(2) Protection = Tariff	(3) Protection = NTB	(4) Protection = Principal Component 1
Lagged protection		0.01***	0.01	0.52***
		(0.003)	(0.01)	(0.08)
Lagged protection*				
Lag		−0.001	−0.004**	−0.01
		(0.001)	(0.002)	(0.02)
Time trend	−0.02***			
	(0.001)			
Time trend*Lag	0.01***			
	(0.001)			
Constant	3.98***	2.87***	2.75**	2.18***
	(0.04)	(0.28)	(1.33)	(0.19)
State Fixed effects	Yes	Yes	Yes	Yes
Year Fixed effects	No	Yes	Yes	Yes
Observations	591	150	150	150
R-squared	0.79	0.91	0.90	0.92

Notes: Robust standard errors in parentheses. ***$p < 0.01$, **$p < 0.05$, *$p < 0.1$. Data are for years 1987, 1993, and 1999 for each of 15 Indian states. Lag is equal to one if state is a lagging state, zero otherwise. Tariffs and NTBs are expressed in percentage points. A 50 per cent tariff implies that the tariff variable equals 50.

specifications (4.1) and (4.2) for the overall sector. A discussion of the pros and cons of these alternative measures can be found in Hasan et al. (2007). The results with our alternative poverty measures are presented in Tables 4.7 and 4.8, both of which are structured exactly like Tables 4.4, 4.5, and 4.6.

The results are qualitatively similar. We find strong evidence that trade liberalization has reduced poverty across all states in India. The coefficient on the lagged protection measure is positive and significant except in one case where the ODR poverty measure is used to measure poverty and the NTB measure to capture protection. The coefficient on lagged protection interacted with the lagging state dummy is always negative and significant except in the case of the ODR measure of poverty where the tariff or the first principal component is used to measure protection. Tables 4.7 and 4.8 support the idea that the poverty-reducing impact of trade liberalization is weaker in lagging states than in leading ones.

Thus, looking overall across all three poverty measures, there seems to be a fair amount of evidence in support of a poverty-reducing effect of trade liberalization across all states, but the effects turn out to be smaller for the lagging states. As explained earlier, this could be due to poorer transmission of world prices and protection in the lagging states as well as greater distance to ports and poorer quality roads in such states. In addition, factor markets probably work better and more smoothly in the leading states. Similar reasons also lead to decreases in the tariff rate leading to bigger reductions in poverty in the urban than in the rural sector of leading states, that is, there is probably better transmission of world prices and protection to urban areas where factor markets are also more efficient.

Price Transmission in India

After finding the differential impacts of trade on poverty and measures of well-being across lagging and leading states, we need to identify the sources of these differential effects. A likely source is poor transmission of world prices and protection, with the extent of the lack of transmission being different in lagging and leading states. Lagging states are not as well connected to ports as are leading states. Also, the quality of roads and their connections to main highways may be much poorer in lagging states. To confirm the correlation between distance from ports and the likelihood of being classified as lagging as opposed to leading, we ran a regression of the logarithm of inverse distance from ports on the lag dummy and found that moving from a leading to a lagging state reduces mean inverse distance by about 25 per cent (increases distance by 25 per cent). The coefficient on Lag is significant at the 10 per cent level.

We next investigate directly the degree of incompleteness of transmission of world prices and protection and the degree to which this differs across lagging and leading states by running specification(4.3). Table 4.9, columns 1 and 2, present results for the rural sector and columns 3 and 4 present results for the urban sector. Our objective is to find out whether the impact of a tariff on unit prices differs between lagging and leading states. In columns 1 and 3, we present results for specification (4.3) for the rural and urban sector respectively with (1 + tariff) and (1 + NTB rate) as our protection measures. If transmission of trade policy to domestic prices is less perfect in lagging states, we would expect the interaction between the trade protection measures and the lagging state dummy to be negative. From columns 1 and 3, we see that this is indeed the case for the tariff measure. In all cases, protection and

TABLE 4.9   Price Transmission Regressions Dependent Variable: Log (Unit Price for Sector)

	Rural sector		Urban sector	
	(1)	(2)	(3)	(4)
Log (1+tariff)	0.60*	0.77***	0.61	0.81
	(0.32)	(0.27)	(0.47)	(0.50)
Log (1+tariff)* Lag	−0.26	−0.36*	−0.08	−0.45*
	(0.43)	(0.20)	(0.53)	(0.25)
Log (1+NTB)	−0.17		−0.21	
	(0.20)		(0.24)	
Log (1+NTB)* Lag	0.11		0.39	
	(0.34)		(0.36)	
Log (world price)	0.28	0.28	0.54**	0.53**
	(0.31)	(0.32)	(0.21)	(0.21)
Log (world price)* Lag	−0.22	−0.21	0.0003	0.01
	(0.15)	(0.14)	(0.11)	(0.11)
Log (exchange rate)	−0.38***	−0.35**	−0.06	−0.05
	(0.15)	(0.15)	(0.10)	(0.10)
Log (inverse distance)* Log (1+tariff)	−0.006	−0.006	−0.10	−0.10
	(0.07)	(0.07)	(0.11)	(0.12)
Log (inverse distance)* Log (world price)	−0.06	−0.06	−0.006	−0.006
	(0.07)	(0.07)	(0.05)	(0.05)
Constant	4.39***	4.17***	2.55***	2.51***
	(0.67)	(0.60)	(0.46)	(0.46)
State fixed effects	Yes	Yes	Yes	Yes
Observations	265	265	266	266
Number of states	15	15	15	15
R-squared	0.13	0.13	0.19	0.19

Notes: Bootstrap standard errors in parentheses ***p < 0.01, **p < 0.05, *p < 0.1. Data are for years 1988, 1994, and 2000 for 16 goods in each of 15 Indian states. Lag is equal to one if state is a lagging state, zero otherwise. Tariffs and NTBs are expressed in fractions. For instance, a 50 per cent tariff implies that tariff = 0.5

its interaction have the right signs, but we have statistical significance for only half of these relevant terms in these two columns of Table 4.10. Subject to the caveat that not all coefficients are precisely estimated, we can say from columns 1 and 3 that for the rural sector, a 1 per cent increase in (1 + tariff) implies a 0.60 per cent increase in the unit price in leading states but a 0.34 per cent increase in the unit price in the lagging states. For the urban sector, a 1 per cent increase in (1 + tariff) implies a 0.61 per cent increase in the unit price in the leading states but a 0.53 per cent increase in the unit price in the lagging states. For the NTB protection measure, however, the coefficients are not estimated precisely. Hasan et al. (2007) point out that the statistical insignificance of the NTB term might be caused by the fact that the NTB measure is a coverage ratio, and it is not clear what exact functional form captures its transmission into domestic prices.

In columns 2 and 4, we drop the NTB measure and the interaction between the NTB measure and the lagging state dummy. The results support our hypothesis that transmission is less perfect for lagging states than for leading ones. The coefficient on (1 + tariff) is positive and it is significant for the rural sector. The coefficient on the interaction between (1 + tariff) and the lagging state dummy is now negative and significant at the 5 per cent level for both rural and urban sectors. Results indicate that for the rural sector, although a 1 per cent increase in (1 + tariff)[9] implies an increase in domestic unit price of 0.77 per cent for leading states, it is only 0.41 per cent for lagging states. For the urban sector, a 1 per cent increase in (1 + tariff) implies an increase in the domestic unit price of 0.81 per cent for leading states but an increase of 0.36 per cent for lagging states. In all our regressions, the exchange rate enters with a negative coefficient that is significant for the rural sector but not for the urban sector. The coefficients on the inverse distance interacted with (1 + tariff) and coefficients on the inverse distance interacted with the world price are always negative but never significant.

We conclude that there is evidence of less than perfect price transmission in lagging versus leading states, with some estimates suggesting that this is an even greater issue in rural areas. This result makes sense if connectedness is a larger problem for rural areas than urban ones, which is not unreasonable in most developing countries.

Exports in India

Having found evidence for the imperfect transmission of prices and protection and for this effect to be stronger in lagging states, we next focus on one of the channels through which this imperfect transmission affects development. One of the ways this happens is through the differences in the product mix. At the very basic level, the degree of specialization in export-oriented goods might be different in the lagging and leading

[9]For our price transmission regressions, we express tariff rates and NTB rates as fractions. In other words, a 50 per cent tariff implies that our tariff measure is 0.5. At a 50 per cent tariff, a 1 per cent increase in (1 + tariff) is a 3 per cent increase in our tariff measure.

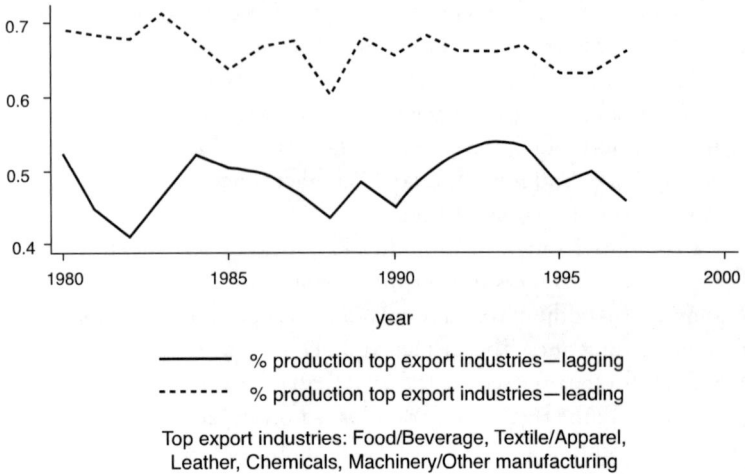

FIGURE 4.1   Production of Export Goods in Leading
and Lagging States

Sources: Annual Survey of Industries (ASI) production data;
NBER–UN World Export Import Data (Feenstra and Lipsey 2005).

states. In Figure 4.1, we plot output, which is measured by net value added in export industries, as a percentage of total output in leading and lagging states over time.

Export industries are food/beverages, textile/apparel, leather, basic chemicals, and machinery/other manufacturing.[10] The share of export goods in total output is larger for leading states for all years. Further, we employ specification (4.4) to study if, after controlling for time-specific shocks, leading states produce more export goods than lagging states. We regress output—which is measured by net value added in an industry in a state in a given year—as a proportion of total output of that state in that year on national exports of an industry, as a percentage of total national exports in a given year, on this export ratio measure interacted with the lagging state dummy and on year fixed effects.

Results shown in Table 4.10 provide evidence that leading states specialize more in export goods in comparison with lagging states. The interaction between exports and the lagged state dummy is negative and strongly significant showing that leading states specialize in the

[10]These industries have the largest export shares in the Feenstra, Lipsey, and colleagues NBER–UN World Export Import data (1980–97).

TABLE 4.10   Production of Export Goods in Lagging Versus Leading States Dependent Variable: Output in Industry-state/ Total State Output

	(1)
Exports in industry/total exports	0.44***
	(0.02)
(Exports in industry/total exports)*Lag	–0.14***
	(0.03)
Constant	0.05***
	(0.01)
State/Industry fixed effects	No
Year fixed effects	Yes
Observations	3348
R-squared	0.12

Notes: Robust standard errors in parentheses.
***p < 0.01, **p < 0.05, *p < 0.1.
Data are for years 1980 to 1997 for 16 Indian states in 12 broad industry groups
Lag is equal to one if state is a lagging state, zero otherwise.

production of export goods. This is not surprising because the lowering of protection through trade liberalization is transmitted more to leading states and, therefore, we have greater specialization in those states.

Productivity in Indian Manufacturing

The second proximate cause for the difference in the impact of trade on development across the lagging and leading states is possibly the difference in the productivity effects of trade liberalization. We use the production function approach with total factor productivity (TFP), depending on the various trade policy variables and their interactions with the lagging state dummy showing the differential effect mentioned earlier. As explained earlier, by increasing competition, trade can also force firms to be more efficient and can make them invest more in R&D. Thus productivity is expected to increase through trade, unless the loss in market size for domestic import-competing firms offsets this effect. However, due to the differential transmission across states, the effect of trade liberalization on productivity might differ across leading and lagging states. Also, factor markets can be more rigid in the lagging states, coming in the way of resource reallocation in response to trade liberalization.

Table 4.11, column 1, presents results for specification (4.5). We find evidence that productivity in Indian manufacturing has been rising, as shown by the positive and significant coefficient of the trend variable. The

TABLE 4.11   Trade Liberalization and Productivity
Dependent Variable: Log (Net Value Added)

	(1)	(2)	(3)
Log (capital stock)	0.39***	0.42***	0.42***
	(0.01)	(0.02)	(0.02)
Log (employment)	0.69***	0.63***	0.63***
	(0.02)	(0.02)	(0.02)
Time trend	0.0***		
	(0.002)		
Time trend* Lag	−0.01**		
	(0.003)		
Lag		−0.25	−0.12
		(0.18)	(0.23)
Log (tariff)		−0.41***	
		(0.10)	
Log (tariff)* Lag		0.03	
		(0.04)	
Log (NTB)			0.16**
			(0.08)
Log (NTB)* Lag			0.03
			(0.06)
Constant	4.82***	6.18***	5.28***
	(0.18)	(0.43)	(0.35)
State fixed effects	Yes	No	No
Industry fixed effects	Yes	Yes	Yes
Time fixed effects	No	Yes	Yes
Observations	4672	2592	2592
R-squared	0.92	0.91	0.91

Notes: Robust standard errors in parentheses. ***p < 0.01, **p < 0.05, *p < 0.1. Data are for 16 Indian states in 18 broad industry groups. Data for column 1 are for years 1980–97. Data for columns 2 and 3 are for 1988–97. Lag is equal to one if state is a lagging state, zero otherwise. Tariffs and NTBs are expressed in percentage points. A 50 per cent tariff implies that the tariff variable equals 50.

coefficient on the time trend interacted with the lagging state dummy is negative and significant, suggesting that the increase in productivity has been much smaller for the lagging states. Column 2 presents results for specification (4.6) with the tariff rate as the protection measure. The coefficient on the tariff is negative and strongly significant. A 1 per cent decrease in the tariff rate increases productivity by 0.41 per cent across all leading states but only by 0.38 per cent in the lagging states (if we disregard the insignificance of the interaction term). The coefficient on the interaction term between the tariff and the lagging state dummy is not estimated precisely.

To check for robustness of our results, we use NTB rates as another measure of protection in our productivity regression. We present results in column 3. The results are not qualitatively different. The NTB rate enters with a negative coefficient that is significant at the 5 per cent level. The coefficient on the NTB rate interacted with the lagging state dummy is positive but not significant. To conclude, while there is strong evidence that trade liberalization has had a productivity-enhancing effect across all states and industries, we find weak evidence that the increase in productivity due to trade liberalization is smaller in lagging states.

Trade and Poverty in South Asia

We now want to see whether our results hold more generally for South Asia as a whole. Here we are constrained by data availability. But we try to do the best we can given the data available. We try to investigate whether the trend rate of growth in GDP per capita and the HDI and rate of reduction in poverty change as a result of trade liberalization. Also, we want to see whether the change is in the desired direction and whether the actual magnitude of the change depends on the population size of the lagging regions relative to leading regions, on the average distance of the various regions to the capital, and on the coastline relative to the overall national boundary. Thus, indirectly, we might be able to infer whether lagging regions grow faster or slower and whether the rate of reduction in poverty is slower or faster in them upon trade liberalization. Thus, we use specifications (4.7) and (4.8) to address these issues, and the results obtained from running these specifications are presented in Table 4.12.

In Table 4.12, columns 1 and 2, the dependent variable that measures well-being is the log of per capita GDP. In columns 3 and 4, it is a measure of poverty. More specifically, it is the log of the percentage of individuals living in households below the poverty line. In columns 5 and 6, the measure of well-being is the log of the HDI. From columns 1, 3, and 5, in which we regress measures of poverty or of well-being on a trend and the trend interacted with the trade liberalization dummy that equals one post-liberalization, one strong result emerges. Poverty as measured by the percentage of people below the poverty line is decreasing over time and well-being as measured by per capita GDP or the HDI is increasing over time. The coefficient of the trend in the HDI and per capita GDP

TABLE 4.12 Trade, Poverty, and Lagging Regions in South Asia

Variables	(1) ln(GDP per capita)	(2) ln(GDP per capita)	(3) ln(percentage in poverty)	(4) ln(percentage in poverty)	(5) ln(HDI)	(6) ln(HDI)
t	0.05***	0.03***	-0.02**	-0.01	0.01***	0.01***
	(0.005)	(0.006)	(0.01)	(0.02)	(0.003)	(0.002)
$t*T_{ct}$	-0.01***	-0.01***	0.002	0.01	0.002**	-0.0001
	(0.002)	(0.002)	(0.006)	(0.01)	(0.001)	(0.001)
$t*T_{ct}*$(proportion population in lagging regions)		-0.01***		0.01		-0.003*
		(0.002)		(0.01)		(0.002)
$t*T_{ct}*$(coastline/total land boundary)		0.03***		-0.04***		0.01***
		(0.001)		(0.001)		(0.0009)
$t*T_{ct}*$(national average distance to capital)		9.27e-06***		3.03e-06		9.16e-07**
		(6.33e-07)		(2.83e-06)		(3.73e-07)
Constant	5.55***	6.06***	4.40***	3.88***	-1.09***	-1.12***
	(0.16)	(0.18)	(0.29)	(0.74)	(0.08)	(0.07)
Observations	181	119	31	21	171	124
R-squared	0.40	0.60	0.10	0.38	0.35	0.55

Notes: Robust standard errors in parentheses. ***$p < 0.01$, **$p < 0.05$, *$p < 0.1$. Data are for years 1961 through 2007 for eight South Asian countries. t is a time trend and T_{ct} is a time dummy that equals one post liberalization.

regressions are positive and strongly significant, and the coefficient of the trend in the poverty regression is negative and significant.

However, the impact of trade liberalization on trends in poverty and well-being are less obvious. From Table 4.12, column 1, although per capita GDP is increasing over time, it grows more slowly post-liberalization. The coefficient on the interaction term between the trend and the trade liberalization dummy is negative and significant. Specifically, the percentage increase in per capita GDP is less by 1.14 percentage points in the post-liberalization period. However, in the case of HDI, the result is the opposite. The coefficient on the interaction term between the trend and the trade liberalization dummy in the HDI regression is positive and significant and suggests that HDI is increasing over time and that the increase is larger post-liberalization. The annual growth rate of HDI is larger by 0.25 percentage points in the period post liberalization. In column 2, we see from the negative coefficient of the trend and the positive coefficient of the interaction between the trend and the trade liberalization dummy that although the percentage of individuals living in poverty is falling over time, this decrease is smaller post-liberalization. However, the interaction effect is statistically insignificant. We conclude that the impact of trade liberalization on poverty is ambiguous. While evidence suggests that trade liberalization was somewhat negatively correlated with per capita income growth (possibly due to macroeconomic factors that accompany or even trigger liberalization episodes), it seems to help growth in human development.

We now examine whether the impact of trade liberalization differs by the percentage of the population living in lagging regions. Given the lack of data on the various regions within each country, this would be our indirect way of finding out whether lagging regions gain less from trade than leading regions all over South Asia. Table 4.13, columns 2, 4, and 6, decomposes the effect of trade on the trends in poverty and well-being. Here our results are clearer. From column 1, we find that the negative effect of trade liberalization on the growth rate of per capita GDP is exacerbated in countries that have a larger population in lagging regions. The coefficient on the triple interaction between the trend, the trade liberalization dummy, and the percentage of population in lagging regions is negative. Results indicate that a one-point increase in the proportion of population in lagging regions depresses the growth in per capita GDP after trade liberalization further by 0.01 percentage points.[11] Because

---

[11]Note that the proportion of population in lagging regions is measured not in percentage terms but as fraction in our data, that is, the scale is 0–1 and not 0–100.

(a) Inequality

TABLE 4.13a Inequality

(1)	(2)	(3)	(4)	(5)	(6)	(7)	(8)
	Liberalization				Income share of the bottom 20 percent		
Country		1981–5	1986–90	1991–5	1996–2000	2001–5	2006–7
Bangladesh	1996	9.72	9.73	9.35	8.70	8.76	
India	1994					8.08	
Nepal	1991				7.47	6.02	
Pakistan	2001		8.29	8.82	9.33	9.26	
Sri Lanka	1977–83, 1991	8.19	8.95		8.14	6.99	

Source: World Development Indicators (2009).

TABLE 4.13b Poverty

(1)	(2)	(3)	(4)	(5)	(6)	(7)
	Liberalization			% individuals in households below poverty line		
Country		1986–90	1991–5	1996–2000	2001–5	2006–7
Bangladesh	1996	52.50	51.13	56.11	50.47	
India (Rural)	1994	55.60	52.46	43.83		
India (Urban)	1994	47.50	40.77	36.16		
Nepal	1991		68.44		55.12	
Pakistan	2001	65.59	23.87	38.60	29.23	
Sri Lanka	1977–83, 1991	15.01	16.32		13.95	

Source: PovcalNet, World Bank.

this is the effect on the annual rate of growth, over time, this benefit will accumulate and become fairly significant. Similarly, a one-point increase in the proportion of population in lagging regions decreases the annual rate of decline in poverty by an additional 0.01 percentage points, but this is statistically insignificant. Thus a country that has 90 per cent of its population in lagging regions can raise its rate of decline in poverty by about 0.4 percentage points if it reduces this population in lagging areas to 50 per cent. For a country with 300 million poor, this means an additional annual reduction of about 1.2 million poor per year. We find stronger results for HDI in terms of statistical significance but weaker results in terms of the magnitude of coefficients. For countries with a larger proportion of population in lagging regions, trade liberalization negatively affected the growth in HDI.

With regard to our control variables, having a higher ratio of coastline to the boundary seems to either reinforce the beneficial effect of trade liberalization or mitigate the negative trade liberalization effects. In two out of the three regressions, having a higher national average distance to the capital city also seems to either dampen the negative effects of trade liberalization on poverty and well-being and boost the positive effects. This is surprising. However, it is possible that what we need is a measure of 'effective' distance to the capital city, one that takes into account transport costs and infrastructure—for instance, the time taken to travel to the capital city. In the absence of such measures, the distance variable may just be proxying for the size (geographic area) of a country, which captures external or agglomeration economies.

IMPLICATIONS FOR SOUTH ASIA

Many South Asian countries began active trade liberalization in the 1990s: Sri Lanka was an exception and introduced trade reform as early as the late 1970s. India started its liberalization process in 1991 after it had to seek IMF help for a debt crisis. India's tariff and NTB reductions have been gradual. Bangladesh, on the other hand, started in the late 1980s and early 1990s with significant reductions in tariffs and quantitative restrictions, generating concerns domestically of foreign competition hurting import-competing industries. However, Bangladesh has seen fast growth in exports since the 1990s in the textiles, garments, footwear, and leather sectors.

The literature on trade, poverty, and inequality and our current study have several implications for South Asia's trade liberalization experience. One implication is that initial conditions affect the impact that trade liberalization will have on poverty. High-income inequality or spatial inequality will imply fewer benefits from trade liberalization for the poor. Tables 4.13(a) and 4.13(b) show the income share held by the bottom 20 per cent and the percentage of individuals in households below the $1.25 a day poverty line in these countries, respectively, over time, averaged over five-year intervals. Trade liberalization dates are provided in column 2. The figures show that Sri Lanka experienced a slight increase in the percentage of individuals below the poverty line just after liberalization (though poverty fell later). For Sri Lanka, the percentage of poor went up from 15.01 per cent in the 1986–90 period to 16.32 in the 1991–5 period. Focusing on inequality as measured by the income share of the bottom 20 per cent, both these countries either had falling (or relatively stable) income shares of the bottom 20 per cent before liberalization, indicating increasing inequality.

Pakistan's experience on the other hand is different. Income shares of the bottom 20 per cent rose prior to liberalization. The income share rose from 8.82 in the 1991–5 period to 9.33 in the 1993–2000 period. Also, the percentage of poor in Pakistan dropped significantly from 38.60 per cent to 29.23 immediately after reform. Although we cannot make concrete conclusions based on these trends, it appears like increasing inequality prior to liberalization went along with a spike in poverty post-reform before poverty started falling again. Table 4.14 shows some inequality and infrastructure measures for each country for 2006/7. Bangladesh, India, and Nepal show higher regional inequality as measured by above-average poor in the most lagging region as a percentage of the total poor in the economy. For these countries, a priority would be to ensure integration of backward regions and government redistribution programmes to lessen inequality so that the poor may also benefit from trade reforms.

Another implication that emerges from the literature is the importance of infrastructure, credit provision, investment in human capital, flexible labour markets, and better institutions (like rule of law and contract enforcement mechanisms) to ensure that the benefits of trade liberalization reach the poor. From Table 4.14, column 7, Bangladesh, India, and Pakistan perform better than Nepal and Sri Lanka in terms of overall infrastructure. In terms of road and rail density, however, India, Pakistan, and Sri Lanka fare better than Bangladesh and Nepal. Bangladesh, Pakistan, and Sri Lanka seem to have above-average airport (with paved runway) coverage, while Bangladesh has better port coverage than the rest. While more and better ports facilitate trade, higher rail

TABLE 4.14   Infrastructure and Inequality Indicators for 2007

(1)	(2) Surface area (km square) /airports	(3) Rail density (kms per 100 km square)	(4) Road density (kms per 100 km square)	(5) Poor in most lagging region as % of country's poor	(6) Index of shipping difficulties	(7) Infrastructure index (1 = worst performer, 5 = best performer)	(8) Ports (number)	(9) Coastline (kms)/ports
	(2007)	(2006)	(2006)	(2006)	(2006)	(2007)	(2007)	(2007)
Bangladesh	9600	2.10	183.80	28.20	112	2.29	2	290
India	13527.82	2.10	113.80	12.20	79	2.90	8	875
Nepal	14718	0	12.20	12.40	151	1.77	0	0
Pakistan	8748.35	1.10	33.50	1	94	2.37	2	523
Sri Lanka	4686.43	2.20	150.50	4	60	2.13	2	670
Mean	10256.12	1.50	98.76	11.56	99.20	2.29	2.80	471.60

Source: World Bank (2009a).

TABLE 4.15   Adult Literacy in South Asia

Country	1991–5	1996–2000	2001–5
Bangladesh	35.32		47.49
India	48.22		61.01
Nepal	32.98		48.59
Pakistan		42.85	46.44
Sri Lanka			90.68

Source: World Development Indicators (2009)·

and road density help to reduce transportation costs to lagging regions, thereby ensuring the transmission of world prices to these regions. Hence, it is important to ensure both.

While Bangladesh has better overall infrastructure and better airport and port coverage, developing road and rail density might help target the benefits of trade liberalization towards the poor in Bangladesh's lagging regions. Pakistan appears to have better infrastructure overall and Sri Lanka lags behind in port coverage. India, Pakistan, and Sri Lanka also have smaller indexes of shipping difficulties, which can be a crude measure of institutions. Nepal and Bangladesh have large indexes. Shipping difficulties might arise as a result of the quality of infrastructure at the ports or due to corruption and other institutional failure at the border (customs). Given that Bangladesh performs fairly well with respect to its infrastructure indicators, shipping difficulties might be an indication of corrupt officials or red tape at the border. Further research in this area might help uncover precise policy implications. Table 4.15 gives average literacy rates across five-year periods from 1991 to 2005. Sri Lanka has the highest literacy rates with 90 per cent literacy in the 2000–5 period, and the other South Asian countries seem to have made significant progress in spreading literacy (Nepal went from 33 per cent literacy in the 1991–5 period to 49 per cent literacy in the 2000–5 period). However, literacy rates in India, Nepal, and Pakistan are still low. Continued efforts to increase literacy rates and focus on investment in higher and technical education will promote better distribution of trade gains to the poor by allowing domestic industry to benefit from cheap capital imports to improve production technologies.

CONCLUSION

We find evidence that, for India, poverty has been decreasing over time in Indian states but more slowly in lagging states. While there is strong evidence that trade liberalization led to a decline in poverty

across all leading states, there is evidence that either this decline arising from trade liberalization was smaller or that there may not have been a decline in poverty due to trade liberalization in the lagging states. We see that though productivity has been increasing in Indian manufacturing across all states, it has been increasing more slowly in lagging states. Our results indicate strong evidence that trade liberalization has increased productivity in Indian manufacturing. However, there is weak evidence that the increase in productivity because of trade liberalization has been smaller in lagging states.

Transmission of tariffs to domestic prices in India seems to be less perfect in lagging states, especially in rural areas. We propose that this might be due to poor infrastructure in these states as measured by distance of the state capital from all ports. Results show that leading states in India specialize primarily in export goods.

We use our results for India to examine the importance of regional inequality in availing the benefits of trade reform for the South Asia region as a whole. Measuring regional inequality by the percentage of population in South Asian countries that lives in lagging regions, we find strong support for the hypothesis that more regionally integrated economies are better able to exploit gains from liberalization. We also draw policy implications of the literature and our empirical analysis for South Asia.

Our study confirms that though trade liberalization brings gains, there is scope for policy to ensure that these gains are distributed more equally. Our results highlight the importance of developing infrastructure, including equipped ports, better and more extensive roads, and communication links in exploiting the gains from trade.

REFERENCES

Aghion Philippe, Robin Burgess, Stephen Redding, and Fabrizio Zilibotti. 2006. 'The Unequal Effects of Liberalization: Evidence from Dismantling the License Raj in India', NBER Working Paper No. 12031, National Bureau of Economic Research, Cambridge, MA.

Baldwin, Robert. 2003. 'Openness and Growth: What is the Empirical Relationship?', NBER Working Paper No. 9578, National Bureau of Economic Research, Cambridge, MA.

Bhagwati, J. 1978. *Foreign Trade Regimes and Economic Development: Anatomy of Exchange Control Regimes*. Cambridge, MA: Ballinger.

Deaton, Angus. 2003. 'Adjusted Indian Poverty Estimates for 1999/2000', *Economic and Political Weekly*, 25: 322–6.

Deaton, Angus and Jean Dreze. 2002. 'Poverty and Inequality in India—A Re-examination', *Economic and Political Weekly*, 7: 3729–48.

Dollar, David. 1992. 'Outward-Oriented Developing Economies Really Do Grow More Rapidly: Evidence from 95 LDCs, 1976–1985', *Economic Development and Cultural Change*, 40 (3): 523–44.

Edwards, Sebastian. 1998. 'Openness, Productivity and Growth: What Do We Really Know?', *The Economic Journal*, 108 (447): 383–98.

Feenstra, Robert C. and Gordon H. Hanson. 1996. 'Globalization, Outsourcing and Wage Inequality', *American Economic Review*, 86: 240–5.

Feenstra, Robert, Robert Lipsey, Haiyan Deng, Alyson C. Ma, and Hengyong Mo. 2005. 'World Trade Flows', NBER Working Paper No. 11040, National Bureau of Economic Research, Cambridge, MA.

Frankel, Jeffrey and David Romer. 1999. 'Does Trade Cause Growth?', *American Economic Review*, 89 (3): 379–99.

Fujita, M., P. Krugman, and A.J. Venables. 1999. *The Spatial Economy: Cities, Regions, and International Trade*. Cambridge, MA: MIT Press.

Goetz, Stephen J. 1992. 'A Selectivity Model of Household Food Marketing Behavior in Sub-Saharan Africa', *American Journal of Agricultural Economics*, 74: 444–52.

Haddad, Eduardo, A. and Fernando S Perobelli. 2004. 'Trade Liberalization and Regional Inequality: Do Transportation Costs Impose A Spatial Poverty Trap?', Paper No. 131, Proceedings of the 32nd Brazilian Economics Meeting, Brazilian Association of Graduate Programs in Economics Sao Paulo.

Harrison, Ann. 2006. 'Globalization and Poverty', Mimeo, University of California–Berkeley.

Hasan, Rana, Devashish Mitra, and Beyza Ural. 2007. 'Trade Liberalization, Labor-Market Institutions and Poverty Reduction: Evidence from Indian States', *India Policy Forum*, 3: 71–122.

Hasan, Rana., M. G. Quibria, and Yangseon Kim. 2003. 'Poverty and Economic Freedom: Evidence from Cross-Country Data', *East-West Center Working Paper*.

Irwin, Douglas and Marko J. Tervio. 2002. 'Does Trade Raise Income? Evidence from the Twentieth Century', *Journal of International Economics*, 58: 1–18.

Krueger, A. 1978. *Foreign Trade Regimes and Economic Development: Liberalization Attempts and Consequences*. Cambridge, MA: Ballinger.

Minot, Nicholoas. 1998. 'Distributional and Nutritional Impact of Devaluation in Rwanda', *Economic Development and Cultural Change*, 46 (2): 379–402.

Ozler, Berk, Gaurav Datt, and Martin Ravallion. 1996. *A Database on Poverty and Growth in India*. Washington, D.C.: World Bank.

Panagariya, Arvind. 2008. *India: The Emerging Giant*. New York: Oxford University Press.

Pandey, Mihir. 1999. 'NCAER Report on Trade Protection in India', National Council of Applied Economic Research, New Delhi.

Pavcnik, Nina and Pinelopi K. Goldberg. 2004. 'Trade, Inequality and Poverty: What Do We Know? Evidence from Recent Trade Liberalization Episodes in

Developing Countries', NBER Working Paper No. 10593, National Bureau of Economic Research, Cambridge, MA.

Porto, Guido G. 2006. 'Using Survey Data to Assess the Distributional Effects of Trade Policy', *Journal of International Economics*, 70 (1): 140–60.

Ramaswamy, K.V. 2003. 'Globalization and Industrial Labor Markets in South Asia: Some Aspects of Adjustment in a Less Integrated Region', *Indian Journal of Labor Economics*, 46 (2): 253–74.

Ravallion, Martin. 2001. 'Growth, Inequality and Poverty: Looking Beyond Averages', *World Development*, 29 (11): 1803–15.

Rodrik, Dani and Francisco Rodriguez. 2001. 'Trade Policy and Economic Growth: A Skeptic's Guide to the Cross-National Evidence', in Ben Bernanke and Kenneth S. Rogoff (eds), *Macroeconomics Annual 2000*. Cambridge, MA: MIT Press for NBER.

Rodrik, Dani, Arvind Subramanian, and Francesco Trebbi. 2002. 'Institutions Rule: The Primacy of Institutions over Geography and Integration in Economic Development', Department of Economics Working Paper, Harvard University.

Sachs Jeffrey D., Andrew Warner, Anders Aslund, and Stanley Fischer. 1995. 'Economic Reform and the Process of Global Integration', *Brookings Papers on Economic Activity*, 1: 1–118.

Topalova, Petia. 2004. 'Trade Liberalization and Firm Productivity: The Case of India', IMF Working Paper No. WP/04/28, International Monetary Fund, Washington, D.C.

United Nations Development Program. 2008. *Human Development Report 2007/2008*. United Nations Development Program.

Wacziarg, Romain and Karen H. Welch. 2003. 'Trade Liberalization and Growth: New Evidence', NBER Working Paper No. 10152, National Bureau of Economic Research, Cambridge, MA.

Winters, Alan L., Neil McCulloch, and Andrew McKay. 2004. 'Trade Liberalization and Poverty: The Evidence So Far', *Journal of Economic Literature*, XLII: 72–115.

World Bank. 2009a. *World Development Report*. Washington, D.C.: World Bank.

———. 2009b. *World Development Indicators*. Washington, D.C.: World Bank.

5

Is Growth Constrained by Institutions?

Ana M. Fernandes, Maddalena Honorati, and Taye Mengistae

A good institutional environment provides the opportunities and incentives for firms to invest, create jobs, and expand, which are key for growth and poverty reduction (World Bank 2005). A growing consensus among academics and policymakers suggests that good institutional performance is indeed fundamental for economic development. A large body of cross-country empirical work has identified the importance of institutional quality for either growth or income levels.[1] Mauro (1995) and Knack and Keefer (1995) document the relationship between corruption and economic growth, while Hall and Jones (1999) and Rodrik et al. (2004) show that institutions exert an important causal effect on per capita incomes across countries.[2]

In this chapter, we examine the institutional quality of South Asian countries and the consequent development impact. Figure 5.1 shows a strong positive correlation between levels of per capita income and a widely used measure of institutional quality—that is, the 'rule-of-law' indicator of Kaufmann et al. (2005). The measure captures perceptions of the likelihood that property will be expropriated by the state, the likelihood that contracts will be enforced, the likelihood that property is secure from

---

[1]Another strand of the literature on institutions and growth has followed a historical perspective—for example, North and Weingast (1989) and Delong and Shleifer (1993).

[2]The analysis in this chapter draws heavily on Fernandes and Kraay (2007).

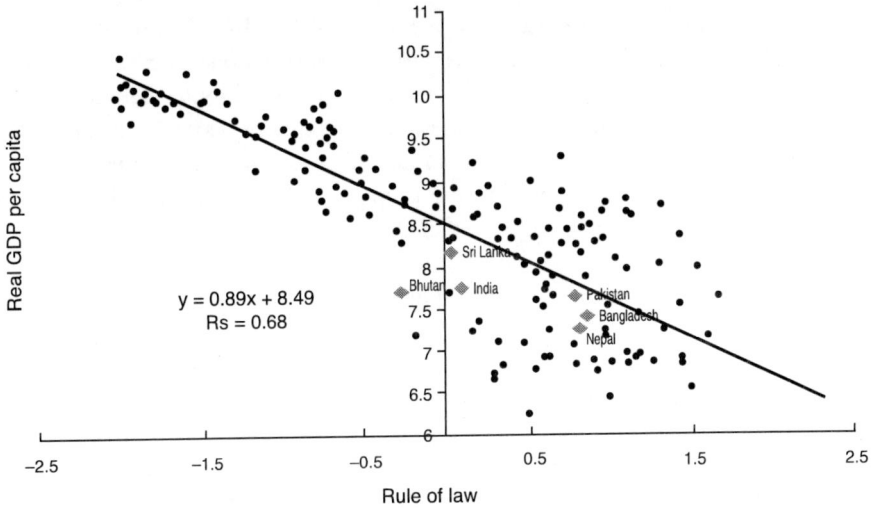

FIGURE 5.1   Rule of Law and Per Capita Incomes

Source: Fernandes and Kraay (2007).
Note: Real Gross Domestic Product (GDP) per Capita refers to the log of real GDP per capita in 1996, and Rule of Law to 2004. Higher values of the Rule of Law measure correspond to worse outcomes.

crime, and so on.[3] Countries with worse institutional quality are on average poorer than countries with good institutional quality. Bangladesh, Nepal, and Pakistan have fairly poor scores on this measure of institutional quality, which place them in the bottom quartile of all countries, whereas Bhutan, India, and Sri Lanka fare much better, around the median of all countries worldwide. A striking feature in Figure 5.1 is that all South Asian countries fall below the simple regression line of per capita incomes on measures of institutional quality. This suggests that, despite recent rapid growth, these countries have not yet reached the per capita incomes typical of countries with similar levels of institutional quality.

To dig deeper into the link between institutional quality and development, we follow Acemoglu and Johnson (2005) in distinguishing between (i) 'property rights institutions' that capture the extent to which private property is secure from predation by the state (for example, through expropriation, or from corrupt officials demanding bribes

[3]The authors combine information from a large number of cross-country sources measuring the perceptions of individuals, firms, commercial risk rating agencies, non-governmental organizations (NGOs), think-tanks, and multilateral development banks.

in exchange for favours to firms or individuals) and (ii) 'contracting institutions' that capture the effectiveness of institutions such as the judicial system used to enforce contracts or mediate disputes between private parties. The former can be viewed as institutions that mediate the 'vertical' relationship between firms or individuals and the state, while the latter mediate the 'horizontal' relationship among firms and individuals (for example, between debtors and creditors).

This chapter examines how countries in South Asia fare on these two key dimensions of institutional quality and how this affected their economic performance. To statistically identify the causal effect of institutional quality on development, it is crucial to exploit the cross-country variation in the quality of the two types of institutions, which is driven by their deep historical determinants. Regarding property rights institutions, Acemoglu et al. (2001) argue that their present strength can be traced to the interaction between countries' geographic features and their colonial experience. In countries where settler mortality was low, it was in the interests of the colonial powers to create institutions that protected property rights, at least those of the occupying settlers, and these institutions have persisted. Their measure of settler mortality in the eighteenth and nineteenth centuries across countries is used as the deep historical determinant of property rights institutions. Regarding contracting institutions, Djankov et al. (2003) show that countries that inherited common-law legal traditions tend to have more effective courts, in the sense that they have simpler and faster procedures and fairer outcomes. An indicator variable for British legal origins is used as the deep historical determinant of contracting institutions.

South Asian countries tend to fare poorly on the two dimensions of institutional quality. India has fairly average performance on 'contracting institutions' when looking at all countries, but it stands out as being one of the poorest performers among countries with British legal origins, a deep determinant of this type of institutions. By contrast, India fares reasonably well on measures of 'property rights institutions'. The reverse is true for Bangladesh, which stands out for having quite poor 'property rights institutions' but reasonable 'contracting institutions'.

Controlling for the deep historical determinants of the two types of institutions, the chapter shows that 'property rights institutions' matter much more for development than do 'contracting institutions'. The rationale for this finding is that private parties can respond to weak formal contracting institutions by developing alternative informal institutions but have little recourse to alternatives when they face a predatory state.

For this reason, contracting institutions appear to matter less for long-run growth than secure property rights institutions. We show where South Asian countries fall in the causal relationship between these two types of institutions and economic performance. India stands out for having a large negative residual, suggesting that even India's good performance on 'property rights institutions' has not yet had the development impact that cross-country analysis would suggest. By contrast, Bangladesh stands out in the opposite direction, with a predicted level of per capita income based on its institutional quality that is much lower than its actual per capita income levels. One interpretation for these findings is that India has a great deal of scope for future growth given its relatively good institutional performance, whereas Bangladesh's current relatively high income levels (given its weak institutional quality) are more likely to be unsustainable.

Good institutional quality plays a crucial role in fostering economic development across countries and in South Asia in particular. By relying on aggregate indicators, one assumes that the institutional environment is similar across locations within a country, when in fact important heterogeneity may be based on local governance. Many rationales can be proposed for why institutional quality will vary at the local level, even if institutional quality has an important national dimension. For example, in large countries such as India or Pakistan, the decentralization of economic policymaking likely leads to important differences in the enforcement of various types of institutions across states and cities depending on the political power, the quality of local government officials, and the degree of corruption.

A growing body of research and policy work considers more disaggregated evidence on the importance of institutions. Banerjee and Iyer (2005) show that Indian districts in which property rights were historically given to landlords had lower levels of investment and productivity than districts in which property rights were assigned to cultivators, arguing that this reflects the greater security of tenure in non-landlord districts. Country-specific Investment Climate Assessments performed recently by the World Bank as well as the study by Dollar et al. (2005) establish an important role for the institutional environment in explaining differences in firm performance within and across South Asian countries. World Bank (2009) shows that 76 per cent of explained productivity differentials among firms in the formal manufacturing sector in India can be traced to investment climate factors. That study links differences in growth of leading and lagging states to investment climate reforms and shows that infrastructure and institutions have been the main bottlenecks to private sector development in India. The study concludes that institutional factors related to red tape, corruption, and crime had the largest negative impact on firm productivity, although infrastructure constraints have dominated investment climate discussions.

For the purposes of this book, the relevant question is 'how important are the disparities in the institutional environment within South Asian countries across lagging regions and leading regions?'[4] Evidence provided elsewhere in this book shows that crime and conflict are escalating and infrastructure bottlenecks are particularly serious in lagging regions relative to leading regions in South Asia. We consider several dimensions of the institutional environment: finance, property rights, and regulatory costs. We document the differences in institutional quality across lagging regions and leading regions along these dimensions based on measures taken from the World Bank Enterprise Surveys (WBES)—a large cross-country manufacturing firm-level data set—and from the World Bank *Doing Business* indicators.

The evidence suggests that the quality of the institutional environment in the lagging regions of South Asia is substantially poorer than that in the leading regions of the continent.[5] First, we show that businesses have poorer access to formal finance in lagging regions. Second, property rights seem to be significantly less secure in lagging regions. Third, it looks like there are more administrative hurdles or regulatory costs required to set up a business in South Asia's lagging regions than in leading regions. Fourth, although it is not obvious from the firm-level surveys or from the *Doing Business* indicators that labour regulation is any more stringent in lagging than in leading regions, there is some evidence that employment protection laws are more stringent or more rigorously enforced in India's lagging states than they are in the country's leading states.

The conspicuous differences in the various dimensions of the institutional environment between lagging regions and leading regions of South Asia can explain the divergence in economic performance across the two types of regions. Poor institutional quality is one important reason why the share of lagging regions in manufacturing activity is so low. The low investment in South Asia's lagging regions can be at least partly traced to

---

[4]The definition of lagging and leading regions follows that used in the previous chapters in the book.

[5]In related research, Fernandes (2009) shows that the differences in institutional quality within countries in South Asia are much higher than those observed within countries in East Asia.

insecure property rights in those regions. Fernandes and Pakes (2008) show that firm-level employment is typically smaller in lagging states of India than in leading states for given levels of total factor productivity, capital intensity, and wage rate. More stringent labour regulation may be impeding job creation more in lagging states than in leading states of India.

The development of lagging regions has been hampered by poor institutions related to access to credit, time taken to set up a business, security of property rights, and labour laws. Using WBES data on firms in Bangladesh, India, Pakistan, and Sri Lanka, this chapter provides concrete evidence on the relationship between the quality of 'contracting institutions' and 'property rights institutions' and economic performance at the firm level. For firms in Bangladesh, India, Pakistan, and Sri Lanka, we find that property rights institutions have a more detrimental effect on performance—measured by sales per worker—than contracting institutions. A possible interpretation for this finding is that firms can find ways to contract around poorly performing contracting institutions, while this is not possible for weak property rights institutions. Our evidence supports this interpretation: in locations with weaker institutional quality, firms resort more frequently to informal channels—for example, belonging to a business association and using it to resolve business disputes—to get around institutional weaknesses.

Overall, our evidence at the aggregate level as well as at the micro level suggests that institutional quality does matter for economic development in South Asia. The poor performance of countries such as Bangladesh and Pakistan on corruption suggests that this is an area for which reforms, although difficult, are likely to have substantial impact. Our evidence for India points to deficiencies in 'contracting institutions', which we primarily measure as weaknesses in the ability of courts to settle business disputes, but which can be interpreted more broadly as failures in the overall regulatory environment. While cross-country evidence suggests that institutional weaknesses in this dimension have smaller development impacts than do 'property rights institutions', there are surely returns to improvements in this area. In fact, our firm-level evidence suggests that firms need to develop alternative strategies to circumvent weak 'contracting institutions', and while we do not provide direct evidence, it is plausible that these alternative strategies are inefficient compared with the benchmark of good 'contracting institutions'.

The important degree of heterogeneity in the institutional environment across South Asia's lagging regions and leading regions is a source of the divergence in economic outcomes across the two types of regions. The weaker security of property rights in lagging regions relative to leading regions of South Asian countries is likely to have been a major rationale for underinvestment in those lagging regions. Economic agents are unwilling to invest in fragile conflict-ridden lagging regions where returns cannot be appropriated. Only once conflict is reduced and law and order restored, will growth pick up in lagging regions.

Institutional reforms seem to be needed to improve the business environment of lagging regions to make them more attractive to more manufacturing investment and employment. Governments may have limited influence over geography but have a much more decisive influence over the security of property rights, the functioning of financial and labour markets, the approaches to regulation, and broader features of governance such as corruption. This said, quick growth results cannot be expected from institutional reforms in the lagging regions of South Asia. Institutional reforms will take time to design, implement, and become effective. Hence, economic growth in South Asia's lagging regions will continue to be hampered by a poor institutional environment and will take a long time to reduce poverty. Thus, regional policy in South Asia needs to cover direct interventions such as fiscal redistribution and the promotion of investment in human capital (as a 'mobile asset') in lagging regions to reduce their shortfall in welfare and well-being in relation to leading regions.

The rest of the chapter is organized as follows. 'Institutional Quality and Development' discusses the link between institutional quality and development at the aggregate level. 'Regional Differences in the Institutional Environment' discusses the differences in institutional environment within South Asian countries. 'Do Institutions Matter for Firm Performance?' examines the effects of poor institutional quality for firms in South Asia. The last section concludes.

INSTITUTIONAL QUALITY AND DEVELOPMENT

The starting point for studying the role of institutional quality for development is the strong positive correlation between measures of institutional quality and log-levels of per capita income shown by Figure 5.1. All six South Asian countries for which we have data fall below the regression line in the figure. Bangladesh, Nepal, and Pakistan have similar fairly poor scores on the measure of 'rule of law', which place them in the bottom quartile of all countries, whereas Bhutan, India, and Sri Lanka fare much better, around the median of all countries worldwide. Two questions arise in the interpretation of Figure 5.1. Should we interpret it 'horizontally' and conclude that South Asian countries have much better institutional quality than expected given their relatively low income levels (that is, emphasize the fact that the countries fall to the left of the regression line)? Or should we interpret it 'vertically' and conclude that South Asian countries have substantially lower income levels than expected given their governance performance (that is, emphasize the fact that the countries fall below the regression line)?

Sorting out these questions requires an understanding of the causal relationship between institutions and per capita incomes, not merely the correlation shown in Figure 5.1. Another problem of interpretation relates to the measure of institutional quality. Do countries that fare poorly on this measure have a high risk of expropriation by the state? Or do they fare poorly because private contract enforcement is weak or crime is an issue? Do all these distinct ingredients of 'rule of law' matter equally for development outcomes? From the definition of 'rule of law', it is clear that this aggregate measure combines—and conflates— the two conceptions of institutional quality related to 'property rights institutions' and 'contracting institutions' considered by Acemoglu and Johnson (2005).

We consider empirical proxies for the two distinct types of institutions. To measure the (absence of) good property rights institutions, we use the Kaufmann et al. (2005) measure of corruption. While perceptions of corruption are not related to the institutions themselves, the prevalence of corruption is a good proxy for the absence of well-functioning institutions that limit the arbitrary exercise of state power. Since corruption is defined as the use of public office for private gain, the taking of bribes by public officials can be thought of as the expropriation of private property by the state. We orient this variable such that higher values correspond to more corruption. To measure contracting institutions, we use a measure of the functioning of the courts, which is an estimate of the number of days and the number of formal procedures that are required to resolve a hypothetical business dispute between two private parties over an unpaid commercial debt based on the World Bank *Doing Business* indicators. This measure emphasizes statutory or *de jure* procedures that must be followed, and it does not attempt to measure the *de facto* procedures that actually are followed. These may differ significantly from the *de jure* ones, particularly in countries where courts are corrupt.[6] Higher values in terms

[6]The possibility of corruption in the courts raises an interesting question: Does this signal the failure of property rights institutions or contracting institutions? The answer is surely a bit of both. On the one hand, bribes paid by private parties to judges who are public officials represent state expropriation as discussed earlier. And at the same time corruption makes the conflict resolution services provided by courts less efficient.

of the length of time and the number of procedures required to settle a business dispute correspond to worse contracting institutions.

Deep Historical Determinants of Institutional Quality

The simple correlation between institutions and per capita incomes in Figure 5.1 does not tell us anything about causation. It could be that better institutional quality causes higher incomes, or it could be that richer countries can 'afford' better institutions. The direction of causality can be sorted using instrumental variables, which should explain cross-country differences in institutional quality but should have little direct effect on per capita incomes today.

Hence one needs to identify deep historical determinants for the two types of institutions that can be used to statistically identify their causal effects on development. As mentioned earlier we use the deep historical determinant for 'property rights institutions,' proposed by Acemoglu et al. (2001): mortality rates of European settlers around the world in the eighteenth and nineteenth centuries.[7] The argument is that in countries where settler mortality was low, it was in the interests of the colonial powers to create institutions that protected property rights, at least those of the occupying settlers, and these institutions have persisted. In contrast, in countries where settler mortality was high, colonial powers were interested only in extracting wealth and had no interest in developing any kind of formal institutions.[8] As a deep historical determinant for 'contracting institutions', we follow, as mentioned earlier, Acemoglu and Johnson (2005) in using data on the legal traditions of countries. The insight is that countries with British legal origins tend to have much more streamlined procedures for dispute resolution, as opposed to the highly formalized and codified procedures in countries with French legal origins. This effect is reflected in the complexity of current dispute resolution mechanisms.

In Table 5.1 we summarize the relationship between these deep historical determinants and institutional quality. We regress our four

[7]We use an expanded data set on settler mortality based on on-going work by Kaufmann et al. (2005), who extend the Acemoglu et al. (2001) estimates of settler mortality to geographically proximate countries with similar climates that were not included in the original analysis.

[8]The different experiences of British colonial power in the Gold Coast in West Africa versus in Canada or New Zealand provide examples of these two extremes. These experiences show that these early differences in institutions cast long shadows that are still seen in cross-country differences in modern institutions.

measures of institutions—rule of law, corruption, number of procedures, and number of days—on the two instrumental variables—settler mortality and a dummy variable identifying countries with British legal origins. We include dummy variables for Bangladesh, India, Pakistan, and Sri Lanka that capture the extent to which these South Asian countries differ significantly from the average relationship estimated using a large cross-country sample of 82 countries. The main regressions of interest appear in Table 5.1, columns 2 and 3. For corruption, we find that settler mortality enters significantly and positively: countries with higher settler mortality 200 years ago have worse corruption in 2004, which we interpret as worse 'property rights institutions'. We also find that British legal origin is significantly associated with the complexity of dispute resolution procedures, as measured by number of procedures, or number of days. Countries with British legal origins have substantially lower values for these two measures, indicating that they tend to have better 'contracting institutions'.

TABLE 5.1   Regressions of Property Rights and Contracting Institutions on Historical Determinants

	Dependent Variable			
	Rule of law	Corruption	Number of procedures	ln(number of days)
British legal origin	−0.268	−0.268	−9.886	−0.321
	(0.173)	(0.177)	(3.436)***	(0.143)**
ln(settler mortality)	0.336	0.327	1.154	0.084
	(0.078)***	(0.078)***	(1.158)	(0.054)
India	0.057	0.384	13.604	0.433
	(0.173)	(0.188)**	(2.465)***	(0.110)***
Bangladesh	0.696	1.029	2.161	0.248
	(0.160)***	(0.171)***	(2.649)	(0.107)**
Sri Lanka	−0.125	0.111	−9.813	0.437
	(0.161)	(0.172)	(2.636)***	(0.107)***
Pakistan	0.846	1.029	19.92	0.383
	(0.184)***	(0.202)***	(2.376)***	(0.115)***
Observations	82	82	82	82
R-Squared	0.34	0.32	0.22	0.14

Source: Fernandes and Kraay (2007).
Notes: Ordinary least squares (OLS) estimation is used. Robust standard errors appear in parentheses. All measures of institutional quality are oriented so that higher values correspond to worse institutions. ***represents significance at 1 per cent and **represents significance at 5 per cent.

Of particular interest for this chapter is how countries in South Asia fare in the relationships shown in Table 5.1. All four countries have British legal origins, and so in assessing the quality of their 'contracting

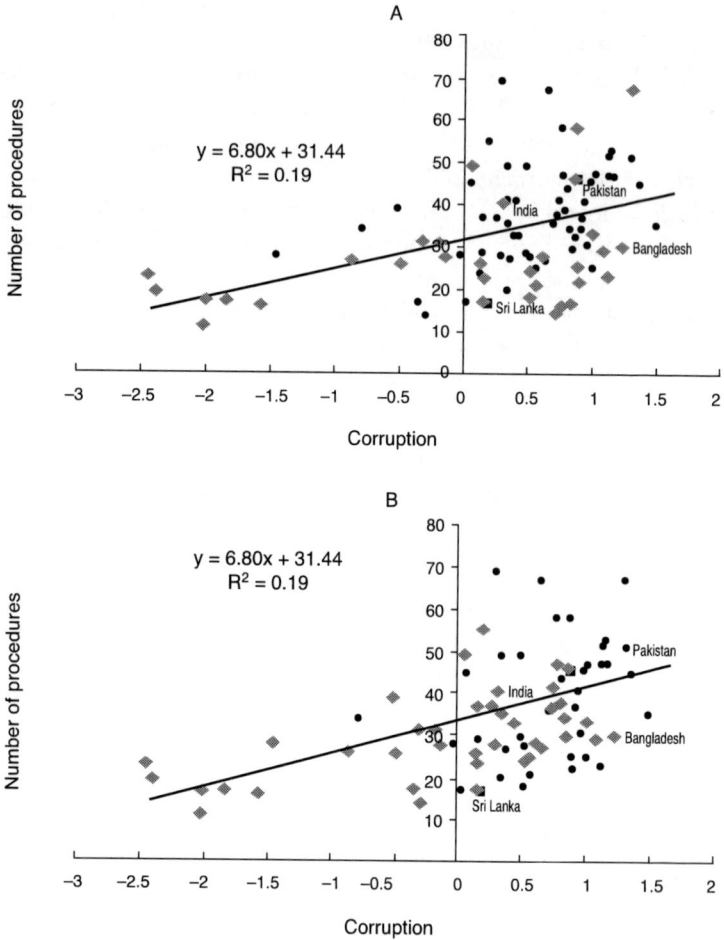

FIGURE 5.2   Property Rights and Contracting Institutions
in South Asia

Source: Fernandes and Kraay (2007).
Notes: All variables refer to 2004. Corruption is oriented so that higher values correspond to worse outcomes. In the top panel the large dots identify countries with British legal origins. In the bottom panel the large dots identify countries with lower-than-average settler mortality.

institutions' one should focus on how they fare relative to other countries with British legal origins. The dummy variables for India and Pakistan in Table 5.1 are positive and highly significant, which tells us that these countries have substantially worse contracting institutions than other countries with British legal origins. For number of procedures, for example, the estimated coefficients imply that in India and in Pakistan it takes 13.6 and 19.9 days longer (respectively) to resolve a business dispute than it does in a typical British legal origin country. This is summarized graphically in Figure 5.2. In both panels of this figure, we plot corruption on the horizontal axis, and number of procedures on the vertical. In the top panel (see Figure 5.2A), the large dots identify countries with British legal origins. Although both India and Pakistan are around the middle of the pack for all countries taken together on 'contracting institutions' as measured by number of days, they are in the worst five performers among the group of countries with British legal origins. In short, India and Pakistan both perform quite poorly on this measure of institutional quality.

Turning to 'property rights institutions', the dummy variables for Pakistan and Bangladesh in Table 5.1 are large, positive, and significant. The interpretation of this is that these two countries have particularly poor performance on the corruption variable, even after taking into account the deep historical determinants of this type of institution. This is visually striking from Figure 5.2B. In this panel, the large dots correspond to countries with low settler mortality. We should expect that the historical situation in these countries was favourable to developing strong 'property rights institutions'. However, Bangladesh and Pakistan stand out as being among the worst performers of all countries in this group, suggesting fundamental problems with corruption.

In summary, the cross-country data suggest that Pakistan stands out for its poor performance in both types of institutions. Bangladesh stands out for having poor performance on property rights institutions, but reasonable performance on contracting institutions, whereas the converse is true for India. Finally, Sri Lanka has good contracting institutions but only average property rights institutions.

Institutional Quality and Development: Identifying Causation

The next step is to assess how these differences in institutional quality have translated into economic development, as summarized by real gross domestic product (GDP) per capita. We report the results of the instrumental variables estimates of the causal impacts of these two types of institutions on real per capita GDP in Table 5.2.[9] Consistent with the findings of Acemoglu and Johnson (2005), we find a clear pattern that 'property rights institutions', as proxied by corruption, have a large and significant causal impact on development, while 'contracting institutions', as proxied by either number of procedures or number of days, matter much less. The magnitude of the effect of institutions on development is large. For example, a one-standard-deviation improvement in corruption, corresponding roughly to the difference between Sri Lanka and Pakistan or Bangladesh, would result in incomes that are higher by a factor of six in the long run. The result that 'property rights institutions' matter much more than 'contracting institutions' is quite intuitive. A key feature of

TABLE 5.2   Regressions of GDP per Capita on Property Rights and Contracting Institutions

	Dependent variable ln(GDP per capita)	
Corruption	−1.843	−2.231
	(0.419)***	(0.632)***
Number of procedures	0.07	
	(0.038)*	
ln(number of days)		2.467
		(1.500)
India	−0.661	−0.633
	(0.269)**	(0.354)*
Bangladesh	1.185	1.121
	(0.494)**	(0.420)***
Sri Lanka	1.068	−0.651
	(0.607)*	(0.490)
Pakistan	−0.137	0.704
	(0.341)	(0.219)***
Observations	82	82

Source: Fernandes and Kraay (2007).
Notes: Instrumental variables estimation is used. Robust standard errors are in parentheses. Corruption is oriented so that higher values correspond to worse outcomes. *** represents significance at 1 per cent, ** represents significance at 5 per cent, and * represents significance at 10 per cent.

[9]A technical point that should be noted based on Table 5.1 is that settler mortality is a good predictor of 'property rights institutions' but not of 'contracting institutions', while the opposite is true of British legal origins. This is crucial for the instrumental variables strategy in Table 5.2 to work. If both instruments predicted both types of institutions, then they would not be helpful for isolating the separate causal effects of the two types of institutions.

'contracting institutions', such as the courts, is that firms and individuals have a variety of opportunities to circumvent them if the services they provide are weak. For example, firms might rely on business associations or informal networks to enforce contracts if the courts are ineffective or slow. In contrast, it is much more difficult for firms to 'contract around' a predatory state when property rights institutions are weak.

It is again of interest to see how the four South Asian countries differ from the average relationship in Table 5.2. Consider, for example, the regression that uses the number of days to proxy for 'contracting institutions'. Here we see a striking pattern in the dummy variables for the four countries. Bangladesh and Pakistan stand out for having significant positive residuals, while India stands out with a modestly significant negative residual. The interpretation of this pattern is that Bangladesh and Pakistan have per capita incomes that are substantially higher than one would expect given their institutional quality in these key dimensions. The point estimates suggest that Bangladesh and Pakistan have per capita incomes that are between two and three times higher than their weak institutional performance would suggest based on average cross-country relationships. In contrast, India's per capita income is only about half of what one might expect given its per capita income. Finally, Sri Lanka falls more or less on the average cross-country relationship, with a dummy variable that is not significantly different from zero.

How do we interpret these findings? The clearest findings we have are that India is much poorer than one would expect based on the cross-country relationship between institutions and economic performance. Conversely, Bangladesh, and to a lesser extent Pakistan, is far richer than one would expect. A somewhat naive interpretation of this evidence focusing on these countries alone might be that institutional quality simply does not matter for these countries. After all, our evidence suggests that Bangladesh and Pakistan have attained quite high per capita incomes despite poor institutional quality, whereas India has lagged in this respect despite its relatively good performance on the 'property rights institutions' that matter most for growth. This interpretation is however too narrow, because it ignores the strong cross-country evidence that 'property rights institutions' do matter on average for economic performance. A more nuanced view might be that institutions do in fact matter for growth, but in the case of India, they have not yet delivered their full development impact. The 'good news' in this interpretation is that India has considerable room to grow based on its reasonably good 'property rights institutions'. The flip side of this is a rather more gloomy

192   The Poor Half Billion in South Asia

view for Bangladesh and Pakistan, where one could argue that their past income gains, whatever their source, are fragile because they are not supported by commensurately strong 'property rights institutions'. Based on our reading of the evidence on institutions and growth, we prefer the latter interpretation. We recognize, however, that cross-country analysis based on these rather crude proxies for 'property rights institutions' and 'contracting institutions' can only bring us so far in understanding what the causes and consequences of institutional weaknesses are. They provide relatively little guidance for policy advice. In the rest of the chapter, we turn to disaggregate evidence on the differences of institutions within countries and their role for firm performance.

REGIONAL DIFFERENCES IN THE INSTITUTIONAL ENVIRONMENT

This section documents the divergence in institutional quality across lagging regions and leading regions in South Asian countries. These differences in institutional indicators may go a long way towards explaining the poor economic performance of South Asia's lagging regions and in particular its manufacturing underinvestment.

Finance

Developed financial markets connect firms to lenders and investors willing to fund their ventures and share some of the risks (World Bank 2005). If financial markets function well, they give firms of all types the ability to seize promising investment opportunities. They reduce the reliance of firms on internally-generated cash flows and on money from informal sources. Well-functioning financial markets impose discipline on firms, forcing them to be efficient. Inadequacies in financial markets create barriers for entrepreneurs to invest productively and grow and hence for the development of the locations where they operate.

Table 5.3 presents for each South Asian country the average of several institutional indicators related to finance in each of its lagging regions, in all its lagging regions, in all its leading regions, and in all its regions based on the WBES data.[10] Columns 1 to 3 document that access to formal finance is significantly poorer for manufacturing firms operating in lagging regions than it is for firms operating in leading regions in all

[10]The WBES used to be known officially as Investment Climate Surveys. Appendix A5.1 describes in detail the WBES data set, including sample sizes, sector coverage, and variable definitions. For each type of region, the indicators shown are computed as an average across all firms covered by the survey located in that region.

South Asian countries. For example, firms are less likely to use bank loans in lagging regions both to finance working capital as well as to finance fixed investments. Firms in lagging regions are less likely to use trade credit for those same purposes than are their counterparts in leading regions. Information asymmetries tend to be the reason for inadequacies in financial markets. These asymmetries are likely to be much higher in the lagging regions than in the leading regions of South Asia.

TABLE 5.3   Indicators of Access to Finance

	% of working capital financed by bank loans (WBES data)	% of fixed investment financed by bank loans (WBES data)	% of working capital financed by trade credit (WBES data)	% of managers rating access to finance as a significant business obstacle (WBES data)
Bangladesh				
Rajshahi	16		5	19
Khulna	16		3	5
Sylhet	5		2	10
Barisal	10		1	19
All Lagging Regions	12		3	13
All Leading Regions	26		4	31
Mean Difference Test	8.7*		1.28*	7.6*
All Bangladesh	22		4	26
India				
Bihar	24	27	5	16
Jharkhand	14	23	17	31
Madhya Pradesh	11	33	5	21
Orissa	42	44	5	36
Rajasthan	33	15	8	18
Uttar Pradesh	28	27	13	11
All Lagging Regions	26	27	10	23
All Leading Regions	34	35	8	10
Mean Difference Test	6.37*	3.86*	–2.25*	–8.3*
All India	31	32	9	15
Pakistan				
Quetta				37
Peshawar	9	1	1	24

(contd...)

Table 5.3 (contd...)

	% of working capital financed by bank loans (WBES data)	% of fixed investment financed by bank loans (WBES data)	% of working capital financed by trade credit (WBES data)	% of managers rating access to finance as a significant business obstacle (WBES data)
All Lagging Regions	5	1	1	30
All Leading Regions	5	8	5	39
Mean Difference Test	0.04	2.25*	2.96*	2.05*
All Pakistan	5	6	5	38
Sri Lanka				
Kandy	14	11	4	10
Matale				0
Puttalam	20	19	11	6
Badulla	40	0	0	0
Monaragala				100
Ratnapura	0	7	0	12
Kegalle	7	10	5	20
All Lagging Regions	13	10	4	11
All Leading Regions	25	17	11	16
Mean Difference Test	3.27*	1.66	2.89*	1.13
All Sri Lanka	23	15	10	15

Source: Authors' calculations using the WBES dataset.
Notes: The mean difference test reports the *t*-statistic on the equality of means test.
*indicates that the average of the indicator in leading regions is significantly different from the average of the indicator in lagging regions at a 5 per cent confidence level.

Table 5.3 shows that, in India, a significantly higher proportion of managers complain about access to finance in lagging relative to leading regions than in Bangladesh and Sri Lanka, where the reverse is true. In Sri Lanka, the rate of complaints by firm managers about access to finance does not differ much by type of region.

Security of Property Rights

Secure property rights link effort with reward, ensuring that all types of firms (small or large, formal or informal) will be able to reap the fruits of their investments (World Bank 2005). The better protected are property rights, the stronger is the link between effort and reward and hence the greater are the incentives to open new businesses or invest in existing businesses.

Table 5.4 shows for each South Asian country the average of various institutional indicators related to the security of property rights across types of regions based on WBES data and *Doing Business* indicators. According to firm managers' perceptions, corruption in India is more pervasive in its lagging regions than it is in its leading regions. The difference in averages across the two types of regions is statistically significant. However, the situation is somewhat different in other South Asian countries, where more or less the same proportion of firm managers complains about corruption as an obstacle to business success in the lagging regions as in the leading regions. In fact, in Sri Lanka, the data show that a significantly higher proportion of firm managers complain about corruption in leading regions relative to lagging regions. The rates of firm managers' complaints against tax administration follow a similar pattern, whereby the rate is significantly higher for lagging regions in India

TABLE 5.4   Indicators of Security of Property Rights

	% of managers rating corruption as a significant business obstacle (WBES data)	% of managers rating tax administration as a significant business obstacle (WBES data)	% of top managers' time spent dealing with government officials (WBES data)	Days to register property (DB data)	Score of confidence in the judiciary on scale of 1 to 6 increasing (WBES data)
Bangladesh					
Rajshahi	51	20	2.8		3.5
Khulna	54	23	4.3	373	3.2
Sylhet	42	30	2.2		3.2
Barisal	54	11	2.0		3.2
All Lagging Regions	50	22	2.9	373	3.3
All Leading Regions	55	31	4.4	408	3.3
Mean Difference Test	1.9	3.58*	5.11*		0.79
All Bangladesh	53	29	4.0	425	3.3
India					
Bihar	50	18	24.8	119	3.7
Jharkhand	21	17	18.1	86	4.5

(contd...)

Table 5.4 (contd...)

	% of managers rating corruption as a significant business obstacle (WBES data)	% of managers rating tax administration as a significant business obstacle (WBES data)	% of top managers' time spent dealing with government officials (WBES data)	Days to register property (DB data)	Score of confidence in the judiciary on scale of 1 to 6 increasing (WBES data)
Madhya Pradesh	28	31	7.5		4.1
Orissa	48	26	8.2	123	4.3
Rajasthan	36	44	10.2	56	3.9
Uttar Pradesh	23	46	17.9	43	3.7
All Lagging Regions	31	32	13.7	85	4.1
All Leading Regions	26	25	12.1	88.5	4.0
Mean Difference Test	−2.6*	−3.8*	−2.68*		−0.33
All India	28	27	12.6	62	4.0
Pakistan					
Quetta	34	39	4.8	93	2.2
Peshawar	47	55	7.9	46	2.4
All Lagging Regions	41	48	6.6	69.5	2.3
All Leading Regions	40	46	10.7	45.5	3.0
Mean Difference Test	−0.28	−0.52	3.71*		4.4*
All Pakistan	40	46	10.1	50	2.9
Sri Lanka					
Kandy	5	0	3.5		4.1
Matale	0	0	0.0		4.8
Puttalam	0	6	2.4		4.8
Badulla	17	0	5.7		3.6
Monaragala	0	50	6.0		4.0
Ratnapura	12	12	4.2		3.6
Kegalle	13	7	8.8		3.9
All Lagging Regions	8	6	4.5		4.1
All Leading Regions	19	14	3.7		4.0
Mean Difference Test	2.54*	2.19*	−1.83		−0.56
All Sri Lanka	17	12	3.8		4.0

Source: Authors' calculations using the WBES dataset and the *Doing Business* data.
Note: The mean difference test reports the *t*-statistic on the equality of means test.
*indicates that the average of the indicator in leading regions is significantly different from the average of the indicator in lagging regions at a 5 per cent confidence level.

but is larger in leading regions in Bangladesh, Pakistan, and Sri Lanka, and significantly so in the case of Bangladesh and Sri Lanka.

Following up on the discussion in 'Institutional Quality and Development', we include corruption under the property rights heading, because we view the prevalence of corruption as a proxy for the security of property rights. Property rights also appear to be less secure in lagging regions more consistently across South Asian countries in terms of a second indicator in Table 5.4, namely, the *Doing Business* indicator of the time it takes to register property. The overall India reference point for this indicator is 62 days. This contrasts with 123 days for the lagging state of Orissa, 119 days for Bihar, and 89 days for Madhya Pradesh. However, it has to be noted that the time to register property is in fact lower than the national average for the lagging regions of Uttar Pradesh (43) and Rajasthan (56). Likewise, the national reference time of 50 days to register property in Pakistan contrasts with 93 days for Quetta, although it takes fewer days than the national reference to register property in Peshawar, the largest city of another lagging region. The weaker security of property rights in lagging regions relative to leading regions of South Asian countries results in lower risk-adjusted expected rates of returns, hence providing a rationale for low investment rates in those lagging regions.

Overall, the security of property rights is poorer in South Asia's lagging regions. This likely may explain why firms invest at a smaller rate in those regions: firms are likely to attach greater risk premiums to investment projects than their counterparts would in leading regions.

Regulatory Costs

The way governments regulate firms and transactions both within and at their borders plays a big role in shaping the institutional environment. Sound regulation addresses market failures that inhibit productive investment. Often, however, governments pursue regulatory approaches that impose unnecessary costs, which increase uncertainty and risks and that erect unjustified barriers to competition (World Bank 2005). The challenge faced by governments is how to regulate without undermining the opportunities and incentives for firms to invest productively and create jobs and thus contribute to growth and poverty reduction.

Table 5.5 shows for each South Asian country the average of various institutional indicators related to regulatory costs across types of regions based on WBES data and *Doing Business* indicators. As shown in column 1, only a small proportion of businesses seem to complain about business licensing requirements in South Asian countries, both in lagging regions

TABLE 5.5   Indicators of Regulatory Costs

	% of managers rating licensing require-ments as a significant business obstacle (WBES data)	Days to start a business (DB data)	% of managers rating labour regulation as a significant business obstacle (WBES data)	% of managers rating customs and trade regulations as a significant business obstacle (WBES data)	Days to clear customs (Imports) (DB data)	Days to clear customs (Exports) (DB data)
Bangladesh						
Rajshahi	10	–	2	10	20.7	1.5
Khulna	5	30	2	6	6.5	5.9
Sylhet	9	–	0	3	20.0	–
Barisal	8	–	0	8	7.1	6.0
All Lagging Regions	8	30	1	6	11.8	5.2
All Leading Regions	12	37	3	13	10.6	8.8
Mean Difference Test	2.34*	–	2.43*	3.7*	–0.52	1.49
All Bangladesh	11	36.3	3	11	10.6	8.6
India						
Bihar	18	41	14	12	–	2.0
Jharkhand	2	46	8	3	0.0	5.0
Madhya Pradesh	14	–	8	16	–	–
Orissa	7	52	5	13	12.0	14.5
Rajasthan	18	42	32	34	11.7	9.2
Uttar Pradesh	8	42	11	30	11.8	13.5
All Lagging Regions	10	44.8	14	19	10.6	10.7
All Leading Regions	9	43.7	15	13	14.1	17.5
Mean Difference Test	–1.08	–4.47*	0.61*	–4.31*	1.02	3.87*
All India	9	44.1	14	15	13.6	15.2

(contd...)

Table 5.5 (contd...)

	% of managers rating licensing requirements as a significant business obstacle (WBES data)	Days to start a business (DB data)	% of managers rating labour regulation as a significant business obstacle (WBES data)	% of managers rating customs and trade regulations as a significant business obstacle (WBES data)	Days to clear customs (Imports) (DB data)	Days to clear customs (Exports) (DB data)
Pakistan						
Quetta	22	25	12	20	–	8.5
Peshawar	5	23	11	41	21.1	10.3
All Lagging Regions	13	23.9	11	32	21.1	10.0
All Leading Regions	15	23.4	16	24	17.2	9.7
Mean Difference Test	0.69	−7.23*	1.37	−1.97*	−0.79	−0.08
All Pakistan	15	23.5	15	25	17.7	9.7
Sri Lanka						
Kandy	0	–	29	0	4.5	25.0
Matale	0	–	0	0	–	–
Puttalam	0	–	0	0	–	1.2
Badulla	8	–	25	17	7.5	6.5
Monaragala	50	–	0	100	–	–
Ratnapura	6	–	35	18	2.0	–
Kegalle	7	–	13	7	5.3	3.5
All Lagging Regions	4	–	19	9	5.3	7.7
All Leading Regions	8	–	27	16	4.1	7.5
Mean Difference Test	1.07		1.55	1.69*	−0.63	−0.04
All Sri Lanka	7	–	26	15	4.1	7.6

Notes: 'Mean difference test' reports the t-statistics on the equality of means test. * indicates that the average in leading regions is significantly different from the average in lagging regions at 5 per cent level.

as well as in leading regions. In Bangladesh, however, a significantly higher proportion of firm managers complain about business requirements in leading regions compared with lagging regions.

Regarding firm managers' complaints about labour regulation in Table 5.5, column 3, the proportions are significantly higher in leading than in lagging regions in Bangladesh and India. In Pakistan and Sri Lanka, the differences between the two types of regions are small. Some evidence for India suggests that employment protection laws are more stringent or more rigorously enforced in the country's lagging states

TABLE 5.6   Indicators of Labour Regulations in India

	Laws on hiring and firing	Chapter Vb—mandating firms with more than 100 workers to request permission from government to fire workers	Laws on procedures for resolution of industrial disputes
Leading Regions			
Andhra Pradesh	More restrictive		Less restrictive
Delhi			
Gujarat			More restrictive
Haryana			
Karnataka	More restrictive	More restrictive	Less restrictive
Kerala			Less restrictive
Maharashtra	More restrictive	More restrictive	
Punjab			
Tamil Nadu			Less restrictive
Lagging Regions			
Bihar			
Jharkhand			
Madhya Pradesh	More restrictive		Less restrictive
Orissa	More restrictive	More restrictive	
Rajasthan	More restrictive	More restrictive	Less restrictive
Uttar Pradesh			
West Bengal	More restrictive	More restrictive	More restrictive

Source: Authors' compilation based on Ahsan and Pages (2007: Appendix).
Notes: The classification of states according to the restrictiveness of their labour regulations is based on Indian states' amendments to central labour laws as of 2004. 'More restrictive' indicates that the given state's amendments made the specific law become more restrictive (more favourable to workers) than the central labour law.

than they are in its leading states (see Table 5.6). The table documents the type of labour regulation prevailing in each lagging and leading state of India drawing on the study by Ahsan and Pages (2007). In different years between 1949 and 2004, many states in India made amendments to two types of central labour laws: (i) laws that regulate the procedures for the resolution of industrial disputes and (ii) laws that affect hiring and firing. In several cases, these amendments made the laws become more restrictive, for example, by making layoffs more expensive. Table 5.6 suggests that lagging regions in India more often than not made amendments to make their labour laws more restrictive than central labour laws. This may have contributed to the finding that the underemployment of labour is greater in India's lagging regions. Fernandes and Pakes (2008) show more underutilization of labour, thus evidence of more market distortions, in Indian states with more restrictive labour laws.[11] Because labour laws stringently affect only those firms with more than 100 workers, they should not be viewed as the major institutional problem hampering manufacturing development in lagging regions. Rather, weaknesses in other institutional factors must play an important role.

Starting a business seems to take significantly longer (on the books) in some of India's lagging regions than it does in Delhi. According to the *Doing Business* indicator, it takes 33 days to set up a business in Delhi, which is much lower than what it takes in many of the lagging regions in India—for example, 42 days in Uttar Pradesh and Rajasthan, 46 days in Jharkhand, 41 days in Bihar, and 52 days in Orissa. Likewise, dealing with licenses and permits seems to require more time in the lagging regions of Bihar (377 days), Jharkhand (522 days), and Orissa (240 days) than it does in India as an average (224 days).

Finally, the proportion of firm managers complaining about customs and trade regulations as obstacles to business is significantly higher in lagging regions in India and Pakistan, although the reverse is true in Bangladesh and Sri Lanka. Also, the number of days needed to clear customs according to the *Doing Business* indicators is larger in lagging regions in Bangladesh, Pakistan, and Sri Lanka.

DO INSTITUTIONS MATTER FOR FIRM PERFORMANCE?

It seems intuitive to argue that the great variability in institutional quality across lagging regions and leading regions within South Asian countries

[11]Basu (2006) proposes a theoretical framework that is consistent with these findings.

202 The Poor Half Billion in South Asia

(identified in 'Regional Differences in the Institutional Environment') must be a driver of the divergence in economic performance across the two types of regions. Nevertheless, in this section, we provide some suggestive evidence of how weaknesses in property rights institutions and in contracting affect firm performance in South Asian countries. The findings inform on whether the cross-country evidence on the importance of the two types of institutions discussed in 'Institutional Quality and Development' hold up at the micro level.

To perform this exercise, we identify empirical proxies at the firm level that proxy for contracting institutions and property rights institutions based on WBES data. We use firms' perceptions about the quality of the courts and the judiciary system in respecting rights in business disputes to capture 'contracting institutions' and firms' views on the importance of corruption as an obstacle to business to capture 'property rights institutions'.[12]

To assess how institutional weaknesses affect firms in South Asian countries, we regress firm-level sales per worker (in logs) on location-industry averages institutional quality.[13] Sales per worker is a measure of labour productivity and varies substantially across industries within each country because of differences in capital intensity and in production processes. Our regressions therefore include industry-fixed effects to control for such industry differences. We include in our regressions only those firms that have been in operation for more than 15 years. The purpose of this choice is to make the measure of sales per worker close to a long-run measure of firm growth, in a similar vein to what is done in

---

[12]Fernandes and Kraay (2007) show that the aggregate data and the micro data on institutional quality are consistent with one another. If one averages the firm-level data in each country to obtain 'micro-founded' macro measures of the quality of 'property rights institutions' and 'contracting institutions' and relates those in a regression framework to their corresponding macro proxies (treating each country as an observation) positive and significant correlations are obtained.

[13]Conceptually, contracting and property rights institutions should be exogenous to a given firm. Our analysis, however, is based on firm-level perceptions of institutional quality, and thus there is a potential endogeneity problem in relating firm-level performance to those perceptions. On the one hand, firms with better performance may be more aware of the difficulties that weak institutions cause and therefore may complain more about those. On the other hand, firms with better performance may be able to undertake actions to avoid dealing with the weak institutions. This endogeneity would lead to biased estimates of the relationship between institutional quality and firm performance. The consideration of averages of the institutional measures at the location-industry level mitigates this endogeneity problem.

'Institutional Quality and Development', in which a country's real GDP per capita is used as a proxy for that country's long-run growth.[14]

According to Table 5.7, for firms in Bangladesh, India, Pakistan, and Sri Lanka, property rights institutions have a more detrimental effect on performance than contracting institutions. The coefficients in column 3 indicate that firms in a location-industry cell with worse property rights institutions by one standard deviation (that is, a location-industry cell for which corruption is more important as an obstacle to business) would have on average 6.6 per cent lower sales per worker than firms in a location-industry cell with (sample) average property rights institutions.[15] We note, however, that weak contracting institutions have a negative effect

TABLE 5.7   Firm Performance, Contracting, and Property Rights Institutions

| | Dependent variable | | |
	Sales per worker	Sales per worker	Sales per worker
Functioning of judiciary with respect to business disputes	−0.012		−0.002
	(0.063)		(0.063)
Corruption as an obstacle to business		−0.066	−0.066
		(0.062)	(0.062)
Country dummies	Yes	Yes	Yes
Industry dummies	Yes	Yes	Yes
Observations	1820	1820	1820
R-Squared	0.91	0.91	0.91

Source: Fernandes and Kraay (2007).
Note: OLS estimation is used. Robust standard errors in parentheses.
***represents significance at 1 per cent and **represents significance at 5 per cent. The dependent variable is the logarithm of sales per worker with sales converted to US dollars. The variables 'functioning of judiciary with respect to business disputes' and 'corruption as an obstacle to business' are normalized to have a mean of 0 and variance of 1. The independent variables are averages of these normalized variables for location-industry cells. The regressions include only firms that are older than 15 years of age. Outliers in the sales per worker distribution for each industry and country (top and bottom 2 per cent) are eliminated from the regressions.

[14]In the cross-country data, the argument is that per capita income levels across countries were not very different in the distant past, and so cross-country differences in levels of per capita income reflect differences in countries' very long-run growth performance.

[15]The measures of contracting and property rights institutions included in the regressions are normalized to have a zero mean and a standard deviation of one.

on firm performance, albeit six times smaller than that of property rights institutions. This firm-level evidence of a link between performance and institutional quality is less clear-cut than the earlier cross-country evidence, which likely reflects a variety of weaknesses in the firm-level data. In particular, the important variability of institutional quality across locations and industries may still be lower than the variability of institutional quality across countries used in 'Institutional Quality and Development' to identify the impact of institutions on cross-country incomes.

One hypothesis that emerges from the cross-country evidence can be investigated using the firm-level data—that is, poor contracting institutions do not have a strong impact on growth because firms can find ways to contract around poorly performing institutions in this dimension; however, that is not possible in the case of weak property rights institutions that allow governments to prey on the private sector. We investigate the

TABLE 5.8   Getting Around Weak Contracting Institutions

	Dependent variable				
	Member-ship in business association	Import-ance of dispute resolution by business association	Percentage of working capital financed by infor-mal sources	Percentage of invest-ment financed by informal sources	Percentage of over-due pay-ments not resolved by courts
Functioning of judiciary with respect to business disputes	0.146** (0.071)	0.273*** (0.074)	0.011** (0.005)	0.018* (0.010)	0.133 (0.111)
Country dummies	Yes	Yes	Yes	Yes	Yes
Industry dummies	Yes	Yes	Yes	Yes	Yes
Observations	4038	2052	1908	1164	328
R-Squared		0.21	0.02	0.04	0.11

Source: Fernandes and Kraay (2007).
Notes: Probit estimation is used in the first column (marginal effects shown) and OLS estimation in the other columns. Robust standard errors are in parentheses.
***, **, and * indicate significance at 1 per cent, 5 per cent, and 10 per cent confidence levels, respectively.
***represents significance at 1 per cent, ** represents significance at 5 per cent, and *represents significance at 10 per cent.
The variable 'functioning of judiciary with respect to business disputes' is normalized to have a mean of 0 and variance of 1. The independent variable is the average of these normalized variables for location-industry cells.

extent to which firms are able to use informal channels in Bangladesh, India, Pakistan, and Sri Lanka to get around weak contracting institutions (see Table 5.8). The informal channels considered are as follows: belonging to a business association, using the business association to resolve business disputes with customers or suppliers, using informal sources of finance for working capital and for investment needs, and solving overdue payments problems by alternative mechanisms instead of courts.

Table 5.8 provides strong evidence that in locations and industries in which the quality of contracting institutions is weaker, firms resort to different informal ways to get around them. For example, firms operating in location-industry cells with worse contracting institutions by one standard deviation (that is, where the functioning of the judiciary in business disputes is worse) are 14.6 per cent more likely to belong to a business association than firms in a location-industry cell with (sample) average contracting institutions. Also, in locations and industries in which the weak quality of the judicial system makes it difficult to enforce debt contracts, firms resort to the use of informal credit channels.

CONCLUSION

This chapter examined the evidence on institutions and growth in South Asian countries at the macro and micro levels, distinguishing between two key dimensions of institutional performance: property rights institutions and contracting institutions. First, we show that while India has poor performance on 'contracting institutions', it fares reasonably well on measures of 'property rights institutions'. The reverse is true for Bangladesh, which stands out for having quite poor 'property rights institutions' but reasonable 'contracting institutions'. Second, we show that 'property rights institutions' matter more for economic growth across countries than 'contracting institutions'. Relative to this strong empirical regularity, India stands out for having a large negative residual, suggesting that even India's good performance on 'property rights institutions' has not yet had the development impact that cross-country analysis would suggest. In contrast, Bangladesh stands out in the opposite direction, with a predicted income level based on its institutional quality that is much lower than its actual income level. A possible interpretation of these findings is that India has a great deal of scope for future growth given its good institutional performance, whereas Bangladesh's current relatively high income levels (given its weak institutional quality) are more likely to be unsustainable. Third, using micro data, we document important differences in institutional quality within South Asian countries. We show that lagging regions exhibit a substantially poorer institutional environment. Firms are more difficult and more costly to set up in those regions, and once set up, they have greater difficulties in raising formal external finance than their counterparts in leading regions. Property rights are less secure in lagging regions according to several indicators. In the case of India, employment protection laws seem to be more restrictive in lagging states than in leading states. Fourth, using micro data, we confirm the importance of property rights institutions for firm performance in Bangladesh, India, Pakistan, and Sri Lanka and we show how firms in these countries are able to circumvent weaknesses in 'contracting institutions', by resorting frequently to informal channels, such as using business associations for dispute resolution.

Institutional reforms are needed to improve the business environment of lagging regions and make them more attractive for manufacturing investment. Governments can have a decisive influence over the security of property rights, the functioning of financial and labour markets, the approaches to regulation, and broader features of governance such as corruption. This said, no quick growth results can be expected from institutional reforms in the lagging regions of South Asia. Institutional reforms will take time to design, implement, and become effective. Thus, economic growth in South Asia's lagging regions will continue to be hampered by a poor institutional environment and will take a long time to reduce poverty. Thus, regional policy in South Asia needs to cover direct interventions such as fiscal redistribution and the promotion of investment in human capital (as a 'mobile asset') in lagging regions to reduce their shortfall in welfare and well-being in relation to leading regions.

APPENDIX A5.1: WORLD BANK ENTERPRISE SURVEYS DATA SET

This analysis uses data from the World Bank Enterprise Surveys (WBES) for Bangladesh, Bhutan, India, Nepal, Pakistan, and Sri Lanka, which are surveys of establishments conducted since 2000. The surveys share a similar sampling design that involves the selection of a stratified random sample of establishments from each country based on location and industry. The surveys collect detailed information on establishment characteristics such as size, age, and accounting variables, as well as perception-based and objective measures of the institutional environment (for example, access to finance, corruption). The surveys cover essentially formal establishments in the manufacturing sector. The number of establishments (with usable data) covered by the WBES data set is 1500 in Bangladesh, 2286 in India, 965 in Pakistan, and 450 in Sri Lanka.

The WBES variables used in the analysis in 'Do Institutions Matter for Firm Performance?' are computed as follows:

- 'Functioning of Judiciary with Respect to Business Disputes' is based on the rating of the statement 'I am confident that the judicial system will enforce my contractual and property rights in business disputes' by the firm ranging from 1 = Fully Disagree to 6 = Fully Agree.

- 'Corruption as an Obstacle to Business' is an assessment of corruption based on 'how problematic is' corruption 'for the operation and growth' of the firm ranging from 0 = No Obstacle to 4 = Major Obstacle.

- 'Importance of Dispute Resolution by Business Association' is an assessment of the value of the services provided by the business association regarding the resolution of disputes with officials, workers, or other firms by the firm ranging from 0 = No Value to 4 = Critical Value to the firm.

- 'Percentage of Working Capital Financed by Informal Sources' indicates how much of the firm's working capital needs were financed from an informal source such as a moneylender.

- 'Percentage of Investment Financed by Informal Sources' indicates how much of the firm's investments were financed from an informal source such as a moneylender.

- 'Percentage of Overdue Payments Not Resolved by Courts' is the percentage of firm disputes about overdue payments in the last two years that were not resolved by court action.

REFERENCES

Acemoglu, D. and S. Johnson. 2005. 'Unbundling Institutions', *Journal of Political Economy*, 113: 949–95.

Acemoglu, D., S. Johnson, and J. Robinson. 2001. 'The Colonial Origins of Comparative Development', *American Economic Review*, 91: 1369–401.

Ahsan, A. and C. Pages. 2007. 'Are All Labor Regulations Equal? Assessing the Effects of Job Security, Labor Dispute and Contract Labor Laws in India', Social Protection Discussion Paper No. 0713, World Bank, Washington, D.C.

Banerjee, A. and L. Iyer. 2005. 'History, Institutions, and Economic Performance: The Legacy of Colonial Land Tenure Systems in India', *American Economic Review*, 95: 1190–213.

Basu, K. 2006. 'Labor Laws and Labor Welfare in the Context of the Indian Experience', in A. De Janvry and R. Kanbur (eds), *Poverty, Inequality and Development*. Norwell, MA: Kluwer.

Delong, J. and A. Shleifer. 1993. 'Princes or Merchants? City Growth before the Industrial Revolution', *Journal of Law and Economics*, 32: 671–702.

Djankov, S., R. La Porta, F. Lopez-de-Silanes, and A. Shleifer. 2003. 'Courts', *Quarterly Journal of Economics*, 118: 453–517.

Dollar, D., M. Hallward-Driemeier, and T. Mengistae. 2005. 'Investment Climate and Firm Performance in Developing Economies', *Economic Development and Cultural Change*, 54: 1–31.

Fernandes, A. 2009. 'Comparing Property Rights Institutions, Contracting Institutions, and Growth in South Asia and East Asia', in S. Ahmed and E. Ghani (eds), *Accelerating Growth and Job Creation in South Asia*. New Delhi: Oxford University Press.

Fernandes, A. and A. Kraay. 2007. 'Property Rights Institutions, Contracting Institutions and Growth in South Asia: Macro and Micro Evidence', in S. Ahmed and E. Ghani (eds), *South Asia Growth and Regional Integration*. Delhi: Macmillan India Ltd.

Fernandes, A. and A. Pakes. 2008. 'Evidence of Underemployment of Labor and Capital in Indian Manufacturing', in S. Ahmed and E. Ghani (eds), *Accelerating Growth and Job Creation in South Asia*. New Delhi: Oxford University Press.

Hall, R. and C. Jones. 1999. 'Why Do Some Countries Produce So Much More Output per Worker than Others?', *Quarterly Journal of Economics*, 114: 83–116.

Kaufmann, D., A. Kraay, and M. Mastruzzi. 2005. 'Governance Matters IV: Governance Estimates for 1996–2004', Policy Research Working Paper No. 3630, World Bank, Washington, D.C.

Knack, S. and P. Keefer. 1995. 'Institutions and Economic Performance: Cross Country Tests Using Alternative Measures', *Economics and Politics*, 7: 207–27.

Mauro, P. 1995. 'Corruption and Growth', *Quarterly Journal of Economics*, 110: 681–712.

North, D. and B. Weingast. 1989. 'Constitutions and Commitment: The Evolution of Institutions Governing Public Choice in 17th Century England', *Journal of Economic History*, 49 (803): 832.

Rodrik, D., A. Subramanian, and F. Trebbi. 2004. 'Institutions Rule: The Primacy of Institutions over Geography and Integration in Economic Development', *Journal of Economic Growth*, 9: 131–65.

World Bank. 2009. *India Investment Climate Assessment*. Washington, D.C: World Bank.

———. 2005. *World Development Report 2005: A Better Investment Climate for Everyone*. Washington, D.C.: World Bank.

6

Education Policies and Outcomes in Lagging Regions

Dhushyanth Raju[†]

South Asia has poor outcomes in human development in general and in education in particular. Using one prominent measure, the region as a whole receives a score of 0.611 in the United Nations Development Program's Human Development Index (HDI), with most of the countries in the region (for example, Bangladesh, India, Nepal, Pakistan) clustered together among the lower half of countries classified as having achieved a medium level of human development (UNDP 2007). This overall score ranks the region higher than Sub-Saharan Africa, but lower than all other world regions.

The HDI, however, belies the true picture with respect to education levels in the region. It becomes apparent when the HDI is decomposed into its constituent indices (income, health, and education) that what differentiates South Asia from Sub-Saharan Africa is much more its levels of income and life expectancy than its level of education: South Asia has a value of 0.598 versus 0.571 for Sub-Saharan Africa in the education index of the HDI.[1] This suggests that education systems in South Asia are generally underperforming relative to the region's level of economic development.

[†]The author thanks Amit Dar and Michelle Riboud for guidance and helpful discussions and Deepa Sankar for assistance with the data for India.
    [1]The education index in HDI is constructed using national statistics on literacy and school enrolment.

On the positive side, South Asia has made tangible progress over the last two decades in raising its level of human development, including its level of education. As Figure 6.1 shows, the HDI values of countries in the region have increased over the period 1975–2005, with comparatively large and small relative increases in Nepal and Sri Lanka, respectively.[2] Over this period, the increases in country HDIs are undoubtedly partly attributable to the increases in the proportions of children attending school and completing higher levels of schooling. As Figure 6.2 shows, gross and net enrolment rates at the primary and secondary levels in the region have in general increased over the 1990s and 2000s, though clearly some countries have made larger strides than others.[3] Conversely, on the negative side, South Asia appears likely to miss meeting the Millennium Development Goal (MDG) target of universal primary education by 2015 (see statements in recent Global Monitoring Reports by the World Bank).

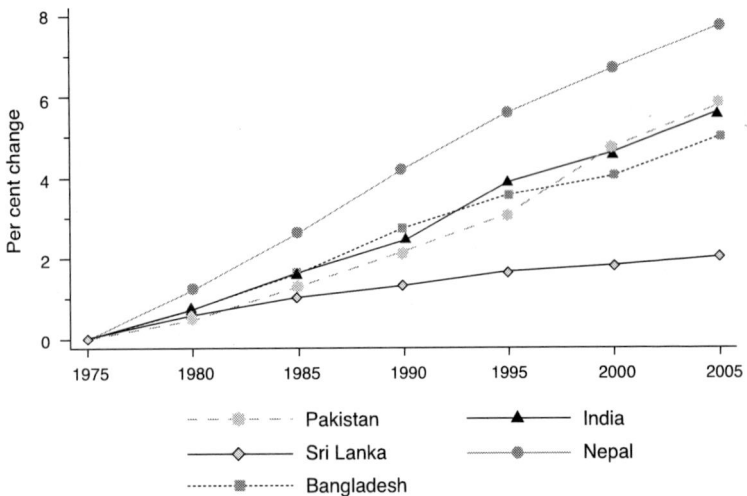

FIGURE 6.1   Evolution of HDI Values, South Asian Countries
(1975–2005)

Source: UNDP, Human Development Report (2007).

[2]Note that the starting points for Nepal and Sri Lanka in 1975 were dramatically different.

[3]However, given the composite nature of the HDI, without further investigation, it is difficult to quantify how much of the change in HDI is attributable to changes in the constituent components of gross enrolment and adult literacy in each of the countries.

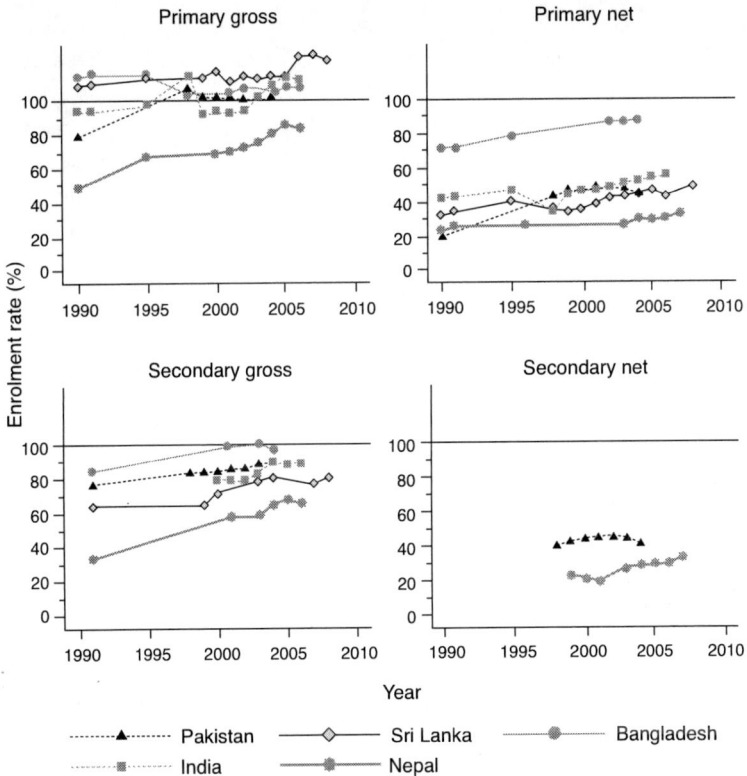

FIGURE 6.2   Evolution of Enrolment Rates, South Asian Countries

Source: UNESCO Institute for Statistics.

Instead of comparing South Asia with other developing regions or even countries in South Asia with one another, this chapter looks within South Asian countries and across major subnational administrative entities—states in India, provinces in Pakistan and Sri Lanka, and divisions in Bangladesh—to shed light on the nature of the education development problem in the region. Specifically, the chapter aims to answer three questions. The first question is whether there are significant differences in educational outcomes between two types of subnational areas: economically-leading and economically-lagging areas.[4] The second question is how these differences (if any) between leading and lagging

[4]The classification of subnational areas into economically-leading and -lagging areas is provided in Chapter 1 of this volume.

areas have evolved over the recent past, and, specifically, whether there has been convergence or divergence in education outcomes between subnational areas over time. The third and final question is what potentially explains any salient cross-sectional gaps and recent trends in education outcomes between leading and lagging areas. The search for potential explanations principally comprises of examining whether the existing literature documents systematic differences in the demand and supply factors of schooling (that is, child, household, school, and educational system characteristics) across subnational areas, including in government allocations and expenditures towards public education. These questions are motivated by the wide recognition that increasing attainment and achievement serve as an important instrument for reducing poverty (measured multidimensionally) and stimulating economic growth. Thus, lagging subnational areas may stand to gain sustained benefits in terms of these outcomes if their education systems successfully deliver the needed quantities and quality of human capital.

It is important to note at the outset that the scope and ambition of the chapter are circumscribed in three ways. First, due to the deficiency of relevant data, the questions posed in this chapter are only examined in Bangladesh, India, Pakistan, and Sri Lanka; additionally, the extent of the answers to the questions varies across these countries depending on the richness of the available data and empirical findings. Second, the chapter focuses exclusively on education at the primary and secondary levels. This choice is motivated mainly by (i) the fact that there generally continues to be acute shortfalls in education at these levels in the region (this is shown later) and (ii) while governments typically attempt to extend primary and secondary schooling to a broad range of rural and urban communities, public and private universities and colleges are typically concentrated in urbanized and urbanizing areas.[5] To the extent that urbanization rates differ across leading and lagging areas, the distribution of higher education institutions will also differ across these areas. Third, the chapter remains decidedly descriptive and does not attempt to make any causal claims on what drives any observed differences in levels and changes in education outcomes between leading and lagging areas.

[5]For example, 75 per cent of colleges and general universities are in urban centres (Government of Pakistan 2006).

PATTERNS AND TRENDS IN EDUCATION OUTCOMES

This section attempts to answer three specific questions. First, are there presently differences between leading and lagging areas within South Asian countries in terms of three key educational indicators: (i) school participation rates among children; (ii) school attainment as measured by school completion rates among selected young adult cohorts; and (iii) student achievement as measured using test scores? These indicators reflect both quantity and quality measures of human capital development. Second, if there are current differences between leading and lagging areas, what are the main features of these differences? Third, how have the differences (if any) between leading and lagging areas evolved over the recent past? Where possible, differences in outcomes in leading and lagging areas are examined not only for the general child population, but also for traditionally-disadvantaged sub-populations in the region such as girls, poor children, rural children, and tribal children (the latter for India only).

When primary data (household sample survey data with national coverage and representative at least at the level of the major subnational area) are used to answer the questions in this section—such as with school participation and completion measures in Bangladesh, India, and Pakistan—divisions, states, and provinces are pooled into leading and lagging area groups in each country and group averages estimated. When secondary data are used, such as with student achievement in all countries or with all educational indicators in Sri Lanka, answering these questions entails looking for general patterns and trends across individual leading and lagging areas.

School Participation

Participation is simply defined as the share of children of a given age group (6–10 years; 11–14 years) reported to be attending any formal schooling institution (for example, private or public; secular or religious) at the time of the survey. The age groupings considered correspond to the typical ages for primary and secondary schooling in the region.[6]

To begin, looking *across* countries, the evidence suggests that Sri Lanka has a significantly higher school participation rate than

[6]These groups have slight deviations. For example, the official age for primary schooling in Pakistan is 5–9 years and 10–14 years for secondary schooling, but examining which ages typically populate primary and secondary schools suggests that the more appropriate age groupings are 7–11 and 12–16 years.

Bangladesh, India, and Pakistan. Roughly 93 per cent of children aged 5–14 years were in school in this country; these ages represent the compulsory ages of schooling in Sri Lanka (Arunatilake 2006). Statistics from 2002 also show that there appears to be little difference in primary school enrolment rates by gender, rural/urban, and consumption expenditure quintiles (World Bank 2005d). Sri Lanka is followed, in turn, by India, where its participation rate in 2004/5 among children aged 6–10 and 11–15 years was 87 per cent and 78 per cent, respectively, Bangladesh (71 per cent and 70 per cent in 2005), and Pakistan (62 per cent and 60 per cent in 2004/5). In Bangladesh, participation rates for boys and girls are similar if not slightly higher for girls; in contrast, in both India and Pakistan, girls have significantly lower participation rates, with the disadvantages increasing with child age. There are also significant rural disadvantages in India and Pakistan; these disadvantages are only weakly present in Bangladesh. Bangladesh, India, and Pakistan also exhibit significant disadvantages for poor children relative to rich children, with the disadvantages increasing with child age. The poverty disadvantage is greatest in Pakistan: participation rates were 48 per cent and 85 per cent (a 32 percentage-point difference) among poor and rich children aged 6–10 years, respectively; the participation rate drops to 40 per cent for poor children aged 11–15 years, while it remains virtually unchanged for rich children.

Looking within countries, India presents a clear-cut picture of persistent disadvantages for lagging states vis-à-vis leading states in school participation, with signs of weak convergence in trends over the recent past. Data from 2004/5 show that, relative to leading states, lagging states had significant shortfalls in school participation for children aged 6–10 and 11–15 years—this finding applies to the full child population as well the key disadvantaged sub-populations of girls, rural children, tribal (Scheduled Tribe) children, and poor children (see Table 6.1). Looking back in time, these shortfalls for lagging states were present in 1999–2000 as well. Over the period 1999/2000–2004/5, the trends show that participation rates have risen significantly in leading as well as lagging states, with lagging states either maintaining ground with leading states (for example, parallel trends for rural and poor children) or marginally gaining ground on leading states, narrowing the gap somewhat (for example, convergence from below for tribal children).

Like India, in Pakistan, lagging provinces in general have lower participation rates than leading provinces in school participation. However, the picture is somewhat more nuanced—the shortfall is

TABLE 6.1   School Participation Rates, India

Sample	1999/2000	2004/5	Yearly % point change, 1999/2000–2004/5	Yearly % change, 1999/2000–2004/5
PANEL 1: Ages 6–10				
All				
Leading	0.831	0.935	0.021	0.024
Lagging	0.678	0.811	0.027	0.036
% point gap	0.153	0.124		
Female				
Leading	0.796	0.925	0.026	0.030
Lagging	0.616	0.801	0.037	0.054
% point gap	0.180	0.124		
Rural				
Leading	0.811	0.928	0.023	0.027
Lagging	0.651	0.780	0.026	0.037
% point gap	0.160	0.148		
Scheduled Tribes				
Leading	0.765	0.857	0.018	0.023
Lagging	0.573	0.755	0.036	0.057
% point gap	0.192	0.102		
Poorest quintile				
Leading	0.732	0.902	0.034	0.043
Lagging	0.548	0.727	0.036	0.058
% point gap	0.184	0.175		
PANEL 2: Ages 11–15				
All				
Leading	0.794	0.824	0.006	0.007
Lagging	0.697	0.735	0.008	0.011
% point gap	0.097	0.089		
Female				
Leading	0.748	0.797	0.010	0.013
Lagging	0.626	0.660	0.007	0.011
% point gap	0.122	0.137		
Rural				
Leading	0.770	0.805	0.007	0.009
Lagging	0.669	0.720	0.010	0.015
% point gap	0.102	0.085		

(contd...)

Table 6.1 (contd...)

Sample	1999/2000	2004/5	Yearly % point change, 1999/2000–2004/5	Yearly % change, 1999/2000–2004/5
Scheduled Tribes				
Leading	0.705	0.743	0.008	0.011
Lagging	0.564	0.617	0.011	0.018
% point gap	0.141	0.125		
Poorest quintile				
Leading	0.666	0.738	0.014	0.020
Lagging	0.553	0.625	0.014	0.025
% point gap	0.113	0.112		

Notes: 1999–2000 and 2004–5 statistics are obtained from the 55th and 61st rounds of the National Sample Survey, respectively. These surveys are representative at the state and urban/rural levels.

notably severe in one of the disadvantaged sub-populations examined, namely, girls. Data from 2004/5 show that school participation rates are significantly lower in the lagging provinces—for children aged 6–10 years, the deficit is 8.5 percentage points; for children aged 11–15 years, it is 6.4 percentage points (see Table 6.2).

Focusing on the selected disadvantaged sub-populations, the deficit appears to be large and significant for girls: 16.6 and 17.9 percentage points for girls aged 6–10 and 11–15 years, respectively. In contrast, the differences between leading and lagging provinces for rural and poor children are not significant. In the case of rural children, this finding is largely the result of the participation rates for leading provinces falling to the levels of lagging provinces, suggesting a larger rural–urban divide in participation rates in leading provinces.

Unlike India, the evidence for Pakistan suggests that the shortfalls in school participation for lagging provinces worsened over the recent past. Data from 1998/9 show that the position of lagging provinces vis-à-vis leading provinces mirrors that in 2004/5: the shortfalls in participation rates for girls are large and significant while the differences for rural and poor children are not. On the positive side, over the period 1998/9–2004/5, participation rates rose in leading as well as lagging provinces for all the disadvantaged sub-populations examined. However, the growth rates in both absolute and relative terms were larger for leading provinces, resulting in the trends for leading and lagging provinces diverging over

TABLE 6.2   School Participation Rates, Pakistan

Sample	1998/9	2004/5	Yearly % point change, 1998/9–2004/5	Yearly % change, 1998/9–2004/5
		PANEL 1: Ages 6–10		
All				
Leading	0.521	0.637	0.019	0.034
Lagging	0.474	0.553	0.013	0.026
% point gap	0.047	0.085		
Female				
Leading	0.465	0.595	0.022	0.042
Lagging	0.354	0.429	0.013	0.033
% point gap	0.111	0.166		
Rural				
Leading	0.457	0.575	0.020	0.039
Lagging	0.446	0.522	0.013	0.027
% point gap	0.011	0.053		
Poorest quintile				
Leading	0.311	0.495	0.031	0.081
Lagging	0.278	0.424	0.024	0.072
% point gap	0.033	0.072		
		PANEL 2: Ages 11–15		
All				
Leading	0.529	0.609	0.013	0.024
Lagging	0.497	0.544	0.008	0.015
% point gap	0.032	0.064		
Female				
Leading	0.442	0.538	0.016	0.033
Lagging	0.321	0.359	0.006	0.019
% point gap	0.122	0.179		
Rural				
Leading	0.445	0.527	0.014	0.029
Lagging	0.469	0.512	0.007	0.015
% point gap	−0.024	0.015		
Poorest quintile				
Leading	0.290	0.412	0.020	0.060
Lagging	0.324	0.374	0.008	0.024
% point gap	−0.034	0.039		

Notes: 1998/9 and 2004/5 are obtained from the 1998/9 Household Integrated Survey and 2004/5 Social and Living Standards Measurement Survey, respectively. These data are representative at the province and urban/rural levels.

time. This finding applies to the total child population as well as to the selected disadvantaged sub-populations.

Differing from India and Pakistan, in Sri Lanka, there does not appear to be significant variation in participation rates between the leading Western province and the rest of the provinces (all lagging). If at all, there appears to be weak evidence of a difference in participation rates between the civil war-ravaged North-Eastern province and the Western province. Though not directly comparable to the participation rate statistics reported for the other countries, data reported by World Bank (2005d) indicate that the primary enrolment rate is 97 per cent for Sri Lanka, with most provinces clustered closely to this figure. The only notable exception is the North-Eastern province, which has a primary enrolment rate of 92 per cent. Junior secondary school participation rates exhibit greater variation but this is driven principally by the difference between the Western and North-Eastern provinces rather than expanding differences between the other lagging provinces. The rates range from a low of 73 per cent in the North-Eastern province to a high of 87 per cent in the Western and Southern provinces. Senior secondary school enrolment rates between the provinces show relatively less variation: the national net enrolment rate is 50 per cent and provincial net enrolment rates range from 46 per cent (Uva, North-Central province) to 52 per cent (Western province). Evidence on the evolution of primary enrolment rates over time suggests that Sri Lanka had attained virtually full participation at the primary level at least as far back as 1990/1, again with little variation between provinces (World Bank 2005d).

Bangladesh paints a strikingly peculiar picture compared to the other countries examined: the sole leading division in Bangladesh (namely, Dhaka division) fared worse than rest of the divisions (all lagging) in the country in terms of school participation in the recent past. Dhaka division has however largely caught up with lagging divisions, the latter where participation rates have shown, at best, marginal increases over time. Using data from 2005, the school participation rates for children aged 6–10 and 11–15 years between Dhaka division and lagging divisions are similar for the full child population as well as for the selected disadvantaged sub-populations of girls, rural children, and poor children (see Table 6.3). For example, the participation rate for children aged 6–10 years was 69.9 per cent and 70.8 per cent for Dhaka division and lagging divisions, respectively. Looking back over the period 2000–5, it appears that participation rates between Dhaka division and lagging divisions have converged from below over time; this convergence from

TABLE 6.3   **School Participation Rates, Bangladesh**

Sample	2000	2005	Yearly % point change, 2000–5	Yearly % change, 2000–5
PANEL 1: Ages 6–10				
All				
Leading	0.627	0.699	0.014	0.022
Lagging	0.698	0.708	0.002	0.003
% point gap	−0.071	−0.009		
Female				
Leading	0.642	0.717	0.015	0.022
Lagging	0.710	0.718	0.002	0.002
% point gap	−0.068	−0.001		
Rural				
Leading	0.593	0.695	0.020	0.032
Lagging	0.699	0.695	−0.001	−0.001
% point gap	−0.106	0.000		
Poorest quintile				
Leading	0.441	0.581	0.028	0.057
Lagging	0.594	0.602	0.002	0.003
% point gap	−0.154	−0.021		
PANEL 2: Ages 11–15				
All				
Leading	0.621	0.695	0.015	0.023
Lagging	0.665	0.697	0.006	0.009
% point gap	−0.044	−0.002		
Female				
Leading	0.690	0.721	0.006	0.009
Lagging	0.725	0.745	0.004	0.005
% point gap	−0.034	−0.024		
Rural				
Leading	0.607	0.695	0.018	0.028
Lagging	0.662	0.693	0.006	0.009
% point gap	−0.056	0.002		
Poorest quintile				
Leading	0.486	0.507	0.004	0.009
Lagging	0.511	0.520	0.002	0.003
% point gap	−0.025	−0.012		

Notes: 2000 and 2005 statistics are obtained from the 2000 and 2005 Household Income and Expenditure Surveys, respectively. These surveys are representative at the division and urban/rural levels.

below has been for the leading division of Dhaka, while the participation rates for lagging divisions have essentially remained stagnant over this period. Further, depending on the specific sub-population examined, this convergence trend for Dhaka division has been sufficiently strong over this period to either completely erase its deficits or gain significant ground against lagging divisions. For example, in 2000, the rural areas in lagging divisions had a participation rate among children aged 6–10 years of 69.9 per cent, whereas the participation rate for the corresponding sample in Dhaka division was a significant 10.6 percentage points lower—this deficit was entirely erased by 2005.

School Attainment

School attainment is measured here in terms of school completion, and reflects the quantity of human capital acquired via the formal education system. Where primary data are used, primary (grades 1–5) and secondary school (grades 6–10) completion rates (conditional on any institutional schooling) are estimated for individuals aged 15–19 and 20–4 years, respectively. It is important to note that, unlike with school participation, standard measurements of school completion rates can misstate differences in attainment between leading and lagging areas in the presence of significant internal migration.

As discussed previously, participation provides information on whether the child is in or out of school in the state, province, or division where the child is a resident at the time of the survey, while completion may provide information on the extent of schooling acquired in a different state, province, or division from the one the individual is a resident at the time of the survey.[7] In a setting where migration out of lagging areas and into leading areas is both a strong and widespread feature in the region (see Chapter 8 in this volume), observed differences in completion rates between leading and lagging areas can be biased—whether differences are upwardly or downwardly biased will depend on whether migration is stronger among the more educated or less, respectively. This caveat should be kept in mind as the results on the patterns and trends in subnational completion rates do not account for population migration patterns across state, division, or province lines.

In India, similar to the story for school participation rates, school completion rates in lagging states are currently lower than in leading

---

[7]Typically, standard household surveys do not collect detailed schooling/migration history data which would enable splicing what level of schooling was acquired in the current subnational area of residence and what level was acquired elsewhere.

states; however, in contrast to the participation story, over the recent past, changes in completion rates in lagging states have either managed to keep pace with or lost ground to leading states. Primary and secondary school completion rates are significantly lower in lagging districts than in leading states (see Table 6.4). This is true in both 1999/2000 and 2004/5. For example, with respect to primary school completion rates in 2004/5, the shortfalls for lagging states range from 16 to 22 percentage points across the sub-populations examined; with respect to secondary school completion rates in the same year, the shortfalls range from 8 to 17 percentage points. However, while both primary and secondary school completion rates have increased in both leading as well as lagging states over 1999/2000–2004/5, lagging states are, at best, maintaining ground (for example, parallel trends among rural children); in some cases, they are marginally losing ground (for example, divergence in trends among poor children).

Likewise, in Pakistan, similar to its participation story, school completion rates are lower in lagging provinces. Moreover, the shortfalls in lagging provinces appear to be particularly severe for young females. In 2004/5, the shortfalls in lagging provinces for primary and secondary school completion rates were 3.8 and 7.5 percentage points, respectively (see Table 6.5). Among the disadvantaged sub-populations of interest, the shortfalls were large and significant for females—for example, among female youth, the secondary school completion rate was 14 percentage points lower in lagging provinces.

While primary and secondary completion rates have increased in leading as well as lagging provinces in Pakistan, whether there has been convergence or divergence across provinces appears to depend on the specific education completion level and sub-population. Over the period 1998/9–2004/5, primary and secondary school completion rates in both leading and lagging provinces have increased; the increases have been particularly dramatic for primary school completion rates, with both leading and lagging provinces posting double-digit per cent growth annually (see Table 6.5). How lagging provinces have fared vis-à-vis leading provinces with respect to completion rates depends on the level and sub-population under consideration. For primary school completion rates, the evidence suggests that leading provinces either maintained ground with (for example, parallel trends for poor youth) or gained ground on (for example, convergence from below for young females) leading provinces. For secondary school completion rates, the evidence is more mixed: lagging provinces have either maintained ground with (for

TABLE 6.4   School Completion Rates, India

Sample	1999/2000	2004/5	Yearly % point change, 1999/2000– 2004/5	Yearly % change, 1999/2000– 2004/5
PANEL 1: Primary completion, ages 15–19				
All				
Leading	0.756	0.818	0.012	0.016
Lagging	0.608	0.659	0.010	0.016
% point gap	0.148	0.159		
Female				
Leading	0.696	0.790	0.019	0.026
Lagging	0.505	0.572	0.013	0.025
% point gap	0.191	0.218		
Rural				
Leading	0.712	0.783	0.014	0.019
Lagging	0.555	0.627	0.014	0.025
% point gap	0.157	0.156		
Scheduled Tribes				
Leading	0.622	0.705	0.017	0.025
Lagging	0.429	0.510	0.016	0.035
% point gap	0.193	0.195		
Poorest quintile				
Leading	0.569	0.695	0.025	0.041
Lagging	0.400	0.503	0.021	0.047
% point gap	0.169	0.192		
PANEL 2: Secondary completion, ages 20–4				
All				
Leading	0.352	0.383	0.006	0.017
Lagging	0.235	0.250	0.003	0.012
% point gap	0.117	0.133		
Female				
Leading	0.293	0.345	0.010	0.033
Lagging	0.155	0.179	0.005	0.029
% point gap	0.138	0.166		
Rural				
Leading	0.275	0.304	0.006	0.020
Lagging	0.170	0.195	0.005	0.028
% point gap	0.105	0.109		

(contd...)

Table 6.4 (contd...)

Sample	1999/2000	2004/5	Yearly % point change, 1999/2000–2004/5	Yearly % change, 1999/2000–2004/5
Scheduled Tribes				
Leading	0.240	0.230	–0.002	–0.008
Lagging	0.149	0.103	–0.009	–0.071
% point gap	0.091	0.127		
Poorest quintile				
Leading	0.141	0.181	0.008	0.051
Lagging	0.080	0.100	0.004	0.046
% point gap	0.061	0.081		

Notes: 1999/2000 and 2004/5 statistics are obtained from the 55th and 61st rounds of the National Sample Survey, respectively. These surveys are representative at the state and urban/rural levels.

example, parallel trends for young females), caught up and marginally surpassed (for example, convergence from below for rural youth) or lost ground to (for example, divergence for poor youth) leading provinces. In the aggregate, the evidence suggests that with respect to the secondary school completion rate lagging provinces have lost ground to leading provinces.

In Bangladesh, the evidence suggests that there are no systematic differences in completion rates between Dhaka division and the lagging divisions. In 2005, whether Dhaka division or lagging divisions had a higher school completion rate depended on the completion level and the specific sub-population under consideration. For example, the secondary school completion rate among young females was 5.1 percentage points higher in Dhaka division, whereas the primary school completion rate among poor youth was 6.6 percentage points higher in lagging divisions. Irrespective of their relative rankings, given the extent of survey sampling error, the differences in completion rates between Dhaka division and the lagging divisions were not found to be statistically significant.

In general, changes in completion rates over the recent past suggest convergence from below for *Dhaka division*. Over the period 2000–5, both primary and secondary school completion rates have increased in all divisions, with the increases larger for the former completion level. Similar to the picture for school participation rates across divisions, with the exception of poor youth for whom the primary school completion rate in Dhaka division lost ground to that of lagging divisions (that is,

TABLE 6.5   School Completion Rates, Pakistan

Sample	1998/9	2004/5	Yearly % point change, 1998/9– 2004/5	Yearly % change, 1998/9– 2004/5
PANEL 1: Primary completion, ages 15–19				
All				
Leading	0.591	0.901	0.052	0.073
Lagging	0.484	0.863	0.063	0.101
% point gap	0.107	0.038		
Female				
Leading	0.492	0.906	0.069	0.107
Lagging	0.257	0.842	0.098	0.219
% point gap	0.235	0.064		
Rural				
Leading	0.492	0.870	0.063	0.100
Lagging	0.447	0.846	0.067	0.112
% point gap	0.045	0.024		
Poorest quintile				
Leading	0.358	0.815	0.076	0.147
Lagging	0.273	0.698	0.071	0.169
% point gap	0.084	0.117		
PANEL 2: Secondary completion, ages 20–4				
All				
Leading	0.293	0.347	0.009	0.029
Lagging	0.248	0.273	0.004	0.016
% point gap	0.045	0.075		
Female				
Leading	0.243	0.305	0.010	0.039
Lagging	0.109	0.165	0.009	0.071
% point gap	0.134	0.140		
Rural				
Leading	0.179	0.225	0.008	0.039
Lagging	0.221	0.236	0.002	0.011
% point gap	0.042	−0.011		
Poorest quintile				
Leading	0.074	0.147	0.012	0.123
Lagging	0.120	0.112	−0.001	−0.011
% point gap	−0.047	0.035		

Notes: 1998/9 and 2004/5 are obtained from the 1998/9 Household Integrated Survey and 2004/5 Social and Living Standards Measurement Survey, respectively. These data are representative at the province and urban/rural levels.

TABLE 6.6   School Completion Rates, Bangladesh

Sample	2000	2005	Yearly % point change, 2000–5	Yearly % change, 2000–5
PANEL 1: Primary completion, ages 15–19				
All				
Leading	0.634	0.770	0.027	0.040
Lagging	0.667	0.727	0.012	0.017
% point gap	−0.033	0.043		
Female				
Leading	0.643	0.794	0.030	0.043
Lagging	0.689	0.779	0.018	0.025
% point gap	−0.047	0.015		
Rural				
Leading	0.572	0.730	0.032	0.050
Lagging	0.654	0.719	0.013	0.019
% point gap	−0.082	0.012		
Poorest quintile				
Leading	0.357	0.488	0.026	0.064
Lagging	0.392	0.554	0.032	0.071
% point gap	−0.035	−0.066		
PANEL 2: Secondary completion, ages 20–24				
All				
Leading	0.267	0.281	0.003	0.011
Lagging	0.224	0.239	0.003	0.012
% point gap	0.042	0.043		
Female				
Leading	0.209	0.241	0.006	0.029
Lagging	0.143	0.190	0.009	0.059
% point gap	0.066	0.051		
Rural				
Leading	0.159	0.184	0.005	0.030
Lagging	0.195	0.201	0.001	0.006
% point gap	−0.037	−0.017		
Poorest quintile				
Leading	0.059	0.063	0.001	0.012
Lagging	0.061	0.066	0.001	0.017
% point gap	−0.001	−0.003		

Notes: 2005 statistics obtained from the 2005 Household Income and Expenditure Survey. 2000 statistics obtained from the 2000 Household Income and Expenditure Survey.

where the trends exhibited divergence from above), the trends for the rest of the examined disadvantaged sub-populations show convergence from below for Dhaka division, to the extent that it erased past deficits. For example, in 2000, rural youth in lagging divisions had a primary school completion rate of 65.4 per cent, whereas the rate for the corresponding sub-population in Dhaka division was 57.2 per cent, a statistically-significant 8.2 percentage-point difference. By 2005, the completion rate for rural youth in Dhaka division had caught up and marginally exceeded the completion rate for the corresponding sub-population in lagging divisions by 1.2 percentage points. With respect to secondary school completion rates, the rates for Dhaka division and lagging divisions largely tracked one another—no statistically-significant differences in completion rates between Dhaka division and the lagging divisions in any of the selected samples in 2000, nor in 2005.

Finally, in Sri Lanka, secondary data from 2002 show that the primary school completion rates were generally similar across the provinces, ranging between 93 per cent in Sabaragamuwa to 96 per cent in the Western province (World Bank 2005d). Moving up to secondary school completion rates, the data suggests greater variation across provinces.[8] Data from 2007 show that the Western province had (close to) the highest rate of students completing basic education (grades 1–9) in the country at 90 per cent (93 per cent) for boys (girls). In the remaining provinces, basic education completion rates varied from a low of 70 per cent (76 per cent) for the Eastern province[9] to a high of 90 per cent (94per cent) for the Southern province for boys (girls), a difference of at least 20 percentage points among lagging provinces.

Achievement

The quality of schooling, as measured by student achievement, is increasingly seen as one of the chief determinants of the long-term socio-economic prospects of individuals (Hanushek and Woessmann 2010, 2008). Unfortunately, data on achievement at the country level in South Asia, leave alone data on achievement at the subnational level within South Asian countries, are highly limited. Bangladesh unfortunately is a casualty of this state of affairs: the country only has national-level annual data on pass rates in its Secondary School Certificate (SSC) and Higher

[8]The corresponding statistics for the North-Eastern province was unavailable.
[9]The North-Eastern province was divided into the Northern and Eastern provinces in 2006.

Secondary School Certificate (HSC) public examinations (BANBEIS 2006).[10] In India, Pakistan, and Sri Lanka, answers to the questions on whether there exist differences in subnational student achievement levels and what explains (the lack of) differences are constructed by piecing together available evidence from (i) small-scale sample-based testing exercises by researchers in selected states and provinces in countries; (ii) some large-scale, sample-based testing exercises undertaken nationwide by governments or NGOs; and (iii) general school-leaving/ entrance examinations. Most of this evidence comes from recent test data, collected in the 2000s. With the exception of Sri Lanka, how subnational achievement levels have evolved over the recent past is not discussed in this section due to the paucity of comparable test data over time.

Unlike with school participation and completion rates for which comparable measurements (both over time and across populations) can be constructed fairly easily by using surveys that ask similar questions, comparing achievement results from different testing exercises (that is, different test populations, testing conditions, and test instrument contents) is less straightforward. Comparable achievement results can, however, be obtained by linking tests based on common test questions and calibrating results to a reference distribution. Efforts at rigorously linking results across tests are highly limited but not entirely missing in South Asia. For example, adjusted results from independent testing (using test questions from the Trends in International Math and Science Study assessment or TIMSS) of grade-9 students in a sample of public and private in selected urban and rural districts in Orissa and Rajasthan, both lagging states, show that average learning levels in these states were significantly below the average for OECD countries (Wu et al. 2009; Das and Zajonc 2008).[11]

There is also some complementary evidence from looser test-result linking efforts. For example, comparisons of the test results of grade-3 students from a sample of private and public schools in selected rural districts in Punjab, a leading province in Pakistan, to TIMSS results for

[10]World Bank (2008) also summarizes the findings from several assessment exercises of primary school-age children. The general finding is that they generally perform far below curriculum levels, with a significant shares completing primary school without acquiring basic competencies.

[11]Given the significantly lower participation rates of children in school in India vis-à-vis OECD countries, especially at this level, the difference in mean learning levels is likely to be an underestimate (if, for example, children with the lower learning abilities have dropped out) of the difference in average learning levels in the underlying populations.

grade-4 students show that the average achievement level in Pakistan is significantly below the achievement level internationally, a shortfall that the majority of students in the country never recover from given that they terminate their schooling in primary grades. Further, it appears that the poor achievement performance of Pakistan vis-à-vis other countries cannot be attributed to differences in curriculum standards (Andrabi et al. 2009). Within the region, comparisons of test results between primary school students in rural Punjab, Pakistan, to primary school students in rural Uttar Pradesh and Madhya Pradesh, the latter both lagging states in India, suggest that average learning levels are largely comparable across the two countries (Das et al. 2006). Further, comparisons of test results for these primary students in rural Punjab, Pakistan, to Pratham's Annual Status of Education Report (ASER) test results for students in rural districts in Indian states suggest that the average learning level in rural Punjab places the Pakistani province roughly in the centre of the distribution of learning levels across Indian states (Andrabi et al. 2008).

Beginning with Pakistan, there is growing evidence that learning levels at the primary and secondary levels in the country are poor, significantly below curriculum levels across a range of subjects. These findings are obtained from government testing (via the National Education Assessment System (NEAS) program) of a sample of grade-4 students in public schools across the country as well as independent testing of a sample of primary school students in private and public schools in selected rural districts in the leading provinces of Punjab and Sindh (Andrabi et al. 2008; Saiens 2008; Das et al. 2006; Government of Pakistan 2006).

While learning levels of children in Pakistan are low in general, the available evidence suggests that there does not appear to be systematic differences in learning levels across provinces. For example, results from NEAS testing of grade-4 students in 2005 show that scaled scores in mathematics ranged from a mean of 443 for Balochistan, a lagging province, to a mean of 402 for Sindh, a leading province; moreover, only Sindh's mean was significantly different from the national mean (Government of Pakistan 2006). This finding sharply contrasts with the findings of significant deficits in school participation and completion levels in lagging provinces relative to leading provinces.

NEAS also finds that, on average, rural students do worse than urban students and female students do better than male students in the test. The finding that female students do just as well as or better than male students in terms of learning is corroborated by other independent research which shows that the female advantage in learning remains largely intact even after accounting for a range of individual, household, village, and school characteristics (Andrabi et al. 2008; Saiens 2008). While we know from earlier in the chapter that there is a female disadvantage in school participation and completion rates in both lagging and leading provinces in Pakistan, and that this disadvantage is particularly severe in lagging provinces, the published statistics from NEAS are not sufficiently disaggregated to infer whether the female advantage in learning performance found nationally differs systematically by province, more specifically, between leading and lagging provinces.

Similar to Pakistan, the limited evidence from India also suggests that learning levels are generally low. For example, results from independent testing of grade-4 students in a sample of public primary schools in selected rural districts in Madhya Pradesh and Uttar Pradesh, both lagging states, show that average learning levels of students were significantly below curriculum standards (Das et al. 2006).

Evidence from recent annual independent testing of children aged 6–14 years in district-representative samples of households across rural India by the NGO Pratham—reported in their publication, the Annual Status of Education Report (ASER)—also suggests low learning levels across much of rural India. For example, the 2008 ASER data show that 67 per cent of rural children in grades 3–5 can read at the grade-1 level and 55 per cent of rural children in grades 3–5 can at least subtract numbers (Pratham 2009).

The available evidence from India also suggests that there does not appear to be a discernible pattern of learning differences between lagging and leading states. For example, ASER data show that there are lagging states as well as leading states with low and high shares of primary school students with minimum levels of competency in language and mathematics, with the range of student competency rates across states largely overlapping (see Figure 6.3). For example, the 2008 ASER data show that the share of rural students in grades 3–5 who could read at grade-1 curriculum levels ranged from 45.7 per cent (Tamil Nadu) to 85.9 per cent (Kerala) among leading states and from 50.7 per cent (Uttar Pradesh) and to 91.7 per cent (Madhya Pradesh) among lagging states. Similarly, the share of rural children in grades 3–5 who can do at least simple subtraction ranged from 29.3 per cent to 80.6 per cent among leading states and from 35.2 per cent (Uttar Pradesh) to 92 per cent (Mizoram) among lagging states (Pratham 2009, 2007).

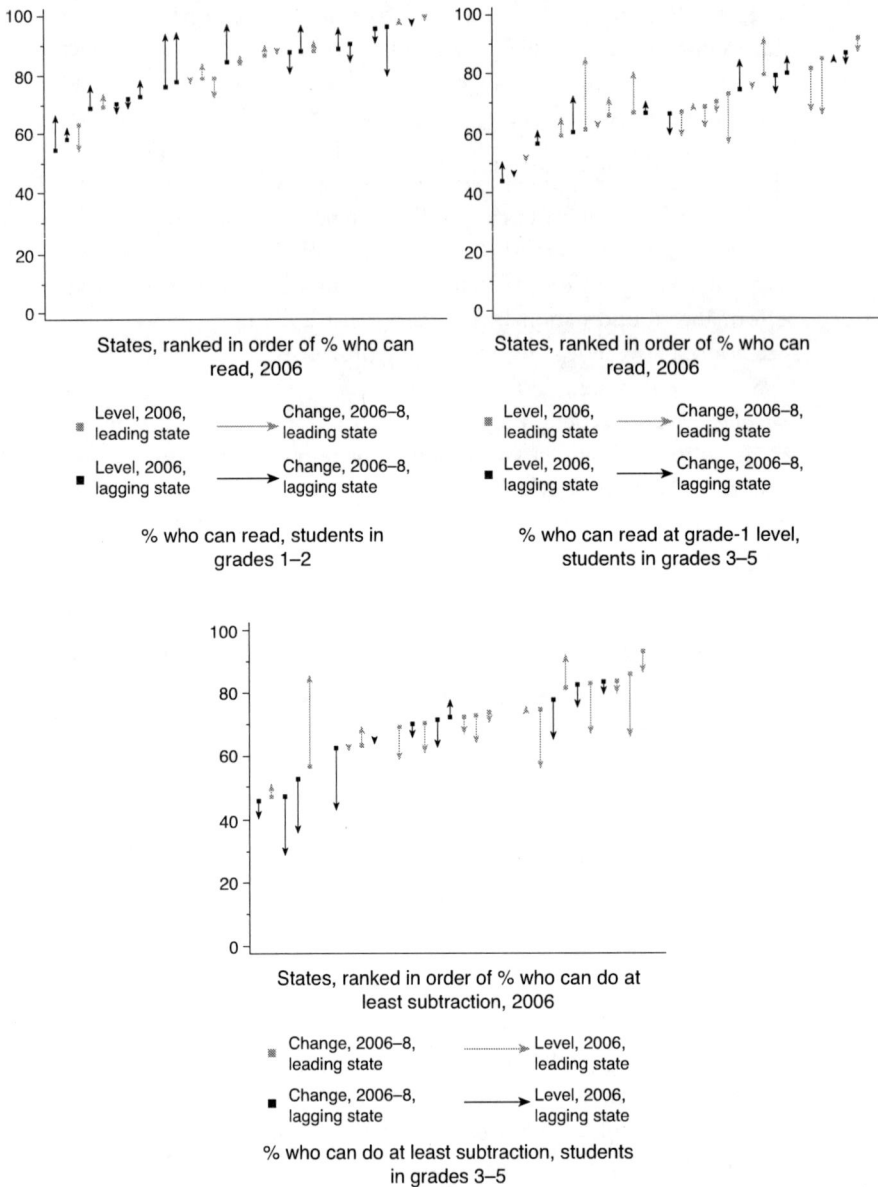

States, ranked in order of % who can read, 2006

| Level, 2006, leading state | Change, 2006–8, leading state |
| Level, 2006, lagging state | Change, 2006–8, lagging state |

% who can read, students in grades 1–2

States, ranked in order of % who can read, 2006

| Level, 2006, leading state | Change, 2006–8, leading state |
| Level, 2006, lagging state | Change, 2006–8, lagging state |

% who can read at grade-1 level, students in grades 3–5

States, ranked in order of % who can do at least subtraction, 2006

| Change, 2006–8, leading state | Level, 2006, leading state |
| Change, 2006–8, lagging state | Level, 2006, lagging state |

% who can do at least subtraction, students in grades 3–5

FIGURE 6.3   Minimum Competency Rates in Language and Mathematical Assessments among Rural Primary School Students, Indian States (2006 and 2008)

Source: Annual Status of Education Reports, Pratham.

Short-term changes in student competency rates as measured using ASER data for 2006 and 2008 show both declines and increases (with some states displaying fairly large jumps). However, similar to the story on the student competency levels across states, there does not appear to be systematic differences in either the magnitude or direction of changes in student competency rates between leading and lagging states.[12]

While Sri Lanka has been much more successful in getting children to school and keeping them there through the primary and secondary cycles than, for example, both India and Pakistan, like these two countries, it has struggled to attain satisfactory learning levels. For example, 2003 data from achievement tests of students who had completed grade 4 in a nationally-representative sample of public schools show that 37 per cent, 10 per cent, and 38 per cent of tested students achieved mastery in their native language, English, and mathematics, respectively (Aturupane et al. 2007). Low levels of achievement are also reflected in the student pass rates of the competitive General Certificate of Education (CGE) examination at the ordinary (O/L) and advanced levels (A/L). The national pass rates in the GCE O/L and A/L examinations in 2002 were 37 per cent and 56 per cent, respectively. These pass rates are particularly low given that GCE candidates are likely a highly positively-selected group—only the best students take these examinations (increasing selectivity is probably an important explanation behind the higher pass rate associated with the A/L examination relative to the O/L). An analysis of trends over the 1990s shows that the O/L pass rates have risen over time, while A/L pass rates have fluctuated in the 50–60 per cent range (World Bank 2005d).

Despite its low learning levels, differences across provinces in Sri Lanka are starker than with its quantity indicators of schooling; in fact, as shown previously, the latter indicators are largely fuzzy across provinces. This finding directly contrasts with the findings for India and Pakistan, where subnational differences in the quantity indicators (participation and completion) are sharp while subnational differences in student achievement are fuzzy. Normalized test scores indicate that

[12]The large changes in competency rates in such a short period in some states raise the question on how reliable the data are. The ASER reports do not provide information on the extent to which sampling variability explains observed differences in competency rates across states at a given point in time or changes in student competency rates across time for a given state. In addition, the ASER reports suggest improvements over time in the extent of survey coverage of districts across states as well as in field survey administration performance—this may be an important part of the explanation for the jumpiness in estimates over time.

the Western province, the leading province in the country, significantly outperformed all other provinces across all three subjects, and that the North-Eastern province significantly underperformed relative to the other provinces. For example, the mean score in mathematics in the Western province was 0.44; the mean score in the North-Eastern province was −0.34; and the rest of the provinces had means ranging from −0.19 to 0.01 (Aturupane et al. 2007). With the GCE examinations, pass rates in the O/L examination range from a low of 31–2 per cent in Uva, North-Eastern, Central, and North-Central provinces, all lagging provinces, to a high of 48 per cent in the Western province. There is a much greater degree of uniformity in A/L pass rates—the pass rates range from 52 per cent in Uva province to 58 per cent in the North-Eastern and North-Western provinces; the Western province had a pass rate of 54 per cent (World Bank 2005d).

There is also fairly strong evidence that, over the recent past, learning levels in Sri Lanka are increasing as well as converging between provinces. Specifically, learning levels for lagging provinces are converging from below to that of the Western province. Data from testing grade-4 students

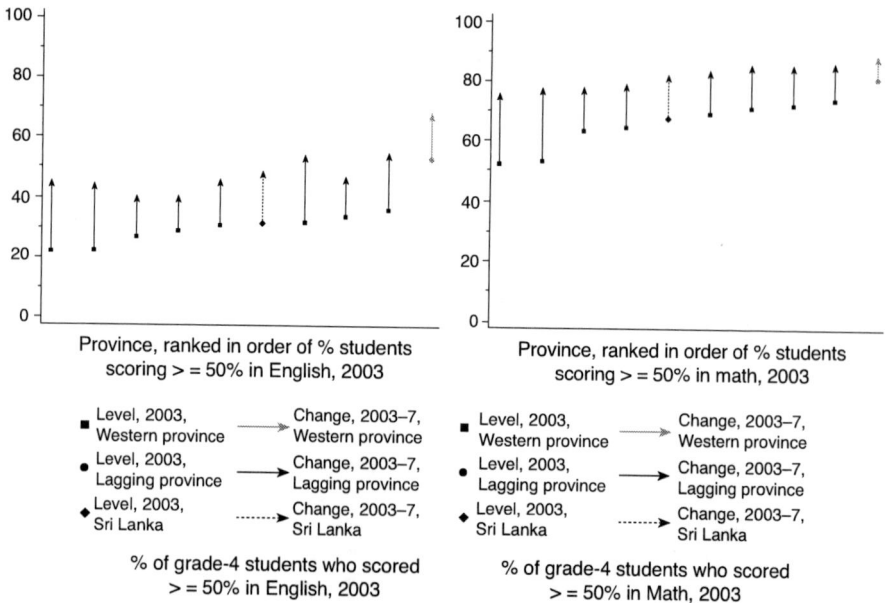

FIGURE 6.4   Primary School Student Achievement in Sri Lanka Provinces (2003 and 2007)

Source: National Education Research and Evaluation Center, University of Colombo.

show that the shares of students who scored at least 50 per cent in English and mathematics have significantly increased in all provinces over the period 2003–7 (see Figure 6.4). For example, the Western province, which was the best performing province in 2003, saw its share of students scoring at least 50 per cent in mathematics increase from 81 per cent in 2003 to 87 per cent in 2007; the Eastern province, which was the worst performing province in 2003, saw its corresponding share increase from 52 per cent to 75 per cent. Over this period, the gap in achievement between the Western province and Sri Lanka decreased from 71 per cent to 39 per cent in English and 21 per cent to 9 per cent in mathematics (Aturupane 2008).

EXPLANATIONS FOR PATTERNS AND TRENDS

Bangladesh

The reasons behind the lower levels of school participation and completion in the recent past in (economically-leading) Dhaka division relative to other (economically-lagging) divisions in the country have been a relatively unexplored question. However, the pattern has not gone unnoticed. For example, Al-Samarrai (2007) notes salient differences between divisions in school participation rates at all levels. Importantly, he finds that school participation rates are higher in divisions with higher poverty rates (such as in Barisal, Khulna, and Rajshahi). The author attributes this association to the higher opportunity costs of schooling in the economically stronger and more dynamic divisions engendered by the relative availability and attractiveness of labour market opportunities for children. A similar argument is made by World Bank (2007), which reports research that secondary school participation is negatively associated with child wages. World Bank (2007) also notes disadvantages in education outcomes for metropolitan areas (with Dhaka being the largest such area) relative to rural and non-metropolitan urban areas, with the disadvantage in education outcomes for metropolitan areas particularly severe for children from the poorest household expenditure quintiles.

In addition, some studies argue that the nature of government priorities in education may have been instrumental in constraining education outcomes and progress in metropolitan areas, including Dhaka. For example, World Bank (2007) claims that the government had focused over the 1980s and 1990s on extending education service delivery to the rural poor and introducing transfer and fee waiver programmes to raise their demand for schooling. The various programmes include the

Monthly Pay Order (MPO) system, the Food-for-Education Program (launched in 1993), the Primary Education Stipend Program (launched in 2003), and the Female Secondary School Stipend Program (launched nationwide in 1994). Many of these programmes have benefit structures and qualifying conditions that are viewed as more appropriate and thus more favourable to disadvantaged populations in rural areas. The World Bank report also claims that metropolitan areas suffer from special service delivery issues that have failed to receive adequate government attention and customized responses. One example that is cited is with respect to the MPO system which offers public subsidies to private providers of secondary education (virtually the exclusive provider of secondary education in Bangladesh) to cover the bulk of their recurrent expenditures (mainly teacher and staff salaries) and provides block grants for school construction and maintenance (Asadullah et al. 2007; World Bank 2003a). Given that recurrent costs reportedly are significantly higher in metropolitan areas due to higher teacher salaries and land and building rental prices, the share of expenditures covered by government subsidies under the MPO system is much smaller and, consequently, secondary schools in metropolitan areas are much more reliant on user fees to cover expenditures, likely discouraging both the supply and demand for secondary schooling.

An important source of information that may yield insights into why the Dhaka division differs from other divisions are studies of the determinants of school participation and education attainment in Bangladesh using recent rounds of representative household sample survey data. In general, these studies find that school participation and attainment of children are positively associated with, for example, the education levels of the parents or household head, household income or consumption levels, whether the child is female, and whether the household is Muslim (for example, see World Bank 2008a; Al-Samarrai 2007; World Bank 2005a; Maitra 2003). Additionally, Al-Samarrai (2007) finds that, controlling for the levels of head's education and household income, the head's occupational status also matters, with schooling attainment lower for a daily wage worker relative than for a self-employed worker. The author also finds that the number of secondary schools found locally is positively associated with boys' attainment. World Bank (2005a) finds that the presence of paved roads in the district, household domicile distance to the bus station, and participation in the Food-for-Education Program are positively associated with primary school participation. However, it remains unknown the extent to which the relative levels of these covariates systematically vary between Dhaka division and the other divisions, and, consequently, whether these differences account for a significant share of the observed differences in educational outcomes. One indication is provided by World Bank (2008a) which reports that mean per capita consumption expenditure in the lowest expenditure quintile is lower in metropolitan areas than in rural areas.

There is also some evidence that, depending on the sub-population under consideration, which division the child belongs to matters even after controlling for a range of covariates that are expected to be associated with schooling outcomes, suggesting the role of additional factors in explaining the variation in outcomes across divisions (World Bank 2008a; Al-Samarrai 2007). For example, Al-Samarrai (2007) finds within a regression framework that, barring Sylhet division, all other individual divisions have a higher attainment level than Dhaka division, and that this finding is driven by the boys' sample. Studies have also examined a range of supply-side factors typically not incorporated into education production regressions, and have argued that the efficiency and effectiveness of the education system in Bangladesh have been adversely affected by such issues as the poor quality of instruction, the limited relevance of curriculum, teacher absence and shirking, poor teacher-hiring practices, and limited school accountability to local communities (Chaudhury et al. 2006; World Bank 2003). Again, it remains unclear the extent to which these factors systematically differ between Dhaka division and the rest, and whether these differences account for a significant share of the observed differences in education outcomes.

Finally, there is some evidence which suggests that to shed light on why there are educational differences between Dhaka division and other divisions requires looking within Dhaka division. For example, World Bank (2005a) notes large differences in school participation and completion rates between rural Dhaka, urban Dhaka, and Standard Metropolitan Area (SMA) Dhaka, with the rates for these areas spanning a large segment of the range of rates across divisions. Likewise, World Bank (2007) claims that schooling outcomes in slums and other low-income areas in Dhaka—where a sizeable share of Dhaka's population resides—are extremely poor. Finally, World Bank (2008a) finds that there are substantive differences in the estimated partial effects of relevant covariates (such as parental education) on school attainment between metropolitan areas, rural areas, and non-metropolitan urban areas. These findings collectively imply that particularly poor outcomes in some sub-populations of Dhaka division may be responsible for the division's poor relative performance in the recent past.

Notwithstanding, to the best of our knowledge, there has been no research that has looked at what factors have contributed to Dhaka division catching up in terms of school participation and completion levels with other divisions over the recent period.

India

In India, across all indicators examined (school participation, primary and secondary completion rates), lagging states do worse than leading states, and this finding holds even when the sample is restricted to girls, rural children, tribal children, and children from the poorest household consumption expenditure quintile. Over the recent past, there have been marked inceases in participation among children of primary school-going age and primary completion rates, but only marginal increases in the participation rate among children of secondary school-going age and in the secondary completion rate. Further, gaps between leading and lagging states remain in terms of absolute percentage point differences. However, there appears to be evidence of catch-up from below for lagging states, particularly in primary education. These trends hold for the overall sample as well as when the sample is restricted to girls, rural children, and children from the poorest quintile.

One source of evidence on why these gaps exist between leading and lagging states in India are the several studies on the determinants of school participation and attainment. While not consistent across all studies, many find that school participation and attainment are positively associated with such factors as household adult and parental education, parental occupational status, household wealth and asset levels, home learning environment, child age, and child ability, and negatively associated with household size or number of younger siblings. They also find that, conditional on household wealth and parental schooling, Muslim children are less likely to attend school or attain less education than Hindu children, and similarly that Scheduled Tribe and Scheduled Caste children attend fewer years of school relative to upper-caste groups. Rural children are also less likely to attend to school relative to urban children (Balhotra and Zamora 2005; Kingdon 2002). Jayachandran (2002) finds that school accessibility is positively associated with school participation. To the extent that lagging states are disadvantaged in terms of the levels of these factors, it is likely that they explain the differences in outcomes between leading and lagging states.

Returns to these factors also matter and may play a role in explaining gaps in participation and attainment between leading and lagging states. For example, Balhotra and Zamora (2005) find that the increases in primary school participation found in India over the period 1992–3/1998–9 was entirely driven by changing to returns to relevant factors that potentially explain the child school participation decision. They find that the levels of the factors do not explain any of the positive change. Kingdon (2002) finds that inferior returns to the relevant factors explain 75 per cent of the gender gap in attainment among adults in Uttar Pradesh, a lagging state; the remaining 25 per cent is explained by the inferior levels of these factors. Durraisamy (2002) finds that the returns to schooling have changed particularly for female wage-earners over the period 1983–94. Thus, to the extent that the (changes in the) returns to factors explain the participation and attainment decision and that the (changes in the) returns to schooling differ systematically between leading and lagging states, it is likely that these explain the participation and completion gaps.

Studies also show that the state continues to matter in participation and attainment regressions, even after controlling for a range of child, parent, and household characteristics; this suggests that other factors potentially correlated with the state remain inadequately accounted for and require further investigation. For example, Jayachandran (2002) finds that, after controlling for a range of factors, school participation in states in eastern region are worse than the rest of India. She also finds that states in northern region have higher gender gaps in participation relative to states in the eastern region. Balhotra and Zamora (2005) find that the state dummies in their primary participation and completion regressions are jointly significant and that individual state dummies are highly significant.

Shifting to the supply side, levels and patterns of budgetary allocations and expenditures for public elementary education show that lagging states in general are disadvantaged relative to leading states. Jhingran and Sankar (2009) note that public investments in elementary education in programmes such as the Sarva Shiksha Abhiyan (SSA), which seeks to universalize elementary education, are substantial and have grown dramatically between 2001/2–2004/5, leading to, in general, significant increases in schools, classrooms, and teachers, and improved provision of textbooks, mid-day meals at schools, and in-service training for teachers. However, they find that per capita SSA allocations and per capita expenditures (that is, the utilization of given resources) are significantly lower in many lagging states and districts. In fact, they find that per capita allocations and expenditures are *positively* associated with their education development index (EDI) across districts in India.[13] For example, they find that the majority of districts in the lagging states of Uttar Pradesh, Bihar, and Jharkand have very low EDI values and per capita allocations; the 50 districts with the lowest EDI values had a mean funds utilization rate of 5 per cent, while the 100 districts with the highest EDI values had a mean funds utilization rate of 60 per cent.

Jhingran and Sankar (2009) attribute these patterns to at least three reasons. One, budgets are set largely as a function of the existing stock of schools and teachers (which favour leading states and districts) rather than considering the extent of existing deficiencies in service delivery. Two, weak planning and implementation capacity of governments in lagging states and districts also limit their ability to garner greater resources and use them more effectively for education development. Three, lagging states have struggled to meet their expected shares of expenditures for SSA and other programmes due to their weak revenue-generating capacities.

The extent of weaknesses in accountability in the public education system, which remains the main provider and financier of primary and secondary education in India, may also be behind the outcome gaps between leading and lagging states. Kremer et al. (2005) find that on average 25 per cent of public school teachers were absent, and that when present in school, less than half of them were engaged in teaching. They also find that absenteeism rates and non-teaching rates tend to be higher in lagging states; this despite the fact that, in *real* terms, teacher salaries in lagging states are higher than in leading states. They attribute the high absenteeism and non-teaching rates to weak or the absence of disciplinary actions (such as firing) for such behaviour. They also find that teachers are more likely to be present if school infrastructure is better, and less likely to be present if the schools are remote. To the extent that there are systematic differences in infrastructure quality and school remoteness across leading and lagging states, this may also play a role in explaining differences in absenteeism rates between them. Regardless, absence has negative consequences for schooling outcomes: children are less likely to attend to school; they also learn less as measured by test scores.

---

[13]The EDI is a composite measure based on data on school access, school infrastructure, equity as measured by female educational outcomes, and child participation and completion rates.

The reduction in gaps observed particularly at the primary level between leading and lagging states may also in part be explained by the growing role of the private sector in service delivery, catering to an increasingly wide range of the population. Muralidhran and Kremer (2008) find that private schools tend to locate in villages where the rates of teacher absence and non-teaching activity in public schools are high. They also find that the relative prevalence of private schools is higher in lagging states, suggesting that private schools may be emerging in these areas to address deficiencies in service delivery in the public education system.

Private schools also appear to yield benefits in terms of quality and cost-effectiveness. Private schools have as good or better facilities and amenities as public schools. They hire more teachers, have less multi-grade teaching, and lower student–teacher ratios. Their teachers tend to better educated. Teacher presence and teaching activity rates tend to be higher than for public school teachers, especially when comparing public schools to private schools within villages—this despite the fact that private school teachers get paid a fraction of the salaries received by public school teachers. Finally, student presence and achievement in private schools tend to be higher than those in public schools, even after controlling for a range of relevant characteristics and attempting to address potential selectivity in school choice (Goyal and Pandey 2009; Desai et al. 2008; Mehrotra and Panchamukhi 2008; Muralidharan and Kremer 2008). Desai et al. (2008) also stress that the private school advantage in student learning is not uniform across states—interestingly, it tends to appear in lagging states (such as Bihar, Uttar Pradesh, Uttarkhand, and Madhya Pradesh).

Pakistan

In Pakistan, as discussed in the previous section, participation, completion, and learning levels are generally poor. Further, the evidence suggests that primary and secondary participation and completion rates are *even* lower in lagging provinces than in leading provinces, with the largest inter-provincial gaps present among *females*. While the trajectories over the recent past in these indicators in both lagging and leading provinces are positive, it appears that lagging provinces are generally losing ground in terms of these outcomes; the sole exception is primary school completion rates, where lagging provinces are narrowing the gap from below. Country-wide evidence on learning (currently largely confined to public school students) does not show systematic differences between lagging and leading provinces; notwithstanding, learning levels in general are extremely low (Das et al. 2006).

Do expenditure levels and patterns across provinces play a role in explaining the divide in education outcomes? Budgetary allocations from the central government made to the provinces are based principally on population numbers. Thus, in absolute terms, the populous and leading provinces of Punjab and Sindh receive the highest allocations—this may matter for education development even if, on a per-capita basis, central allocations to the provinces are comparable. The central allocations are topped up by provincial allocations, which vary between 20–30 per cent of total provincial budgets (Husain et al. 2003). The revenue-generating capacity of the provinces will play a role in determining the extent of direct provincial contribution to public education; needless to say, the lagging provinces will be disadvantaged in this respect. In addition, Sabir (2003) finds that while expenditures for public education are progressive at the primary level in Punjab and Sindh; they are not in Balochistan and NWFP. Further, he finds that females are systematically disadvantaged in terms of the incidence of allocations—this has partly to do with the lower relative enrolment among females (which is more acute in the lagging provinces) but also suggests the need to direct expenditures to areas with low female enrolment and initiatives that raise female enrolment.

The current gaps in participation and completion rates between leading and lagging provinces and evidence of a growing divide in these indicators in the recent past may be driven to a large extent by the arrested reach and poor quality of service delivery in the public education system, which remains the main provider of education, particularly in rural areas. Many researchers point to weak accountability for performance to be a major reason behind the poor quality of public education; the explosive growth of private schools in the last two decades is also viewed as a response to the growing demand for better quality schooling among a wide swathe of the population (Andrabi et al. 2006; Arif and Saqib 2003; Aslam 2003). To the extent that accountability structures and practices in public education systematically differ across lagging and leading provinces, they are likely to be a factor in explaining observed outcome differences.

A look at teachers, the major educational resource generally available to children in Pakistan, sheds light on the state of accountability in public education. Andrabi et al. (2008) find that public school teachers in rural Punjab are more qualified and more experienced than private school teachers; they also find that public school teachers are paid several-fold higher than private school teachers both unconditionally *and* conditionally (similar evidence is found by Khan et al. 2005). However, public school teachers have an absenteeism rate that is double that among private school teachers (15 per cent vs 8 per cent). (Comparable absenteeism rates among public school teachers are found by King et al. [2008] in NWFP and Saiens [2008] in rural Sindh). Further, teacher absenteeism, teacher test scores, as well as student test scores by and large do not vary with teacher compensation in public schools, while they do in the private schools, suggesting that pay in public schools is not determined by teacher performance (but rather is a deterministic function of teacher education, experience, and training). The NEAS data analysis by the Government of Pakistan also suggests that teacher qualifications, training, and experience do not explain differences in learning levels among public school students, nor does the provision of many other school resources considered important a priori (Government of Pakistan 2007, 2006). Similar findings are presented by Aslam (2003) and Berhman et al. (1997).

To the extent that the reach of the public (and private) school systems differ across lagging and leading provinces, this factor may also explain participation and attainment differences between these two types of provinces. Evidence shows that, in rural Pakistan, traditionally public schools have been placed by the authorities in wealthier, larger, and more accessible communities. Further, these village factors are likely to weigh more in the decision to set up a middle or secondary school, thus further constraining the availability of these levels of schooling in rural areas (World Bank 2005c).

In addition, there has been a phenomenal growth in private schools in the 1990s and 2000s, with higher growth rates in private schools and private enrolment in rural areas and in lower-income populations (Andrabi et al. 2006; Harlech-Jones et al. 2005; Arif and Saqib 2003). Private schools tend to locate in rural communities that already possess a public primary or secondary school; for example, 85 per cent of private schools in Punjab were established in villages where a boys public primary school was already present (World Bank 2005c). Further, given the heavy reliance on locally-hired female teachers by private schools, Andrabi et al. (2007) find that the probability of a private school being established doubles if the rural community already has a public secondary school that girls can attend—thus the local availability of a pool of minimally-qualified women appears to act as a constraint for extending the reach of the private sector in rural Pakistan. Finally, the survival rates of schools in rural communities with poor socio-economic characteristics appear to be low, suggesting that even if some villages are not disadvantaged in terms of receiving a private school, they may be in terms of keeping that private school alive (Andrabi and Saiens 2009). Thus, Andrabi and Saiens argue that while the patterns of growth in the private provision of education are reducing urban–rural gaps in schooling outcomes, they are exacerbating intra-rural differences along the lines discussed. It is also worth noting that the wide expansion of the private sector may be a Punjab phenomenon—for example, Andrabi and Saiens (2009) show that 65 per cent and 16 per cent of private schools are present in the leading provinces of Punjab and Sindh, respectively. On the other hand, only 1.5 per cent of all private schools are located in the lagging province of Balochistan, home to roughly 5 per cent of the country's population—this is disproportionately low.

The poor educational situation of girls in Pakistan has been the subject of much research in Pakistan. The problem can be easily stylized: girls join school in lesser numbers relative to boys; conditional on joining school, they accumulate less years of schooling than boys (World Bank 2005c); and the cognitive skills of adult females are less than adult males (Alderman et al. 1996).[14] The gender gaps in these indicators also appear to be principally a rural phenomenon. These findings hold both unconditionally and conditionally. Further, evidence from gender-specific regressions for school participation and attainment suggest that various school, village, household, parent, and child characteristics often matter differently between boys and girls (in terms of size and statistical significance of the effects). Factors that have been documented to have gender differential effects (in many cases acting to disadvantage girls) include parental education, household wealth, local labour market conditions, distance to school/local school availability, out-of-pocket schooling expenditures, village infrastructure conditions, and school input availability (see, for example, Holmes 2003; Hazarika 2001; Alderman et al. 1997, 1996).[15] To the extent that the levels of these

[14]Alderman et al. (1996) find that the gender gap in cognitive achievement is driven more by gender differences in joining and staying in school than the quality of schooling when in school.

[15]It is important to note that not all factors disadvantage girls relative to boys. For example, Mansuri (2006) finds that temporary economic migration by adult males have a positive impact on school participation, progression, and attainment, with larger effects for girls relative to boys. These estimated effects are robust to correcting for the potential

factors vary systematically between leading and lagging provinces, these differences are likely to explain differences in the size of the gender gaps between leading and lagging provinces.

A key explanation for gender gaps in the literature is proximity to school, which is a particularly salient issue in rural areas, given that both public and private schooling systems are less extensive than in urban areas, and fail to reach certain types of villages. World Bank (2005c) finds that the probability of school participation declines at an increasing rate with respect to distance for both genders, but the decline is steeper for girls; this result remains even with a multiple regression framework (World Bank 2005c; Holmes 2003). The sensitivity to distance increases with age, with a sharp drop in the probability of schooling after age 13 (a pattern not observed for boys). The statistical evidence on distance to school being a major constraint for girls is corroborated by qualitative data gathered from interviews of mothers (World Bank 2005c). On the flipside, increasing girls' access to schools yields large increases in girls' enrolment as found in an experimental evaluation of the provision of public per-girl subsidies for the establishment and operation of private primary schools in poor neighbourhoods in Quetta, Balochistan (Kim et al. 1999).

Distance to school also interacts with other related factors to further disadvantage girls. It appears that, controlling for distance to school, households spend more on getting girls to schools than boys; these additional costs may be due to the need to provide safe passage for girls. Further, controlling for distance to school, crossing village boundaries (and within villages, crossing settlement or hamlet boundaries) significantly lowers the probability of schooling. The results hold even when the effects are identified based on comparisons between siblings of different genders (Jacoby and Mansuri 2008; World Bank 2005c). In other words, girls without a school in their own village may be severely disadvantaged in terms of participation and attainment. Survey data from 2001/2 shows that 67 per cent of rural primary sampling units had a girls' public primary school versus 87 per cent which had a boys' public primary school (this situation is an marked improvement from the past when the gender divide in terms of local school availability was more severe (see, for example, Alderman et al. 1996).

Finally, while learning levels are low but similar across lagging and leading provinces, given that participation rates differ across leading

---

endogeneity of the migration decision as well as to identifying the effects by comparing siblings within households.

and lagging provinces, the similarities in learning levels may be due to a more positively selected school-going population in lagging provinces relative to leading provinces. This same phenomenon may be behind the finding that learning outcomes of female students are at par or better than those of male students. The private sector may hold the key to raising participation (particularly girls' participation) as well as learning levels. World Bank (2005c) finds that private schools tend to be coeducational and have a high share of female teachers—consequently, the growth rates of private enrolment have been higher for girls than boys. This has contributed to more favourable female–male ratios in private schools relative to public schools. At the same time, evidence shows that learning levels in private schools are on average significantly higher than in public schools, and that this private school advantage in learning remains after controlling for relevant child, parent, household, and village characteristics (Andrabi et al. 2008; Arif and Saqib 2003; Aslam 2003).[16] While private education continues to make inroads in reaching a broader population, the public school system stills continues to serve poor, disadvantaged households. Given that the difference in average learning outcomes between public and private schools is largely driven by the relatively left-skewed learning distribution in public schools, an appropriate public education development policy would be to focus efforts on the poorest quality public schools.

Sri Lanka

Sri Lanka's success in raising participation and completion rates across the board is principally attributed to legislating compulsory education (grades 1–9) in 1997, as well as, concurrently, the expansion of service delivery to provide schooling opportunities up to grade 9 in remote and disadvantaged areas, and community and government campaigns to systematically document and draw in out-of-school children and keep children in school. These efforts encouraged the enrolment and regular attendance of children aged 6–14 years in primary and junior secondary school grades. In 1997, net primary enrolment rate in the country was 96 per cent, with a survival rate until ninth grade of 59 per cent. By 2007, the survival rate had improved to 90 per cent. Further, apart from the Eastern province, where survival rate rose but only to 80 per cent, the rest of the provinces show similar rates, from 89 per cent to 95 per cent. It is

[16]The research so far has not attempted to address potential selection due to unobservables in school type choice.

also impressive that not only have school participation and completion in the North and Eastern provinces remained robust but they have also shown marked growth despite the long-standing civil conflict. Part of this success lies in the strong demand for elementary schooling and the commitment of the government to sustained and reliable education service delivery in conflict areas (Aturupane 2008).

Despite these successes, differences do continue to exist in participation and completion between provinces, particularly at the secondary school level. Surveys show that out-of-school children are largely composed of those from the conflict areas in the country; within non-conflict areas, these children are largely from economically-disadvantaged areas such as the estate sector—in lagging provinces. A significant share of out-of-school children and their households point to the low quality of schooling as a strong deterrent to schooling, with low quality associated with lagging provinces due to the relatively lower quality of human and physical resources there (Aturupane 2008; World Bank 2005d). Using community and household sample survey data from 1999–2000, Arunatilake (2006) finds that a child aged 5–14 years is less likely to attend school if the child (i) comes from a poor household; (ii) has a household head who is a farmer or unemployed; (iii) is non-Sinhalese; (iv) resides in a fishing or farming community; and (v) resides in a community with teacher vacancies. Clearly, these factors disadvantage lagging provinces as the economic base of these provinces is principally agriculture and fishing, and these provinces face problems with teacher deployment and attendance and have higher poverty rates than the Western province. The parameter estimates for the provincial dummies in the participation regression were not reported by Arunatilake (2006)—this would have been useful in ascertaining if the province continued to have some explanatory power after controlling for the included set of individual, household, and community characteristics.

A number of policies have likely contributed to lagging provinces closing the gap with the Western province in secondary school participation and completion rates, as well as in achievement levels. These include (i) competitive scholarships at the end of the primary cycle to enable students from disadvantaged primary schools to access better quality secondary education; (ii) university quotas for students from disadvantaged households and areas; (iii) the establishment of centres across the country for professional development for teachers; and (iv) the requirement that all new teacher hires complete a three-year pre-service teacher education programme or hold a university degree. The last policy has resulted in the number of untrained teachers in the public school system declining from 45,000 in 1997 to 2,000 (less than 1 per cent of the total teaching workforce) in 2003 (World Bank 2005d).

Another policy that has likely helped improve the extent and quality of service delivery in lagging provinces is the progressive central government financing of education. In 2000, the government shifted to a formula-based system in which central allocations for recurrent expenditures (mainly salaries) were determined on a per student basis, with adjustments for school size (enrolment), school level, and the size of the deficit in the physical stock implied by established quality input norms. This change in expenditure allocation rules reduced the allocation variation between schools with similar characteristics from 300:1 in 1996 to 1:15 in 2002, with accompanying reductions between provinces. The main beneficiaries of this change in rules were clearly lagging provinces. For example, central government financing of provincial education ranges from 45–50 per cent in the Western province to 100 per cent in the North-Eastern province. Other lagging provinces that are particularly poor such as Uva, North-Central, and Southern provinces also receive significant central transfers to supplement their limited own-revenue generation. The upshot of these flows is that public expenditure per student (relative to provincial per capita income) is often several times higher in lagging provinces than in the Western province (Aturupane 2008; World Bank 2005d; Arunatilake and de Silva 2004).

Despite the increases in attainment and achievement, differences do continue to exist. Learning level differences across provinces are attributable to differences in the quality of schooling and the level of economic development. The Western province has better schools, better teachers, and richer households who are able to provide more assistance for education than lagging provinces. Tight government budgetary constraints in recent years have limited capital expenditures in education. This has affected investments in basic amenities in rural schools as well as in quality-related inputs such as science laboratories, information technology, and libraries. Recurrent expenditures are almost exclusively on teacher and administrator compensation. The remaining funds go towards textbooks, school uniforms, and utility payments. Consequently, there is little left for professional development of teachers and academic support for schools. This situation again disadvantages lagging provinces more, given their lower quality of human and other resources (World Bank 2005d).

Private investments in education also likely contribute to attainment and achievement differences between lagging provinces and the Western province. Households invest significant resources in education. Data from 1995/6 show that private expenditures on education were roughly 23 per cent of public expenditures on education. The data also show that 93 per cent of total private expenditures on education are made by the non-poor, with 52 per cent of the total made by households in the richest quintile. These expenditures are primarily for tutoring services (45 per cent of total unit private education expenditures), and are often made by households to offer their children an advantage in various examinations (secondary school scholarship examinations, GCE O/L, GCE A/L, and university entrance examinations) and to compensate for deficient teaching and learning quality in schools. Given that the Western province is richer, this puts the province in advantageous position (World Bank 2005).

Sri Lanka has also struggled with teacher deployment across the country as teaching positions in rural areas and economically-disadvantaged areas are unattractive. While teacher–student ratios do not show significant variation across provinces, they mask the problem of deployment as the lack of attractiveness of positions in (the poorer and more rural parts of) lagging provinces is considered to contribute to the higher turnover of teachers, higher teacher absenteeism rates, and the inability to retain subject specialists in key subjects such as English, science, and mathematics. Within provinces, there is also the problem of overstaffed urban schools and understaffed rural schools. The government has attempted to address this problem of high turnover by requiring new teacher hires to be placed in disadvantaged schools for 3–5 years. One effect of this policy has been the replacement of older, more experienced teachers by younger, less experienced teachers, with a potentially detrimental effect on the quality of teaching. Monetary incentives for working in undesirable locations were started to motivate teachers to take and keep their positions in these locations but these incentives were shortly dismantled due to budgetary constraints (World Bank 2005d).

CONCLUSION

While South Asia has made significant progress in the last decades in raising participation and attainment, the region as a whole still suffers from poor outcomes, and is likely to miss meeting the education MDGs. Looking with South Asian countries, between economically leading and lagging subnational areas, the evidence suggests that schooling indicators in lagging areas in India and Pakistan are worse than in leading areas, with the lagging-area disadvantage particularly large for girls in Pakistan. Further, with the exception of primary school participation and completion in India, the gaps between leading and lagging areas in these two countries appear not to have narrowed over the recent past. In Bangladesh, there does not appear to be differences in participation and attainment outcomes between the leading division of Dhaka and the other divisions (all lagging) in the country; in fact, the leading division had poorer outcomes in the recent past, but has managed to catch up from below. Finally, the provinces in Sri Lanka appear to have comparable outcomes at the primary and secondary level; there is also evidence of lagging provinces catching up with the leading Western province in student achievement. Where differences exist, they are likely to be between the lagging North and Eastern provinces (which were until recently under conflict) and the leading Western province. In general, it appears that the battle of closing the education divide between lagging and leading areas (where they exist) has shifted from the primary level to the secondary level and higher.

In countries where lagging areas trail leading areas in participation and attainment, disadvantages in the levels of factors (both demand and supply side) that promote these outcomes are likely to play an important role in explaining the poorer performance of lagging areas. The estimated marginal returns to these factors may also partly explain the poorer performance in lagging areas. While the public education systems in Bangladesh and Sri Lanka have explicitly tried (and successfully so) to tackle deficiencies in lagging areas by actively targeting financial resources and initiatives in infrastructure expansion and upgradation, teacher deployment and development, provision of other schooling inputs, and incentives for households to stimulate the demand for schooling, much more has to done by India and Pakistan in reorienting public education development efforts towards addressing the needs in lagging states and provinces.

Targeting resources to lagging areas may not be sufficient. Accountability issues may also be more serious in lagging areas, contributing to the poorer quality of service delivery. Fixes in this domain may also be required to improve public education performance in attracting out-of-school children, retaining students, and ensuring minimal and rising achievement. The private expenditures for schooling by households as well as the rapid and expansive growth in the private provision of primary and secondary education may be in response to shortcomings in the public school systems, particularly in terms of schooling quality. This response may cut both ways. It can contribute to widening differences between leading and lagging (such as may be the case due to higher investments in private tutoring in the leading Western province or private schools situating in villages with better endowments in Pakistan and India). It can also contribute to narrowing gaps (such as may be the case due to the relatively higher infusion of private schools in lagging states in India and the higher learning levels achieved by them vis-à-vis public schools). The issues in system accountability and market competition in education clearly require further analysis. It may also be fruitful for policymakers to concentrate on seeking to troubleshoot governance issues and leverage emerging opportunities in the financing and provision of schooling to engender better educational outcomes in their countries in general, and in lagging areas within in their countries in particular.

REFERENCES

Alderman, Harold, Jere R. Behrman, Shahrukh Khan, David R. Ross, and Richard Sabot. 1997. 'The Income Gap in Cognitive Skills in Rural Pakistan', *Economic Development and Cultural Change*, 46: 97–122.

Alderman, Harold, Jere R. Behrman, David R. Ross, and Richard Sabot. 1996. 'Decomposing the Gender Gap in Cognitive Skills in a Poor Rural Economy', *Journal of Human Resources*, 31 (1): 229–54.

Alderman, Harold, Peter F. Orazem, and Elizabeth M Paterno. 2001. 'School Quality, School Cost, and the Public/Private School Choices of Low-Income Households in Pakistan', *Journal of Human Resources*, 36 (2): 304–26.

Al-Samarrai, Samer. 2007. 'Changes in Educational Attainment in Bangladesh, 2000–2005', background paper for the Bangladesh Poverty Assessment, World Bank, Washington, D.C.

Andrabi, Tahir, Jishnu Das, and Asim Ijaz Khwaja. 2007. 'Students Today, Teachers Tomorrow? Identifying Constraints on the Provision of Education', unpublished working paper.

———. 2006. 'A Dime a Day: The Possibilities and Limits of Private Schooling in Pakistan', Policy Research Working Paper No. 4066, World Bank, Washington, D.C.

Andrabi, Tahir, Jishnu Das, Asim Ijaz Khwaja, Tara Vishwanath, and Tristan Zajonc. 2008. *Learning and Educational Achievements in Punjab Schools: Insights to Inform the Policy Debate.* Washington, D.C: World Bank.

Andrabi, Tahir and Corinne Saiens. 2009. 'The Rise of Private Schooling in Pakistan—Findings from School Census Data', unpublished working paper.

Arif, G. M. and Najam Us Saqib. 2003. 'Production of Cognitive and Life Skills in Public, Private and NGO Schools in Pakistan', *Pakistan Development Review*, 42 (1): 1–28.

250   The Poor Half Billion in South Asia

Arunatilake, Nisha. 2006. 'Education Participation in Sri Lanka—Why All are Not in School', *International Journal of Educational Research*, 45: 137–52.

Arunatilake, Nisha and Roshani de Silva. 2004. 'Overview of Education Budgeting and Resource Allocation Processes in Sri Lanka', Commonwealth Education Fund, London.

Asadullah, Mohammad Niaz, Nazmul Chaudhury, and Amit Dar. 2007. 'Student Achievement Conditioned upon School Selection: Religious and Secular Secondary School Quality in Bangladesh', *Economics of Education Review*, 26: 648–59.

Aslam, Monazza. 2003. 'The Determinants of Student Achievement in Government and Private Schools in Pakistan', *Pakistan Development Review*, 42 (4): 841–76.

Aturupane, Harsha. 2008. 'Celebrating 60 Years of Progress and Challenges in Education in Sri Lanka', paper presented at the 60th Anniversary Celebrations of Sri Lanka organized by the Council of Education in the Commonwealth, London.

Aturupane, Harsha, Paul Glewwe, and Suzanne Wisniewski. 2007. 'The Impact of School Quality, Socio-economic Factors and Child Health on Students' Academic Performance: Evidence from Sri Lankan Primary Schools', unpublished working paper.

Bangladesh Bureau of Educational Information and Statistics (BANBEIS). 2006. *Bangladesh Educational Statistics 2006*. Dhaka: BANBEIS.

Behrman, Jere R., Shahrukh Khan, David Ross, and Richard Sabot. 1997. 'School Quality and Cognitive Achievement Production: A Case Study for Rural Pakistan', *Economics of Education Review*, 16 (2): 127–42.

Bhalotra, Sonia and Bernarda Zamora. 2005. 'Growth in School Enrollment and Completion Rates in India', UNU-WIDER Working Paper.

Chaudhury, Nazmul, Jeffrey Hammer, Michael Kremer, Karthik Muralidharan, and F. Halsey Rogers. 2006. 'Missing in Action: Teacher and Health Worker Absence in Developing Countries', *Journal of Economic Perspectives*, 20 (1): 91–116.

Das, Jishnu, Priyanka Pandey, and Tristan Zajonc. 2006. 'Learning Levels and Gaps in Pakistan', Policy Research Working Paper Series No. 4067, World Bank, Washington, D.C.

Das, Jishnu, and Tristan Zajonc. 2008. 'India Shining and Bharat Drowning: Comparing Two Indian States to the Worldwide Distribution in Mathematics Achievement', Policy Research Working Paper Series No. 4644, World Bank, Washington, D.C.

Desai, Sonalde, Amaresh Dubey, Reeve Vanneman, and Rukmini Banerji. 2008. 'Private Schooling in India: A New Educational Landscape', India Human Development Survey Working Paper No. 11.

Durraisamy, P. 2002. 'Changes in Returns to Education in India, 1983–94: By Gender, Age-cohort, and Location', *Economics of Education Review*, 21: 609–22.

Government of Pakistan, Ministry of Education. 2007. *National Education Assessment 2006*. Islamabad: Government of Pakistan.

———. 2006. *National Education Assessment 2005*. Islamabad: Government of Pakistan.

Goyal, Sangeeta and Priyanka Pandey. 2009. 'How do Government and Private Schools Differ? Findings from Two Large Indian States', South Asia Human Development Sector Report No. 30, World Bank, Washington, D.C.

Hanushek, Eric A. and Ludger Woessmann. 2010. 'Education and Economic Growth', in Dominic J. Brewer and Patrick J. McEwan (eds), *Economics of Education*, pp. 60–7. Amsterdam: Elsevier.

Hanushek, Eric A. and Ludger Woessman. 2008. 'The Role of Cognitive Skills in Economic Development', *Journal of Economic Literature*, 46 (3): 607–68.

Harlech-Jones, Brian, Musa Baig, Shamshad Sajid, and Shams ur-Rahman. 2005. 'Private Schooling in the Northern Areas in Pakistan: A Decade of Rapid Expansion', *International Journal of Educational Development*, 25: 557–68.

Hazarika, Gautam. 2001. 'The Sensitivity of Primary School Enrollment to the Costs of Post-Primary Schooling in Rural Pakistan: A Gender Perspective', *Education Economics*, 9 (3): 237–44.

Holmes, Jessica. 2003. 'Measuring the Determinants of School Completion in Pakistan: Analysis of Censoring and Selection Bias', *Economics of Education Review*, 22: 249–64.

Husain, Fazal, Muhammad Ali Qasim, and Khalid Hameed Sheikh. 2003. 'An Analysis of Public Expenditure on Education in Pakistan', *Pakistan Development Review*, 42 (4): 771–80.

Jacoby, Hanan and Ghazala Mansuri. 2008. 'Crossing Boundaries: Caste, Gender, and Schooling in Rural Pakistan', unpublished working paper.

Jayachandran, Usha. 2002. 'Socio-economic Determinants of School Attendance in India', Center for Development Economics Working Paper No. 103, Delhi School of Economics, New Delhi.

Jhingran, Dhir and Deepa Sankar. 2009. 'Addressing Educational Disparity: Using District Level Education Development Indices for Equitable Resource Allocations in India', Policy Research Working Paper 4955, World Bank, Washington, D.C.

Khan, Shahrukh Rafi, Sajid Kazmi, and Zainab Latif. 2005. 'A Comparative Institutional Analysis of Government, NGO and Private Rural Primary Schooling in Pakistan', *European Journal of Development Research*, 17 (2): 199–223.

Kim, Jooseop, Harold Alderman, and Peter F. Orazem. 1999. 'Can Private School Subsidies Increase Enrollment for the Poor?' The Quetta Urban Fellowship Program, *World Bank Economic Review*, 13 (3): 443–65.

King, Elizabeth M., Peter F. Orazem, and Elizabeth M Paterno. 2008. 'Promotion With and Without Learning: Effects on Student Enrollment and Dropout Behavior', Policy Research Working Paper No. 4722, World Bank, Washington, D.C.

Kremer, Michael, Nazmul Chaudhury, F. Halsey Rogers, Karthik Muralidharan, and Jeffrey Hammer. 2005. 'Teacher Absence in India: A Snapshot', *Journal of the European Economic Association*, 3 (2–3): 658–67.

Kingdon, Geeta. 2002. 'The Gender Gap in Educational Attainment in India: How Much Can Be Explained?', *Journal of Development Studies*, 39 (2): 25–53.

Maitra, Pushkar. 2003. 'Schooling and Educational Attainment: Evidence from Bangladesh', *Education Economics*, 11 (2): 129–53.

Mansuri, Ghazala. 2006. 'Migration, School Attainment and Child Labor: Evidence from Rural Pakistan', Policy Research Working Paper No. 3945, World Bank, Washington, D.C.

Mehrotra, Santosh and Parthasarthi R. Panchamukhi. 2008. 'Private Provision of Elementary Education in India: Findings of a Survey in Eight States', *Compare*, 36 (4): 421–42.

Muralidharan, Karthik and Michael Kremer. 2008. 'Public and Private Schools in Rural India', in Rajashri Chakrabarti and Paul E. Peterson (eds), *School Choice International: Exploring Public-Private Partnerships*, pp. 91–110. Cambridge: MIT Press.

Pradhan, Basanta K. and Shalabh Kumar Singh. 2000. 'Policy Reforms and Financing of Elementary Education in India: A Study of the Quality of Service and Outcome', National Council of Applied Economics Research, New Delhi.

Pratham. 2009. *Annual Status of Education Report (Rural) 2008*. Mumbai: Pratham Resource Center.

———. 2007. *Annual Status of Education Report (Rural) 2006*. Mumbai: Pratham Resource Center.

Sabir, Muhammad. 2003. 'Gender and Public Spending on Education in Pakistan: A Case Study of Disaggregated Benefit Incidence', Conference Paper No. 48, Social Policy Development Centre, Karachi.

Saiens, Corinne. 2008. 'Challenges for the Education Sector in Sindh, Pakistan: Key Messages on Access and Quality', Manuscript, World Bank, Washington, D.C.

Sankar, Deepa. 2008. 'What is the Progress in Elementary Education Participation in India during the Last Two Decades? An Analysis using NSS Education Rounds', World Bank South Asia Human Development Sector Discussion Paper No. 24, Washington, D.C.

United Nations Development Program (UNDP). 2007. *Human Development Report 2007/2008: Fighting Climate Change: Human Solidarity in a Divided World.* New York: Palgrave Macmillan.

World Bank. 2009. *Global Monitoring Report 2009: A Development Emergency.* Washington, D.C: World Bank.

————. 2008a. 'Education for All in Bangladesh: Where Does Bangladesh Stand in Achieving the EFA Goals by 2015.' Bangladesh Development Series Paper No. 24, World Bank, Washington, D.C.

————. 2008b. *Global Monitoring Report 2008: MDGs and the Environment: Agenda for Inclusive and Sustainable Development.* Washington, D.C.: World Bank.

————. 2007. 'To the MDGs and Beyond: Accountability and Institutional Innovation in Bangladesh', Bangladesh Development Series Paper No. 14, World Bank, Dhaka.

————. 2005a. *Attaining the Millennium Development Goals in Bangladesh: How Likely and What Will It Take to Reduce Poverty, Child Mortality and Malnutrition, and to Increase School Enrollment and Completion?* Washington, D.C.: World Bank.

————. 2005b. *Attaining the Millennium Development Goals in Sri Lanka: How Likely and What Will It Take to Reduce Poverty, Child Mortality and Malnutrition, and to Increase School Enrollment and Completion?* World Bank Report No. 32134-LK, World Bank, Washington, D.C.

————. 2005c. 'Pakistan Country Gender Assessment: Bridging the Gender Gap: Opportunities and Challenges', World Bank Report No. 32244-PAK, World Bank, Washington, D.C.

————. 2005d. *Treasures of the Education System in Sri Lanka: Restoring Performance, Expanding Opportunities, and Enhancing Prospects.* Colombo: World Bank.

————. 2003a. 'Bangladesh Public Expenditure Review', Report No. 24370-BD, World Bank, Washington, D.C.

————. 2003b. 'Secondary Education in India', World Bank South Asia Human Development Sector Discussion Paper No. 2, World Bank, Washington, D.C.

Wu, Kin Bing, Pete Goldschmidt, Christy Kim Boscardin, and Deepa Sankar. 2009. 'International Benchmarking and Determinants of Mathematics Achievement in Two Indian States', *Education Economics*, 17 (3): 395–411.

II
A New Approach to
Reducing Poverty

7

Is Decentralization Helping the Lagging Regions?

Lakshmi Iyer, Ejaz Ghani, and Saurabh Mishra

DECENTRALIZATION: FISCAL, ADMINISTRATIVE, POLITICAL

The previous chapters have demonstrated the large differences between lagging and leading regions of South Asia in terms of per capita income, poverty rates, and levels of human capital. How can government policies help the lagging regions to catch up with the leading regions? One obvious way is to provide the right business environment for the private sector to make investments. This would include things like improving the regulatory environment, taking steps towards market integration of lagging regions with leading ones, providing connectivity through transport and communication investments, and ensuring macroeconomic stability. Another way is to intervene directly in sectors or locations in which the private sector is reluctant to invest. Such intervention can take many different forms, such as providing subsidies for investments in lagging regions, investing in developing human capital in the lagging regions, or compensating for the regional variation in growth and industry patterns by using transfer payments. An alternative strategy could be to devolve greater policy powers to local governments, which may be able to implement policies more suited to local conditions.

In this chapter, we review whether the current decentralization arrangements are working to the benefit of the lagging regions of

South Asia. Our primary focus will be on the arrangements for fiscal decentralization: the revenue-raising and expenditure powers assigned to the different levels of government (national, provincial, local), as well as the system of inter-state transfers conducted by the national government. We will review, theoretically and empirically, the potential consequences of different degrees of fiscal decentralization. We then evaluate whether the system of inter-state transfers has worked to promote equity between lagging and leading regions in the countries of South Asia.

Later in this chapter, we consider how much authority should be shared with subnational governments so they can make social investments most effectively. This refers to the domain of administrative decentralization. Local governments can be expected to have better information about local conditions, and hence design and implement more appropriate policies than a centrally designed one-size-fits-all system. On the other hand, local governments, especially in poor institutional settings, may be more subject to capture by narrow local interests and may end up implementing policies that benefit a small local elite. In places with low levels of human capital, local governments may not have the administrative capacity to make use of development funding—that is, in some situations greater administrative decentralization can undercut the benefits provided by inter-state transfer funds.

A key aspect of fiscal and administrative decentralization is that it can create competition between state governments with regard to taxation and other policies. This competition can take a beneficial form when states compete to reduce red tape or improve social services. This can also take a 'race-to-the-bottom' approach if states compete in wasteful ways to attract investments, such as offering larger and larger subsidies or relaxing environmental regulations. The analysis of inter-jurisdictional competition is beyond the scope of this chapter.

We briefly examine political decentralization, which refers to people's power to choose their representatives for different levels of government. Greater political decentralization can lead to a greater voice for people in government decisions and also can increase the perceived legitimacy of governments. This encourages greater trust and cooperation between government agencies and citizens, leading to better policy outcomes. Such an increase in trust and legitimacy can be key to increasing political stability. On the downside, the constraints of electoral politics can lead to some biases—for example, a move to favour policies with short-term payoffs at the cost of longer-term investments. We review the empirical evidence from India's Panchayati Raj programme, which brought political decentralization to the village level in the 1990s.

We begin by reviewing the arrangements for fiscal decentralization across South Asian countries. Throughout this paper, we will examine the decentralization patterns in detail for India, Pakistan, Sri Lanka, and Bangladesh. Data availability issues for Nepal and Afghanistan, as well as the lack of well-defined arrangements for decentralization in these conflict-affected regions, prevent us from completing a detailed analysis for these countries.

FISCAL DECENTRALIZATION IN SOUTH ASIA

Fiscal decentralization refers to the powers of subnational governments to set and collect taxes, make spending decisions, and borrow from higher levels of government or the market. Viewed from this lens, there is considerable diversity in fiscal decentralization arrangements across the South Asian countries. A typical cross-country measure of fiscal decentralization is the share of total revenues or expenditures that are collected by subnational governments. We briefly review these measures for South Asian countries compared with the rest of the world, before describing the fiscal decentralization arrangements in specific South Asian countries.

We see that India is quite decentralized compared with the world average: subnational (state and local) governments collect 34 per cent of all government revenues and are in charge of 52 per cent of total government expenditures (see Table 7.1). The other South Asian countries—Bangladesh, Pakistan, and Sri Lanka—are extremely centralized in terms of revenue powers, with subnational governments having the authority to collect less than 10 per cent of total revenues. Subnational governments are responsible for a much lower proportion of total expenditures compared with India. Consistent with the high degree of revenue centralization, subnational governments are dependent on transfers and grants from the federal government for the bulk (more than two-thirds) of their revenue.

India

The degree of revenue and expenditure decentralization usually is specified by constitutional provisions. The Indian Constitution explicitly divides the powers over different areas of legislation between the

TABLE 7.1   Extent of Fiscal Decentralization in South Asia and the World

Country	% of government revenue raised by subnational governments	% of government expenditure done by subnational governments	Transfers to sub national units as a share of sub-national revenues
India	33.6	52	39
Bangladesh	<2	3–4	64–70
Pakistan	7.3	30.3	81.1
Sri Lanka	7	12	82.5
World	21.7	29.1	32.5
China	59.7	81.5	35
Canada	52.2	59.7	21.3
USA	41.1	49.3	28.9
Mexico	23.5	23.1	47

Sources: India, Canada, Mexico and World figures are from GFS (1999); USA and Mexico figures are from GFS for 2000; Sri Lanka figures from World Bank (2006) for the year 2004; Bangladesh figures estimated from World Bank (2009a); Pakistan figures are for 2000 (for comparability), and are computed by authors from National and Provincial budget documents. World average is based on the 41 countries present in the GFS database.

national and state governments, including the powers of taxation and expenditure. The national government has exclusive powers over subjects such as defense, railways, currency, banking, and insurance, as well as the exclusive right to levy taxes on corporations and on non-agricultural income. This is in contrast to federal countries, such as the United States or Canada, where states also levy income taxes. A portion of the taxes collected by the central government is given back to the states as part of tax-sharing arrangements (fiscal devolution). This results in de facto inter-state transfers of resources, because the share of tax revenue a state receives from this divisible pool is not necessarily the same as the share it contributes. Such systems of inter-state transfers are a common feature of many federal systems. We examine inter-state transfers in greater detail in the next section.

State governments in India have power over police, public health, local government, agriculture, and sales taxes. State governments also have a 'concurrent list' for which the national and state governments have joint decision-making power; this list includes subjects such as education, economic and social planning, criminal law, trade unions, and bankruptcy. Two provisions further strengthen the balance of power towards the national government: all residual legislative powers have been assigned to the national government,[1] and in cases of conflict between national and state laws, the national law is expected to prevail. Although subnational governments have more levels, such as the village-level Panchayati Raj institutions, these lower levels currently have limited autonomy in administrative matters and few sources of independent revenue.

The relative balance between the central and state governments has been relatively stable over time. Figure 7.1 shows that the shares of revenue and expenditures controlled by states have remained steady for the past decade.

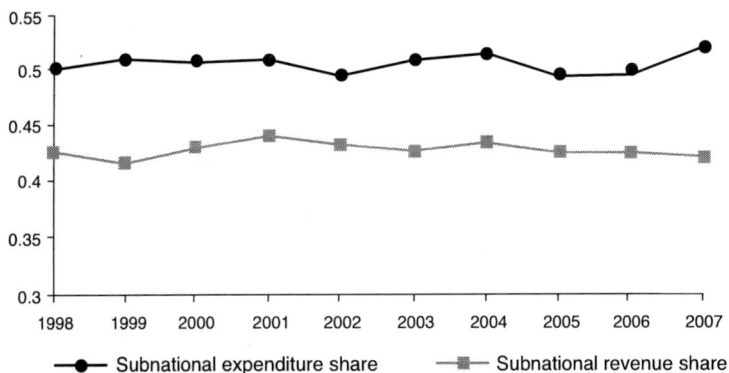

FIGURE 7.1   Subnational Revenue and Expenditure Shares, India

Sources: Government of India 2008a; budget data for individual states.
Note: Figures are based on states' share of total revenue expenditures and total revenue receipts.

Pakistan

In Pakistan, more than 90 per cent of all taxes are collected by the federal government; these are then shared between the federal and provincial governments on the basis of a revenue-sharing formula. In 2006, provinces were given 45 per cent of the total taxes collected by the federal government, with this proportion set to increase by one percentage point in the next five years. Provincial governments have a few independent sources of revenue, such as stamp duties, motor vehicle taxes, land revenue, and user charges on government services (Ahmed et al. 2007). In terms of expenditures, subnational governments undertake 30 per cent of all government expenditures. The discrepancy between

[1]The US Constitution explicitly assigns the residual powers to the states.

the revenue share and the expenditure share indicates clearly that the subnational governments are strongly dependent on transfers from the federal government to manage their finances.

This high degree of centralization in Pakistan's fiscal system has been relatively stable over the past decade. We see that the subnational share of revenues has remained steady, while the subnational share of expenditures has declined slightly (see Figure 7.2). This is consistent with the institutional setting, for which there are no major initiatives to decentralize any of the federal fiscal powers to the provinces. The major areas of institutional change have been in the system of fiscal transfers from the federal government to the provinces, as well as a significant move towards administrative decentralization from the provincial government to local governments.

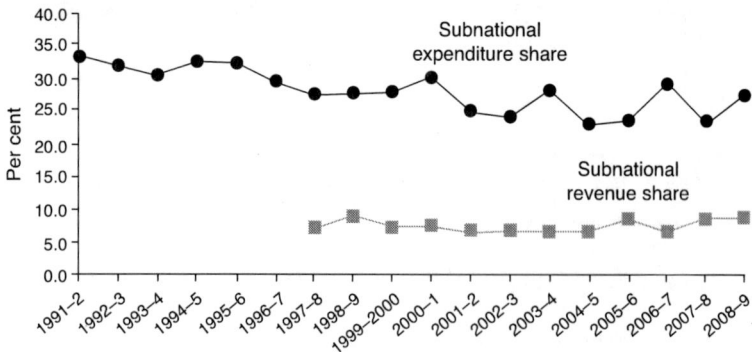

FIGURE 7.2   Provincial Revenue and Expenditure Shares
over Time, Pakistan

Sources: Government of Pakistan, Finance Accounts (1984–5/1997–8), Combined Finance Accounts (1990–1/1998–9), and budget documents for subsequent years.

Sri Lanka and Bangladesh

Sri Lanka is one of the most centralized countries in the world in terms of both revenues and expenditures, with subnational governments having a limited role to play either in collecting taxes or in disbursing government expenditure. Sri Lanka was a unitary state from the days of British rule until the 1980s. In 1987, under the pressure of growing ethnic conflict and demands for regional autonomy, the constitution was amended to create provinces as an intermediate level of government, between the national government and the local governments. Provincial governments are responsible for internal law and order, education, health, housing, agriculture, and irrigation, among other things. Despite this broad list, provincial and local government spending accounts for only 12 per cent of total national expenditure. The central government's encroaching on provincial responsibilities is an added concern. For instance, the Ministry of Education has established national schools in many provinces, which are perceived to have more resources and to be of higher quality than the schools run by the provincial government (World Bank 2006).

In terms of revenue, provincial and local governments raise only 7 per cent of total government revenue in the country. The provinces are constitutionally permitted to raise revenues from business turnover tax, stamp duties, excise duties, and motor vehicle licenses, while all other major sources of revenue (value added tax [VAT], income and corporate taxes, excise taxes, and trade duties) are assigned to the central government. As inferred from this institutional setting, provincial governments are heavily dependent on grants and other transfers from the central government to bridge the gap between their expenditures and revenues; in 2004, less than 20 per cent of provincial government budgets were obtained from their own resources.

In terms of fiscal decentralization, Bangladesh is one of the most centralized countries in the world. The central government collects almost all taxes, and subnational governments obtain most of their revenues through transfers from the central government. Subnational governments are not responsible for any large share of overall government expenditures.

Table 7.2 summarizes the main heads of revenue and expenditure for the subnational governments in South Asia. Important to note is that interest payments and salaries constitute the two largest components of subnational governments' expenditures in all these South Asian countries. This means that little of the subnational government's budget is available for specific development initiatives. This relative lack of fiscal space for development is apparent at the central government level: interest payments, defence, and salaries constitute the three major areas of expenditure in South Asia.

The extent of fiscal decentralization has implications for the national government's ability to use fiscal transfers to help the lagging regions. For instance, if 100 per cent of the government revenues are raised and 100 per cent of expenditures are spent by subnational governments (that is, there is complete fiscal decentralization), then the federal government has limited scope to help the lagging regions by fiscal means. Lagging regions

TABLE 7.2   Major Revenue Sources and Expenditure Categories for National and Subnational Governments in South Asia

Country	Major revenue sources of central government	Major revenue sources of subnational governments	Major heads of expenditure for central government	Major heads of expenditure for subnational governments
India	Income and corporation taxes, excise duties, customs	Sales taxes, stamp duties, tax devolution and grants from central government	Interest payments, defence, salaries, food and fertilizer subsidies	Interest payments, education, health, police, agriculture, irrigation and power.
Pakistan		Tax devolution and grants from federal government; stamp duties, user charges on government services	Interest payments, defence, education, irrigation, transport, subsidies, grants	Interest payments, grants and investments, general administration, law and order, education, health, agriculture, irrigation, roads and bridges
Sri Lanka	VAT, income tax, excise taxes, trade duties	Grants from federal government, business turnover tax, stamp duties	Interest payments, defence	Salaries, transfers and grants
Bangladesh	Income, VAT, and customs taxes	Transfers from federal government, property taxes, user fees	Salaries, interest payments, subsidies and transfers, development	Salaries, road construction, agriculture

Sources: For India, Government of India (2008a), Tables 2.1 and 3.1; for Pakistan, Government of Pakistan, Combined Finance Accounts (1990–1/1998–9) and budget documents for years onward; for Sri Lanka, World Bank (2006, chapter 2); for Bangladesh, World Bank (2009a).

thus have to depend more on their own revenues to undertake productive investments or provide public services. On the other hand, if there is complete centralization of finances, then the national government has the scope to transfer some of the revenues obtained from leading regions for the benefit of lagging regions through a system of inter-state transfers.

INTER-STATE FISCAL TRANSFERS

In practice, all federal states have some system of inter-state transfers, and subnational governments are dependent on these transfers to a greater or lesser degree. In the most decentralized country (Canada), transfers to subnational governments account for only 21 per cent of subnational governments' revenues. This channel is substantially greater in India: transfers from the central government account for 39 per cent of subnational governments' revenues; the corresponding figure for Pakistan is 81 per cent, which is consistent with the institutional arrangement of most revenues being collected by the federal government.

In this section, we review the varying arrangements for inter-state transfers in the South Asian countries. In all of these countries, the central government transfers resources to subnational governments. The amounts and types of such transfers are defined by country-specific institutions.

India

Indian states obtain resources from the central government in three main ways. The first consists of tax shares and grants decided by a non-political Finance Commission, which makes recommendations every five years. In 2004, the Twelfth Finance Commission decided that 30.5 per cent of central government tax revenues would be given back to the states over the period 2005–10; this was a small increase over the 29.5 per cent set by the Finance Commission. Dividing up these funds among the states is done by means of an explicit Finance Commission formula, which places weights on factors such as the state's area (10 per cent), population (25 per cent), per capita income (50 per cent), and other factors including the state's own revenues as a fraction of state domestic product (7.5 per cent). Tax devolution in India is thus geared to assign more funding to lagging regions, which in India are poorer and more populous.

The second source of funding is from the Planning Commission, which is in charge of formulating national five-year plans and makes grants and loans for implementing state development plans. The Planning Commission functions as follows. It works out five-year-plan investments for each sector of the economy and each state. With this plan as background, the states work out their respective development plans for each year; these plans then are approved by the Planning Commission. Since 1969, these funds have been awarded to states on the basis of a consensus formula devised by the National Development Council, which includes the prime minister and the chief ministers of all the states. This formula gives maximum weight to state population (60 per cent) and the gap between state per capita income and national average (25 per cent). About 30 per cent of all Planning Commission funds are earmarked for 11 'special category' states.[2]

Third, in various ministries, the central sector and centrally-sponsored schemes give grants to their counterparts in the states for specified projects either wholly funded by the centre (central sector projects) or requiring the states to share a proportion of the cost (centrally-sponsored schemes). These grants are wholly discretionary and often are not coordinated with Planning Commission transfers, although they are meant to serve similar objectives.

In addition to these explicit transfers from the central government to the states, a number of 'hidden' or 'implicit' transfers arise from the large subsidies given by the central government for food and fertilizer. Additionally, subsidized borrowing resources for the states are provided by either the central government or government-owned financial institutions and tax exportation. In 2007–8, the central government had budgeted about 1.34 per cent of overall gross domestic product (GDP) to be paid out in subsidies, the bulk of which were paid for subsidized food sales through the Food Corporation of India, and for fertilizers. States in India could borrow from the market only with permission of the central government, which decided the overall volume of borrowing in consultation with the Reserve Bank of India. Because most states depended on sales taxes for their revenue, the consumers in poorer states might have ended up paying much higher taxes than the producers in more affluent states—referred to as 'tax exportation' (Rao and Singh 2005).

The largest component of fiscal transfers in India comes from the tax-sharing schemes, where the Finance Commission has an explicit mandate to help poorer states. Figure 7.3 shows these different components of the transfers from the central to the state governments in India, as of 2006–7. At the same time, the discretionary transfers and the subsidies put together are almost as large as the tax shares. The Finance Commission transfers

[2]These are Arunachal Pradesh, Assam, Himachal Pradesh, Jammu & Kashmir, Manipur, Meghalaya, Mizoram, Nagaland, Sikkim, Tripura, and Uttarakhand.

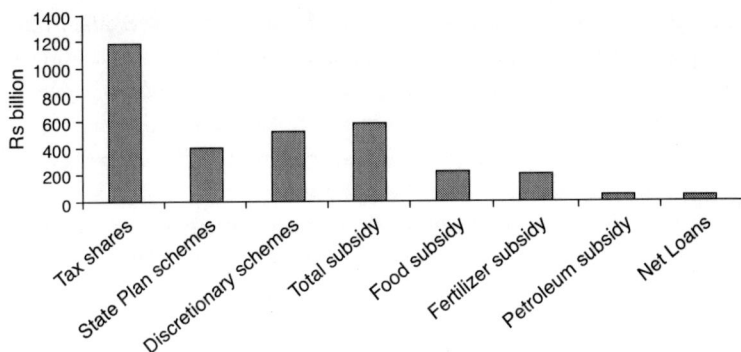

FIGURE 7.3   Transfers from Central to State Governments in India
(2006–7)

Source: Government of India (2008a).

are explicitly geared to providing larger allocations for lagging regions,
but it is not clear whether these other types of inter-state transfers will
necessarily be geared towards the lagging regions. For instance, it could be
that the leading regions are better at lobbying the centre for discretionary
grants, or they are able to meet the benchmarks of these schemes better
than lagging regions, and hence obtain more resources from these means.
We will examine this question explicitly in the next section.

In 1992, a constitutional amendment in India mandated further
decentralization to elected councils at the village and district levels. This
Panchayati Raj initiative included provisions for fiscal decentralization,
but the details were left to the states for implementation. We will review
the functioning of Panchayati Raj institutions in the section 'Political
Decentralization'. The overall picture is that most Panchayati Raj institutions
are heavily dependent on state government for their revenues, and they
have not developed many independent sources to raise revenues.

Pakistan

In Pakistan, subnational governments are present both at the provincial
level and the local (district) level. The 1973 Constitution of Pakistan
provides for the establishment of a National Finance Commission,
consisting of the federal and provincial finance ministers, to decide on
revenue-sharing matters between federal and provincial governments.
Between 1975 and 1996, only certain federal taxes were subject to such
sharing, and the provincial share was 80 per cent. In 1996, a major

change included all federal taxes in this divisible pool of resources, but the provincial share was drastically reduced to 37.5 per cent, leading to major fiscal problems in the provinces. In 2006, this share was revised upwards to 45 per cent by President Parvez Musharraf to address these fiscal concerns. Currently, this share is set to increase by one percentage point each year until it reaches 50 per cent.

The National Finance Commission is the counterpart of the Finance Commissions in India. However, there are three key differences in the functioning of these institutions in the two countries. In Pakistan, the commission is composed of political representatives, in contrast to India, where it is non-political and staffed by bureaucrats. Partly as a result of this, the National Commission in Pakistan has made only three recommendations in the last 35 years, whereas in India, 11 Finance Commissions have made recommendations that have been largely accepted by the central government. The main stumbling block in Pakistan appears to be a lack of agreement among the commission members; in fact, in 2006, President Musharraf made the decisions regarding tax sharing after the commission failed to reach a consensus (Ahmed et al. 2007). The third main difference is the criteria for distributing tax revenue across subnational units. In Pakistan, the main criterion is population, compared with India's formula scheme, which gives a substantial weight to underdevelopment in addition to population and other factors. The population criterion means that Pakistan's most populous province, Punjab, gets nearly 60 per cent of the divisible pool. In the most recent allocation, an adjustment has been made to this rule, whereby the provinces of Sindh and the North-West Frontier Province (NWFP) receive a higher-than-population share of sales tax revenue, while two-thirds of all grants-in-aid are allocated to the poor provinces of Balochistanand NWFP ('Order No. 1 of 2006' 2006).

The tax-sharing scheme constitutes the bulk of federal transfers to provinces, as we can see in Figure 7.4. In addition to the tax-sharing schemes, all royalties generated from oil and gas production and hydroelectric projects are collected by the federal government, but then are transferred back to the provinces. The federal government makes grants to the provinces for development and non-development reasons.

An important facet of decentralization in Pakistan is the role played by local governments. The relative power and importance of the local governments in regard to the provincial governments has been changed several times through the history of the country, mostly to achieve political goals. Local body elections were encouraged in 1979

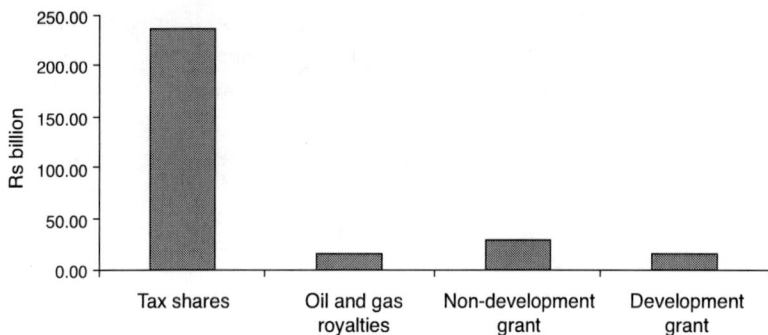

FIGURE 7.4   Transfers from Federal to Provincial Governments,
Pakistan (2004–5)

Sources: Government of Pakistan, Finance Accounts (1984–5/1997–8), Combined
Finance Accounts (1990–1/1998–9), and budget documents for years onward.

by the government of Zia-ul-Haq, which led to a widespread system
of patronage politics and a rise in the tensions between provincial and
local politicians. Partly as a result of this, local bodies were suspended
between 1993 and 1998.

In 2000, President Musharraf revived the local bodies, significantly
increasing political decentralization (by holding direct elections to local
bodies) as well as giving them significant administrative powers over such
subjects as education and health. However, there was no corresponding
fiscal decentralization. Expenditures on these topics continued to be met
out of provincial funds, and local bodies were dependent for funding
on the decisions of newly constituted Provincial Financial Councils,
which devolved some of the provincial revenue downwards. The result is
a great deal of ambiguity regarding the dividing line between provincial
and local authority and potentially overlapping or conflicting service
functions (World Bank 2002). It is notable that no functions of the federal
government were devolved in this exercise, which appeared to have been
motivated strongly by the military's need for legitimization of state control.
The fact that this happened during a period in which there were no elected
provincial governments suggests that this was a means to centralize power
in a non-elected federal government (Cheema et al. 2006).

Sri Lanka

In Sri Lanka, provinces are highly dependent on the central government
transfers for their budgetary needs, because their revenue-raising capacity

is strictly limited. As in India and Pakistan, a statutory body called the Finance Commission makes recommendations on the allocation of resources between federal and provincial governments, and on the further allocation across provinces. The Finance Commission consists of the governor of the central bank, the secretary to the treasury and three other members. Article 154R of the constitution of Sri Lanka specifies that the objective of the Finance Commission is to 'achieve balanced regional development', by taking into account the population of each province, the per capita income, and the need to reduce, progressively, economic and social disparities and the gap between the province's per capita income and that of the richest province.

Fiscal transfers from the central government come in four major ways. The first is the block grant, which is meant to cover the cost of wages and salaries in excess of subnational governments' revenues. This is determined by subtracting estimated provincial revenues from the budgeted recurrent wage expenditures. This is the single largest source of fiscal transfers to subnational governments (see Figure 7.5). Estimates of provincial revenues and budgeted expenditures are prepared by the Finance Commission. A new reform in 2005 specifies that the salaries of upper-level civil servants must be paid out of provincial revenues.

Three types of grants are meant for capital expenditures. The Provincial Service Development Grants (PSDG) is given for capital projects, which are proposed by the provinces and selected and approved by the Finance

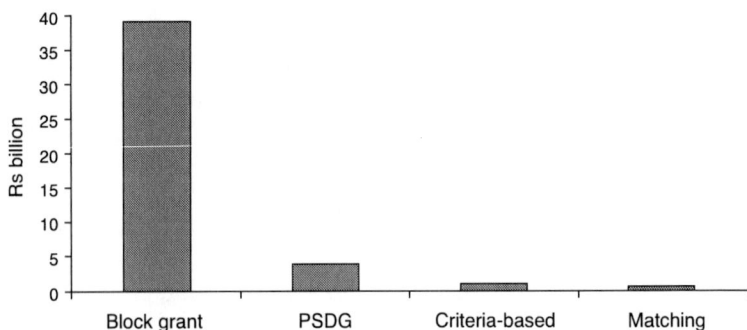

FIGURE 7.5   Transfers from Federal to Provincial Governments, Sri Lanka (2004)

Source: World Bank (2006).

Commission in a somewhat non-transparent process. The criteria-based grants are allocated across provinces in a formula-based manner, which gives weight to a diverse set of factors including per capita income and its difference from the richest province (20 per cent), unemployment (15 per cent), poverty (10 per cent), education (15 per cent), and infant mortality (7.5 per cent). This is the only part of the fiscal transfers that is directed explicitly to benefit the lagging regions, but it accounts for less than 2 per cent of the total fiscal transfers. Finally, the province can access matching grants when they raise revenues in excess of a benchmark. This is a small amount, but provincial governments enjoy complete autonomy in its use.

Bangladesh

In Bangladesh, the high degree of fiscal centralization means that transfers from higher levels of government are the most important source of financing for most local governments. There are four broad categories of transfers: earmarked sectoral grants; grants for specific transfer programmes, such as Food for Works or Old Age Pensions; block development grants; and recurrent expenditure grants, which cover expenses such as salaries for elected officials and staff. Of these, only the block grants have explicit allocation criteria, taking into account population, physical area, poor communication, literacy, nutrition level, and unemployment. This, however, accounted for a relatively small share of local government revenue (less than 6 per cent).

Table 7.3 summarizes the key features of the system of inter-state transfers across South Asian countries. This table serves as a quick reference and is not a substitute for understanding the full context of the institutional arrangements described earlier.

FISCAL TRANSFERS FOR LAGGING REGIONS

In most countries, one of the stated objectives of a system of inter-state transfers is to ensure equity across subnational regions. This is important for both economic and political reasons. Economically, poorer regions have a lower base of economic activity to tax, and typically end up having lower revenues. This revenue constraint can prevent them from investing in human and physical capital and can hamper the delivery of government services. Achieving horizontal equity through fiscal transfers is thus a way to ensure a 'level playing field' as far as government services are concerned. This can be particularly important if the government

TABLE 7.3 Fiscal Transfer Arrangements in South Asia

Country	Tax devolution decisions	Share of subnational governments in federal taxes	Grant decisions	Criteria for fiscal transfers	Borrowing by subnational government
India	Finance Commission	30.50%	Planning Commission and central ministries	Population, area, gap between state per capita income and national average	With permission of central government*
Pakistan	National Finance Commission	48% (set to increase to 50% by 2010)	Federal government	Population	With permission of central government*
Sri Lanka	No official tax-sharing scheme		Finance Commission and federal government	Population, per capita income, economic and social disparities	Not allowed
Bangladesh	No official tax-sharing scheme		Federal government		Not allowed

Source: Rao and Singh (2005); World Bank (2009a); World Bank (2006); Ahmed et al. (2007).

Note: *Subnational governments are subject to borrowing restrictions by the central government, if they have outstanding loan balances with the central government. In practice, almost all subnational governments have such outstanding loan balances, and hence their borrowing decisions are effectively controlled by the central government.

services are important inputs into future growth potential, such as in developing a healthy and educated workforce. Growing regional disparities can be a source of political tensions, and fiscal transfers can offset some of this.

On the other hand, the structure of such compensating fiscal transfers can set up some perverse incentives. If provinces feel that the deficit between their revenues and expenditures will be offset by federal transfers (the 'soft budget constraint'), this reduces their incentives to improve revenue collection. A similar disincentive can occur if subnational governments are not given much autonomy over the use of locally generated resources. In this sense, the quest for horizontal equity can blunt incentives for efficiency in both revenue generation and revenue utilization. The system of inter-state transfers can build up resentments from leading regions. As the finance minister of Punjab once asked, 'Why should I pay for Uttar Pradesh's problems?' At an extreme, the quest for regional autonomy can lead to demands for a separate state, as happened in the Indian state of Punjab in the 1980s.

In this section, we examine whether the current system of inter-state transfers is geared towards ensuring horizontal equity across the subnational regions within South Asian countries. Although the optimal degree of horizontal equity will have to balance the incentive constraints mentioned earlier, there is no reason to expect that the system will achieve any equity at all. For instance, it could be the case that richer regions have much higher political clout, and thus they are able to bias all federal transfers toward themselves. This is important to understand, so that we may develop policy recommendations to help lagging regions.

We see that poorer states do receive higher per capita fiscal transfers in India. Figure 7.6a shows the relationship between total fiscal transfers received per capita in 2005–6 against the per capita state domestic product, for the major states of India.[3] We see a significant negative slope, showing that richer states are given substantially lower fiscal transfers. Figure 7.6 includes only the explicit transfers—that is, those given through tax shares, state plan schemes, and other developmental and non-developmental funding. The picture looks quite similar when we include the food and fertilizer subsidies in addition to the explicit transfers (see Figure 7.6b). We have estimated the state-wise allocation

[3]This graph excludes the Special Category states, which are given extra funds by the Planning Commission.

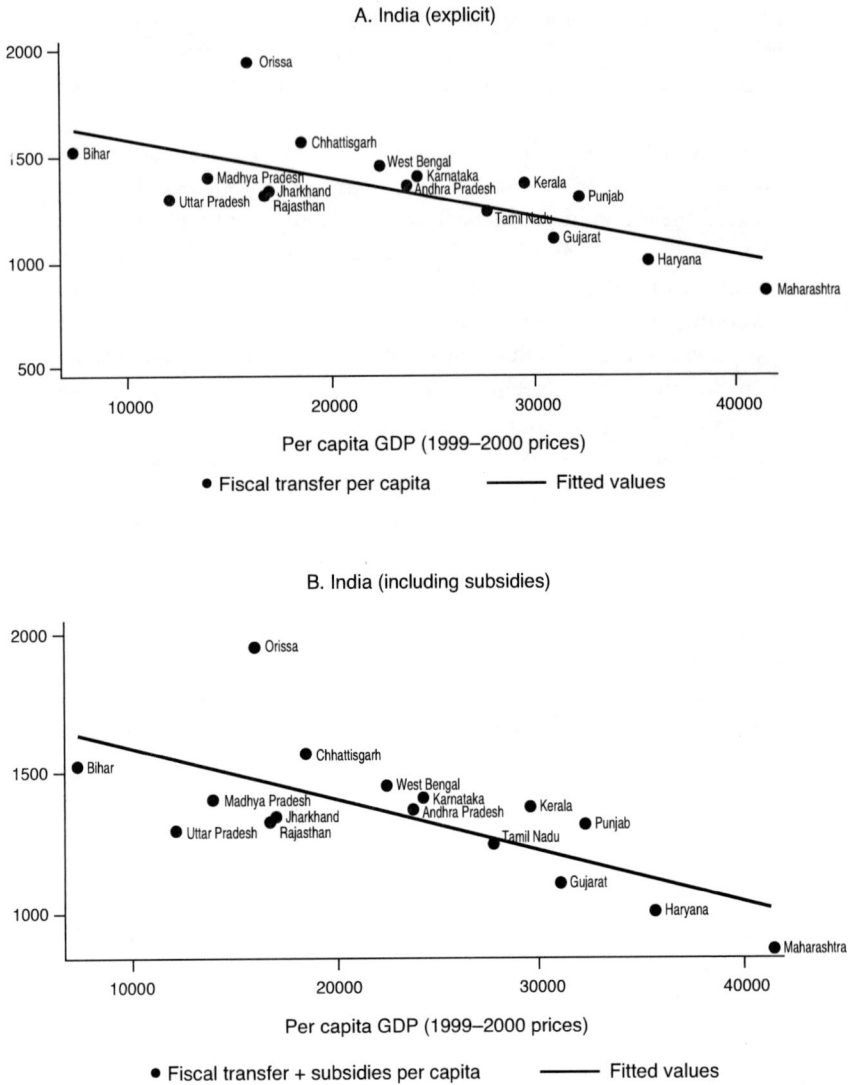

FIGURE 7.6   Lagging Regions and Fiscal Transfers in India (2005–6)

Sources: Government of India (2008a); budget data for individual states for data on subsidies.

Note: GDP per capita is in constant 1999–2000 local currency units.

of the food and fertilizer subsidies to be in the same proportion as the consumption of food and fertilizer in each state.[4]

Looking at the different components of fiscal transfers in India, it becomes clear that the horizontal equity is being achieved only through the tax-sharing schemes of the Finance Commission (see Figure 7.7a). The state plan grants administered by the Planning Commission are not directed towards either the richer or the poorer states (see Figure 7.7b), while the discretionary schemes show higher per capita expenditures in the richer states (see Figure 7.7c). Food subsidies per capita are roughly uniform across poor and rich states, if we assume that all the subsidies are spent in subsidizing sales of food by the Food Corporation of India (see Figure 7.7d). On the other hand, if we allocate food subsidies on the assumption that all the subsidies are spent in food procurement through above-market procurement prices, then we see that highest levels of subsidies are given to the leading states of Punjab, Haryana, and Maharashtra (see Figure 7.7e). The true picture is probably a mix of production and consumption subsidies, but the overall conclusion is that these food subsidies are not significantly higher in poorer regions. If we look at the second-biggest source of subsidies, fertilizers, we see that this benefits richer regions much more than poorer regions, because the richer regions tend to consume more fertilizers (see Figure 7.7f). In this sense, if the subsidies are meant to improve investment levels in lagging regions, they need to be targeted to those regions, rather than to a specific good or service that may turn out to be consumed more in richer states.

In Pakistan, we see poorer regions obtaining a higher level of per capita fiscal transfers (see Figure 7.8a). Which component of fiscal transfers is contributing most to this relationship? We find that the poorer provinces are obtaining a higher tax share per capita (see Figure 7.8b). As described earlier, income tax revenue is shared on the basis of provincial population, whereas sales tax is shared according to a different formula that gives a lower weight to the populous Punjab province. When we examine developmental and non-developmental grants allocated by the federal government, we again see that the lagging regions obtain a higher per capita level of these types of federal transfers (see Figure 7.8c).

---

[4]The government accounts only mention the total amount of food and fertilizer subsidies, not the state-wise allocation. Hence we assume that these are proportional to the amount of food and fertilizer consumption across states. It is possible that most of these food subsidies are spent in procuring food, rather than subsidizing consumption. We therefore show the allocation of food subsidies according to both purchases and sales.

A. Tax Shares

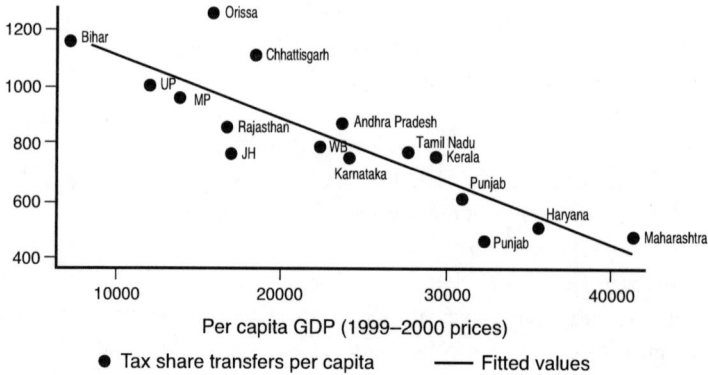

Per capita GDP (1999–2000 prices)

● Tax share transfers per capita   —— Fitted values

B. State Plan Schemes

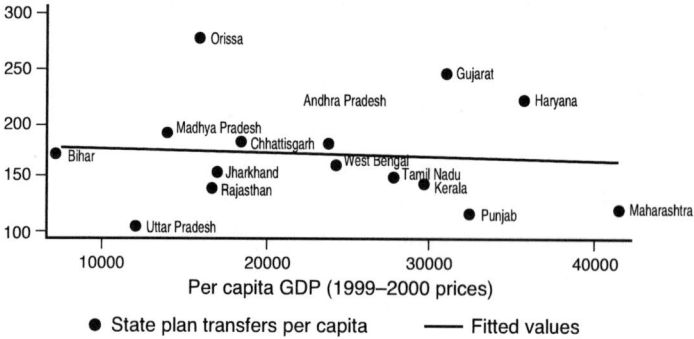

Per capita GDP (1999–2000 prices)

● State plan transfers per capita   —— Fitted values

C. Discretionary Schemes

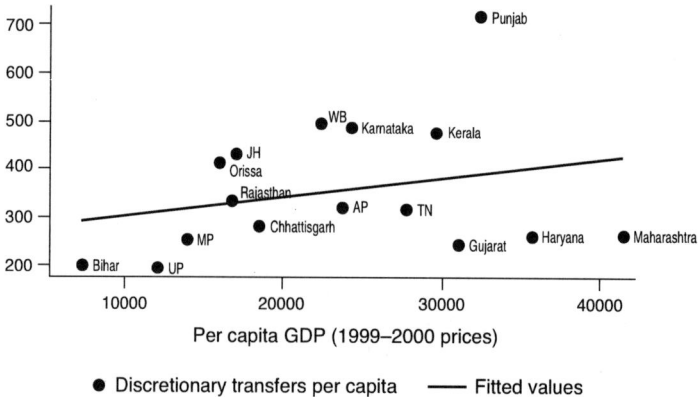

Per capita GDP (1999–2000 prices)

● Discretionary transfers per capita   —— Fitted values

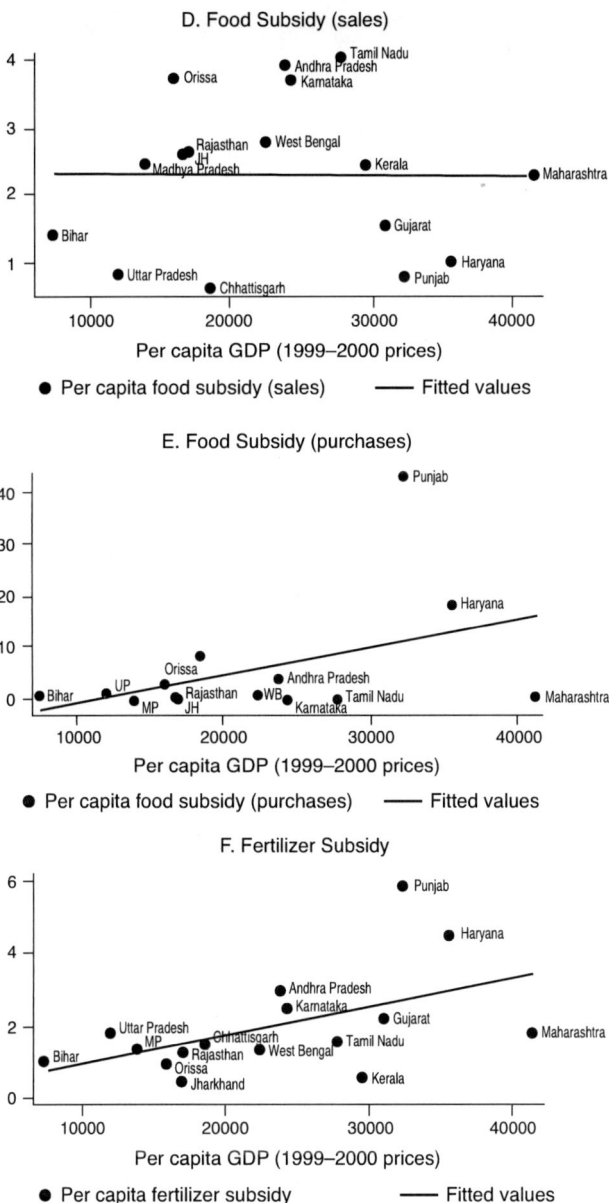

Figure 7.7   Lagging Regions and Types of Fiscal Transfers in India (2005–6)

Sources: Government of India 2008a; budget data for individual states. State-level subsidy allocation is estimated using food grain purchases or sales reported in annual reports published by the Food Corporation of India, 2005–6.

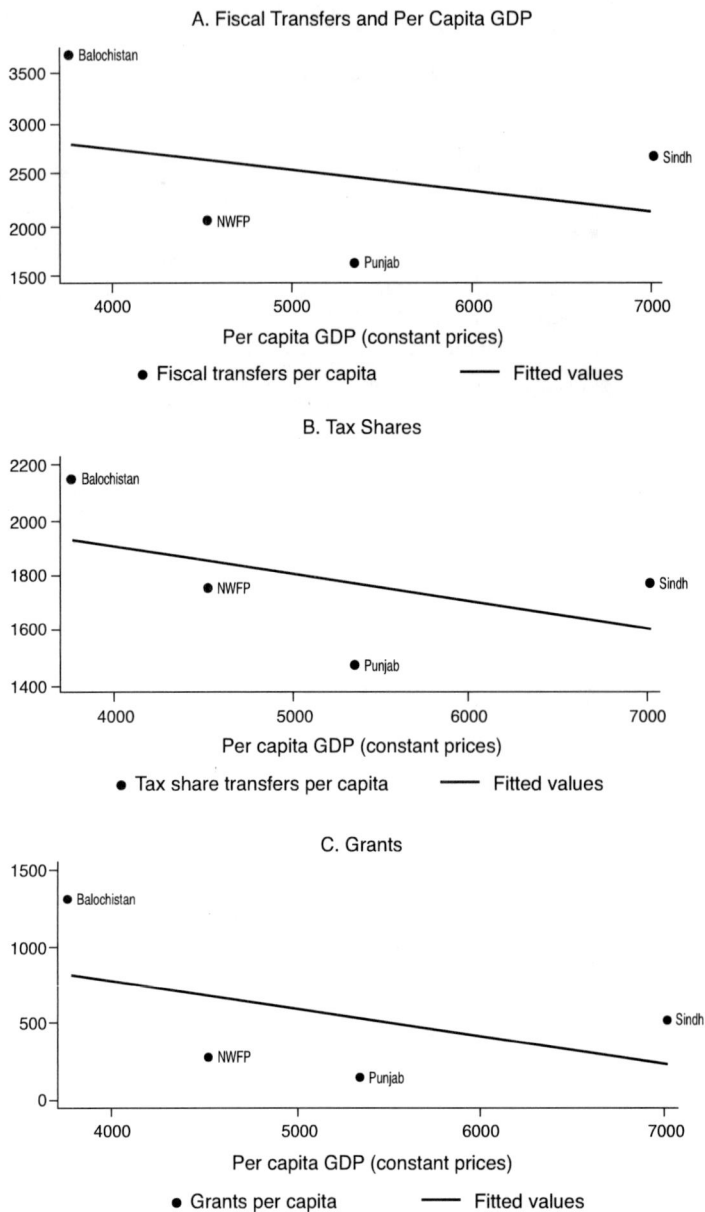

A. Fiscal Transfers and Per Capita GDP

- Fiscal transfers per capita   —— Fitted values

B. Tax Shares

- Tax share transfers per capita   —— Fitted values

C. Grants

- Grants per capita   —— Fitted values

FIGURE 7.8   Lagging Regions and Fiscal Transfers in Pakistan

Sources: Government of Pakistan, Finance Accounts (1984–5/1997–8), Combined Finance Accounts (1990–1/1998–9), and budget documents for years onward.

Consistent with the stated objective of balanced regional development in Sri Lanka, we find that the poorer provinces are given significantly higher levels of federal transfers per capita (see Figure 7.9). This pro-poor bias is seen in all components of the fiscal transfers: block grants, provincial service development grants, and criteria-based grants, where per capita income, poverty, and unemployment are part of the formula for allocating funds. It is notable that the highest levels of per capita funding have been allocated to the north-east province, the centre of a long-running Tamil separatist movement. In this sense, fiscal transfers appear to be attempting to solve a political problem as well.

A matter of concern raised in the recent World Bank's public expenditure report on Bangladesh is that poorer regions are being allocated lower levels of per capita development funding (see Figure 7.10). This is not too surprising, given that no explicit mandates direct resource transfers toward poorer regions for most categories of federal transfers. But it does raise a concern that the fiscal decentralization arrangements are working against ensuring equity across the subnational regions of Bangladesh.

ADMINISTRATIVE DECENTRALIZATION

Administrative decentralization refers to devolving spending authority to subnational governments. Theoretically, this can improve welfare by ensuring better policy choices and better implementation of policy.[5] The idea is that local (subnational) governments have more information about local needs, and they are better placed to choose appropriate policies for the local region to or better identify the targeting of policy. For instance, in implementing a poverty alleviation programme, it is the local government that is likely to know where the poor are concentrated or to know which places need an extra school, and so on. An alternative channel is that local governments are better able to monitor the service providers (local teachers, nurses, and so on), and therefore can ensure better delivery of public services.

Administrative decentralization has two potential downsides. First, local officials may be less competent than those at the national level, perhaps because of insufficient levels of human capital or an inability to manage a lack of social cohesion at the local level. Such lack of

[5]See Seabright (1996), Besley and Case (1995), and Bardhan and Mookherjee (2006a) for a theoretical analysis of administrative decentralization. Bardhan (2002) provides a useful summary of the theoretical and empirical literature on this topic.

A. Fiscal Transfers

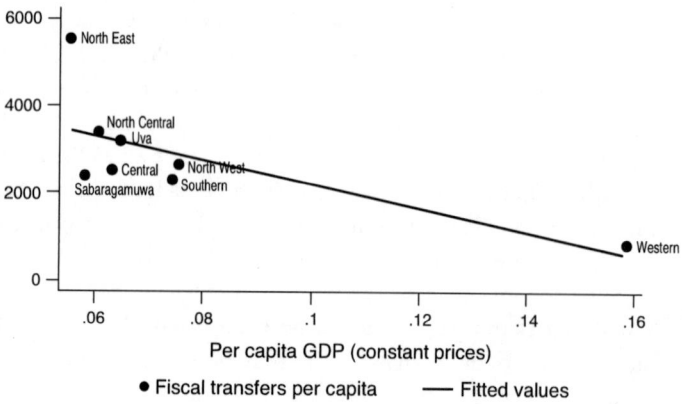

Per capita GDP (constant prices)

● Fiscal transfers per capita   —— Fitted values

B. Block Grants

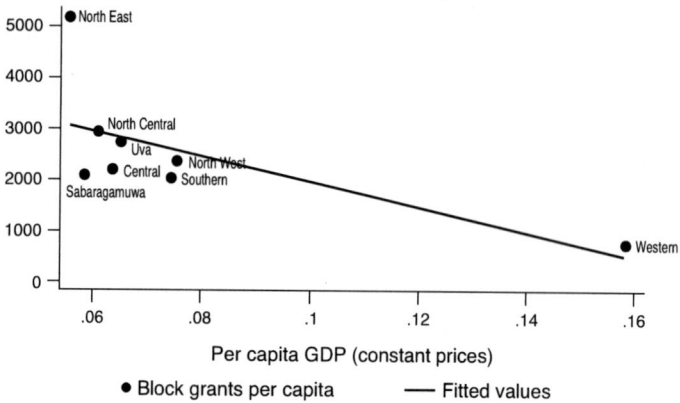

Per capita GDP (constant prices)

● Block grants per capita   —— Fitted values

C. Provincial Service Development Grants

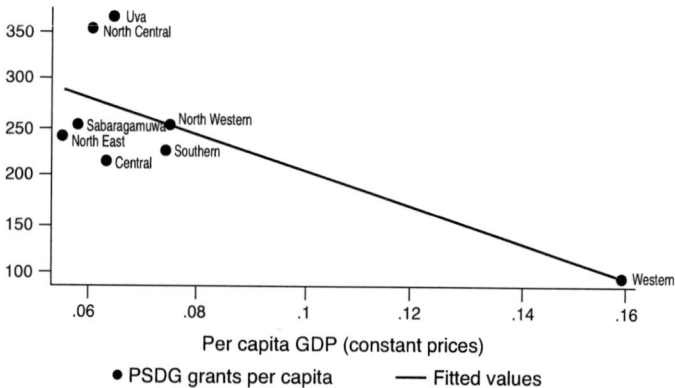

Per capita GDP (constant prices)

● PSDG grants per capita   —— Fitted values

D. Criteria-based Grants

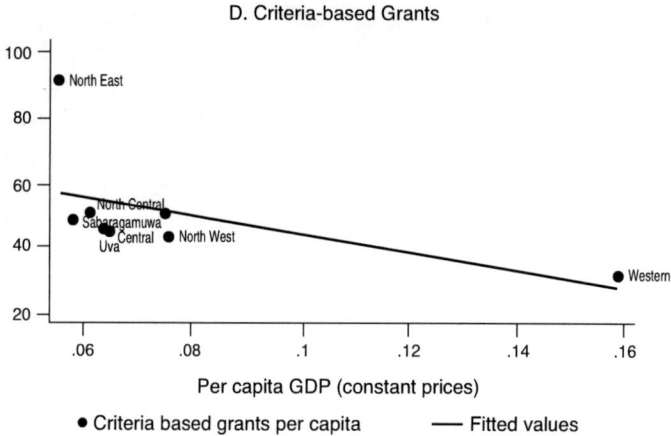

FIGURE 7.9   Lagging Regions and Fiscal Transfers in Sri Lanka

Source: World Bank (2006).

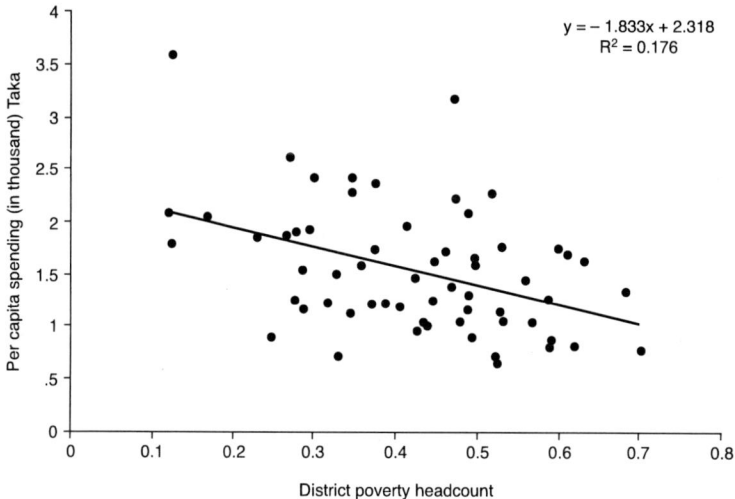

FIGURE 7.10   Per Capita Development Spending across
Districts of Bangladesh

Sources: World Bank (2009a), based on data from Ministry of Finance for fiscal year
2006–7; World Bank staff estimates.
Note: Scatter graph excludes districts with Chittagong Hill Tribes, Rangamati,
Bandarban, and Khagrachhari, which represent outliers in terms of development
spending.

282 The Poor Half Billion in South Asia

administrative capacity is especially likely to be true in the lagging regions and can lead to underutilization or poor utilization of any funds, thereby undermining the effectiveness of fiscal transfers. Second, local officials might be more likely to be 'captured' by local interests and use their administrative power to provide services only to a local narrow elite. A lack of supervisory mechanisms might lead to local officials charging bribes for providing government services. Thus, the net effect of devolving authority to subnational governments may or may not be positive.

How well does South Asia compare with other countries on the extent of administrative decentralization? Using a World Bank data set on Qualitative Decentralization Indicators,[6] we construct the extent to which broad classes of government services have been decentralized to the subnational level. For instance, the broad category of social services includes public health, primary education, secondary education, and tertiary education. Of these four categories, a country that had devolved two of these services to the subnational level is given an administrative decentralization score of 0.5, and so on. The results from this exercise are summarized in Table 7.4.

We find that the extent of administrative decentralization varies across the types of services even within specific countries. There is also considerable variation in whether execution and supervision are both decentralized. For instance, India has devolved the execution of most education programmes to the subnational level, but supervision in many cases is retained at the national level. A similar story follows in Pakistan's administrative decentralization where the implementation of service delivery has been decentralized but the autonomy lies at the centre. Overall, as in fiscal decentralization, we observe that India is more decentralized than the world average, while Pakistan is somewhat less decentralized. Bangladesh is extremely centralized in both execution and supervision of service delivery.

Does greater administrative decentralization lead to better service delivery outcomes? As discussed earlier, the a priori effect is ambiguous, because we do not know whether the advantages of better local information and monitoring will or will not be offset by a greater degree of capture or corruption. Furthermore, the relative effects of these forces will depend

[6]The database can be accessed publicly at http://www1.worldbank.org/publicsector/decentralization/qualitativeindicators.htm

TABLE 7.4   Level of Administrative Decentralization in
South Asia and the World

Execution	Social services	Transportation	Other services	Utility services
Bangladesh	0	0	0	0
India	1	0.40	0.625	0.67
Pakistan	1	0.50	0.5	1
World	*0.44*	*0.31*	*0.28*	*0.48*
Brazil	0.57	0.67	0.33	0.50
China	0.83			
Mexico	0.79	0.42	0.33	0.38
Supervision				
Bangladesh	0	0	0	0
India	0.21	0	0.38	0.50
Pakistan	1	0	0	1
World	*0.19*	*0.26*	*0.12*	*0.35*
Brazil	0.29	0.5	0.33	0.5
Mexico	0.21	0.33	0.17	0.33

Source: Author's calculation using *Qualitative Decentralization Indicators* that have been collected from various sources (World Bank 2008).

Note: A fully centralized governance structure is replaced with a 0, complete local autonomy is replaced with 1, whereas an intermediate structure between fully centralized and local autonomy is referred as 0.5. We take the arithmetic average of the level of devolution for the individual categories. Social Services include the following categories: Housing, Nutrition Programmes, Primary and Preschool Education, Secondary Education, Universities, Public Health, and Hospitals. Transportation encompasses Interurban Highways, Urban Highways, Ports and Navigable Waterways, Airports Railroads, Urban Transportation. Other services are Oil and Gas Pipelines, Public Order and Safety, Police and Irrigation. Utility Services include Drinking Water and Sewerage, Waste Collection, Electric Power Supply, and Telecommunications.

both on local conditions, as well as on the nature of the service being decentralized. In the cross-country data, we do not find any consistent relationship between the degree of administrative decentralization and human capital investments (which reflect the effectiveness of public service delivery). Figure 7.11 shows that the extent of administrative decentralization is positively correlated with education attainment (see Figure 7.11a), but it is not correlated with infant mortality rates (see Figure 7.11b).

A better way to assess the impact of administrative decentralization is to study specific instances, with better data at the local level. A number of recent studies have examined various aspects of administrative

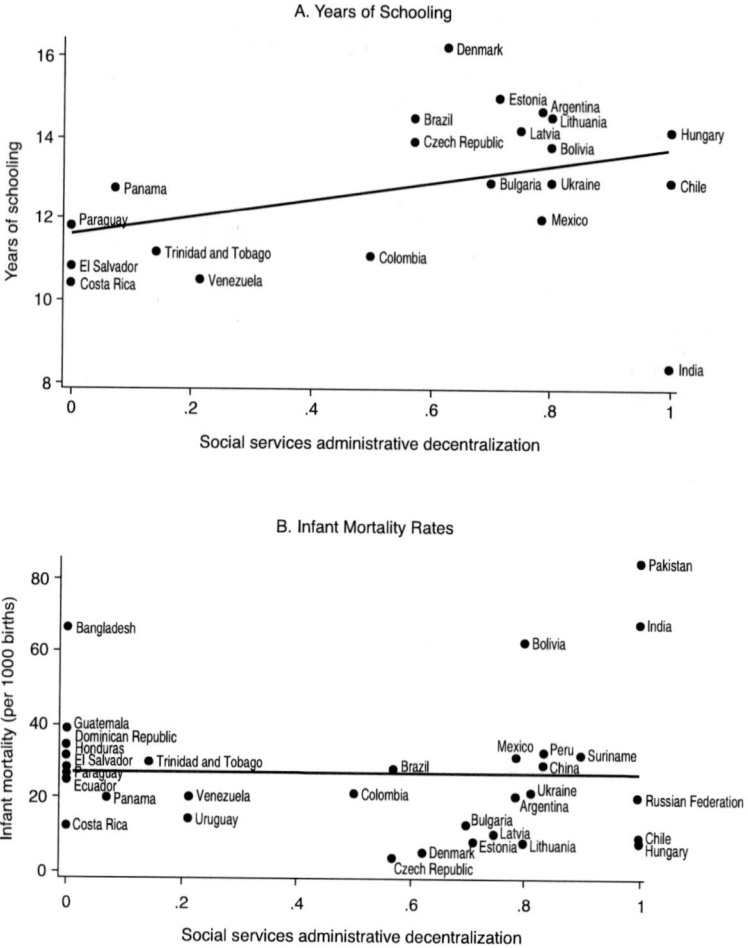

A. Years of Schooling

B. Infant Mortality Rates

FIGURE 7.11 Administrative Decentralization and Development Outcomes (cross-country)

Sources: World Bank (2009b) for development outcome variables; author's calculation using Qualitative Decentralization Indicators that have been collected from various sources (World Bank 2008).

Note: Social services administrative decentralization is a measure of the extent to which the execution of social services has been devolved to subnational governments. Social services include the following categories: housing, nutrition programmes, primary and pre-school education, secondary education, universities, public health, and hospitals. Please see notes to Table 7.4 for details on author's calculation of social service administrative decentralization.

decentralization. The evidence on whether local governments have better information regarding local needs is quite mixed. Some studies find that intra-village mis-allocation of poverty benefits is lower than inter-village mis-allocation, suggesting that local governments do a better job in identifying the poor (see Bardhan and Mookherjee 2006b, on India; Galasso and Ravallion 2005, on Bangladesh). On the other hand, the analysis of Coady (2001) for Mexico finds that most of the benefits of targeting are achieved at the inter-village level, rather than within-village. This is important particularly because the extent of misallocation in poverty targeting programmes is found to be large in many recent studies (Alatas et al. 2009; Galasso and Ravallion 2005).

The evidence for the power of local monitoring to ensure better performance of local governments is particularly weak. Galiani et al. (2008) find that decentralization of schools leads to better student outcomes in better-off provinces and worse outcomes in poorer provinces of Argentina. Olken (2007) finds that top–down auditing by upper levels of government is much more effective than local monitoring in controlling corruption in road-building in Indonesia. Banerjee et al. (2008) find that the local community monitoring of teachers was almost non-existent in India despite the provision of information and training. Linden and Shastry (2009) find that teachers systematically inflate student attendance records to obtain free meals in India. Chaudhury et al. (2006) find that rates of teacher and health worker absenteeism is much higher in the poorer states of India.

Overall, it is not clear whether local governments have certain advantages in either information or monitoring capability when it comes to public service delivery. In fact, we see that poorer states within India spend considerably less on social services, including education and health (see Figure 7.12a). An encouraging sign is that they spend greater amounts as a proportion of their state domestic products, suggesting that higher economic growth might translate into greater social expenditures over the longer term (see Figure 7.12b).

Local governments in poor regions often lack the administrative capacity to make use of the resources at their disposal. We have seen that they are less successful in obtaining funds from the central government if the funds are not routed through the Finance Commission (see Figure 7.7). A case study of Bihar by the World Bank revealed that one-third of Bihar's 533 blocks lacked development officers, and 20 per cent of funds allocated to the state remained unspent (World Bank 2005).

A. Social Services per Capita

B. Social Services (% of GDP)

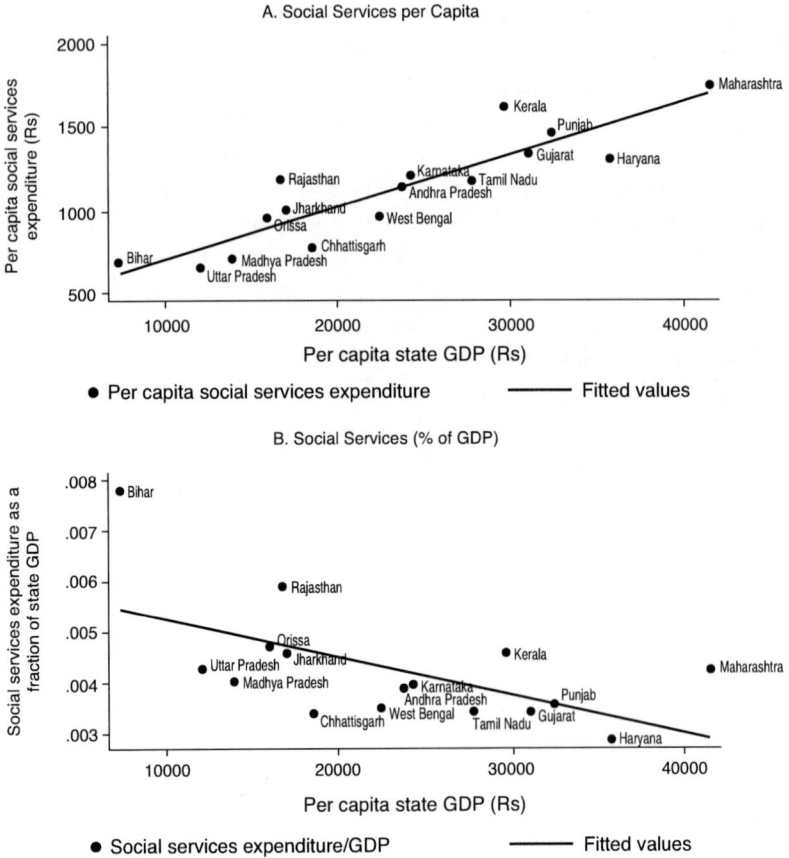

FIGURE 7.12   Social Service Expenditures across Indian States (2006–7)

Sources: Government of India (2008a); budget data for individual states.

POLITICAL DECENTRALIZATION

Another factor in effective service delivery is the extent of political decentralization—that is, the extent to which local governments are elected directly by the citizens. The idea is that political decentralization will make local governments more accountable to the citizens, thereby improving service delivery and governance. Another potential outcome of political decentralization or grassroots democracy is that it might enable the representation of politically disadvantaged sections of society that previously were unable to obtain political representation at higher levels of office. This representation would have the beneficial impact of making government policies more responsive to the needs of such politically marginalized communities. On the other hand, introducing further layers of government officials between the national government and the citizenry might increase the incentives toward corruption, and the lack of coordination between local elected officials and those at higher levels of office might impede effective policy implementation.

The cross-country comparisons of the extent of political decentralization in South Asian countries line up with the comparisons of fiscal and administrative decentralization. India has significantly increased the extent of political decentralization through the 1992 Panchayati Raj Act, which required all states to set up a three-tier system of elected local governments at district, block, and village levels. Other South Asian countries do not offer such levels of direct democracy to their citizens (see Table 7.5).

When we examine the number of tiers of government as an index of political decentralization (because this brings government closer to the people), we find that it is associated with worse human capital outcomes.

TABLE 7.5   Measures of Political Decentralization in
South Asia and the World

Country	Number of tiers (including central)	Per capita number of bottom tier units	Executive at bottom tier directly elected or chosen by directly elected assembly	Executive at second lowest tier directly elected or chosen by directly elected assembly
	(i)	(ii)	(iii)	(iv)
Bangladesh	5	0.49	0	0
India	5	0.25	1	1
Nepal	3	0.18	0.5	0.5
Pakistan	4.5	0.04	0.5	0.5
Sri Lanka	4	0.02	1	0
World	3.72	0.25	0.68	0.42
China	5			
Canada	4	0.15	1	1
USA	4	0.13	1	1
Mexico	3	0.03	1	1

Source: Treisman 2008.
Note: The Treisman database on political decentralization is representative of the mid-1990s. Per capita number of bottom tier units = total number of bottom tier units/population. The executive at bottom tier directly elected variable is set to 0.5 if local councils consist of both elected representatives and members appointed by upper levels of government. If executives are elected, then the bottom tier executive is reflected as 1, whereas if they are nominated it is reflected as 0.

Education attainment is lower and infant mortality is higher in countries that have many tiers of government between the national government and the citizenry (see Figure 7.13). These patterns are reversed, however,

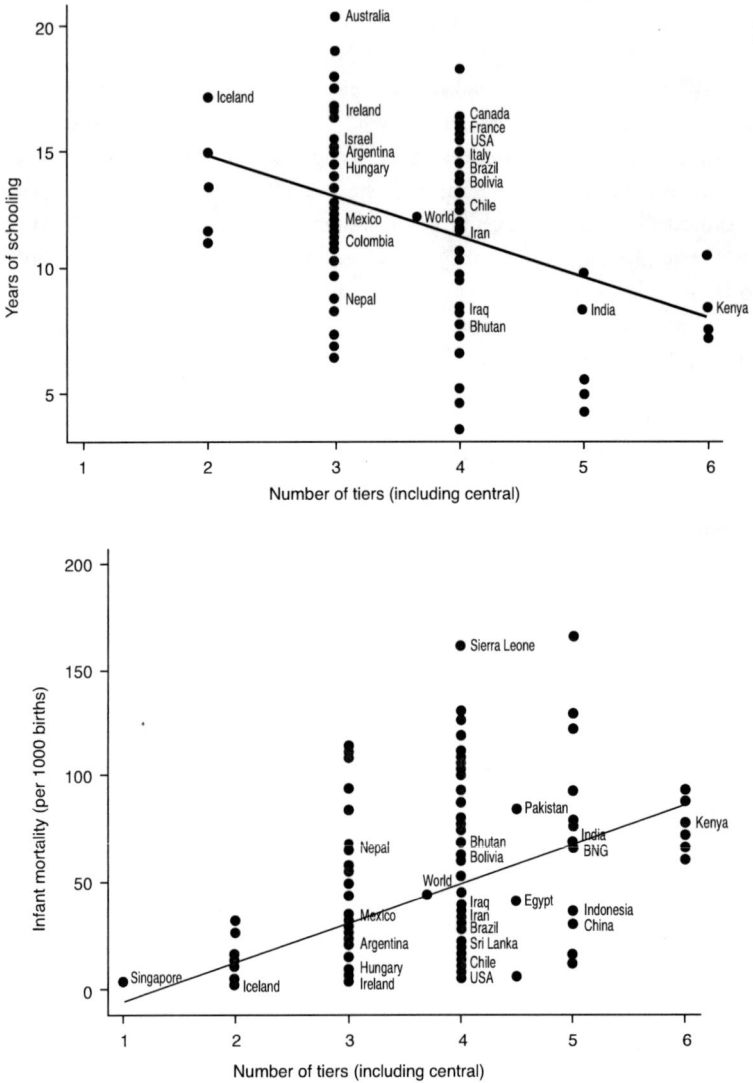

FIGURE 7.13   Number of Government Tiers and Human Capital Investments

Sources: World Bank (2009b); Treisman (2008).

BOX 7.1   The Panchayati Raj in India

In 1992, the Indian constitution was amended to mandate the creation of elected councils below state level. Although such 'Panchayati Raj' institutions had existed for a long time, they had not been able to 'acquire the status and dignity of viable and responsive people's bodies' for a number of reasons, including absence of regular elections, prolonged supersessions, insufficient representation of weaker sections like Scheduled Castes, Scheduled Tribes, and women, inadequate devolution of powers, and lack of financial resources. The constitutional amendment sought to redress these deficiencies by specifying that elections be held every five years, seats be reserved in the local councils for members of Scheduled Castes, Scheduled Tribes, and women, a State Finance Commission be set up to review fiscal devolution to district and village councils, and 29 categories of public service delivery be devolved to these local councils. The legislation thus provided for a significant degree of fiscal, administrative, and political decentralization from the state to local levels.

There has been considerable variation across states in the effective progress of decentralization under this reform. The extent of fiscal decentralization has been quite minimal under this reform, and most Panchayati Raj institutions (district, block, and village councils) have no independent sources of revenue and are overwhelmingly dependent on state governments for their revenue. The progress of administrative decentralization has been extremely uneven across states. As of 2007, only three of India's 28 states had passed executive orders devolving all 29 functions to the local level, as required by the constitutional amendment. These functions included control over education, health, roads, electricity, and poverty alleviation programmes at the local level. Some states had passed orders for the devolution of some of these functions, while seven states had devolved *none* of these functions (Government of India 2008b). This is a stark illustration of the fact that the process of decentralization remains poorly understood: mandating such devolution of power at the national level is clearly not enough to deliver real power to local councils.

The political decentralization part of the Panchayati Raj initiative has made considerable progress. All states in India have now held direct elections to the local councils, although the timing has varied considerably across states. For instance, states like West Bengal with pre-existing local councils were able to hold their first elections under the new regime in 1993 itself, while the state of Bihar had its first Panchayati Raj election only in 2001.

(contd...)

The key aspect of the Panchayati Raj political decentralization, which has been analysed extensively, has been the mandated reservation for women representatives in local councils. This is a key aspect in part because the randomized scheme used in such reservations has facilitated empirical identification of programme effects. The 1992 Act mandates that one-third of all local council seats and all local council head positions be reserved for women. This represents a significant increase in the political representation of women: on average, only 5.5 per cent of all state legislators were women, and women made up fewer than 10 per cent of national legislators.

The empirical results strongly suggest that such mandated reservation for women in local councils can be a powerful means of empowering women. Chattopadhyay and Duflo (2004) use the randomization in the selection of reserved seats at the village level to identify the impact of a woman leader on policy outcomes. They find that women leaders are more likely to provide public goods valued highly by women, such as drinking water. Iyer et al. (2009) find that political empowerment of women leads to greater reporting of crimes against women, an important first step in the investigation and prosecution of such crimes. Furthermore, Beaman et al. (2009) find that the perception of women leaders improves significantly after these villages actually elect women leaders. This is particularly important since it suggests that such interventions can lead to long-term societal changes.

when we replace the number of tiers measure of political decentralization with a dummy for whether local governments are directly elected or not (results not shown). In sum, regarding administrative decentralization, the cross-country data do not yield strong conclusions regarding the effects of political decentralization on public service delivery.

CONCLUSION

This chapter documents the relationship between the federal government and subnational governments in the South Asian countries. This is an important aspect in developing appropriate policies for the lagging regions of South Asia. We find that India is relatively decentralized in terms of fiscal, administrative, and political decentralization, whereas other South Asian countries have a considerably lower degree of decentralization in all dimensions. This indicates a lack of subnational autonomy, and also means that the federal government, if it so wishes, has the capacity to direct resources to the lagging regions to facilitate investments in human capital and institutional reforms.

We draw two main conclusions from our study of decentralization arrangements in South Asia. First, the systems of inter-state fiscal transfers in South Asian countries transfer a greater amount of resources to poorer regions, suggesting that they are acting in the direction of achieving greater equity. An important caveat in this regard is that this is mostly the case when such pro-poor redistribution has explicit rules. Other types of transfers from the central government to subnational governments tend to be skewed toward richer states, the most illustrative examples being India's discretionary schemes and fertilizer subsidies. Therefore, more resources could be transferred to lagging regions so that welfare programmes and human development can be accelerated.

The second main conclusion is that simply directing financial resources to lagging regions may not be sufficient and may need to be complemented with increases in capacity, accountability, and participation at the local level, so that lagging regions can make full use of these resources. A related question is whether fiscal transfers are the right way to help lagging regions. After all, one can make the case that the presence of an inter-state transfer system provides a disincentive for fiscal responsibility by subnational governments, since they can always ask for transfers to compensate for budgetary shortfalls. This big question is beyond the scope of the chapter, but the remaining chapters do examine other ways to help the poor in lagging regions.

REFERENCES

Ahmed, Iftikhar, Mustafa Usman, and Mahmood Khalid. 2007. 'National Finance Commission Awards in Pakistan: A Historical Perspective', Working Paper 2007:33, Pakistan Institute of Development Economics, Islamabad.

Alatas, Vivi, Abhijit Banerjee, Rema Hanna, Benjamin Olken, and Julia Tobias. 2009. 'How to Target the Poor: Evidence from a Field Experiment in Indonesia', Working Paper, Massachusetts Institute of Technology.

Banerjee, Abhijit, Rukmini Banerji, Esther Duflo, Rachel Glennerster, and Stuti Khemani. 2008. 'Pitfalls of Participatory Programs: Evidence from a Randomized Evaluation in Education in India', NBER Working Paper No. 14311, National Bureau of Economic Research, Cambridge, MA.

Bardhan, Pranab. 2002. 'Decentralization of Governance and Development', *Journal of Economic Perspectives*, 16 (4): 185–205.

Bardhan, Pranab and Dilip Mookherjee. 2006a. 'Decentralization and Accountability in Infrastructure Delivery in Developing Countries', *Economic Journal*, 116 (1): 101–27.

———. 2006b. 'Pro-poor Targeting and Accountability of Local Governments in West Bengal', *Journal of Development Economics*, 79: 303–27.

Beaman, Lori, Raghabendra Chattopadhyay, Rohini Pande, and Petia Topalova. 2009. 'Powerful Women: Does Exposure Reduce Bias?', *Quarterly Journal of Economics*, 124 (4): 1497–540.

Besley, Timothy and Anne Case. 1995. 'Incumbent Behavior: Vote-Seeking, Tax-Setting and Yardstick Competition', *American Economic Review*, 85 (1): 25–45.

Chaudhury, Nazmul, Jeffrey Hammer, Michael Kremer, Karthik Muralidharan, and F. Halsey Rogers. 2006. 'Missing in Action: Teacher and Health Worker Absence in Developing Countries', *Journal of Economic Perspectives*, 20 (1): 91–116.

Chattopadhyay, Raghabendra and Esther Duflo. 2004. 'Women as Policy Makers: Evidence from a Randomized Policy Experiment in India', *Econometrica*, 72 (5): 1409–43.

Cheema, Ali, Asim Khwaja, and A. Qadir. 2006. 'Local Government Reforms in Pakistan: Context, Content and Causes', in D. Mookherjee and P. Bardhan (eds), *Decentralization and Local Governance in Developing Countries: A Comparative Perspective*. Cambridge: MIT Press.

Coady, David. 2001. 'An Evaluation of the Distributional Power of Progresa's Cash Transfers in Mexico', International Food Policy Research Institute Working Paper, Washington, D.C.

Galasso, E. and M. Ravallion. 2005. 'Decentralized Targeting of an Anti-Poverty Program', *Journal of Public Economics*, 89: 705–27.

Galiani, Sebastian, Paul Gertler, and Ernesto Schargrodsky. 2008. 'School Decentralization: Helping the Good Get Better, but Leaving the Poor Behind', *Journal of Public Economics*, 92: 2106–20.

Government Finance Statistics (GFS). 2001. Washington, D.C.: International Monetary Fund.

Government of India. 2008a. *Indian Public Finance Statistics 2007–2008*. New Delhi: Ministry of Finance, Government of India.

———. 2008b. *The State of Panchayats 2007–08: An Independent Assessment*. New Delhi: Ministry of Panchayati Raj, Government of India.

Government of Pakistan. Finance Accounts, 1984–5/1997–8. Ministry of Finance, Government of Pakistan.

———. Combined Finance Accounts, 1990–1/1998–9. Ministry of Finance, Government of Pakistan.

———. Budget Documents, 1999–2000/2007–8. Ministry of Finance, Government of Pakistan.

Iyer, Lakshmi, Anandi Mani, Prachi Mishra, and Petia Topalova. 2009. 'Political Representation and Crime: Evidence from India's Panchayati Raj', Working Paper, Harvard Business School, Boston.

Linden, Leigh and Gauri Kartini Shastry. 2009. 'Grain Inflation: Identifying Agent Discretion in Response to a Conditional School Nutrition Program', Working Paper, Wellesley College.

Olken, Benjamin. 2007. 'Monitoring Corruption: Evidence from a Field Experiment in Indonesia', *Journal of Political Economy*, 115 (2): 200–49.

Gazette of Pakistan. 2006. 'Order No. 1 of 2006: An Order Further to Amend the Distribution of Revenues and Grants-in-Aid Order, 1997', 19 January 2006.

Rao, M. Govinda and Nirvikar Singh. 2005. *Political Economy of Federalism in India*. New Delhi: Oxford University Press.

Seabright, Paul. 1996. 'Accountability and Decentralization in Government: An Incomplete Contracts Model', *European Economic Review*, 40 (1): 61–89.

Treisman, Daniel. 2008. 'Decentralization Dataset'. Available at http://www.sscnet.ucla.edu/polisci/faculty/treisman/, accessed in November 2009.

———. 2002. 'Decentralization and the Quality of Government', Working Paper, University of California–Los Angeles.

World Bank. 2009a. *Bangladesh Public Expenditure Review*. Washington, D.C.: World Bank.

———. 2009b. *World Development Indicators*. Washington, D.C.: World Bank.

———. 2008. *Qualitative Decentralization Indicators*. Available at http://www1.worldbank.org/publicsector/decentralization/qualitativeindicators.htm, accessed in November 2009.

———. 2006. 'Decentralization and Service Delivery in Sri Lanka Assessment and Options', Draft Report, World Bank, Washington, D.C.

———. 2005. 'Bihar: Towards a Development Strategy', World Bank, Washington, D.C.

———. 2002. 'Pakistan's Fiscal Decentralization: Issues and Opportunities', World Bank, Washington, D.C.

8

How Important is Migration?

Çağlar Özden and Mirvat Sewadeh

Internal migration, like all other reallocation mechanisms, allows labour to move to geographic areas and economic sectors where the demand and the returns are much higher. These movements tend to be closely related to massive bouts of urbanization seen in many developing countries such as Brazil, China, Mexico, and Turkey and take place in the leading regions of generally fast-growing countries. As a result, internal migration becomes an integral component of economic development and poverty reduction processes in many countries and an important factor for achieving equitable development within a country.[1]

Where does internal migration in South Asia fit in this picture? South Asia has one of the highest population densities in the world, and the region's population continues to grow rapidly, especially when compared with other parts of the developing world. Several countries in the region, especially India, achieved remarkably consistent high growth rates over significant periods of time. Yet, countries in South Asia do not place among the top countries in terms of internal labour mobility. Even with the inclusion of some of the largest cities in the world, their total urban populations are very small relative to the significant rural populations in lagging areas of countries in the region. India especially is frequently cited as a prominent example of limited internal mobility. For example,

[1]See Ozden and Schiff (2007) and Ozden and Schiff (2006) for discussion on link between migration and development.

recent work by Bell and Muhidin (2009) compiles extensive evidence on internal migration and points out that the number of people living outside their district (or province) of birth is around 7 per cent of the population in China, 30 per cent in Brazil, and only 3.5 per cent in India. Bell and Muhidin (2009) provide several other measures of internal mobility that all point out the same patterns. What is particularly striking about low internal mobility in India is that the unskilled account for only a small portion of migrants. Barriers to migration whether geographical (such as distance), policy-induced (such as social entitlement and rural employment programmes), or cultural (such as linguistic differences) are especially difficult for the poor and the low-skilled to overcome. As such, impediments to internal migration are depriving India's poor of access to work opportunities in other states and, consequently, of a path out of poverty.

Many questions immediately emerge on the causes and consequences of the limited internal mobility in South Asia. This chapter aims to address these questions. First, the overall patterns and economic implications of internal mobility in South Asia are presented. The evidence is based on censuses, household surveys, and econometric analysis. In addition to identifying main internal migration corridors and linking these to the leading-lagging regions' differences, the analysis aims to identify the economic impact of internal migration on the migrants, the people left behind in the sending regions, as well as the natives of the receiving regions. Given the scarcity of data on internal migration in most countries in South Asia, this chapter will primarily focus on internal migration in India and will discuss migration in Pakistan and Sri Lanka only briefly.

The second goal is to discuss the role and significance of the forces that encourage mobility and the natural and policy-related impediments that inhibit it. Among the push–pull factors, the most significant are the differences in income and returns to labour. The impediments are transportation costs in addition to cultural assimilation and adaptation costs. In the context of South Asia, the most significant costs are linguistic barriers and rigid social norms. Certain policy measures, such as location-specific social benefit and entitlement programmes, discourage the mobility of the low-skilled and low-income people who rely on them.

The policy discussion on internal mobility and regional disparities is rapidly evolving, and this volume is a contribution towards that debate.[2] Increased social tensions, congestion in urban areas, and strained public

[2]See the *World Development Report* (World Bank 2009), which explores the links between economic geography, concentration, and economic development (also see Mohapatra and Ozden 2010).

services in the receiving regions as well as rapid draining of human capital in the sending regions historically have been presented as evidence proving the harmful consequences of internal migration. However, history has shown many times over that growth and development rarely occur evenly across geographic regions. New technologies, institutions, and production methods tend to favour one region or type of agglomeration over others. And rapid economic growth occurs in places that can best take advantage of these benefits. The key challenge is to establish policies that remove the barriers limiting the movement of resources to their optimal use. At the same time, the positive externalities generated by agglomeration of inputs across the geographic space need to be maximized and the negative externalities caused by changes in concentration levels need to be minimized. In other words, the aim should be to encourage people to move to the right places for the right reasons. The next section presents the main patterns of internal mobility in South Asian countries.

MAIN PATTERNS OF INTERNAL MIGRATION IN INDIA

Internal migration has been a limited but permanent feature of South Asia's labour market. Over the past few decades, tens of millions of people in India, Pakistan, and Sri Lanka, among other countries, moved within national borders either temporarily or permanently in search of better work prospects. The large income disparities between different regions explain the majority of internal migration flows.

The Indian economy exhibits a large variation in terms of income between states, urban and rural areas, and skill levels. Per capita gross domestic product (GDP) of India's richest state, Goa, is seven and a half times that of the country's poorest state, Bihar. With such wide income gaps, migration both within and between states is to be expected. During the 1990s, an approximate 81.6 million Indians migrated within their state of residence, either on seasonal or permanent basis, while some 15.9 million people moved from one state to another. Figure 8.1 presents the main patterns of migration for the largest states in India.

In India, intra-state migration dwarfs inter-state migration as seen in Figure 8.1. For many of the largest states, between 6 per cent and 15 per cent of the population had moved during the 1990s. Inter-state migration is relatively small and, except in the case of Maharashtra, this migration accounts for less than 2 per cent of the population for all of the states. Maharashtra, with its booming economy centred around Mumbai and focused on mostly high-tech service sectors, is the largest migrant-receiving state (in absolute numbers) with emigrants accounting

Migrants as a Share of State Population

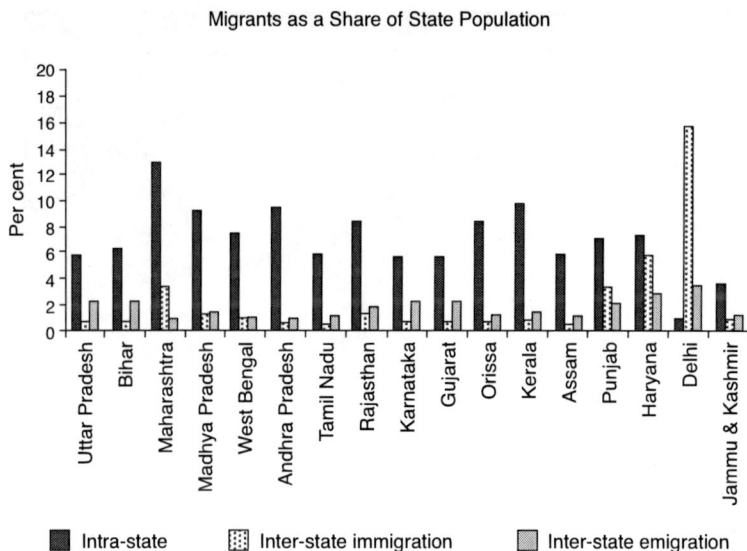

FIGURE 8.1   Main Patterns of Migration 1990s, India

Source: Census of India (2001).

for close to 4 per cent of its population. Punjab and Haryana are other big destinations with emigrants from other states forming close to 4 per cent and 6 per cent of their populations, respectively. Uttar Pradesh and Bihar are the largest migrant-sending states with close to 2 per cent of their populations migrating to other states during the 1990s.

Figure 8.2 highlights the main inter-state migration corridors for India based on the data from the National Sample Survey 55th Round 1999–2000. The small numbers above the arrows represent the number of people above age 15 who migrated to another state during the 1990s. The main destinations from Uttar Pradesh are Maharashtra, Madhya Pradesh, Haryana, and Punjab. For Bihar, the main destinations are Uttar Pradesh and West Bengal.

Figure 8.3 presents the distributions of all inter-state migrants by destination and origin. Uttar Pradesh together with Bihar and Madhya Pradesh are the source of more than 50 per cent of inter-state immigrants during the decade. In terms of destinations, Maharashtra is the largest single destination for inter-state migration, receiving 20 per cent of total inter-state immigrants, followed by Delhi, which is the destination for another 14 per cent of inter-state immigrants.

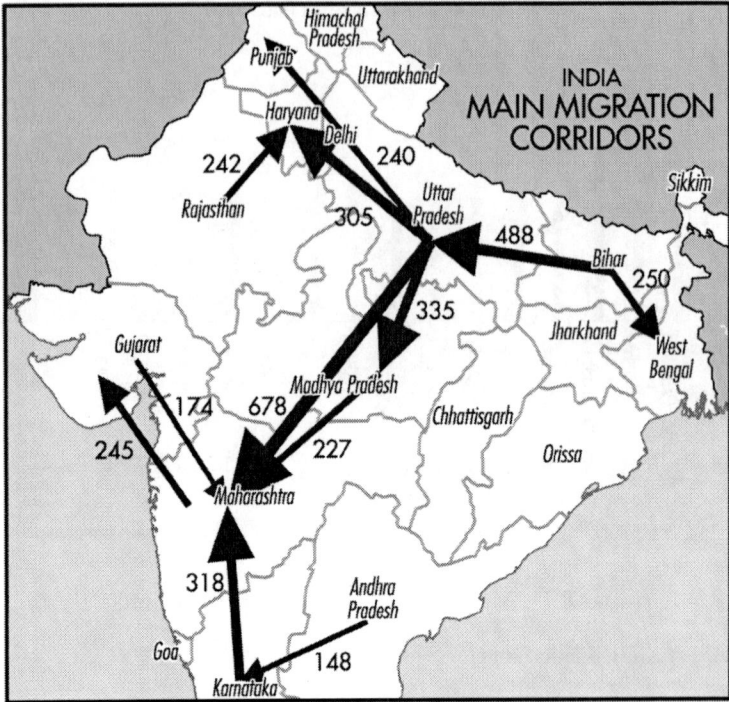

FIGURE 8.2   Main Migration Corridors

Source: National Sample Survey of India, 55th Round, 1999–2000.

Several factors explain the low level of inter-state migration in India. Some of these are policy induced and others relate to cultural and economic characteristics of India, such as the importance of social networks and the linguistic diversity. One of the key issues in internal mobility is how it varies across different education categories. Figure 8.4 presents that proportion of intra-state and inter-state migrants for three separate education categories similar to Figure 8.1. The three education categories consist of people who have (i) primary education or less, (ii) secondary education, and (iii) university education or more. As seen in the unskilled portion of Figure 8.4, 15 per cent of the population of Uttar Pradesh with primary education or less had migrated within the state during the 1990s. Two per cent moved to another state, while 2 per cent came from another state. In Maharashtra, on the other hand, 13 per cent of the primary education group moved within the state and 1.5 per cent left the state, but 4 per cent of this population came from another

Inter-state Emigrants in the 1990s, by State, India

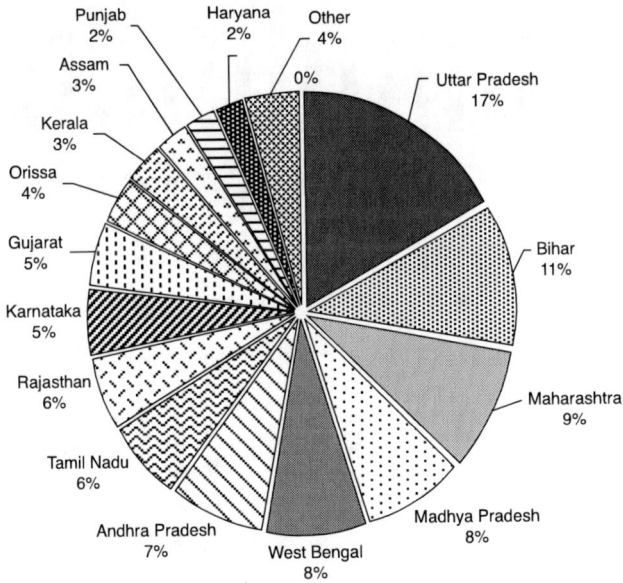

Inter-state Immigrants in the 1990s, by State, India

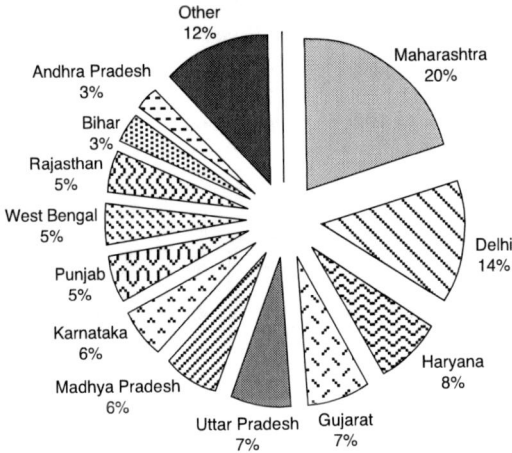

FIGURE 8.3   Distribution of Migrants by Origin and Destination
in India

Source: Census of India 2001.

India: Patterns of Migration among the Unskilled

Inter-state emigration   Inter-state immigration   Intra-state

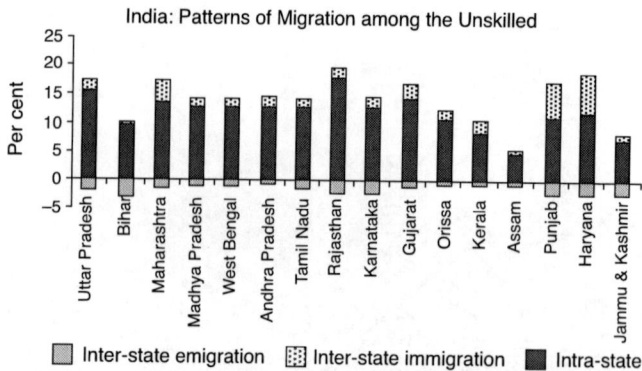

Patterns of Migration for India's Largest States in the 1990s: Medium Skilled

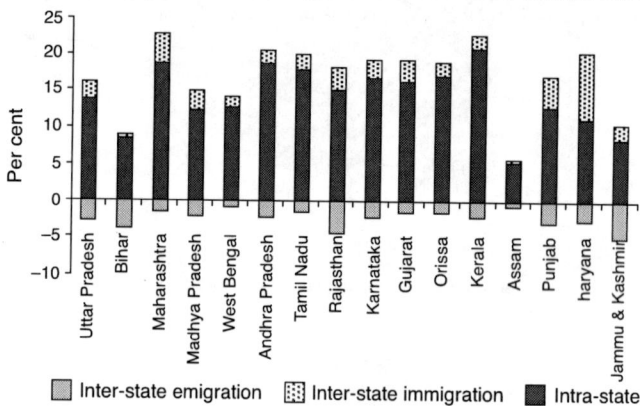

Inter-state emigration   Inter-state immigration   Intra-state

Patterns of Migration for India's Largest States in the 1990s: Highly Skilled

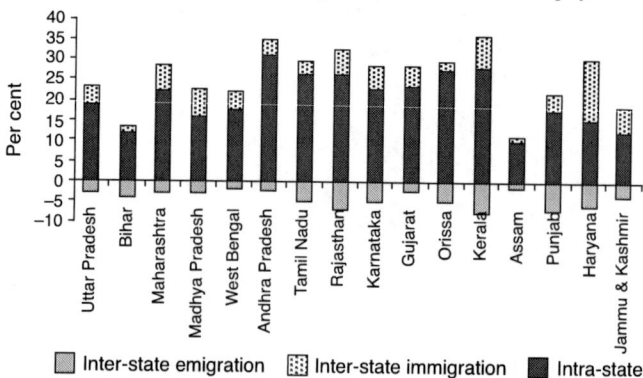

Inter-state emigration   Inter-state immigration   Intra-state

FIGURE 8.4   Migration Patterns by Education Levels

Source: Census of India 2001.

state. In relative terms, Punjab and Haryana have the largest group of emigrants, and Bihar is the largest source of immigrants with primary education. The same pattern is maintained for people with secondary education (the medium-skilled portion of Figure 8.4), but the picture changes with highly educated people (the last portion of Figure 8.4).

The internal mobility of university-educated people in India is higher than the mobility of the unskilled. For example, around 5 per cent of this group has emigrated from their home states to another state. Kerala has the highest level of emigration closely followed by Rajasthan and Punjab. In terms of destination, close to 15 per cent of the population with a university education in Haryana had come from another state in the 1990s. Maharashtra, Madhya Pradesh, and Karnataka are among the main recipients of highly educated migrants.

One of the most important patterns of mobility between leading and lagging regions in India is summarized in Figure 8.5. The inter-state flows between lagging and leading regions[3] by education levels are presented. The largest migration flows are from lagging to leading regions. Close to 4 million people moved from lagging to leading regions (southwest quadrant) while only 1.5 million people migrated from leading to lagging regions (northeast quadrant). Significant mobility also occurs within leading states, with 3.2 million people moving from one leading region to another. One of the key features of Figure 8.5 is the relative high level of mobility among the highly educated portion of society compared with less educated people. More interesting, an especially significant level of migration of highly educated people occurs between leading states. Of the 3.3 million migrants between leading states, almost 15 per cent are highly educated. This level of migration is partially due to an existing larger stock of highly educated people and partially due to increased mobility in these areas.

It is important to examine net gains and losses of each state by level of education. Figure 8.6 summarizes the net movement of migrants in each state by education level as a share of total population with the same level of education.[4] The top portion of the figure shows gains and

[3]The leading states are Andhra Pradesh, Gujarat, Haryana, Karnataka, Kerala, Maharashtra, Punjab, Tamil Nadu, and West Bengal. The lagging regions are Arunachal Pradesh, Assam, Bihar, Madhya Pradesh, Manipur, Meghalaya, Mizoram, Nagaland, Orissa, Rajasthan, Tripura, and Uttar Pradesh.

[4]The net movement for each state was calculated as follows: [share of inter-state immigrants for each education level—share of inter-state emigrants with the same education level]/sum of state's non-migrants, intra-state migrants, and inter-state immigrants with the same education level.

leading   lagging

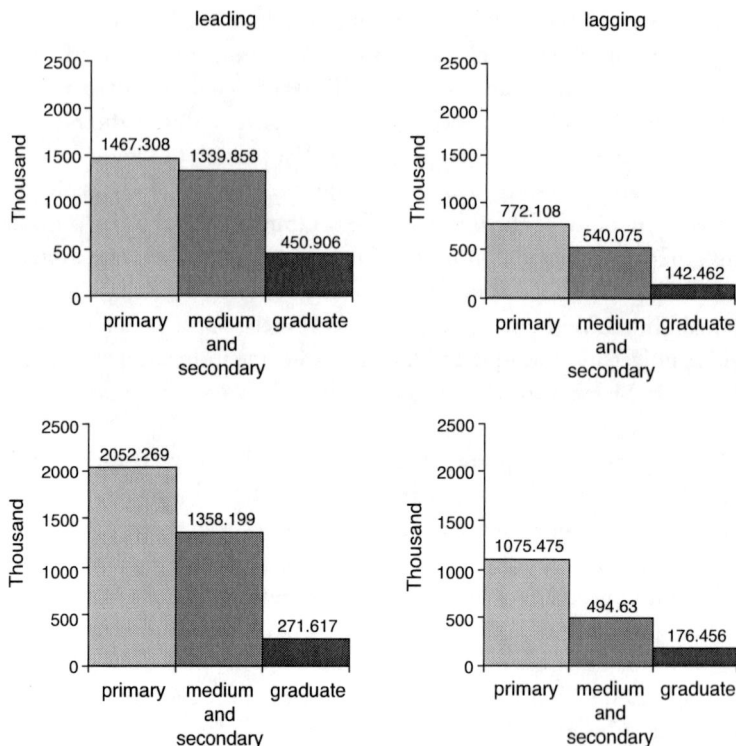

FIGURE 8.5   Inter-state Migration between Leading and
Lagging Regions in India (1990s)

Source: National Sample Survey of India, 55th Round, 1999–2000.
Note: Migrants above the age of 15 have been considered.

losses for leading states and the bottom portion provides gains and losses
for lagging states. Although the loss of educated people is often part of
overall mobility, the net inflow and outflow of the highly educated is
larger than that for other education categories in most states. This pattern
again highlights the higher mobility of the more educated portion of
the labour force.

Among leading states, Haryana has the largest net inflow of immigrants
as a portion of the underlying population for all levels of education. The
net inflow of educated migrants is the highest at around 9 per cent of
the same portion of the labour force. Punjab has the largest net outflow
of educated immigrants among leading state, but it has a net inflow
of migrants with primary and secondary education, mainly because

Net Gain/Loss of Inter-state Immigrants by Educational Level in Lagging States

Net Gain/Loss of Inter-state Immigrants by Educational Level in Leading States

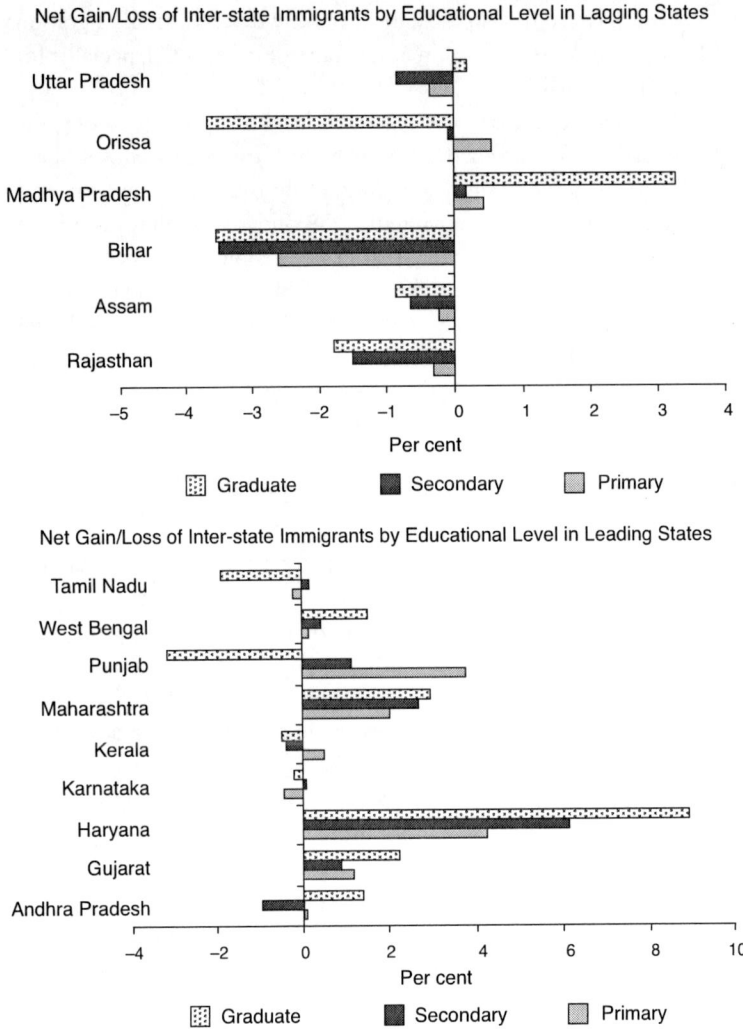

FIGURE 8.6   Net Migration Flows among Leading and Lagging
States by Education Level

Source: Census of India 2001.

the agricultural sector attracts low-skilled labour in the state. With the
exception of Madhya Pradesh, lagging states suffer from a net outflow
of immigrants for all levels of education. The net outflow of educated
immigrants is the highest for Orissa. Interestingly, although Uttar Pradesh
is the largest migrant-sending state, its net outflows are minimal. Because

Uttar Pradesh is also the largest state, it is likely that its overall migration is relatively small. It is also an important destination, especially for migrants from Bihar.

Various reasons explain the increased level of mobility among the highly educated portion of the labour force.[5] The highly educated are more likely to speak English and thus easily overcome the linguistic barriers imposed on inter-state migration. Second, the absolute gains from migration tend to be higher for more educated people, and hence they can overcome the costs of migration more easily. Third, people tend to migrate to acquire education, and they stay in the destination after completing their education. Finally, policy-induced barriers to mobility—such as those related to labour market and social protection—tend to have a smaller impact on the highly educated people.

MAIN PATTERNS OF INTERNAL MIGRATION IN PAKISTAN AND SRI LANKA

Internal migration data also are available for Pakistan and Sri Lanka, but they are significantly limited when compared with India, especially in terms of educational distribution. In Pakistan, the patterns of migration are more concentrated when compared with those in India, but the overall level of mobility is also low (see Figure 8.7). The most populous state, Punjab, with 57 per cent of the population according to the 1998 Census, is the largest source of inter-state emigration in absolute terms. Thirty-seven per cent of all inter-state migrants are from Punjab. On the other hand, Sindh, the second-most-populated state with 24 per cent of the population, is the largest destination with 42 per cent of migrants moving there. Northwest Frontier Province (NWFP), the third largest with 14 per cent of the population, is the largest source of inter-state migrants in relative terms. Thirty-three per cent of all inter-state migrants are from NWFP, which receives only 7 per cent of immigrants.

In Pakistan, internal migration both within and between states and provinces is even more limited than in India (see Figure 8.8). Intra-state immigrants and inter-state emigrants account for less than 5 per cent of the population in each of the major states. Similarly, inter-state immigrants account for less than 4 per cent of the population in all Pakistani states except in Islamabad, where migrants from other provinces make up more than 40 per cent of the province's population.

[5]See Docquier and Marfouk (2007) for a discussion of migration and brain drain.

Pakistan: Inter-state Immigrants in the Last 10 Years, by Province

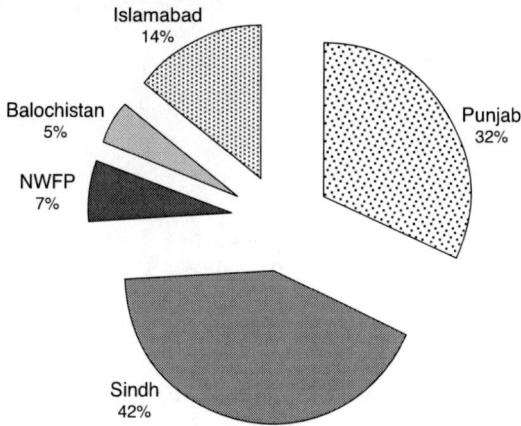

Islamabad
14%

Balochistan
5%

NWFP
7%

Punjab
32%

Sindh
42%

Pakistan: Emigrants in the Last 10 Years, by Province, Pakistan

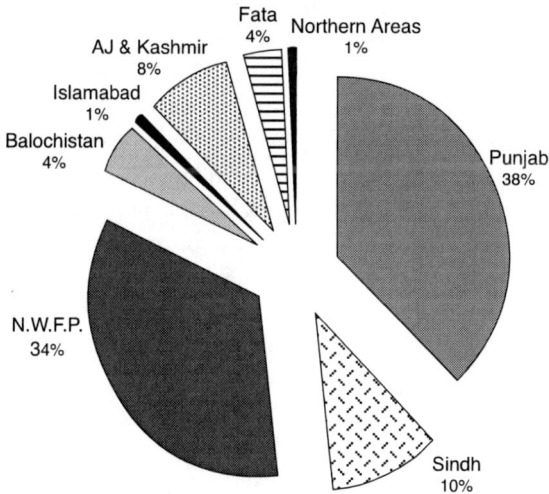

Fata
4%

Northern Areas
1%

AJ & Kashmir
8%

Islamabad
1%

Balochistan
4%

Punjab
38%

N.W.F.P.
34%

Sindh
10%

FIGURE 8.7   Distribution of Migrants by Origin and Destination in Pakistan

Source: Pakistan Census 1998.

The main migration corridors in Pakistan are Punjab–Sindh, NWFP–Sindh, and Punjab–Islamabad (see Figure 8.9). The top map in Figure 8.9 presents the main corridors for the *low-skilled* people and the bottom map presents the main corridors for the *high-skilled* people. The relevant number of migrants (in thousand) is shown above the arrows.

Migrants as a Share of Province Population

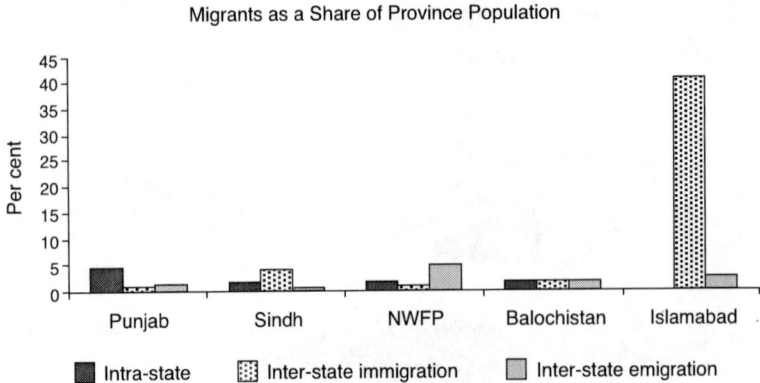

FIGURE 8.8   Main Patterns of Migration in Pakistan

Source: Pakistan Census 1998.

Migration in Sri Lanka is as concentrated as in Pakistan. The western region receives close to 70 per cent of all immigrants in the country, although it has only 30 per cent of the total population. Neighbouring regions—Central, Southern, and North-central—account for the rest of the migrants. In terms of origin, migrants are more evenly distributed. As seen in Figure 8.10, the number of migrants from each region is quite proportional to its share in the overall population. The share of interregional migrants in the overall population ranges from 3 per cent in the Uva region to more than 10 per cent in the western region. Intraregional migration is much more limited in Sri Lanka, accounting for around 3 per cent of the population in all of the main regions. It should be noted that four regions—Northern, North-western, Eastern, and Sabaragamuwa—do not have any officially recorded data on migration because of the internal military conflict.

As with India and Pakistan, overall internal mobility is low in Sri Lanka as well (see Figure 8.11). In the regions for which the data are available, intraregional migration is never above 2 per cent. Similarly, inter-regional migration, even in the Western region, which is the destination of 70 per cent of all migrants, is limited, with the share of emigrants in the total population at only 10 per cent. This limited inter-regional migration is true even in the most important migrant-sending regions, such as Sabaragamuwa, Uva, or the southern region, where only around 6 per cent of the population has migrated to other parts of the country. This low level of migration is especially surprising in a

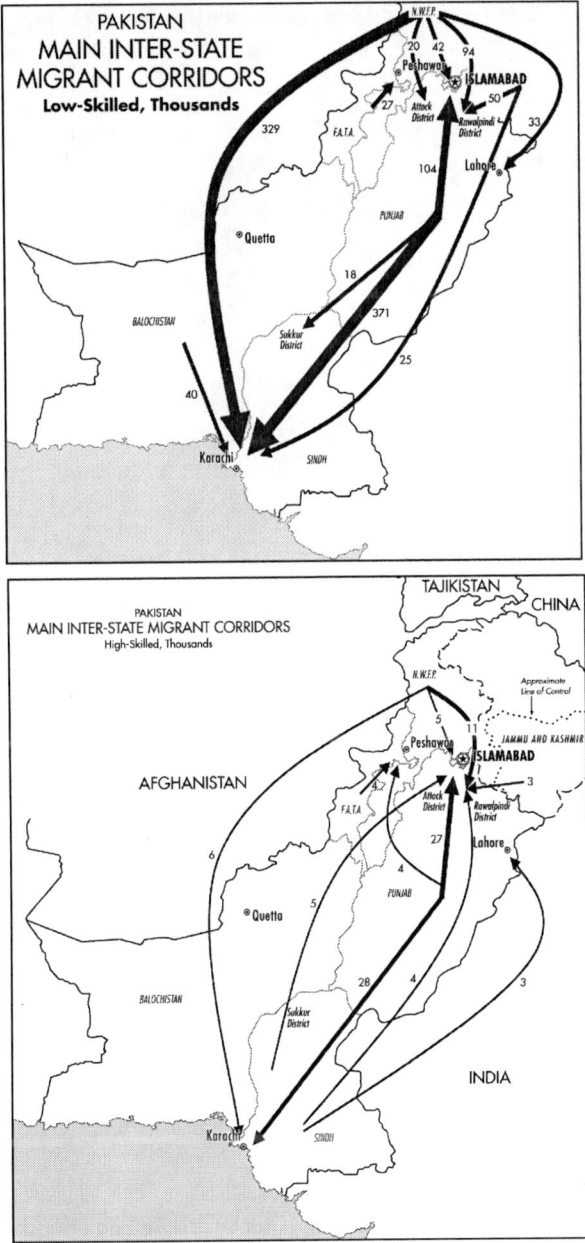

FIGURE 8.9   Main Corridors for the Low-Skilled and High-Skilled

Source: Pakistan Census 1998.

Sri Lanka Internal Immigration in the Last 10 Years

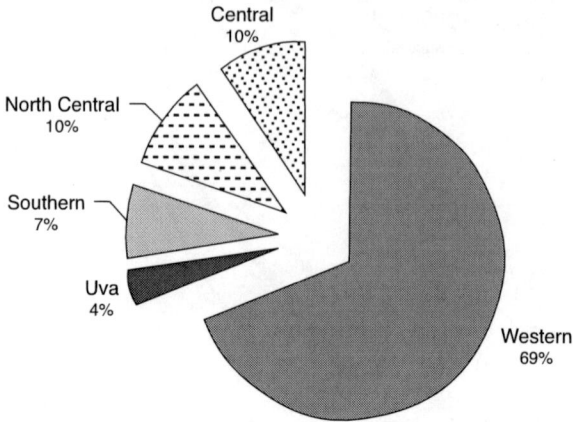

Sri Lanka Emigration in the Last 10 Years by Region

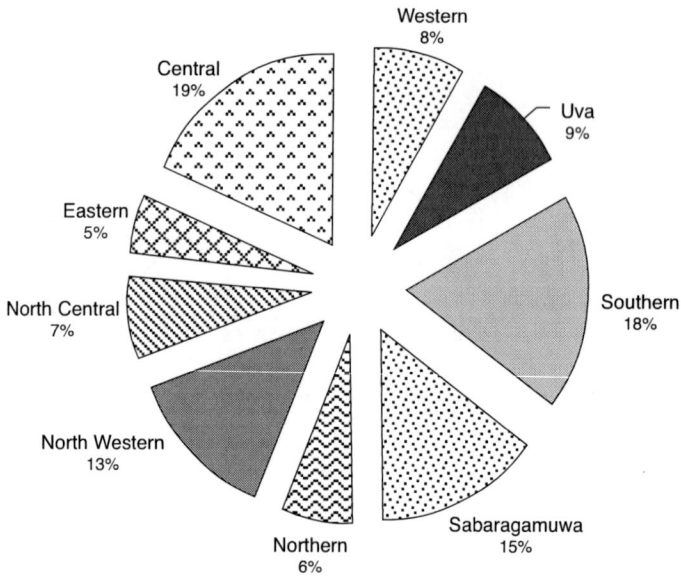

FIGURE 8.10   Distribution of Migrants by Origin and Destination
in Sri Lanka

Source: Sri Lanka Census 2001.

Migrants as Share of Region Population

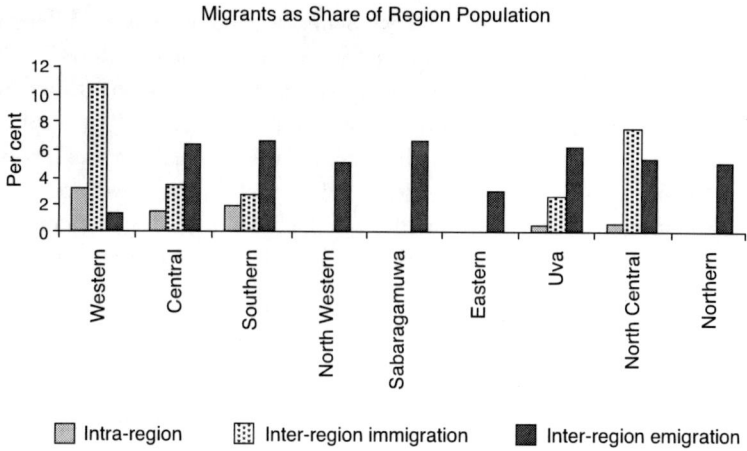

FIGURE 8.11   Main Patterns of Migration in Sri Lanka

Source: Sri Lanka Census 2001.

small country such as Sri Lanka, where the economic activity is quite concentrated and cultural barriers to mobility are relatively low.

Few observations can be discerned from the data and figures presented so far. The most important emerging fact is the extremely low level of internal mobility within India, Pakistan, and Sri Lanka. Inter-state immigration levels are rarely over 6 per cent of the population in the vast majority of the states and regions within these countries. There is significantly more migration from lagging to leading regions, as expected, but not enough to make a significant impact on poverty reduction and welfare improvement. In India, where the most detailed data are available, the more educated segments of the labour force are more mobile as they face lower barriers to migration and enjoy larger gains. However, the main puzzle about the low level of mobility remains. The development challenges faced in lagging regions in South Asia will not be addressed properly without answering this puzzle.

DETERMINANTS OF INTERNAL MOBILITY

Identifying main migration corridors and patterns—especially between leading and lagging regions in each country—answers many questions on the linkages between mobility, development, and poverty reduction. The next crucial and natural question is on the determinants of internal mobility and constraints that limit it. To identify these factors and assess their relative impacts, gravity models of migration flows between different states in India are estimated. In a gravity model, bilateral flows (such as trade, capital, or labour) between two geographic regions (different countries or parts of one country) are functions of the GDP per capita, the population in each region, distance, and other impediments. Gravity equations are among the most widely and successfully employed models in estimating trade and migration flows in the literature. The gravity model estimated in this section takes the following form in equation 8.1:

$$M_{ij} = a + b_1\, GDP_i + b_2 GDP_j + b_3\, POP_i + b_4\, POP_j + b_5\, DIST_{ij}$$
$$+ b_6\, BORDER_{ij} + b_7\, LANG_{ij} + e_{ij} \qquad (8.1)$$

M_{ij} represents different types of migration flows between states i and j. The estimation uses different flows—total migration flows, male-only migration, migration for employment reasons, and temporary migration flows (less than one year). GDP_i is the GDP per capita and POP_i is population in state i. Income gaps are the first obvious determinants of population flows; labour, like other economic inputs, naturally flows from regions with lower to higher wages. High wage gaps in different parts of each country in South Asia are identified and explored in other sections of this volume. So, significant 'pull' factors exist in terms of increased economic opportunities and income gains in leading regions. Similarly, population levels are crucial because larger states naturally will send and attract larger number of people.

Among the impediments that limit mobility are the factors that increase both transportation and assimilation costs. In the case of South Asia, these factors can be quite strong as the physical distances are large; transportation infrastructure is not well developed and significant cultural differences exist between different parts of the countries. $DIST_{ij}$ is the distance between the two states and captures actual cost of mobility. $BORDER_{ij}$ is a dummy variable that takes the value of one if the two states share a common border. This variable has been shown to be an important factor in economic activity between different geographic regions. $LANG_{ij}$ is the share of the population in each state that shares the same native language and aims to capture the cultural costs of mobility. See the results of the regression in Table 8.1

As the results in Table 8.1 indicate, the internal migration flows in India are influenced by a variety of pull and push factors. All the variables are in natural logs, so the coefficients are elasticities. GDP per capita in destination states are the most important factors—a 1 per cent increase in GDP per capita in destination region is associated with a 1.2 per cent

TABLE 8.1   Results of Gravity Estimation of Migration Flows between States in India, 2000

	All Migrants	Male Migrants	Migration for Work Purposes	Migration for Less than 1 Year
GDP per capita at origin (log)	–0.076 [0.083]	–0.162* [0.083]	–0.248*** [0.089]	–0.003 [0.086]
GDP per capita at destination (log)	1.213*** [0.100]	1.403*** [0.092]	1.660*** [0.098]	1.383*** [0.088]
Distance (log)	–1.118*** [0.066]	–1.093*** [0.066]	–1.079*** [0.071]	–0.765*** [0.066]
Dummy for common border	1.022*** [0.119]	0.837*** [0.119]	0.801*** [0.129]	1.090*** [0.128]
Common language	1.218*** [0.128]	1.094*** [0.126]	1.288*** [0.137]	1.401*** [0.131]
Population in origin (log)	0.806*** [0.021]	0.805*** [0.021]	0.846*** [0.022]	0.764*** [0.020]
Population in destination (log)	0.744*** [0.024]	0.709*** [0.024]	0.708*** [0.026]	0.669*** [0.023]
Constant	–2.911*** [0.922]	–2.453*** [0.884]	–3.054*** [0.927]	–4.748*** [0.867]
Origin state dummy variables	No	No	No	No
Destination state dummy variables	No	No	No	No
Observations	992	992	992	992
R-squared	0.833	0.828	0.818	0.816

Source: National Sample Survey of India, 55th Round, 1999–2000.
Notes: GDP = gross domestic product. Robust standard errors are in brackets.
*** represents significance at 1 per cent, ** represents significance at 5 per cent, and * represents significance at 10 per cent.

increase in overall migration (column 1), a 1.4 per cent increase in male migration (column 2), almost 1.7 per cent increase in employment-related migration (column 3), and 1.4 per cent increase in migration for less than one year in duration (column 4). GDP per capita in origin states is not significant in many cases and is barely significant for male and employment-related migration. Distance is a significant impediment—a 1 per cent increase in distances lowers migration flows by slightly over 1 per cent. Similarly, common border and common language increase migration flows for all types of migration. For example, a 1 per cent increase in number of people sharing a common language increases employment-related migration and temporary migration flows by 1.3 and 1.4 per cent, respectively. Finally, populations are significant and indicate that a 1 per cent increase in population levels in both origin and destination regions increases migration flows by around 0.8 per cent.

This simple exercise identifies the importance of different factors affecting migration. Migration for employment reasons is the most sensitive to income differentials—a 1 per cent increase in the gap increases flows by almost 2 per cent (the difference of the coefficients of the GDP per capita variables). Although the analysis was done using Indian survey data, it would be safe to assume that the determinants of labour mobility in other countries in South Asia are very similar to those in India.

Overall, the estimation suggests that significant potential exists for mobility between leading and lagging regions. But the impediments—physical and cultural costs appear to be significant as well, especially for the low-skilled. This is why highly educated people have higher mobility levels. The distance costs are less binding for the highly educated and they all speak English, which lowers the cultural assimilation costs discussed earlier. If increased mobility would contribute to economic development and lower poverty, a clear policy message would be to enact measures to lower these barriers.

POVERTY IMPACTS OF MIGRATION IN INDIA

Migrants are primarily driven by the hope for better lives for themselves and their children. Thus, it is critical to investigate the poverty impact of migration. The best method to assess improvements in welfare resulting from migration is to track migrants over time—especially before and after migration takes place—and compare them with non-migrants. Such time-series data are rarely available, however, and unfortunately this is the case in South Asia. In the absence of panel data that track the economic welfare of immigrants over time, data on per capita household expenditure reported in India's NSS 55th Round are used. For each state, we calculate the average per capita household expenditure—relative to the poverty line—of four groups.[6] These groups are (i) non-migrants, (ii) people who migrated within that state, (iii) people who left that state, and (iv) people who migrated to

---

[6]To control for relative price levels, per capita household expenditure relative to statewide poverty line (rural or urban areas whichever was the relevant one) is used.

that state from other parts of India. This exercise is repeated for three main types of migration flows. These are (i) unskilled migration from rural areas to other rural areas, (ii) unskilled migration from urban areas to other urban areas, and (iii) skilled migration from urban areas to other urban areas.

Rural–Rural Unskilled Migration

In Figure 8.12, the first map shows, for each state in India, the average per capita household expenditure of non-migrant rural households (where the head of household is unskilled—that is, has only a primary education) relative to the poverty line in that state. For example, in Maharashtra, average per capita expenditure of non-migrants is between 20 per cent and 40 per cent above the rural poverty line. The second map presents the relative income of same type of households (rural and unskilled) who have migrated within the state. The average expenditures of these intra-state migrant households are clearly higher than the non-migrant households in many states. The third map is the average per capita expenditures (relative to the poverty line) of the households that have migrated into that state from other states. For example, the average per capita expenditure of intra-state migrants in Maharashtra is between 40 per cent and 60 per cent above the poverty line, whereas the expenditures of migrants from other states into Maharashtra are between 60 per cent and 80 per cent above the poverty line. Finally, the last map shows the average expenditures (relative to poverty line) of the people who left that state to migrate to other states. In short, these maps reveal the welfare levels of different groups of unskilled rural people based on their migration status. For example, out-of-state emigrants are generally better off than intra-state migrant who are, in turn, generally better off than non-migrants.

Urban–Urban Unskilled Migration

The maps in Figure 8.13 present the same analysis for unskilled urban–urban migrants. The first map shows the average relative expenditures of *urban* non-migrants, the correct comparison group. The second map shows the average relative expenditure of migrants who moved from urban areas to other urban areas *within* the same state, while the third map shows migrants who came from urban areas in other states to urban areas in that specific state. Finally, the last map shows migrants who moved from urban areas in that state to urban areas in other states of India. The relative poverty lines used are the urban poverty levels.

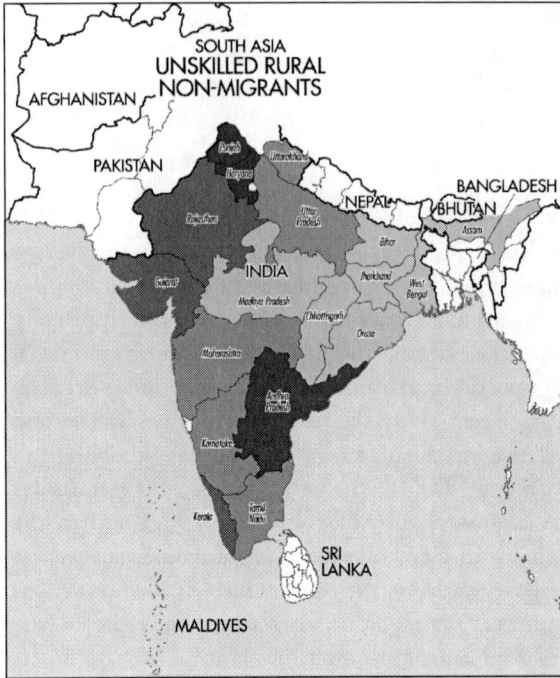

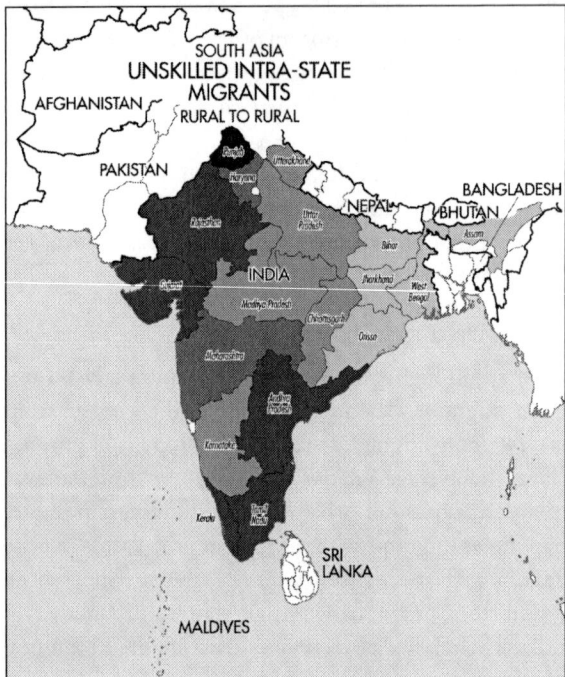

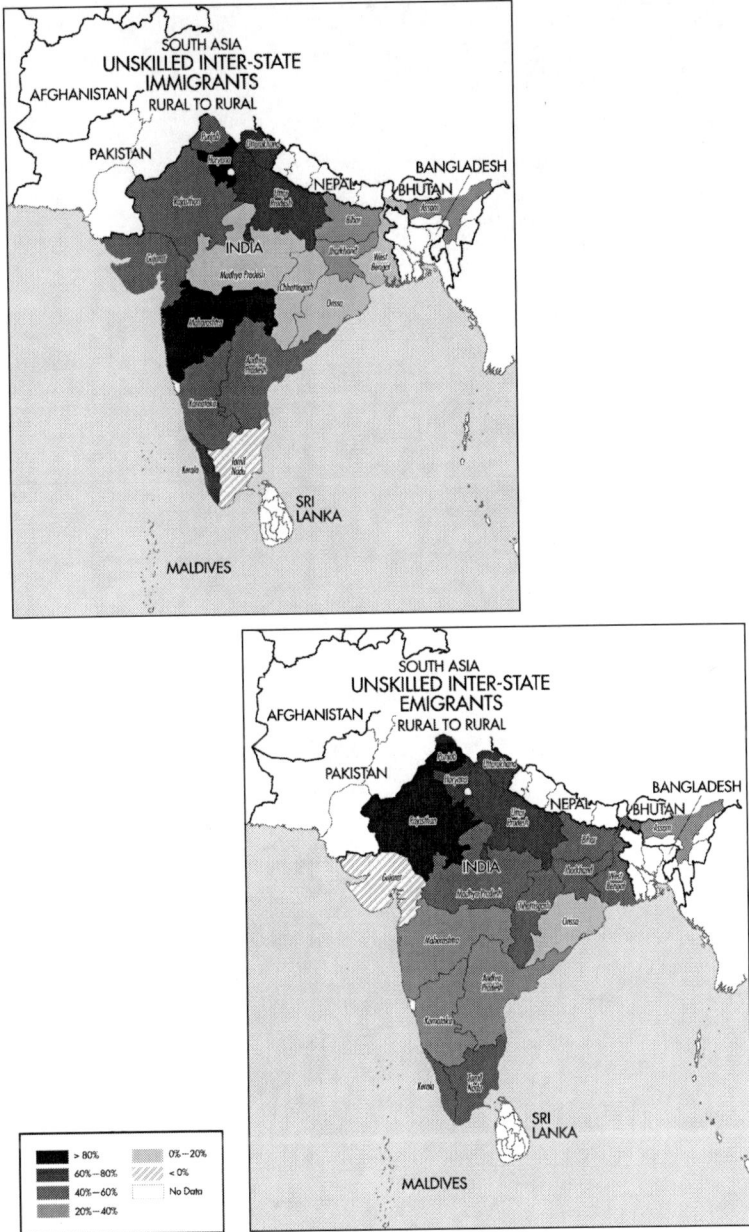

FIGURE 8.12 Income Relative to the Rural Poverty Line of Rural Unskilled Non-migrants and Rural–Rural Unskilled Migrants

Sources: National Sample Survey of India, 55th Round, 1999–2000; authors' calculations.

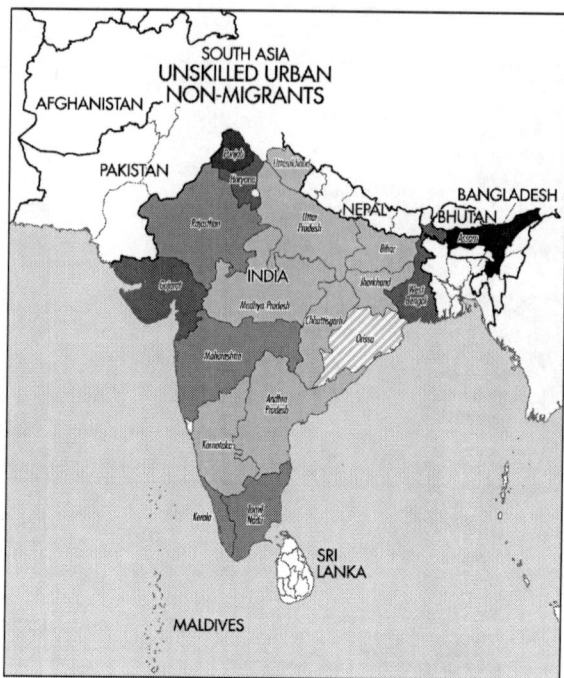

SOUTH ASIA
UNSKILLED URBAN
NON-MIGRANTS

AFGHANISTAN

PAKISTAN

NEPAL

BANGLADESH
BHUTAN

INDIA

SRI LANKA

MALDIVES

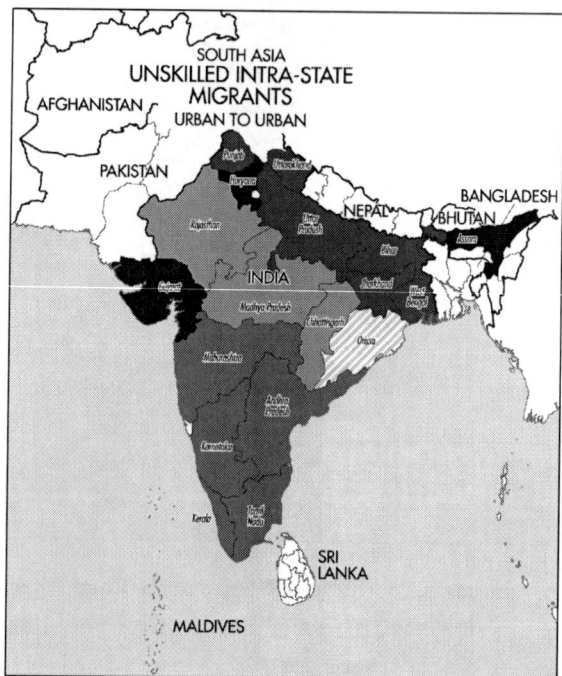

SOUTH ASIA
UNSKILLED INTRA-STATE
MIGRANTS
URBAN TO URBAN

AFGHANISTAN

PAKISTAN

NEPAL

BANGLADESH
BHUTAN

INDIA

SRI LANKA

MALDIVES

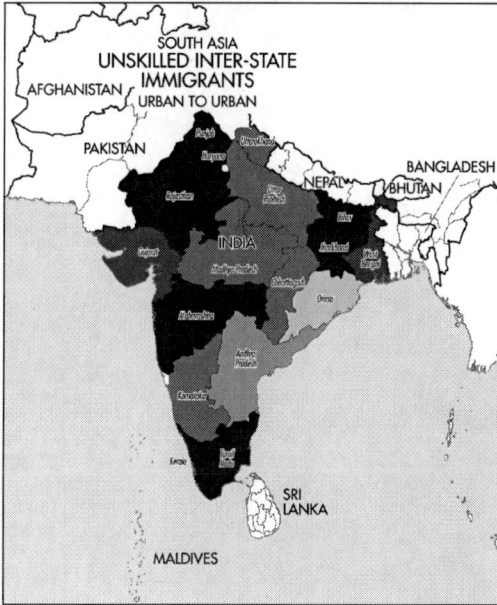

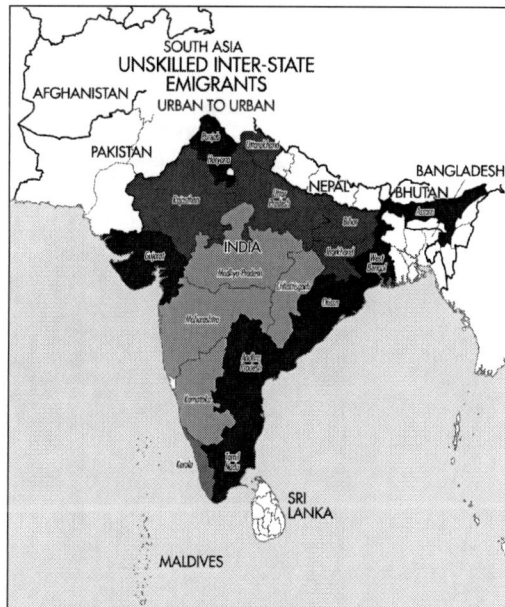

FIGURE 8.13   Income Relative to the Urban Poverty Line of Urban
Unskilled Non-migrants and Urban–Urban Unskilled Migrants

Sources: National Sample Survey of India, 55th Round, 1999–2000; authors' calculations.

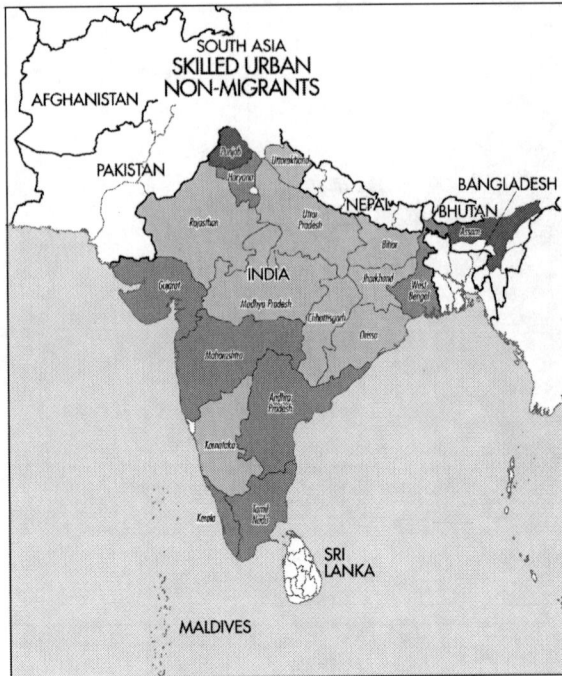

SOUTH ASIA
SKILLED URBAN
NON-MIGRANTS

AFGHANISTAN

PAKISTAN

BANGLADESH

NEPAL   BHUTAN

INDIA

SRI
LANKA

MALDIVES

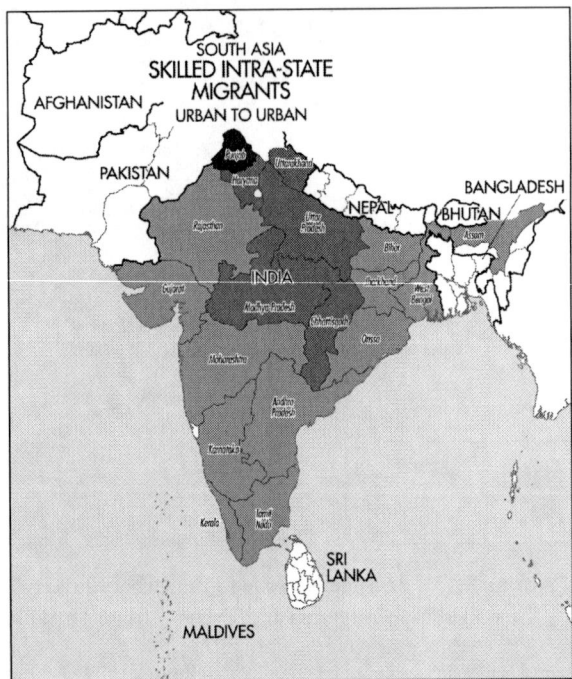

SOUTH ASIA
SKILLED INTRA-STATE
MIGRANTS
URBAN TO URBAN

AFGHANISTAN

PAKISTAN

BANGLADESH

NEPAL   BHUTAN

INDIA

SRI
LANKA

MALDIVES

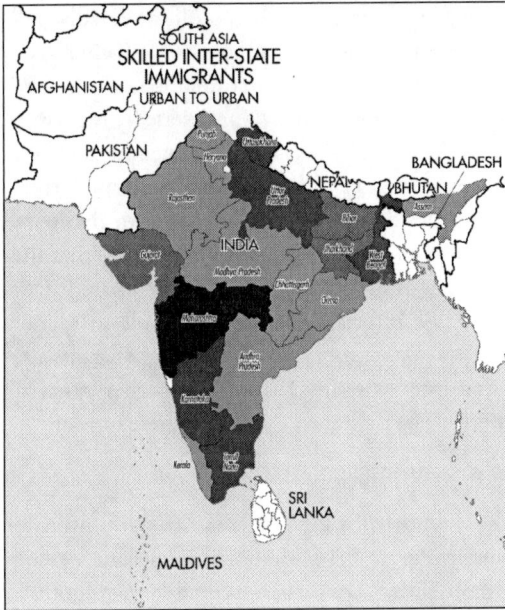

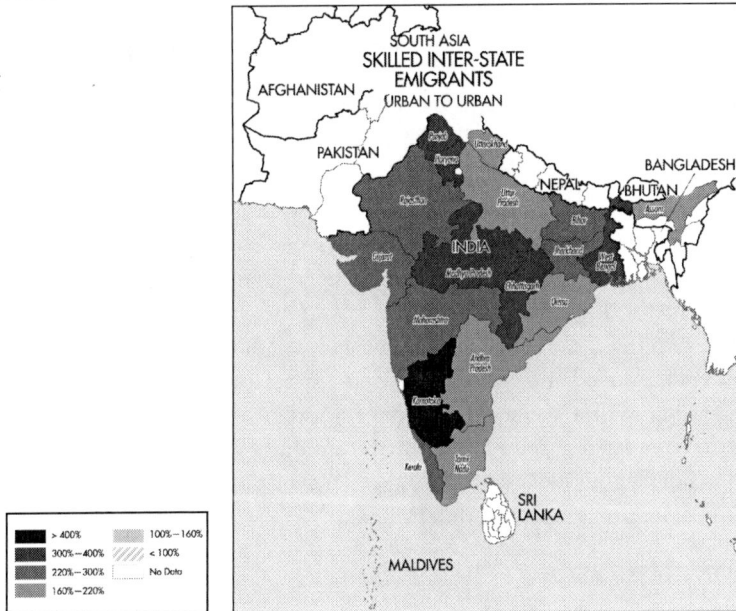

FIGURE 8.14   Income Relative to the Urban Poverty Line of Urban
Skilled Non-migrants and Urban–Urban Skilled Migrants

Sources: National Sample Survey of India, 55th Round, 1999–2000; authors' calculations.

As clearly seen, the intra-state migrants are better off (or equally well off) in almost every state compared with non-migrants. The inter-state migrants are also better off than non-migrants (comparison of the first and third map) in their destination state or their home state (comparison of the first and fourth map). A critical point is that the income gains for urban–urban migration are much higher when compared with rural–rural migration. The change in shades of grey is much stronger in the maps Figure 8.13 relative to the maps in Figure 8.12, which indicates that the urban–urban migration generates higher welfare gains compared with rural–urban migration. Finally, inter-state migration leads to higher welfare gains relative to intra-state migration. These higher gains are mainly due to that fact that inter-state migration faces higher barriers. Thus, the welfare gains need to be higher to overcome these burdens.

Urban–Urban High-Skilled Migration

The final analysis is on the welfare gains for highly skilled (or university educated) migrants. Maps in Figure 8.14 present the relevant welfare comparisons. The first map shows the urban skilled non-migrants, and the second map shows urban–urban intra-state migrants. Similar to previous figures, the last two maps show inter-state migrants. The movement of skilled labour is of particular importance because, as mentioned, it has important social and economic consequences for the source and destination states. Maps in Figure 8.14 show that skilled workers benefit significantly from migration. The biggest winners are those moving from one state to another. Without exception, all skilled inter-state immigrants have much higher per capita expenditure than non-immigrants and, in most states, higher than intra-state immigrants. The benefits of migration for skilled labour are evident even in lagging states. An important issue to examine with relation to skilled migration is whether skilled emigrants from lagging states are better off than those migrating within the state. This has important implications for brain drain from lagging states. With the exception of Bihar, emigrants from all major lagging states do have higher per capita household expenditure than those immigrating within the state.

CONCLUSION

This chapter had two goals. The first was to show that internal mobility in South Asia is quite low. In the three countries analysed, India, Pakistan, and Sri Lanka, inter-state migrants rarely constitute more than 6 per cent of that state's population. Despite large potential gains, people in South Asia stay in their regions. This is not the case in other developing countries, especially China, where migration from lagging to leading regions is part of the overall development process. The main question then becomes, what are the impediments to internal mobility in South Asia? Among these are social and cultural barriers as well as policy-induced restrictions. In the case of India, linguistic barriers can create significant costs, especially for the unskilled and the uneducated. The fact that mobility increases with the education level indicates the importance of these factors. Various policy-induced barriers include labour market restrictions and state-specific social welfare programmes. If migrants are not eligible for certain welfare programmes outside their own state, then they will have lower incentives to move. Similarly, rural landownership laws and rules and urban housing markets create additional mobility costs.

The second goal was to show the welfare gains from mobility. For this, the per capita expenditures of inter-state and intra-state migrants in India (relative to the poverty levels) were compared with those of non-migrants. As clearly seen, intra-state migrants are generally betteroff relative to non-migrants and inter-state migrants are better off relative to both groups. This ranking is generally maintained whether analysing rural–rural and urban–urban migrants or unskilled and skilled migrants. Again, the results of this chapter point to significant welfare gains from internal mobility, which is an important component of economic development process. Although the analysis in this chapter focused on migration within India, the determinants of migrations and the welfare impacts of internal migration in other countries in the region are likely to be very similar to those observed in India.

REFERENCES

Bell, M. and S. Muhidin. 2009. 'Cross-National Comparisons of Internal Migration', Human Development Research Paper No. 2009/30, United Nations Development Program, New York City.

Census of India. 2001. Available at http://www.censusindia.net/, accessed on 31 January 2009.

Docquier, F. and A. Marfouk. 2007 'International Migration by Education Attainment 1990–2000', in C. Özden and M. Schiff (eds), *International Migration, Economic Development and Policy*. Washington, D.C.: World Bank and Palgrave McMillan.

Mohapatra, S. and C. Ozden. 2010. 'Migration and Remittances in South Asia', in E. Ghani (ed.), *The Services Revolution in South Asia*. New Delhi: Oxford University Press.

National Sample Survey of India, 55th Round. 1999–2000. Available at http://
    mospi.gov.in/nsso_4aug2008/web/nsso.htm, accessed on 25 October
    2009.

Ozden, C. and M. Schiff (eds). 2007. *International Migration, Economic
    Development and Policy*. Washington, D.C.: World Bank and Palgrave
    McMillan.

———. (ed.). 2006. *International Migration and Remittances and the Brain
    Drain*. New York: Palgrave McMillan.

Pakistan Census. 1998. Available at http://catalog.loc.gov/cgibin/Pwebrecon.cg
    i?DB=local&BBID=12818875&v3=1, accessed on 25 February 2009.

Sri Lanka Census. 2001. Available at http://www.statistics.gov.lk/PopHouSat/
    index.asp, accessed on 15 January 2009.

World Bank. 2009. *World Development Report*. Washington, D.C.: World Bank.

9

Stimulating Agricultural Growth

Ejaz Ghani and Surabhi Mittal*

Slow agricultural growth is constraining economic opportunities for the vast majority of poor people in lagging regions. Agricultural growth is low due to problems of 'distance', 'division', and 'density', which is more acute in the agricultural sector compared to manufacturing and services sectors. Long-distance, low-economic density, low mobility, and high trade divisions prevent farmers from the benefits of agglomeration and scale economies. Market failures are more widespread in lagging regions. Most lagging regions suffer from poor access to roads, credit, information communication technology (ICT), and trade. Local markets are small, fragmented, and are cut off from global markets due to high transaction or 'informational costs',[1] which deprives producers of better price terms and precludes adoption of more profitable cropping patterns in line with market demand, rather than for self-consumption. Market failures are further compounded by government failures. Farmers in lagging regions are less integrated into state-supported structures, such as, crop and livestock extension systems, price support systems, and provision of credit which help farmers introduce new technologies and expand production range, cooperatives and networks for processing and marketing, and

*We are grateful to Veronica Minaya for research support.
[1]Including various costs arising from asymmetries in information relating to, for example, quality, reliability, contract enforceability, and so on.

security support systems (relative lack of physical and economic security shortens the length of value chains people enter into).

The limits imposed by market failures and state failures are made worse by policy distortions. In Sri Lanka, an effort to introduce self-sufficiency in rice has compelled farmers to specialize in paddy cultivation, which is less profitable and more vulnerable to the weather than other crops. In India, a plethora of subsidies ranging from irrigation to fertilizers to power has meant that very little has been invested in rural infrastructure, and agricultural productivity is suffering. Most subsidies benefit leading rather than lagging regions. Overregulation of agricultural markets have discouraged private investments in farming and encouraged inappropriate use of natural resources such as groundwater.

These problems can be resolved. The limits of poor market access and market failures can be overcome with ICT—mobile phones and Internet—which can make agricultural markets more efficient and transparent and can improve the delivery of agricultural services. ICT can connect small farmers and artisans to global markets. A successful example of this is E-Choupal in India. The gradual introduction of Internet kiosks in villages to provide soybean prices and product-screening services overcame connectivity infrastructure shortcomings, cut out the intermediaries, enhanced market efficiency, increased farmers' profits by 33 per cent, and boosted soybean cultivation by 19 per cent in districts with kiosks by reallocating land from other crop cultivation. Low-cost access to information infrastructure is a necessary prerequisite for the successful use of ICT by farmers, but it is not sufficient. It needs to be backed by a market-oriented, non-discriminatory approach to agriculture in land policy and administration, agricultural research and extension, watershed management, and agricultural marketing. The focus needs to shift from badly targeted, one-size-fits-all input subsidies to the provision of infrastructure, marketing, and technology investments that improve private returns and reduce risk, and to policy support suited to agro-climatic conditions that promote intensification, diversification, non-farm linkages, or exit from marginal lands, as appropriate.

Although these solutions to stimulate and revive agriculture are well known, these problems persist. Reducing agricultural subsidies is often seen as a direct attack on farmers' interests. States in India that ended free power to farmers underestimated the resulting political fallout and promptly reintroduced free power when faced with the prospect of electoral defeat. So this is not simply a matter of 'political will', because almost by definition 'political will' would get defeated at the polls. The solution lies in information and advocacy campaigns to bring out the voice of the suffering poor. New and innovative ways of compensating losers, while raising the productivity of both rich and poor farmers, should be emphasized. Agricultural reform is likely to be a negotiated, slow process, but one that needs to start now. This process can be accelerated with the help of information technology.

This analysis—which is closely related to the three-part geography–institutions–globalization framework of this volume—suggests that policy and investment actions that are customized to fill these gaps are likely to be the most reliable way forward. This approach will build and empower farmers on the ground and expand their production and economic options, and enhance the productivity and profitability of their operations.

IMPORTANCE OF AGRICULTURE IN LAGGING REGIONS

First, agriculture remains the most important source of livelihood and employment in South Asia, often employing up to two-thirds of the labour force. Its importance has declined as its contribution to growth and job creation has declined. This decline is expected with economic development. Rapid growth is associated with a reduced role of agriculture in growth, job creation, and poverty reduction in South Asia (Ghani 2010). Growth process involves structural transformation and the reallocation of resources from low-productivity areas into high-productivity areas. This process enables labour, land, and capital to be reallocated out of agriculture and into manufacturing and services.

The pace of sectoral transformation out of agriculture and into more productive sectors has been slow in South Asia compared with East Asia. Table 9.1 shows that South Asian countries are more dependent on agriculture compared with East Asia. The total share of agriculture in gross domestic product (GDP) for South Asia has declined from 34 per cent in 1980 to 18 per cent in 2008. But it is still nearly double compared with East Asia. Similarly, the share of employment in agriculture in total employment has declined from 67 per cent in 1980 to 52 per cent in 2008. But the pace of decline in employment is much slower compared with the decline in its contribution to GDP.

The pace of spatial transformation is a lot slower in lagging regions compared to leading regions. The lagging regions are more dependent on agriculture both in terms of contribution to the state GDP and employment. Table 9.2 shows that the agricultural sector in lagging regions in India are contributing about 24 per cent to the state GDP

TABLE 9.1   Contribution of Agriculture in South Asia

	Share of agriculture to GDP (%), 1980	Share of agriculture to GDP (%), 2008	Share of employment in agriculture (%), 1980	Share of employment in agriculture (%), 2008
India	35.7	17.6	68.2	55.4
Pakistan	29.5	20.4	58.5	39.9
Sri Lanka	27.6	13.4	52.3	43.1
Nepal	61.8	33.7	93.4	93.0
Bangladesh	31.6	19.1	72.0	47.3
China	30.2	11.3	73.9	62.0
South Asia	34.7	18.0	67.2	52.2
East Asia	28.6	11.9	66.5	55.7

Sources: World Bank (2009); FAO (2009).

TABLE 9.2   Agricultural Sector Contribution in Leading and Lagging Regions of India

	Leading	Lagging
Share of agriculture to State GDP (%), 2004–05	14.25	23.72
Share of employment in agriculture (%)	38.42	62.24

Source: Ministry of Agriculture (2008).
Note: Share of employment in agriculture is computed as total share of agricultural labourers and cultivators to total workers in each state for Census 2001.

and employ about 62 per cent of the workforce in agricultural activities. These numbers are much higher compared to the leading regions.[2] However, spatial transformation is not completely absent in lagging regions. The importance of agriculture to growth has declined over the last three decades in lagging regions too.

Second, big gaps exist in agricultural productivity between lagging and leading regions. These gaps have widened. Figure 9.1 shows that the yields in the lagging regions are a lot lower than in the leading regions of India. It also shows a slower growth than in the leading regions. For wheat, the first Green Revolution improved the yields in lagging regions substantially; overall, however, the yield gaps between the leading and lagging states remained constant. But in the case of rice, the trends are more diverging. Given the limited frontiers of expansion of cultivable area, an increase in yields and the efficient utilization of

[2]The definitions of leading and lagging regions are provided in Chapter 1.

India wheat yield

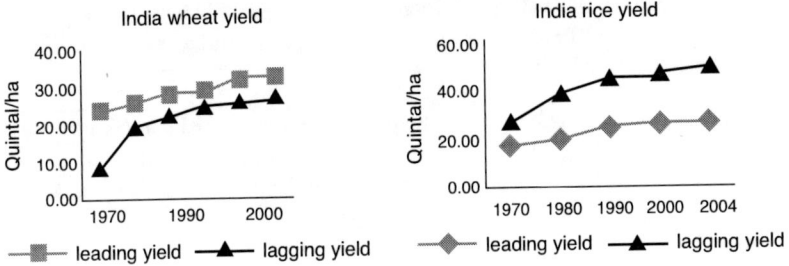

India rice yield

FIGURE 9.1   Diverging Yield in Rice and Wheat in Regions of India

Source: Ministry of Agriculture (2008).
Note: ha = hectare.

resources for sustainable agriculture are the most crucial factors for agricultural sector development.

If lagging regions in India are able to increase their yield to the levels in leading regions then it is likely that their per capita income can increase substantively. Table 9.3 shows that if the existing yield gap of 973.45 kg/ha in rice and 319.32 kg/ha of wheat is reduced then for the existing area of land the lagging regions would be able to increase their per capita production to the tune of around 50 kg for rice and 10.56 kg for wheat. With the increase in yields at the given minimum support price (MSP), the per capita income of paddy cultivators can increase by Rs 372 in lagging regions. Even though the yield differential on wheat is relatively less than that of rice, the per capita income of lagging regions is expected to increase by Rs 100 per person if lagging regions can catch up with leading regions on wheat yield.

The big message is that per capita income of lagging regions in India could increase by nearly Rs 500 per person in lagging regions if the wheat and paddy productivity in lagging regions could be increased to the same level as in leading regions. This highlights the importance of increasing productivity as a measure to improve agricultural incomes and reduce poverty.

Third, farming in lagging regions is a low-income activity that is increasingly unviable, but fewer economic alternatives (for example, in manufacturing and services) are available than in high-income regions. Agricultural production in the lagging regions is dominated by food grains in terms of area cultivated, although they account for a proportionately smaller share of the value of agricultural output. Production is largely oriented towards self-consumption rather than

TABLE 9.3   Estimated Increase in Income with Increase in
Productivity in Lagging Regions, India

Crops	In Lagging Regions		
	Yield gap (kg/ha)	Required per capita increase in agricultural production (kg)	Expected increase in income (Rs per person)
Rice	973.45	49.94	372.07
Wheat	319.32	10.61	106.12

Source: Computed by authors.
Note: The MSP for 2007–8 was Rs 745 per quintal for rice and Rs 1000 per quintal for wheat.

the market, and agricultural diversification is typically low. Livestock is an important source of livelihoods for farm households in the lagging regions. Productivity of livestock is low, and use of veterinary services and improved husbandry practices are limited.

Fourth, farm production in lagging regions is characterized by low use of modern (purchased) inputs, especially seeds and fertilizers. This is related to a combination of factors, including less access to formal credit and a poor network of input and output markets. Extension support (for production and marketing relevant information) is weaker than the national average. Also, farmer literacy (male and female) tends to be lower in the lagging regions. Lagging regions tend to have poorer market connectivity partly because of bad road and other transport and communication infrastructure. Transaction costs and barriers are high (especially with respect to marketing and agribusiness activities), many relating to particular administrative, regulatory, or local fiscal arrangements.

Finally, farmers in lagging regions are more vulnerable to market risks. Production risks relating to weather and natural events as well as pests and diseases are increased because of their higher dependence on rain and because of weaker livestock support systems. Market risks relating to inter-seasonal price volatility and inefficient price discovery arise from high transport and transaction costs and remote and poorly functioning markets.

OPPORTUNITIES AND CHALLENGES

Conventionally, a range of institutional factors impinge on economic activity. These can be seen in two kinds of institutions: (i) those that directly impinge on the agricultural sector production and marketing activities; and (ii) those that indirectly influence resource allocation decisions within the agricultural sector. The first set includes public sector institutions and organized institutions in private or cooperative sector that influence access to the following: (i) inputs, credit, and agricultural risk management; (ii) support services related to crop and livestock production and sales; (iii) output markets; and (iv) and new business and production opportunities (for example, agro-processing, small-scale enterprises, and horticultural crops). The second set of 'institutions' affect the social environment for agricultural sector growth, and are related to issues such as land tenure security, security in appropriating investment returns, transactions costs, institutional rigidities in labour and credit markets, and governance and regulatory regimes.

Growth has been hampered by the poor composition of public expenditures, with public spending on agricultural subsidies, including for food, power, irrigation, and fertilizers, crowding out productivity-enhancing investments, such as research and extension, infrastructure, health, and education. In 1999–2000, agricultural subsidies in India amounted to 3 per cent of the GDP, and were more than seven times the public investments in the sector. Although economic and trade reforms in the 1990s improved the incentive framework, overregulation of domestic trade, including in storage, movement, and enterprise-size controls, have increased costs, price risks, and uncertainty, which undermine the sector's competitiveness. More rapid growth of the rural non-farm sector is also constrained by inadequate and poor quality infrastructure and services.

Most lagging regions lack a strong framework for sustainable water resource management and irrigation service delivery. They lack both the incentives and the policy, regulatory, and institutional framework for efficient, sustainable, and equitable allocation and use of water. Additionally, the regions are not able to internalize the environmental costs of inefficient use. The composition of public expenditures in the irrigation sector has led to the spreading of resources thinly over many incomplete projects with lower priority given to operations and maintenance, leading to the rapid deterioration of existing infrastructure.

Restrictive commodity, input, and factor market policies are squeezing the returns from farming, limiting investments by farmers to increase productivity and income, and discouraging diversification to higher-value and non-farm activities. For instance, restrictive agricultural technology and phyto-sanitary policies as well as a weak research and extension system have hampered farmers' access to technologies and practices to increase productivity and incomes in Sri Lanka. Restrictions on mortgaging, leasing, subdividing, and selling of land granted under the Land Development Ordinance (LDO) have limited the economic benefits from landownership and use of land for diverse livelihood strategies. Weaknesses in land administration have contributed to an insecurity of tenure and an increase in transaction costs. Frequent changes in agriculture trade tariffs have exacerbated domestic price uncertainty.

Poor farmers have limited access to assets. While land distribution has become less skewed, land policy and regulations to increase security of tenure (including restrictions or ban on land rentals or conversion to other uses) have had the unintended effect of reducing access by the landless and discouraging rural investments. State government initiatives to improve land administration through computerization of land records have reduced transaction costs and increased transparency, but also have brought to light operational and institutional weaknesses. India has a wide network of rural finance institutions, but many of the rural poor remain underserved or excluded, as a result of inefficiencies in the formal rural finance institutions, weak regulatory framework, and high transaction costs and risks associated with lending to agriculture.

In Sri Lanka, prompt processing of the LDO amendments are needed to grant full ownership rights to farmers, but potential adverse socio-economic consequences should be carefully identified and mitigated. Because of its sensitivity, consensus building with civil society should be a priority. To implement the national title registration system, the Registration of Titles Act (RTA) needs to be amended as follows: (i) eliminating registration restrictions on co-owned land; (ii) allowing titles for people without ownership documents on the basis of occupancy; and (iii) protecting interests that are difficult to register formally. Land administration also needs to be streamlined for efficient service delivery.

Improved access to rural finance is a priority, although the establishment of a viable rural financial system has to be viewed as a medium-term goal. Ensuring the financial sustainability of the rapidly growing microfinance system is crucial. Commercial banks have only begun operations in Kabul and it will likely be many years before they reach rural Afghanistan, so new products and delivery instruments need to be developed to meet immediate needs.

Agriculture is more vulnerable to natural disasters. Bangladesh is the terminal floodplain delta of three large rivers—Ganges, Brahmaputra, and Meghna. Every year about 20 to 30 per cent, and every few years about 40 per cent, of the country is flooded, causing serious damage to infrastructure, crops, and the overall economy. Projected climatic changes and rise in the sea levels are likely to worsen the situation. Since independence in 1971, the government has made large structural and non-structural investments for protection against floods and cyclones. Issues related to public and private roles and community participation in disaster management and mitigation, environmental protection, and institutional reforms of the Bangladesh Water Development Board (BWDB) still need to be addressed.

MARKET ACCESS

Producers in lagging regions lack access to or have benefited less from state support provided to agriculture, for example, through extension, inputs supply and procurement, or output price and marketing support. In India, only a few states—Punjab, Haryana, and Andhra Pradesh—gain from the price support system for grains, which hardly operate in the lagging regions of the east. They suffer from poor yields, declining productivity, and weakness in the physical structure like infrastructure, including roads, irrigation, and use of fertilizers. The share of investment in agriculture is declining, which affects the development of the agricultural sector in the lagging regions.

Through panel regressions, we test whether the lagging regions show signs of poor access to food, mainly rice and wheat. The regressions focus mainly on one pillar (out of four— availability, access, utilization, and vulnerability) of the food security definition, that is, food access. The regressions take account of changing food consumption behaviours with changes in incomes. Thus, it tries to capture the effect of both the physical availability of food grains and purchasing capability of the households. It helps to look at the household food security issue rather than just the availability of food at the national level. The results are presented for India and for South Asia (variable description in Appendix A9.1) for rice and wheat. The regressions try to capture the effect of both the physical availability of food grains and purchasing capability of the households.

The first equation of the regression checks whether lagging regions face constraints on food consumption, after controlling for the region's food production and income. In the second equation, an interaction term of lagging region dummy and regional production is introduced. This checks the correlation between food consumption and food production in lagging regions as compared to leading ones. The lagging dummy is assigned a value of one for lagging regions and zero for leading regions. Thus, when we create an interaction term, the model rules out any transfer or trading of food from the leading regions to the lagging regions. If the coefficient of the interaction term is positive and significant, then this implies that consumption in the lagging region is closely related to the state's production only. This implies that lagging regions face barriers in trade that prevent them from smoothing consumption over time. In these equations, food production is used an indicator of availability and food consumption is used as an indicator of access to food. The dependent and independent variables are converted into per capita to normalize the effect of population variations in different regions. The interaction term is used to 'prove' that consumption is largely dependent on own production and thus in case of low production the lagging regions become more vulnerable.

South Asia

The data on per capita consumption of rice are available only at the subnational level for India, Pakistan, and Sri Lanka and for wheat only for India and Pakistan. Nevertheless, the regression is representative of South Asia because these three countries account for about 86 per cent of South Asia's population, contribute about 91 per cent to South Asia's GDP, and have about an 82 per cent share in the region's wheat production and 75 per cent share in rice production. The regressions are calculated for the period 2001–6 and then at the two intervals of three years from 2001–3 and 2004–6. Equation 9.1 shows that in the sub-periods the per capita consumption of rice is positively and significantly dependent on the region's production. The linkage is even stronger in 2004–6. This also indicates self-sufficiency (see Table 9.4).

For wheat, the positive and significant relation of wheat consumption to the region's price in the period 2001–3 becomes negative in 2004–6. To test the lack of market access, in equation 9.2, the interaction term is introduced, which is not positive or significant. In fact, in the case of wheat for 2001–3 and for 2001–6, the coefficient is negative and significant, which rules out poor market access. Overall, the income effect is negative but the magnitude of the effect is negligible. Thus, with increases in incomes, the share of rice and wheat in total food consumption would decline, but marginally. Overall, in South Asia, the results do not confirm the situation of a lack of market access for either rice or wheat.

Crop Consumption = α_0 + α_1 Crop production + α_2 Per capita income + α_3 (State Dummies) + α_4 (Time dummy)   (9.1)

Crop Consumption = β_0 + β Crop production + β_2 Per capita income + β_3 (Crop Production * lagging region dummy) + β_4 (State Dummies) + β_5 (Time dummy)   (9.2)

TABLE 9.4 Ordinary Least Squares Results: Regressions for Access to Food (South Asia)

Dependent variable	2001–3 Rice consumption eq1	2001–3 Rice consumption eq2	2001–3 Wheat consumption eq1	2001–3 Wheat consumption eq2	2004–6 Rice consumption eq1	2004–6 Rice consumption eq2	2004–6 Wheat consumption eq1	2004–6 Wheat consumption eq2	2001–6 Rice consumption eq1	2001–6 Rice consumption eq2	2001–6 Wheat consumption eq1	2001–6 Wheat consumption eq2
Independent variables												
Constant	4.62***	4.61***	1.66***	1.96***	3.86***	3.95***	1.46***	1.78***	4.46***	4.28***	1.71***	2.11***
Own production	0.06*	0.05	0.10*	0.17***	0.13*	0.19**	-0.13	0.15***	0.07	-0.02	-0.03	0.18
Per capita income	-0.00	-0.00	-0.00**	-0.00**	-0.00	-0.00	-0.00	-0.00	-0.00	-0.00	-0.00	-0.00
Interaction = (own production * lagging region dummy)	–	0.01	–	-0.30*	–	-0.07	–	-0.63	–	0.13	–	-0.55***
State dummies	-ive***	-ive***	-ive***	-ive***	-ive***	-ive***	-ive***	-ive***	-ive***	No specific trend	-ive***	-ive***
Time dummy	+ive	+ive	+ive	+ive	+ive	+ive	+ive	+ive	+ive	+ive	0.37*	+ive
No. of observations	90	90	57	57	90	90	57	57	180	180	114	114
degree of freedom	57	56	35	34	57	56	35	34	147	146	90	89
R-sq	0.99	0.99	0.99	0.99	0.95	0.95	0.96	0.96	0.97	0.97	0.97	0.97
Adj R-sq	0.99	0.99	0.99	0.99	0.93	0.93	0.93	0.94	0.96	0.96	0.96	0.96
DW stat	1.77	1.77	2.34	2.19	2.18	2.18	2.32	2.30	1.97	1.96	1.92	1.91

Source: Authors' calculation.

Notes: *** = coefficients are statistically significant at 1 per cent level.

** = coefficients are statistically significant at 5 per cent level.

* = coefficients are statistically significant at 10 per cent level.

All variables are in log *t*- statistics in parenthesis. Results are corrected for heteroskedasticity.

Subnational level for India (16), Pakistan (4), and Sri Lanka (9) for rice; and India and Pakistan for wheat.

All variables are in log and are in per capita. Lagging = 1 and Leading = 0.

India

The same exercise is repeated for India at the subnational level. The panel data are built up for 17 states, including the north-eastern states as a combined group for the period 1980–2006 and the sub-periods. Using these data, we again check whether there are indications for poor market access in rice and wheat (see Tables 9.5 and 9.6). In equation

TABLE 9.5   Ordinary Least Squares Results: Regressions for Access to Food (India)

Dependent Variable: Rice Consumption

Year		Constant	Own production	PKY	Inter-action	State dummy	Time dummy	R-sq
1980–2	Eq^1	9.32***	0.07**	−0.55***	–	−ive***	+ive**	0.99
	Eq^2	8.99***	0.04	−0.52***	0.05	−ive***	+ive***	0.99
1983–5	Eq^1	4.91***	0.00	0.01	–	+ive***	−ive***	0.99
	Eq^2	4.93***	0.00	0.01	−0.42	+ive***	−ive***	0.99
1986–8	Eq^1	12.86***	0.28**	−1.11**	–	+ive***	−ive***	0.99
	Eq^2	12.40***	0.23**	−1.07**	0.09	+ive***	−ive***	0.99
1989–91	Eq^1	4.47***	−0.03	0.07	–	+ive***	−ive***	0.99
	Eq^2	4.88***	0.12	0.04	−0.18	+ive***	−ive***	0.99
1992–4	Eq^1	5.08***	−0.13	0.07	–	−ive***	+ive***	0.99
	Eq^2	5.21**	0.00	0.07	−0.15	−ive***	+ive***	0.99
1995–7	Eq^1	7.39***	0.23***	−0.45***	–	+ive***	−ive***	0.99
	Eq^2	7.40***	0.26***	−0.43***	−0.07	+ive***	−ive***	0.99
1998–	Eq^1	−2.29	0.16	0.76	–	−ive	No trend	0.98
2000	Eq^2	−2.52	0.01	0.58	0.49	−ive	No trend	0.98
2001–3	Eq^1	5.70**	0.08	−0.15	–	+ive	−ive***	0.99
	Eq^2	5.78**	0.07	−0.16	0.01	+ive	−ive***	0.99
2004–6	Eq^1	52.21	0.42*	−3.79	–	+ive	+ive	0.93
	Eq^2	51.93	0.35**	−6.78	0.12	+ive	+ive	0.99
1980–	Eq^1	4.66***	0.09***	−0.02	–	−ive*	−ive	0.97
2006	Eq^2	4.37***	−0.01	−0.30	0.18*	−ive*	−ive	0.98

Source: Authors' calculations.

Notes: Interaction = (production * lagging region dummy); Lagging = 1 and Leading = 0; PKY= per capita income; Number of observations = 51; degree of freedom in equation 9.1 is 31 and is 30 in equation 9.2.

*** = coefficients are statistically significant at 1 per cent level; ** = coefficients are statistically significant at 5 per cent level. * = coefficients are statistically significant at 10 per cent level.

All variables are in log and are in per capita. Results are corrected for heteroskedasticity. These results are for state-level data for 16 major states and the north-east as group of seven states (Tripura, Sikkim, Meghalaya, Mizoram, Manipur, Arunachal Pradesh, and Nagaland).

TABLE 9.6   Ordinary Least Squares Results: Regressions for Access to Food (India)

Dependent Wheat Consumption

Year		Constant	Own production	PKY	Inter-action	State dummy	Time dummy	R-sq
1980–2	Eq¹	6.14**	0.07	-0.50	–	+ive***	–ive	0.99
	Eq²	4.35	–0.04	-0.32	0.28**	+ive***	–ive	0.99
1983–5	Eq¹	1.98***	–0.01	-0.01	–	+ive***	–ive	0.99
	Eq²	1.98***	–0.01	-0.01	-0.01	+ive***	–ive	0.99
1986–8	Eq¹	10.75***	0.17**	–1.14***	–	+ive***	+ive***	0.99
	Eq²	10.60***	0.17**	–1.10***	–0.14	+ive***	+ive***	0.99
1989–91	Eq¹	4.37***	0.16**	–0.33**	–	+ive***	+ive	0.99
	Eq²	4.63***	0.14*	–0.37**	0.09	+ive***	+ive	0.99
1992–4	Eq¹	3.93**	0.09**	-0.25	–	+ive***	+ive	0.99
	Eq²	3.82**	0.09*	-0.23	0.01	+ive***	+ive	0.99
1995–7	Eq¹	4.89***	0.07	–0.38**	–	+ive***	+ive	0.99
	Eq²	4.92***	0.06	–0.39*	0.05	+ive***	+ive	0.99
1998–2000	Eq¹	7.27***	0.12***	–0.74***	–	+ive***	+ive***	0.99
	Eq²	7.45***	0.14**	–0.76***	0.04	+ive***	+ive***	0.99
2001–3	Eq¹	7.07***	0.14**	–0.60**	–	+ive***	–ive	0.99
	Eq²	5.39***	0.19**	–0.35*	–0.29**	+ive***	–ive	0.99
2004–6	Eq¹	-9.82	–0.23	1.31	–	+ive***	–ive	0.95
	Eq²	-6.84	–0.40	0.99	–0.44	+ive***	–ive	0.95
1980–2006	Eq¹	2.57***	–0.01	0.08	–	+ive***	–ive	0.98
	Eq²	2.65***	0.02	–0.09	–0.04	+ive***	–ive	0.98

Source: Authors' calculations.
Notes: Same as in Table 9.4.
Number of observations = 45; degree of freedom in equation 9.1 is 27 and is 2 in equation 9.2. Data exclude Kerala and Tamil Nadu.
*** = coefficients are statistically significant at 1 per cent level; ** = coefficients are statistically significant at 5 per cent level; * = coefficients are statistically significant at 10 per cent level.

9.1, the coefficient of the region's production is positive and significant both for rice and wheat. This implies that access to food is primarily met by the region's own food production. In the lagging regions, the income coefficient is negative, indicating that with increasing per capita incomes, consumers have diversified their consumption basket away from the staple commodities. In equation 9.2, the interaction term is introduced, which captures the combined effect of the region's production and the lagging region effect. This interaction term is positive and significant for rice for the period 1980–2006, indicating that consumption in lagging regions is highly correlated with its own production.

Although these results suggest a lack of market access, they do not hold in the sub-periods. In fact, in some of the sub-periods, the interaction term is negative. Interestingly, in the case of wheat, the interaction term is positive and significant in the initial period of 1980–3, indicating poor market access in the lagging regions; however, this term became negative over the years and, for 2001–3, this term is statistically significant and also negative. This suggests that market access to lagging regions for wheat has improved over time. Lagging regions have access to markets outside the region. This implies that wheat trade and transfers do take place between lagging and leading regions. Incompleteness exists in public redistribution from producing to consuming regions, which is evident in the regressions by a positive significant correlation between production and consumption. Such a lack of market access does not appear to be systematically greater in lagging regions. Thus, the regressions present mixed evidence that the lagging regions suffer from the problem of poor market access to food.

So what can be done to improve agricultural growth? Creating a more productive, competitive, and diversified agricultural sector would require a shift in public expenditures away from subsidies towards productivity-enhancing investments. Removing the restrictions on domestic private trade (imposing them only in true emergencies) would also help. The agricultural research and extension systems need to be strengthened in lagging regions to improve farmers' access to productivity-enhancing technologies. This will require (i) fostering pluralistic systems; (ii) improving priority setting; (iii) promoting demand-driven, decentralized, public systems, and public–private partnerships; and (iv) building closer links with domestic and international sources of technologies and knowledge.

There is a growing consensus in the region to reform land policy, particularly land tenancy policy and land administration systems in lagging regions. States that do not have tenancy restrictions can provide useful lessons in this regard. Over the longer term, a more holistic approach to land

TABLE 9.7   Road Density in India (km per 1,000 km^2)

Averages	1980	1990	2000	2006
Leading	752.5	1022.3	1133.7	1196.5
Lagging	551.1	662.4	937.7	969.9

Source: CMIE (2009).

TABLE 9.8   **Per cent Area under Irrigation in India (2005–6)**

	Rice	Wheat	Food grains
Leading State's Average	77.2	70.3	54.7
Lagging State's Average	33.8	66.9	35.6

Source: Ministry of Agriculture (2008).

administration policies, regulations, and institutions is necessary to reduce costs and to ensure security, fairness, and sustainability of the system.

Growth has increased demand for higher-value fresh and processed agricultural products. This opens new opportunities for agricultural diversification to higher-value products (for example, horticulture and livestock), agro-processing, and related services. A careful reorientation of the government's role towards an enabling environment for private sector participation and competition is necessary to make agribusiness and, more broadly, the rural non-farm sector key drivers for growth.

Lagging regions would benefit from building social capital and increased networking to compensate for weak institutions. Scaling up livelihood and community-driven development approaches are critical to build social capital in the lagging regions, promote savings mobilization efforts, promote productive investments and income-generating opportunities, and enable sustainable natural resource management. Direct support to self-help groups, village committees, water user associations, forest user associations, and savings and loans groups can provide the initial 'push' to move towards higher levels of organizations and access to new economic opportunities. Moreover, social mobilization and particularly the empowerment of women's groups, through increased capacity for collective action, will provide communities with a greater 'voice' and bargaining power in dealing with the private sector, markets, and financial services.

CONCLUSION

The lagging regions are served by small, fragmented local markets (with 'thin' trading, low volumes, and high price volatility), and often cut off from the global markets. The challenge is to recast agriculture in the new environment of globalization, rising prices, growing domestic demand, and greater private sector involvement. This will require greater investments to increase farmer yields and profitability and in rural infrastructure, such as irrigation, roads, power, and markets. The tension is not about the lack of resources, but about the fact that the flow of resources that has gone into agriculture has not gone into improving land and labour productivity. There is too much emphasis on providing subsidies rather than investments, whose benefits are regressive across states.

Agriculture can be a key source of growth and poverty reduction, provided there is improvement in the asset position of the rural poor, smallholder farming is made more competitive and sustainable, income sources are diversified towards the labour market and the rural non-farm economy, and successful migration out of agriculture is facilitated. The region needs to rebuild social capital and networking through farmers associations, self-help groups, and water user groups to transform the poor and marginalized farmers into an organized market.

In the next two decades, lagging regions will witness a rural transformation, which is likely to be accelerated with the help of mobile phones and Internet access. The importance of agriculture in job creation and growth will further decline. There is nothing to worry about as long as those who remain in agriculture continue to be productive. Those that leave agriculture will create new challenges of migration, urbanization, and job quality.

APPENDIX A9.1   VARIABLES DEFINITIONS AND DATA SOURCES

Variables	Definitions	Country	Data Sources
Rice/wheat consumption	Average annual per capita consumption of rice/wheat in kg	India	NSS consumer expenditure annual rounds
		Pakistan	Household Integrated Economic Survey, Federal Bureau of Statistics, Division, Ministry of Economic Affairs and Statistics, Government of Pakistan
		Sri Lanka	Department of Census and Statistics, Ministry of Finance and Planning, Sri Lanka
Paddy/wheat production	Annual per capita production of rice/wheat in kg	India	Ministry of Agriculture, Government of India
		Pakistan	Agricultural Statistics of Pakistan, Government of Pakistan

(contd.)

Appendix A9.1 (contd...)

Variables	Definitions	Country	Data Sources
		Sri Lanka	Department of Census and Statistics, Ministry of Finance and Planning, Sri Lanka
Per capita income	Average annual per capita income at state level (in rupees for India regression; in US dollars at PPP for South Asia regression)	India	Centre for Monitoring Indian Economy (CMIE)
		Pakistan	World Bank Calculations
		Sri Lanka	World Bank Calculations
Lagging dummy	Lagging region = 1; Leading region = 0	South Asia	World Bank
Rice interaction term	Paddy Production * lagging dummy	South Asia, India	Authors' computation
Wheat interaction term	Wheat production * lagging dummy	South Asia, India	Authors' computation

Notes: kg = kilograms; NSS = National Sample Survey; PPP = purchasing power parity.

REFERENCES

CMIE (Centre for Monitoring Indian Economy). 2009. Online database (http://www.cmie.com/).

Ghani, Ejaz. 2010. *The Service Revolution in South Asia*. New Delhi: Oxford University Press.

Ministry of Agriculture. 2008. *Agricultural Statistics at a Glance*. New Delhi: Directorate of Economics and Statistics, Ministry of Agriculture, Government of India.

World Bank. 2009. *World Development Indicators*. Washington, D.C.: World Bank.

Contributors

MAARTEN BOSKER is a Post-doctoral Researcher at the University of Groningen and Utrecht University, The Netherlands.

ANA M. FERNANDES is Economist, Trade and International Integration Unit, Development Research Group (DECRG), The World Bank, Washington, D.C.

HARRY GARRETSEN is Professor, International Economics and Business, University of Groningen, The Netherlands.

EJAZ GHANI is Economic Adviser, South Asia Poverty Reduction and Economic Management (SASEP), The World Bank, Washington, D.C.

MADDALENA HONORATI is Economist, Social Protection Team (HDNSP), The World Bank, Washington, D.C.

LAKSHMI IYER is Associate Professor, Business Administration, Harvard Business School, Boston.

PRAVIN KRISHNA is Chung Ju Yung Professor of International Economics, School of Advanced International Studies, and Professor of Economics, Department of Economics, Johns Hopkins University.

TAYE MENGISTAE is Senior Economist, Finance and Private Sector Development, Africa Region, The World Bank, Washington, D.C.

SAURABH MISHRA is a Consultant for South Asia Poverty Reduction and Economic Management (SASEP), The World Bank, Washington, D.C.

DEVASHISH MITRA is Professor of Economics and Gerald B. and Daphna Cramer Professor of Global Affairs, Maxwell School of Citizenship and Public Affairs, Syracuse University.

SURABHI MITTAL is Senior Fellow, Indian Council for Research on International Economic Relations (ICRIER), New Delhi.

ÇAĞLAR ÖZDEN is Senior Economist, Development Research Group (DECTI), The World Bank, Washington, D.C.

DHUSHYANTH RAJU is Economist, South Asia Region Education Department (SASED), The World Bank, Washington, D.C.

MIRVAT SEWADEH is Consultant, Development Research Group (DECTI), The World Bank, Washington, D.C.

ASHA SUNDARAM is Senior Lecturer of Economics, University of Cape Town, South Africa.